# Waterstone's Guide
# to Irish Books

*Edited by Cormac Kinsella*

WATERSTONE'S GUIDES SERIES EDITOR
*Nick Rennison*

# Contents

## Introduction By Cormac Kinsella

The Irish literary heritage is both huge and hugely diverse. The *Waterstone's Guide to Irish Books* is a representation of this diverse heritage and aims to reflect the best that is currently available in Irish writing. There has been no previous attempt by a bookseller to provide a guide to the different elements of Irish writing, one which provides, in an easy-to-use format, information on authors from Lady Gregory to Roddy Doyle, from Jonathan Swift to Patrick McCabe. The guide includes both fiction and non-fiction and, in sections such as poetry and travel, history and art, it aims to be a tool for use by readers whose tastes are as varied as the writing the guide contains. In short, the *Waterstone's Guide to Irish Books* is a wide-ranging introduction to the wealth of Irish writing available.

Basic information about the authors and their works has been provided as well as bibliographic information which will enable the reader to find books more easily. The guide also includes seven articles by established authors in which they reflect on favourite books in a relaxed but insightful fashion. Criteria for inclusion in the guide have been simple. Books should be by Irish writers and about Irish subject matter. Books included should also be readily available on the shelves of our shops or easily obtainable from the publisher.

The research for the *Waterstone's Guide to Irish Books* and the editorial process led me to books that were familiar and also to books that were new and exciting. I hope that anyone buying the guide will also be led to the old, the new and the exciting in the Irish literary heritage.

*The prices quoted from English publishers will be subject to a price change in Irish branches due to the sterling difference.*

## Resolution and Independence by Gerald Dawe

The girls are at their radiant screens,
columns of figures that put them
in touch with the world – Zurich,
Hong Kong, New York, Mulgrave Street.


Qualm at Waterstone's :
*Hold on,* she said,
*I'll put you through to Biography*
*and they'll look for you there.*


*These things are sent to try us*
went through my head
as the street rose to meet me
and I just made Moon's Corner.


There should always be
THE IRISH YEAST CO.
shining in the twilight
of College Street.

# Art & Architecture

## ART AND ARCHITECTURE

BY JANE HUMPHRIES

Such is the wealth of words woven into the rich cultural life of Ireland that the visual arts have tended to be overlooked. Although the shadow of Ireland's literary heritage still looms large, all forms of Irish visual arts are beginning to be reassessed and critically valued as never before. The number of fine publications on the market today echoes this desire to focus on Ireland's visual history.

## CELTIC ART

Celtic Art is one period in Irish Art that has always attracted scholars, probably because the finest remains of both pagan Celtic Art and Christian Celtic Art are to be found on these shores. Hibernia, unlike other parts of Western Europe, escaped early Roman domination and, even with the advent of Christianity, Celtic designs can be traced on stone monuments, pottery, gold, and silver jewellery. This distinctive Celtic style, based on circles, spirals and curved lines is plentiful, and has become omnipresent in today's tourist shops. **Early Celtic Art in Ireland** (0946172374 pb £4.95), **Metal Craftsmanship in Early Ireland** (0946172374 pb £4.95), and **Megalithic Art in Ireland** (094617236 6 pb £4.95) all published by Townhouse are invaluable little books which are specifically interested in local Celtic Art.

Other books tend to have a wider geographical base but incorporate large Irish sections. Thames and Hudson publish a plethora of Celtic Art books; the best value being **Celtic Art** (0714121177 pb £8.99), one of the World of Art Series. Like all the titles in this excellent series it has a fine bibliography. A weightier tome is

**Celtic Art** (050027585 £18.95) by Ruth and Vincent Megaw. This is probably the definitive study in the area, with a comprehensive survey of the period and some fine reproductions. Aidan Meehan is the author of a charming series, which offers practical sources for designing illuminated letters, animal patterns and the like. For those wishing a more detailed read **Celtic Image** (Bradford hb £16.99 0713724803), **Celtic Art** (Constable pb £9.95 0094769001) and **Imagining an Irish Past** ( University of Chicago P. £21.950935573127) are recommended.

The best surviving example of a Christian Celtic Art illuminated manuscript is the **Book of Kells**. It is amazing to think it was crafted in the 8th century as some pages have been preserved so well that the jewel-like illumination still leaps to the eye. It is a truly magnificent book and is housed in Trinity College, Dublin. Unfortunately no book can do justice to the original, but there are many publications which add to our enjoyment of it by offering additional historical information.

**The Book of Kells** (Collins & Brown pb £5.99 1855853124), **The Book of Kells** (Thomas & Hudson pb £9.95 0500277907) by Bernard Meehan and **The Book of Kells: A New Look** (0951865110) are all informative. A book which is educational and aimed at a younger audience is George Otto Simms's **Exploring the Book of Kells** (O'Brien Press pb £6.95 0862781795).

Trinity College, Dublin is also home to another early medieval Gospel book of great historic and artistic value, The Book of Durrow. Written by monks in early Christian Ireland it has had an interesting journey before coming to rest at Trinity and the keeper of manuscripts, Bernard Meehan, has written a well-documented book, which takes us on a guided tour of this masterpiece, **The Book of Durrow** (1860590063 £9.99). Bringing the two books together is George Henderson's **From Durrow to Kells** (Thames & Hudson hb 0500234744 £41.80) which is a well-documented, interesting read but, despite being the most expensive, it has no colour plates to study.

# General Irish Art

*As an introduction to the general personalities, fashions and movements in Irish art through the centuries the following books serve as good general texts: –*

## BRUCE ARNOLD

**Irish Art**
pb £6.95 050020148X

This book is one of Thames and Hudson's World of Art series and very good value in terms of the information provided for the price charged. Because of the size of the book reproductions are small and not always in colour, but they do serve as excellent springboards from which to venture into more specialist areas. The author, Bruce Arnold, is a well-known Irish art critic who knows and loves his subject and conveys this to the reader. Although constrained by space the book deals with everything from Celtic Art to Jack Yeats and the moderns and the many illustrations highlight the author's major points. The number of contemporary artists continues to grow and the section on today's work is perhaps the weakest. However inclusions of Camille Souter and Edward McGuire's work are welcome, although it is a pity their work is shown in black and white rather than colour. Minor criticisms aside, here is the perfect start to explore Irish Art.

## BRIAN FALLON

**Irish Art 1830–1990**
Appletree Press £20.00
0862814383

Concentrating on the period 1830-1990 Brian Fallon, the retired chief art critic of The Irish Times, has provided the reader with a lyrical and knowledgeable commentary on Irish art in the period. 'For even culturally well-informed people, Irish art got no further than the Book of Kells more than a millennium ago,' he states, and proceeds to illustrate why this was the case. Recalling nineteenth century artists, such as Francis Danby, Daniel Maclise and William Mulready, back into the Irish fold, examining the allure Europe, particularly France, held for artists like Nathaniel Hone and Roderick O'Connor, tracing the by now famous Irish Literary Revival artists such as John Lavery, William Orpen and Walter Osborne, and ending in what he terms 'the modern epoch', Fallon has produced an interesting read.

## CATHERINE MARSHALL

**Irish Art Masterpieces**
Gazelle £19.95 0883632950

Many of the best-known images from Irish Art are included in this excellent book – Sarah Purser's portrait of 'Maud Gonne', Harry Clarke's stained glass 'Eve of Saint Agnes', the quintessential western landscape of Paul Henry's 'Lakeside Cottages', Mainie Jellet's cubist 'The Virgin of Eire' and, on a more contemporary note, Dorothy Cross's fabulous 'Shark Lady in a Balldress' and Rita Duffy's 'Mother Ireland and Mother Ulster'.

## Contemporary Irish Art

In the last decade, the number of Irish artists to make an impact on the national and international art scene has been phenomenal. Ireland has also become a base for foreign artists to work from, thus creating a broader spectrum for ideas to be exchanged and enabling the country to make a profound mark on the contemporary art circuit.

## BRIAN KENNEDY

**Irish Painting**
Town House £14.99
0948524650

For lovers of Irish art this book is a treat. Graced with a cover of 'Mrs Lavery Sketching' by John Lavery (one of the sixty-five artists studied here), the book includes concise biographies at the front section and the rest of the book is given over to the scrutiny of favourite masterpieces in glorious detail. Particular sections of works are magnified to examine technique and brushstrokes. The book also has a splendid bibliography but it does not include any recent Irish art.

## LIAM KELLY

**Thinking Long: Contemporary Art in Northern Ireland**
0946641773 £25.00

As the title suggests this is a thoughtful study of art practice in the North of Ireland during a period of acute political and social change – from the late 1970s to the early 1990s. The author examines over 80 artists from a wide variety of media, who have both lived and worked in the North or whose work is a reaction to it. Excellent layout and content in each chapter, with comprehensive artists' biographies, a fine bibliography, notes and references combine to make a brilliant book.

## DOROTHY WALKER

**Modern Art in Ireland**
1874675775 £25.00

Dorothy Walker has gained a reputation as an enthusiastic arts commentator in Ireland and this is very much her voice on the subject. Extremely informative, bursting with enthusiasm, sprinkled with cheeky anecdotes and many fine colour plates, this is a tour de force of modern Irish art history.

From Dorothy Walker, Modern Art in Ireland

## Academic Art History

For the art historian there are many fine academic works. Listed here are a few particularly interesting publications, which are primarily aimed at the scholar. **The School of Art in Dublin since 1790** (0717120597 hb £40.00), John Turpin's fine study of the formation, expansion, development and personalities involved in the Dublin School of Art is an interesting read, as is **Visual Politics: Representation of Ireland 1750-1930**, by Fintan Cullen (Cork University Press 185918023X £25.00). A multi-disciplinary approach to Ireland's pictorial tradition from the seventeenth to the twentieth centuries and how it complements and challenges written representation of national identity is offered in a series of essays called **Visualising Ireland**, edited by Adele M. Dalsimer (Faber pb 0571198139 £10.99). **The Arts and Crafts Movements in Dublin and Edinburgh 1885-1925** (Irish Academic Press 0716525798 £29.50) is a finely catalogued, exquisitely illustrated study of two cities at the forefront of the Celtic revival. **Irish Public Sculpture** (Four Courts Press £29.95 1851822747) is an informative and well-researched book by Judith Hill, which tells the intriguing story of public art in Ireland from the Celtic period to today. It is a fascinating tale, and the whole debate about public art and its role is explored.

## Watercolours

Irish Watercolorists have gained international fame and it is a medium in which particular artists have excelled. Two books, which are good on the subject, are **Two Hundred Years of Watercolours** (National Gallery 0903162393 pb £3.00) and **Three Hundred Years of Irish Watercolours and Drawings** (Orion 0753802066, £14.99), a particularly pleasing book, written with great clarity by Patricia A. Butler. The period covered is from 1660 to 1960 and includes a wide range of artists and their work. It is the drawings which make for the most interesting viewing, especially William Conor's street scenes of Belfast, drawn in crayon and of course Sarah Purser's drawings of John Butler Yeats. **Irish Watercolours and Drawings** (National Gallery of Ireland 0903162563 £25.00) and **Watercolours in Ireland** (Edinburgh Press 0091783690 £45.00) are also worth checking out.

## Galleries/Collections

The National Gallery of Ireland has many books about the paintings hung on its walls. From a small guide at £3.00 (0906162784), ideal for tourists, to specialist volumes – Illustrated Summary Catalogues at £70.00 – the gallery publishes many fine books. These include Marie Bourke's **Exploring Art at the National Gallery of Ireland** (0903162679 £9.95) **Brocas Collection** by Patricia Butler (0907328261 £14.99) and **Crazy About Women** by Paul Durcan (090316258X £9.95), a celebration by the poet of his favourites from the gallery.

A catalogue of the Collection at the Irish Museum of Modern Art is at the moment in preparation. It will be a fully illustrated catalogue of the fabulous Permanent Collection housed at the Royal Hospital, Kilmainham. The Gallery has published and co-published with other galleries many catalogues to accompany exhibitions. These include **The Collection: Figuration** which has work by, among others, Antony Gormley, Kathy Prendergast, Eithne Jordan and Robert Ballagh, **Artists' Work Programme**, about the forty plus artists who have taken part in the galleries programme since 1995, **Hughie O'Donoghue: Paintings and Drawings** and the recent exhibition **After The Party: Andy Warhol Works 1956-1986**, with texts by IMMA's director, Declan McGonagle.

The Hugh Lane Gallery, Municipal Gallery of Modern Irish Art has two books, which tell the history of the Gallery and give details of the permanent collection. One for adults, **Images and Insights** (0951424637 £?) and one for children, **Picture This!: Looking At Art in the Hugh Lane Municipal Gallery** by Daire O'Connell. Other publications to accompany exhibitions are of a particularly high quality and make beautiful collectors' items. **Anne Madden: Trajectories 1995-1997**, with an essay by the Sunday Tribune art critic Aidan Dunne, is a pleasure to read and a great keepsake as are **Ramus: Botanic Gardens Exhibition, Ian Joyce** and **Oona Hyland** and, in association with the Ormeau Baths Gallery, **Belfast Banquet** by Rita Duffy.

The Douglas Hyde Gallery, housed in Trinity, brings some of the most exciting contemporary exhibitions to Dublin. They frequently publish catalogues to accompany these. **The Bread and Butter Stone** (0907660584 £ 9.95) is one such publication, which concentrates on ten artists who have worked closely with the Gallery. Among the artists are Christian Boltanski, Annette Messanger, Wolfgang Laib, Marlene Dumas, Richard Tuttle and Dorothy Cross and the book contains an essay by the Gallery's director John Hutchinson. For Irish Art enthusiasts the gallery produces a number of excellent pamphlets with superb accompanying text to assist greater understanding of the artist's work. The sculptress Éilis O'Connell's **Steel Quarry** (0907660290 £4.95), Patrick Hall's **Mountain** (0907660541 £4.95) and Paul Mosse's **Partial** (0907660614 £5.95) are just a few examples.

The Crawford Municipal Art Gallery, Cork's collection is published in **Irish Art 1770-1995** (Murray 0946647897 £15.00) This is a large format book featuring important essays on Irish Art and has wonderful colour plates of all the major artists' work included in the gallery.

Limerick City Gallery of Art publishes a beautifully produced book to accompany the National Collection of Contemporary Drawing, part of its permanent collection. An ever expanding and fine collection, which includes such interesting work as Mary Fitzgerald's skilful Four Square 7, Gerda Fromel's Untitled Drawing 1 and Kathy Prendergast's Untitled is well served by the book (0946641714 ).

Sligo Art Gallery has no catalogue for a permanent collection but each year it produces a catalogue to accompany the small ioncas small works exhibition and for anyone interested in new work it is a fine wee publication. Another annual exhibition, which is recorded in a catalogue, is EV+ A. Based in Limerick, this offers audiences three strands of contemporary art practice – open, young and invited - and is nationally and internationally recognised. The accompanying catalogue is published by Gandon and is an example of their dedication to the contemporary Art scene in Ireland.

Many smaller galleries around the country are now publishing catalogues of a very high quality which feature contemporary artists who may not as yet be included in a major publication. The Green On Red Gallery, in Dublin, publish elegant catalogues, little works of art in their own right. One particularly fine one is of the work of painter Mark Joyce, with accompanying text by Paul Durcan. The wittily titled **The Fiction of a Coherent Iconography: The Installation Work of Finola Jones,** who is a very interesting and thought provoking artist, is a gorgeous little book, as is a lovely, simple reminder of Alice Maher's Ombres – three drawings on charcoal paper.

As the interest in Irish Art swells, it is reassuring to know that many corporate organisations have begun to collect and support the artistic community by purchasing work. The State itself has, in the last decade, in the guise of the Office of Public Works, been a patron of the visual arts. A catalogue of work acquired by the OPW is available, **Art In State Buildings** (070637198 £15.00) which lists the paintings, prints, applied art works, public sculpture and where they are exhibited. It is particularly good at identifying public art like Kathy Prendergast's design for wrought iron gates in Dublin Castle and Eric Pearce's furniture in the dining rooms of government buildings. AIB (Allied Irish Bank) have also a very fine eye for collecting and their acquisitions are published in **AIB ART** (095266008 £15.99.)

## Major Artists

There are two dictionaries of Irish Artists that are useful sources and standard works. The most up to date one is **Dictionary of Irish Artists** by Theo Snoddy (Wolfhound Press 0863275621 £50.00) which is fully comprehensive. However an art book collector's dream is the two-volume set, **Dictionary of Irish Artists** (07165244422 £45.00), published by Irish Academic Press. It appeared first in 1913 and, whilst not a reliable guide for modern artists, it is a treasure trove to art historians.

### HARRY CLARKE
### (1889–1931)

An absolutely fantastic symbolist artist and the master of stained-glass windows. His 'The Eve of Saint Agnes' can be viewed at the Hugh Lane Gallery.

**Life and Work of Harry Clarke**
Irish Academic Press
0716525348 £19.95

*Nicola Gordon Brown*
**Harry Clarke**
Douglas Hyde Gallery £4.95

### WILLIAM CROZIER
### (b.1930)

A glorious painter, who grapples provocatively with the dichotomy between abstract and figurative painting. His palate is bold and lush, inspired by the landscapes of West Cork, where he lives.

### PAUL HENRY
### (1876–1958)

Henry trained at Belfast School of Art and was influenced by the work of Whistler and Jean Francois Millet. After a period in London he moved with his artist wife, Grace, to Achill Island, in County Mayo. He began painting local people harvesting seaweed, gathering turf, and fishing. Known as the sky, bog, and turf painter, he became a victim of his own success, as the Western landscape he wished to capture became increasingly associated with an idealistic romantic view, and favoured by tourists. It was his fascination with light and his desire to capture the atmospheric affect on the landscape, which still radiates from his canvas. His wife was also a very fine painter, and it is interesting to contrast her rather brutal view of the land with Henry's own.
Town House, in association with National Gallery of Ireland 0948524227 £4.95

## MAINIE JELLETT
### (1897–1944)

Influenced by William Orpen at the Dublin Metropolitan School of Art she later studied under Walter Sickert at the Westminster School of Art. Here she met fellow artist and life-time friend, Evie Hone. Together they studied at Andre Lhote's academy in Paris and later became pupils of one of the original cubists, Albert Gleizes. Both Jellet and Hone embraced cubism. Jellet, however, was the genius, remaining true to the theory of the logical progression of colours and forms; 'translation and rotation'. Fra Angelico inspires many of her works and the spiritual core of the work is still strongly communicated. For years her modernist approach was treated harshly by Dublin critics but today her intelligent work has been reassessed and her greatness as one of the best cubist exponents recognised, as has her dedication to revolutionising art in Ireland.

## BRUCE ARNOLD

**Mainie Jellett and the Modern Movement in Ireland**
0300054637 £45.00

## NATHANIEL HONE, THE ELDER (1718–1784)

Known for his exquisite enamel miniatures and fine oil portraits, he was a successful artist in his lifetime and his complex satire in the execution of some of his work continues to make him interesting today. A fine example of such boldness is his satire of Sir Joshua Reynolds in the famous picture 'The Conjuror'.

**Nathaniel Hone**
Town & Country Hse.
0948524367 £4.95

## JOHN LAVERY
### (1856–1941)

Born in Belfast, Lavery was orphaned at an early age and sent to Scotland to be educated in Ayrshire. He ran away to Glasgow where he apprenticed for a photographer and later enrolled at art classes. In 1883 he went to join the artists' colony of Grez-sur-Loing returning in 1885 with the reputation of a sophisticated modernist. He became a very successful portrait painter and after the death of his first wife moved to London. His life was to change in 1910 when he met Hazel Martyn, a beautiful young American artist, thirty years his junior. Lavery was inspired by her opaque beauty and she became his favourite model. Indeed his portraits of Hazel, with her haunting beauty and the red, purple and gold colour harmonies which he favoured in painting her, are most enchanting today.

**Sir John Lavery**
0862414407 £14.95

## LOUIS LE BROCQUY (b.1916)

Another self-taught artist, Le Brocquy has become one of the most highly regarded living Irish artists. His style is delicate, spare and carefully considered. He is best known for his head image series, a series depicting famous literary heroes like Beckett and Joyce.

**Irish Landscape**
0946641293 £25.00
**Head Images**
0946641587 £25.00
**Louis Le Brocquy**
1873654464 £15.00

## WILLIAM JOHN LEECH (1881–1968)

After studying under Walter Osborne, Leech moved to France in 1903, where he lived for some years. His painting – 'A Convent Garden, Brittany' – has become one of the most popular paintings in Ireland. His love of colour and flamboyant style made him an exciting painter. Sincerity and sensitivity are communicated in his work.

*Denise Ferran*
**William John Leech: An Irish Painter Abroad**
Merrell Holberton 1858940346 £29.95

## ALISTAIR MACLENNAN (b.1943)

Is the artist his art or the art the artist? An extremely thought-provoking performance and conceptual artist MacLennan has been influential to many through his teaching and his work. He himself is the canvas for his ideas to flow and the more people know about how interesting these ideas are the better.

**Coming To Meet:**
Project Press £10.00

## ALICE MAHER (b.1956)

Known for her fine drawings and gently challenging paintings, which are highly personal and slightly subversive, this very intelligent artist is continually redefining the medium in which she works. Her latest multi-media and sculptural work confirms her as one of the most exciting Irish artists around.

**Profile: Alice Maher**
Gandon pb 094664165X £7.50

## RODERIC O'CONOR (1860–1940)

Probably Ireland's first modernist painter, he was classically educated in England before returning to Ireland to enrol at the Metropolitan School of Art. He went to Paris and studied under Carolus- Duran, moving to the artists colony at Grez-sur-Loing, which was linked with the School of Pont Aven, presided over by Paul Gauguin. O'Conor was reputedly a complex character and his work reflects this.

*Johnathan Bennington*
**Roderic O'Conor: A Biography with a catalogne of his work.**
Irish Academic Press
0716524929 £14.95
*Paula Murphy*
**Roderic O'Conor**
hb 0948524383 £4.95

## TONY O'MALLEY
### (b.1913)

Born in Callan, Co Kilkenny he is a self taught artist, who went to live in St Ives in the 1950s. He returned to Ireland, with Jane, his wife in 1990. A fine abstract artist, his palate of greys, blacks and lavenders make wonderful compositions. His response to history motivates his sense of space.

**Tony O'Malley Ed. Brian Lynch**
Scolar Press hb 1859282350
£40.00
**Tony O'Malley**
Gandon 0946641404 £3.95
**Tony O'Malley – Painter**
**In Exile?**
£7.50 Arts Council Publication

## WALTER OSBORNE
### (1859–1903)

The son of a well-known animal painter, William Osborne, his paintings have become very popular, displaying charm yet avoiding sentimentality. Like most Irish artists of the time he spent time abroad in England and Europe and has been described as the first Irish Impressionist. A particularly good outdoor painter, he died tragically, at an early age, of pneumonia.

**Walter Osborne**
Town House 0948524235 £4.95

## SARAH PURSER
### (1848–1943)

Born in Dublin and educated in Europe this remarkable artist is best known for her fine pastel portraits. In Paris she met Degas, and his influence is apparent in her work. In 1890 she was elected as an honorary member of the Royal Hibernian Academy at a time when women were not allowed full membership. When this rule changed she became the first woman elected member. Her vigour and strength of character resulted in many changes in the way art was appreciated in Ireland and she was instrumental in the growth of the history of art course at Trinity. Sarah Purser was a pioneer, and a fine portrait painter to boot.

*John O'Grady*
**Life and Works of Sarah Purser**
Four Courts Press 1851822410
£29.95

## NANO REID (1900–1981)

The artistic reputation of this Drogheda painter is beginning to grow, becoming as famous as her reputedly caustic tongue. Known as a Celtic Bohemian and an Irish eccentric, her artistic legacy is as great as her character. Her pen and ink drawings are charming.

**Nano Reid**
0952479206 £15.00

## WILLIAM SCOTT
### (1913-1989)

Known as a primitive realist he is best known for his still life paintings. The simple construction and harmonious colours created a pleasing canvas. Modigliani, Chardin, Cezanne and Braque influenced him.

*Lynton Norbert*
**William Scott**
Bernard Jacobson Gallery
1872784038 £14.95

## SEAN SCULLY

A wonderful simplicity and eastern influence flow from the work of this artist, which is mesmerising to behold and at the essence is a deep spirituality, or as he himself has said, an emotional glue. It is indeed intoxicating stuff and the more one delves into his work, the more engrossing and gratifying it becomes. Of particular interest are the Catherine paintings. Each year the artist chooses a painting which he thinks is indicative of his best work of that year and he retains it for his private collection, named after his partner, Catherine Lee.

**Sean Scully: The Catherine Paintings**
Modern Art Museum of Fort Worth 092986509X £26.00

*Ned Rifkin*
**Sean Scully: Twenty Years**
Thames & Hudson 0500092494 £24.95

# CHARLES TYRELL (b.1950)

'An animated lyrical abstraction underlined by geometric structures' is how his work is described. Tyrell has been influenced by Morris Louis and Richard Diebenkorn and of particular interest is his Borderland series from the late 1980s.

**Charles Tyrell**
Gandon 0946641412 £3.99
**Charles Tyrell Paintings 1993**
Gandon 0946641439 £4.95

# LEO WHELAN (1892–1956)

Whelan studied under William Orpen whose other pupils included Sean Keating, Margaret Clarke and Patrick Tuohy. Unlike many Irish artists he never left Ireland and lived throughout his life at 65 Eccles Street. Many of his paintings depict a simple domestic arena and in his figurative work he pays special attention to the detail of hands.

# JACK B. YEATS (1871–1957)

Regarded as the finest painter Ireland has ever produced, he began his career as a draughtsman and illustrator. Born in London, he spent much of his childhood in Sligo, and with his brother, William Butler Yeats, he became part of the Irish Revival and provided sketches for Synge's series of articles in the Manchester Guardian in 1905. When he began to use oils, his work became freer and more vibrant; the famous thick, energetic brush strokes became his style. A very literal painter, he was fond of symbolising horses – depicting, loyalty, freedom and intelligence and this is most common in his later work. As Samuel Beckett said of him, 'One can simply bow, wonder struck'.

*T.E. Rosenthal*
**Art of Jack B. Yeats**
Andre Deutsch pb 0233989528 £14.99

*Hilary Pyle*
**Yeats: Portrait of an Artistic Family**
Merrell Holberton hb1858940400 £35.00

*John Booth*
**Jack B. Yeats: A Vision of Ireland**
House of Lochar hb 0946537909 £35.00

*Hilary Pyle*
**Jack B. Yeats: Watercolours**
Irish Academic Press hb 0716524775 £20.00

*Hilary Pyle*
**Jack B. Yeats: Cartoons**
Irish Academic Press hb 0716525216 £37.50

*Bruce Arnold*
**Jack Yeats**
Yale UP hb £25.00 0300075499

Works series from Gandon Editions are really well presented short studies of individual artists, with an interview or essay and high quality reproductions of the 'works'.

**Gwen O'Dowd**
£3.95 0946641390

**Michael Mulcahy**
pb £3.95 0946641471

**Tony O'Malley**
pb £3.95 0946641404

**John T Davis**
pb £3.95 0946641323

**Charles Brady**
pb £3.99 0946641307

**Seán McSweeney**
pb £7.50 0946641617

**Charles Tyrell**
pb £3.99 0946641412

**Patrick Graham**
pb £3.95 0946641226

**Andrew Folan**
pb £3.99 0946641161

**Michael Scott 1905-1989**
pb £3.99 0946641315

**Anita Groener**
pb £3.99 0946641501

**Eithne Jordan**
Irish pb £3.95 0946641420

**James Scanlon**
pb £3.95 0946641536

**Martin Gale**
pb £3.95 0946641498

**Dermot Seymour**
pb £3.95 094664148X

**Patrick Hickey**
pb £3.99 0946641153

**Mary FitzGerald**
pb £3.95 0946641234

**Michael Cullen**
pb £3.950946641242

**Maud Cotter**
pb £4.95 0946641633

**Patrick Hall**
pb £3.99 0946641331

**Vivienne Roche**
pb £3.95 0946641145

Gandon Editions also publish the brilliant Profile series, which is a medium format and includes a critical essay on the artist, and interview and of course high quality reproductions.

**Pauline Flynn**
pb £7.50 0946641722

**Seán Mcsweeney**
pb £7.50 0946641617

**Eil's O'Connell**
pb £7.50 096641870

**Siobhán Piercy**
pb $7.50 0946641900

**Mary Lohan**
pb £7.50 0946641889

## Practical Resource Books

There are a number of art books on the market, which offer practical information. An excellent reference book is **Guide to Exhibition Venues in Ireland** (0906627605 £5.95). This little book tells you of all the major and minor galleries, the times they open and their geographical location. **Organising An Exhibition** (0906627435 £3.00) and **Handle With Care** (0906627443) offer excellent information about setting up exhibitions and looking after art works and The Arts Council publish a number of books and leaflets on subjects like tax and the artist. It also produces a Directory of Arts Managers in Ireland and other useful information. Every year **The Irish Arts Review, ed. Homan Potterton** (Irish Arts Review 0952387662 hb £35.00 and 0952387670 pb £22.50) contains a catalogue of what Irish Paintings, sculptures, crafts, furnishings etc. have sold and forms the annual report of the art world.

# Architecture
by Jane Humphries

Like other countries, the architectural landscape of Ireland tells us much about cultural, economic, social and historical influences at work. From the Celtic era, to modern day Ireland, a rich heritage has been left behind. *Architecture in Ireland* by *Maurice Craig* (0708944965 £22.95), *Building On The Edge* (0946641749 £ 12.50), *Irish Art and Architecture* (0500277079 £16.00) are all good general architecture books, tracing a history of architectural theories and ideas. *Field Guide To The Buildings of Ireland* (1874675813) *and Buildings of Ireland* (014071085X £35.00) are two very good resource books as is *Buildings of Ireland* (014070817 £25).

So we will begin on a potted architectural history tour of Ireland and the books which accompany the trail.

Ireland, like Scotland had a large number of castles and fortifications. Listed here are a number of titles, which make for interesting browsing.

*Castles of Britain and Ireland* (0715302426 £20.00), *Irish Castles and Fortification* (1898256128 £24.95), *Irish Castles* (0852210108 £12.00), *Castles in Ireland* (0415165377 £29.95). *Irish Castles* (090034668X £2.95). *Castles and Strongholds of Ireland* (1871731151 £7.50).

After the Celtic clan system, Christianity came to Ireland, and with it monastic architecture. *Early Irish Monasteries* (094617248X £5.95), *Cistercian Monasteries of Ireland* (030037376 £45.00) are worth checking out. Later Christian architecture can be found in *Cathedrals of Ireland* (0853894523 £17.50), and three volumes of *Irish Churches by Leask Dundalg* costing £18.00 each, (0852210167, 0852210116, 0852210125).

There are a number of books, which lament the end of the great Irish house. *Vanishing Country Houses Of Ireland* (0946641781 £19.95), *Follies and Gardens of Ireland* (0300055773 £40.00), *In Ruins* (0316879274 £18.99)

And those which specialise in particular subjects such as *Irish Stone Bridges* (0716524651 £29.90), *Bright Light White Water* (about Lighthouses*)* (1874597642 £14.99), *Irish Hospital Architecture* (1873820313 £10.00) and *Dublin, A Grand Tour* (0297822217 £14.99), which is a visually lush tour of Georgian Dublin.

This brings us to the most exciting time in Ireland for architecture since James Gandon's Custom House. Contemporary architecture in Ireland is making an impression on the urban and rural landscape, indicating the new economic strength of Ireland, its European feel and tremendous confidence of spirit. *20$^{th}$ Century Architecture In Ireland* (3791317199 £39.99), *Dublin: A Recent Guide to Architecture* (189985830X £5.95), *Making A Modern Street* (0946641194 £9.50) and a great series of New Irish Architecture Awards published by Gandon Press which tell us of this architectural Zeitgeist.

After that frantic romp around the bookshelves here are a few books which are particularly good.

*A Companion Guide to Irish Architecture 1837–1921* (0716525135 £ 19.95)

The author of this very informative book, Jeremy Williams, has written a truly interesting and resourceful book. For anyone interested in Ireland's architecture of the post Georgian period, this is a treat. A Gazetteer, in the true sense of the word, he has produced a thoughtful, easy to use, resource book, with plenty of handy maps, laced with charming drawings, many of which are penned by his hand. From Antrim to Wicklow, the book contains valuable information about artists, craftworkers, builders and, of course, architects. An ideal companion to both scholars and the lay person, wishing to glean an insight into this period. All in all a rare gem, which shines through as a labour of love by its author. Many will love exploring its pages, discovering much about the architectural heritage of favourite Irish counties.

*Irish Georgian* (Thames & Hudson 050007020 £16.95)

Ireland has its fair share of gracious Georgian dwellings, and this book brings together the best examples from the period. Looking at houses, both big and small which includes villas and cottages, the book is sectioned into five areas –

Origins, Interiors, Colours, Ingredient and Virtuosi – to explore the major characteristics and features of the time. With some fabulous colour photographs and interesting text, this is a fine testimony to Irish Georgian style.

*McGarr and Ní Eanaigh* (0946641994 £7.50)

Gandon editions – appropriately named after the architect James Gandon- have a Profile series on contemporary architects. Like the series for artists, these consist of a critical appraisal, an in conversation section and then a generous dollop of illustrated colour plates. A mouth watering combination. The choice of spotlighting the architectural practice of Michael McGarry and Sibhan NiEanaigh is a good one. They are innovative architects who have contributed greatly to the modern architectural landscape – Poodle Bridge, Temple Bar, Tain Interpretative Centre etc. Here there is an excellent essay about the architects, titled Pragmatic Idealists, by Raymund Ryan which is an enlightening evaluation of their work to date.

*O'Donnell and Tuomey* (0946641986 £7.50)

Another one of Gandon's Profile series, this times concentrating on the architectural practise of Sheila O'Donnell and John Tuomey. an inspiring group of Irish contemporary architects, their most famous projects being, the Irish Film Centre, IMMA, National Photography Centre and Gallery of Photography. They have stamped their design style firmly on the face of Temple Bar, making it the fabulous space we know today. Included here are a number of insightful essays and excellent design plans. Fantastic viewing and thought provoking prose make another worthwhile Profile.

*Temple Bar: The Power Of An Idea* (1874202095 £20)

Everything you ever wanted to know about Temple Bar, but were too drunk to care. From its roots as an inner city community, to the present day chic artists playground, the book consists of a collection of essays, which tackle questions like living in the area and then concentrates on the designs of the Group 91 architects, who designed the contemporary area. Lots of stunning photographs, insights into cultural projects like Arthouse, Designyard and Gallery of Photography but for once, not a stag party in sight.

*ARIS: Temple Bar Gallery and Studios* (0951914626 £15)

   With a front cover of the magnificent oval staircase of the new Temple Bar artist studios, this could be misleading, as the book is actually a homage to those artists who first inhabited the area. A legacy to the artists who first made Temple Bar Dublin's Left Bank, it is good to see them listed with examples of their work, their vision as the original pioneers of this arty area remembered. Aidan Dunne tells the tale, of how they got the new studios built, with great insight and knowledge. Temple Bar has gone beyond the wildest dreams of those who dared to dream to bring its existence.

*Michael Scott : Architect in (casual) conversation with Dorothy Walker* (Gandon094664151X £25)

   It is fitting that casual here is in brackets, for what comes from reading this book, which was constructed by a series of interviews with the architect from 1978-1980, is what an amazingly affable and conversational person Michael Scott was. Not only was he such a likeable chap, he influenced Irish twentieth century architecture and arts like nobody else. One of the great personalities of his age, this book is a wonderful insight into the man and his ideas.

# Autobiography & Memoirs

**Collins Gem Famous Irish Lives**
Harper Collins pb £3.50
0004709403
With over 150 entries,
including writers, politicians,
scientists and sports
personalities, this is the
handiest biographical
reference book available.
The book includes clear
text, some line drawings
and an index by profession
of the personalities.

## GERRY ADAMS (b.1948)

Born into a republican family in Belfast and educated in local
schools he became involved in the Republican movement in
the 1960s mainly with the West Belfast Action Housing
Committee and the Northern Ireland Civil Rights Association.
In 1972, he was held on the Maidstone prison ship before being
moved to Long Kesh. After his release, he became president of
Provisional Sinn Féin, following a split with the Official IRA.
He has been a Westminster MP for West Belfast since 1987.

**Before the Dawn**
Heineman hb £7.99 0434003417
**Falls Memories**
Brandon Press pb £6.99 0863220134
**Irish Voice**
Brandon Press pb £9.99 1902011015

## JONATHON BARRINGTON

**Personal Sketches**
Ashfield Press pb £9.95
190165804X

First published in 1827, this is a lively memoir about the ascendancy in 18th Century Ireland from an insider's point of view. Rituals like marriage markets, duels and characters like Wolfe Tone are presented in a racy, gossipy style.

## PATRICK BOLAND

**Tales From a City Farm Yard**
Boland pb £5.95 0952673703
This is a collection of auto-biographical stories set in the Liberties area of Dublin's South inner city during the 1940s. Told through the small boy's eyes, the stories tell of a past way of life where pigs, cows, hens and horses were kept in the small gardens of the city's houses.

## ROSITA BOLAND

**Sealegs: Hitch-Hiking the Coast of Ireland Alone**
New Island Books pb £6.95
1874597006

In this autobiographical travelogue Boland, having spent some years abroad, came back to Ireland and travelled around the country recording the stories told by people that she met.

## CHRISTY BROWN (1932–1981)

Memoirist, novelist and poet Christy Brown was born in Dublin, where he lived all his life. He suffered from cerebral palsy, but managed to overcome his disability and reveal a major literary talent. He managed to use a typewriter with his left foot, thus the title of his bestselling memoir. *My Left Foot* is a very important portrait of Dublin working class life in the 1940s and 1950s as well as being the moving story of a strong individual who was determined not to be discouraged by an overwhelming handicap. He drew heavily on his experiences for his novel *Down all the Days* which displays his great talent for descriptive detail and mood. Both books enjoyed a huge revival in the early 1990s following the success of Jim Sheridan's film, starring Daniel Day Lewis as Christy Brown.

**My Left Foot**
Minerva pb £5.99 0749391774
**Down All the Days**
Minerva pb £6.99 0749391790 (novel)

## NOEL BROWNE

**Against the Tide**
Blackstaff Press pb £13.99
0717114589

*Against the Tide* is one of the
more important political
memoirs of 20th century
Ireland. Medical doctor and
government minister, Browne
(1915-1996) was responsible
for setting up the sanitoria
which effectively eradicated
tuberculosis in Ireland.
He also clashed with the
Catholic hierarchy over his
proposed health scheme
which would entitle everyone
in Ireland to free health care
without a means test. This
clash led to his resignation in
1951. *Against the Tide*
chronicles his early life in
Athlone, his student days in
England, his time in
government and his very
personal but acute
commentary on the state of
leftist politics in Ireland.

## GABRIEL BYRNE

**Pictures in my Head**
Wolfhound Press pb £7.99
0863274625

A fascinating memoir from a
talented actor, this movingly
describes his life from
growing up in Crumlin to his
successful career in
TV and film. Written with
good humour, this book
also takes a wry look at the
Hollywood film industry
as well as providing an
introspective narrative from
one of Ireland's foremost
acting talents.

## WILLIAM CARLETON

**Autobiography**
White Row Ltd pb £7.95
1870132750

Carleton (1794-1869) was
one of the most important
19th century men of letters.
Though educated in a hedge
school, Carleton traveled
from Co.Tyrone to Maynooth
to study for the priesthood.
However, he soon decided
against this, married and
converted to Protestantism.
He wrote pen portraits of
contemporary Irish country
life for a variety of journals
including *The Nation* and
*The Dublin University
Magazine*. These pieces were
later collected and published
as *Traits and Stories of the Irish
Peasantry* which made him
famous. Written in the year
before he died, though
unfinished, his *Autobiography*
is a moving testament to
many lives led in grim
subsistence by Irish people in
colonial Ireland in the 19th
century.

## MONICA CARR

**Country Diary**
Cork Publishing Ltd. pb £7.99
1860769551
This is a collection of pieces written on a weekly basis for the Farming Independent during the 1950s. Monica Carr was born Mary Norton in Dunlavin, Co Wicklow in 1922; her weekly column delighted many readers because of its enthusiasm for country life and its numerous recipes.

## SR SARAH CLARKE

**No Faith in the System**
Mercier Press pb £9.99
1856351602
In 1976 Sr Sarah Clarke gave up teaching and went to work full time with prisoners in English Gaols. Her memoir records her early life in Athlone and why she gave up teaching to devote her time to the pastoral care of prisoners.

## GERRY CONLON

**Proved Innocent**
Penguin pb £6.99 0140230629
*Proved Innocent* is a harrowing memoir written by one of the Birmingham Six, wrongly accused of bombing an English pub in 1972. Falsely imprisoned for 16 years, Conlon in this book movingly describes the soul-destroying wait for final vindication against the huge weight of a prejudiced English legal system.

## CHRIS CONROY

**Beggar in Paradise**
Mentor pb £12.99 0947548920
This is a memoir of the fifteen years that Conroy spent living with the Incas in Peru. Conroy gives a fascinating insight into the lives of the Incas in the twentieth century.

## ELAINE CROWLEY

**Cowslips and Chainies: A Memoir of Dublin in the 1930s**
Lilliput Press pb £6.99
1874675805
*Cowslips and Chainies* is a classic of its kind. Recalling both the joy and the trauma of her childhood in a charming prose that never seeks to sentimentalize, Crowley narrates the way Dublin was when she was growing up. Remembering the Iveagh Market in its heyday, the 1932 Eucharistic congress and the awful time at the death of her father, Crowley has given the 1990s reader a rare insight into a forgotten time.

## PADDY DOYLE

**The God Squad**
Black Swan pb £6.99
0552135828

Born in 1951 and orphaned at the age of four, Paddy Doyle was ordered to be taken into the 'care' of an industrial school, where he was physically, psychologically and sexually abused by his religious keepers. His trauma led to physical reactions and these in turn have led to his permanent disability. *The God Squad* is his memoir of his institutionalization and the awful treatment he received from both Church and State. This book, as moving as it is harrowing, is written without bitterness and as a result manages to evoke in the reader a huge range of emotions unmatched in contemporary Irish memoir.

## TERESITA DURKAN

**Goldenbridge: The View From Valparaiso**
Veritas pb £6.99 1853903035

Sister Teresita Durkan, now working in South America has written a memoir in reaction to the controversy surrounding the allegations of systematic abuse by the nuns running the Goldenbridge orphanage during the 1960s. Accused by many of being an apologetic defense of the actions of her colleagues, Durkan herself asserts that, although there was hardship, there was no system of abuse while she was working there.

## ELIZABETH, COUNTESS OF FINGALL

**Seventy Years Young**
Lilliput Press pb £10.00
0946640742

This is a wonderfully colourful memoir of the late ninteenth and early twentieth century Irish Catholic ascendancy. Written by Daisy Burke who married the 11th Earl of Fingall of Killeen Castle, Co. Meath, the book covers a vitally important period of modern Irish history, from the 1916 Rising, the Civil War and into the 1920s. Many of the great contemporary cultural/political figures from Charles Stuart Parnell to George Bernard Shaw and W.B. Yeats are brought to life in its pages.

## JOHN FLEETWOOD

**In Stitches: The Diary of a Student Doctor**
O'Brien Press pb £5.99
0862783836

In this humorous account of going through medical school, John Fleetwood carefully notes all the mistakes, some funny, some serious which rounded off the education of this talented doctor. It could be said that this account takes the old maxim of learning by your mistakes a little too far.

## ROBIN FLOWER
### (1881–1946)

**The Western Island Or The Great Blasket**
Oxford University Press pb £5.99 0192812343

Robin Flower was an Oxford-educated local historian, translator and naturalist who spent a number of years on the Great Blasket, an island off the Kerry coast. This is his memoir of his time there and the book is an important record of life on an island that is no longer inhabited.

## BOB GELDOF

**Is That It?**
Penguin pb £6.99 014009363X
This is a movingly honest
memoir from the Dublin
born singer/songwriter. The
book very effectively captures
the cultural moments through
which Geldof lived, from
1960s Dublin through 1970s
hippy London to punk and
The Boomtown Rats. It also
provides the inside story of
the phenomenally successful
Band-Aid campaign to raise
money for famine relief
in Ethopia.

## ANNABEL DAVIS GOFF

**Walled Gardens: Scenes From an Anglo-Irish Childhood**
Eland pb £8.99 0907871429
This is a portrait of the
Anglo-Irish in the 1940s and
1950s. Davis-Goff grew up
in a society that still had
servants and regularly went
fox-hunting but the house
had no central heating and
the roof leaked constantly.
The author also tells the
poignant story of the collapse
of her parents' marriage
against a background picture
of fading glory and
crumbling walls.

## OLIVER ST JOHN GOGARTY (1878-1957)

Poet, dramatist, memoirist,
nose and throat surgeon,
Gogarty was born in Dublin.
He was educated at
Clongowes Wood College and
the Medical School of Trinity
College, Dublin. He was a
close friend of James Joyce
and in the autumn of 1904,
he shared the Martello tower
in Sandycove Co. Dublin with
Joyce and another friend
from England. This period
was immortalized in the
opening chapter of *Ulysses,*
where the Buck Mulligan
character is based on Gogarty.
He wrote three plays which
were produced for the Abbey
theatre. He became a member
of the Irish senate and was
kidnapped by republicans
during the Civil War. He
emigrated to America in 1939
and lived there until he died.
Both of his memoirs, as well
as displaying a formidably
jaunty, though never flippant
style, are very important
historically as they provide an
inimitable portrait of many
of the historical and literary
characters of the time whom
Gogarty knew.

**As I Was Going Down Sackville Street**
O'Brien Press pb £7.99
0862783941
**Tumbling in the Hay**
O'Brien Press pb £7.99
0862784727

## JOE GOOD

**Enchanted by Dreams**
Brandon Press pb £9.99
0863222250
Joe Good (1895-1962) fought
in the GPO during the 1916
rising. He was an associate of
Michael Collins and was one
of the team sent to London
in 1918 to assassinate
members of the English
cabinet. His memoir,
*Enchanted by Dreams,* is a lively
retelling of an often
adventurous life.

## ELIZABETH GRANT

**The Highland Lady in Ireland**
Canongate pb £7.99
0862413613
First published in 1898 this
is an account of Grant's life
while she lived in Ireland
during the 1840s. She came
to Ireland when she married
Colonel John Smith and gives
both acute and irreverent
accounts of the Irish people
that she met.

## MAURICE HAYES

Maurice Hayes's book *Black Puddings and Slim* is a charming memoir of a ten year old boy who has just moved to Downpatrick from the countryside. The book is a nostalgic paean to the country life that the author remembers. Hayes went on to write *Minority Verdict* which is a much tougher, political book about life in the Irish Civil Service.

**Black Puddings and Slim: A Downpatrick Boyhood**
Blackstaff Press pb £8.99
0856405906
**Minority Verdict: Experience of a Catholic Public Servant**
Blackstaff Press pb £12.99
0856405485

## JOHN KELLY

**Cool About the Ankles**
Blackstaff Press pb £7.99
0856405914
The successful compere of Today F.M.'s nightly Eclectic Ballroom has written an idiosyncratic book. *Cool About the Ankles* consists of sardonically humorous reflections/memoirs from a Manhattan hotel room about a number of topics including jazz, soccer, Woody Allen and Co. Monaghan. Part travelogue, part memoir and diary, the book shows Kelly's quirky and captivating sense of humour throughout.

## BRIAN KEENAN

**An Evil Cradling**
Vintage pb £7.99 009999030X
Born in Belfast in 1950, Brian Keenan went to teach in Beirut in 1985 and was kidnapped by fundamentalist Shi'ite terrorists in 1986. He was held for five years in often appalling conditions and *An Evil Cradling* is the result of his coming to terms with his lost years. Not just a straight day-to-day chronicle of his captivity, this book is a moving meditation on the nature of cruelty, captivity and hope.

"Hunger-strike is a powerful weapon in the Irish psyche. It powerfully commits back into the hunger-striker's own hands the full sanction of his own life and of his will. I was desperate for information."
Brian Keenan – An Evil Cradling

## CHRISTY KENNEALLY

Christy Kenneally has written two captivating memoirs about his life. *Maura's Boy* describes his life after his mother died, when he was ten years old, and the way that his loving father, Dave, reacted. It is a magical description and evocation of Ireland in the late 1940s and early 1950s. His next book describes the life he led in his early twenties, as a young deacon in Cork, working with incurables in St. Patrick's Hospital.

**Maura's Boy: A Cork Childhood**
Mercier Press pb £6.99
1856351513
**The New Curate**
Mercier Press pb £6.99
1856351998

## GEORGE KENNEDY

**Not All At Sea**
Morrigan pb £22.00
0907677975

The naval architect and yacht designer has written a memoir detailing his early life working on naval craft during World War II. In the 1960s, he returned to Ireland and was the first person to realise the potential of the River Shannon as a tourist area and went ahead with his idea of building a fleet of river cruisers.

## EAMON MACTHOMÁIS

**Me Jewel and Darlin' Dublin**
O'Brien Press pb £7.99
0862783895

This is a classic Dublin memoir, vividly describing a child's world and the old ways of the city. Pawnshops, Dublin slang, Phoenix Park and the sights and smells of the old city centre are described in vivid and varied detail.

## MAUD GONNE MACBRIDE

**Servant of the Queen: Reminiscences**
Colin Smythe pb £8.95
0861403673

Probably most famous as the subject of W.B.Yeats's unrequited love, Maud Gonne MacBride was also a prominent nationalist, journalist and, on the evidence of *Servant of the Queen,* a gifted memoirist. Describing her life and a pivotal period of Ireland's history, in clear, vibrant prose, this book provides both an insight and introduction to the history of 20th Century Ireland.

## JAMES MACINTYRE

**Three Men on an Island**
Blackstaff Press hb £20.00
0856405825

The artist James Macintyre's beautifully illustrated memoir is the celebratory story of a summer spent on the island of Inishlacken off the West coast of Ireland in the company of his friends, the artists Gerard Dillon and George Campbell. Recording the arguments, disappointments, conversations and laughter of a formative summer in all three of their lives, MacIntyre's memoir is a warm testament to friendship.

## LYN MADDEN

**Lyn A Story of Prostitution**
Attic pb £7.99 0946211450

This is a harrowing memoir by a woman who worked as a prostitute in Dublin during the early 1980s. Written with journalist June Levine, and detailing the abuse she received at the hands of her partner and her clients, *Lyn* gives the reader an important awakening to and education about a side of Dublin that contemporary society is all to happy to ignore.

## JULIAN MADIGAN

**Agony of Ecstasy**
Poolbeg pb £5.99 1853716820

This is the story of Madigan's involvement with hash, acid, speed and finally ecstasy. His book also describes the way that his father rescued him from the horror.

## HUGH MAXTON

**Waking: An Irish Protestant Upbringing**
Laglan Press pb £7.95
1873687915

*Waking* is the often untold story of the non-Catholic but non-Anglo-Irish community in Ireland. Written in a gentle, realistic prose, Maxton's book also describes the after affect of his father's death in 1961 and gently evokes the ordinary lives of his community with a rare, affecting charm.

## FRANK MCCOURT

**Angela's Ashes**
Flamingo pb £7.99 000649840X

*Angela's Ashes* is one of the publishing sensations of recent years. It tells the story of Frank McCourt and his family growing up in Limerick in the 1930s. Never shirking from telling the story as it really was, McCourt marries elements of humour and tragedy with a rare effectiveness. The book starts with the story of how his parents came to be married and of his early life in New York and then his life in Limerick before he, in his early twenties, took the boat back to America.

*Nuala O'Faolain, journalist and memoirist, hails Frank McCourt's Angela's Ashes as an
instant classic of modern Irish writing.*

There has never been an Irish book with a destiny like *Angela's Ashes*. It arrived on the
scene from nowhere; the work of a nobody, and proceeded to lay claim to a territory
where no-one had been before. In itself, it neither set off to scale the heights of art
nor settled for the mild plain of the conventionally popular. It isn't *Ulysses,* though its
worm's-eye Limerick is as impeccably remembered as Joyce's Dublin. It isn't, on the
other hand, a reassuring moral tale, such as Maeve Binchy tells, to huge international
success. Yet such as it uniquely is, it has had and even surpassed Maeve Binchy's
popular success, while being certain to join *Ulysses* among the classics of Irish writing.
It defies categorisation. It is memoir, yet shaped as much by Frank McCourt's artistry
as by recall. The growing-up it describes is almost grotesquely underprivileged, yet it
is mediated to the reader by a sensibility so profoundly humorous that it makes that
reader helpless with laughter. It is utterly Irish, yet there is nothing narrowly local
about its appeal, and it has sold in millions all over the world, including in countries
where English is not spoken and Ireland barely heard of. It calls out its story from
down at the bottom of society, a place which most of the systems of the world have
decreed not to have a voice – the place of the pauper underclass. Angela, the mother
in *Angela's Ashes* owns a few things. Jam-jars, for instance, in which she serves her
family's drinks of tea. Old coats, to put on their bed. She is one with all the women in
the world who have two bowls, or a tin plate and a mug, or a single blanket, and
nothing else to furnish wherever they call home. The child Frank and his brothers are
one with all the barefoot children, or children in home-made boots, who stare out at
us with bewildered eyes from photographs of the ghettoes of the poor.

Even readers who neither know nor care about material poverty, know the other
kinds of disempowerment the McCourt children know. All children must depend on
the strength and goodness of their parents. All children are helpless when the
parents fail in these things, as Frank McCourt's parents failed. When his father drank
the money for their food and medicine, he was every father who though painfully
loved, did not love enough. Not that Malachy McCourt didn't try. Few things in
*Angela's Ashes* are more tellingly done than the glimpses of the father's dumb inner
life, in his long walks, his refusal to eat, his leaving them to go back to England,
to his real life as a drunk, on Christmas Day. Most readers hardly notice how
effectively Frank McCourt does quiet things like that, overwhelmed as they are by the
book's unforgettably painful passages, like the surviving little twin, Eugene, searching
for his brother, who is dead – calling Ollie's name, at first whenever he sees a fair-
haired child, and then, losing hope, 'He doesn't say Ollie anymore. He only points.'
And then Eugene dies himself. God asks too godddam much of this family, as a
passing doctor says. He took the mother's hope, and the children's trust, when they
searched Brooklyn for their errant breadwinner. He took the lives of the children too
frail to survive the bad housing and the inadequate food of a poor family made

destitute by alcoholism. He almost took the life-chances of the boys who survived. But above all, He took the fellow with the odd manner from Northern Ireland, and the sweet, feckless Limerick girl he got pregnant, and He handed them lives in which on even the longest walk it would not be possible to make out the operations of justice or mercy. And when Malachy disappeared, there was nowhere for Angela to go but further down. Begging outside the priests' house. Selling her pride to her cruel cousin.

But even as the parents decline, the boys grow up, vigorous as weeds reaching for the light. The glory of the book is its double perspective – the reader sharing the doctor's outraged and heartbroken overview of the McCourt family, but at the same time looking up at the rich life of that family and its place and time, from the point of view of the child Frank. The wake, for instance, for poor little dead Eugene, is peopled by the fierce Granny, the uncle who hasn't been right since he was dropped on his head, and the uncle who was gassed by the Germans and doesn't give a fart, and as an event it is lent magic by food and drink – and, as always in *Angela's Ashes*, is closely observed. The child is dead, but the room is warm. And the room is often the scene of tenderness, humour, and a creativity even of idiom so unforced that the family doesn't even know that these are gifts, which it possesses. The same is true of Limerick city itself – on one level so hard and hypocritical: on another, so eccentric in social character that people of absolutely no property can survive there. Survive, even, with wit, as in the savage verbal antics of the teachers Frank encounters. Survive in good company – because the boys with whom the McCourts share the great events of childhood, like saying the Rosary over a dead greyhound because it is very likely a Catholic greyhound, or trying to see a girl's body – are not much better off than they. Survive with grace, as in the scene with the much worse-off Clohessys, where Angela sings a last 'Oh, the Nights of the Kerry Dancing' with the dying man in whose arms she once danced light as a feather.

The Clohessys, like the McCourts, are within their fate. They live it as it comes. But if their world is full of suffering borne as uncomplainingly as if it were deserved, it is also full of goodness. From the Jewish and Italian neighbours in Brooklyn, to the policemen in Dublin, to Mr. Timoney in Limerick who introduces Frank to literature, to the Franciscan who relieves him of his guilt about his dead lover Theresa, individual people shine in the mire like stars. But the saviour of Frank McCourt – and all that in him which made *Angela's Ashes* – was not a person but a place. The United States of America is the heroine of this book – longed for for years as the place of health and opportunity, and entered (as it transpires) through the accident of a few hours with a generous party girl from Poughkeepsie, triumphant with joyful love-making. If, therefore, this is a great Irish book, it is also one which could not have existed without America. The suffering is Irish: the genial entertainer who puts it before us is Irish-American. That word has long been synonymous with the trite and the kitsch: *Angela's Ashes* reclaims it for the true heart and for art.

## ELIZABETH MCCULLOUGH

**Square Peg: An Ulster Childhood**
Marino pb £8.99 1860230652
This is Elizabeth McCullough's memoir of her life growing up outside Belfast from the 1930s, through World War II and on into the post-war years. She left her rural surroundings and went to work in the photography department at Queen's University where she met the writers John Luke and John Hewitt. She then took off on travels around Ghana, the USA and Tanzania with the man she eventually married.

## AIDAN O'HARA

**I'll Live Til I Die: The Story of Delia Murphy**
Drumlin pb £10.95 187343717X
This is the life story of Delia Murphy, the singer who laid the way for the folk music revival in Ireland. The book recounts her meetings with various luminaries including Joyce, Yeats and Erwin Rommel.

## DERVLA MURPHY

**Wheels Within Wheels**
Penguin pb £6.99
014005448040
Best known for her travel books Dervla Murphy has also published this memoir of her early life in Ireland. Examining the relationship she had with her parents, the book tells of her having to leave boarding school at the age of fourteen to look after her ailing mother, and of her early yen for travel. Murphy has written a charming and affective book which serves as interesting counterpoint to her travelogues.

## SEAMUS MURPHY

**Stone Mad**
Blackstaff Press pb £9.99
085640617
This is Murphy's account of the seven years he spent as an apprentice stonemason in Cork. Now one of Ireland's most respected sculptors, Murphy decided to spend time with a stonemason while studying in the Crawford School of Art. His charming and touching memoir is a great portrait of the eccentric and colourful masons he met.

## THOMAS O'CROHAN

**The Islandman**
Oxford University Press pb £5.99 0192812335
Originally published as An tOileánach and translated by Robin Flower, this memoir is a very important record of growing up on the Great Blasket island and of the island's daily life. Born in 1856 and living until 1937, O'Crohan experienced the huge change in life of the Blaskets as the modern world slowly encroached on the microcosm that was the island. He was married in 1878 and had ten children. *The Islandman* narrates the harshness of daily life with great dignity.

## PHIL O'KEEFE

*Down Cobbled Streets* is a charming and lively evocation of Dublin in the 1930s, a world where draymen delivered barrels of Guinness to pubs daily. These autobiographical stories were first broadcast on RTE radio. The sequel, *Standing at the Crossroads,* describes her early working life in 1950s Dublin and recalls the aura of the Metropole Dancehall and Gate theatres with lively detail.

**Down Cobbled Streets:
A Liberties Childhood**
Brandon Press pb £6.95
0863222137
**Standing at the Crossroads**
Brandon Press pb £7.99
0863222315

## MAURICE O'SULLIVAN

**Twenty Years a Growing**
Oxford University Press pb
£6.99 0192813250
Maurice O'Sullivan (Muiris î Sœilleabháin 1904-1950) was born on the Great Blasket Island but spent some time as an infant in an orphanage in Dingle when his mother died. He returned to the island at the age of six and stayed until his early twenties, when he joined the Gardaí Síochána. He wrote his island memoir while based in Galway and it was published in 1933. He spent the rest of his life in Galway where he drowned in 1950.

## GEORGE O'BRIEN

*Dancehall Days* is a great memoir set in Dublin in the early 1960s. Escaping fom his rural upbringing, the young O'Brien hit the dancehalls of the city centre with gusto and his anecdotal and lively story is a great evocation of Dublin at the time. O'Brien moved to London at the end of the decade and worked in a pub on the Lambeth Road. His second book, *Out of Our Minds,* recalls his life at the time and tells the story of his discovery of Jimi Hendrix and sojourns in Paris and Oxford. Both memoirs are funny, unsentimental and successfully avoid the pitfalls of distorted hindsight.

**Dance Hall Days**
Blackstaff Press pb £7.99
085640523X
**Out of Our Minds**
Blackstaff Press pb £7.99
0856405418

## MICHEAL O'GUIHEEN

**A Pity Youth does not Last**
Oxford University Press pb
£5.99 019281320X
This book recalls O'Guiheen's life on the Great Blasket island and compares the island of his youth to the island he had to leave as an adult. The great sadness inherent in witnessing the demise of one's community is recorded with poignancy and his fond memories of his mother, Peig Sayers are compelling.

## PATRICK O'SULLIVAN

**I Heard the Wild Birds Sing: A Kerry Childhood**
Anvil pb £4.95 0947962557
This book describes O'Sullivan's life in Callinafarcy, a small village between Milltown and Killorglin in Co. Kerry. A mixture of memoir, local history and study of folklore, O'Sullivan's book beautifully evokes an age and way of life that have disappeared.

## NUALA O'FAOLAIN

**Are You Somebody?**
New Island pb £7.99
1874597464

Before the publication of her
memoir Nuala O'Faolain was
best known for her incisive
political and social journalism
which features every week in
her column in the Irish
Times, as well as her books
programme. But nothing
could have prepared the
Irish, English and American
public for the poignancy and
truth of *Are You Somebody?*
Detailing her early life,
her relationship with her
parents, dealing with the
difficulties of boarding
school, O'Faolain is never
afraid to tell her reader the
truth, which makes painful if
gripping reading. She paints
great portraits of Dublin in
the 1950s, Oxford in the
1960s and her unhappy life
in 1970s London. The book
includes a selection of her
best journalism for the Irish
Times. The latest edition also
has an afterword written a
year after the book was first
published, in which O'Faolain
discusses the rare emotional
reactions she got from people
who read the book.

## JOHN QUINN

**My Education**
Town House pb £12.99
1860590632

This book consists of the
transcripts of a fascinating
series of radio interviews
which ran between 1991 and
1996 in which Quinn asked
many writers, politicians and
famous personalities about
their formative education.
Interviewees include Noam
Chomsky, Garret Fitzgerald,
Marilyn French, Brendan
Kennelly and Tony O'Reilly.

## PEIG SAYERS
**(1873–1958)**

The Oxford UP book is the
record of Sayers's life as
dictated to her son Micheal
O'Guiheen. Though born in
Dunquin, Co. Kerry, Sayers
(1873-1958) moved to the
Great Blasket after she
married Pádraig O'Gaoithú
and through her storytelling
became the most celebrated
of all the Blasket islanders.
Detailing the death of half of
her children by drowning as
well as recording her own
daily life, Sayers's memoir is
both tragic and compelling.
This book differs from the
other Blasket memoirs in that
it also includes many stories
from the folklore of the island.
*Peig* offers further, previously
unpublished stories.

**An Old Womens Reflections**
Oxford University Press pb
£5.99 0192812394
**Peig**
Edco pb £6.99 0861674405

## RAYMOND SMITH

**Urbi Et Orbi And All That**
Mountcross pb £9.95
0952667401

*Urbi et Orbi and All That* is Smith's humorous memoir of his experiences when working as a foreign and diplomatic correspondent with Independent Newspapers. Working in countries like the USA , the Lebanon and Zaire and covering the Pope's visit to Ireland in 1979, Smith has seen much of the world and his anecdotes are always amusing and acute.

## ALICE TAYLOR

The first of Alice Taylor's highly successful memoirs, *To School Through the Fields,* detailed her early life in rural Co. Cork and is a tribute to a quiet, simple way of life that has all but disappeared. Written in clear, engaging prose, Taylor's memoirs effectively recorded the experiences and feelings of a whole generation. Since the huge success of this first book, Alice Taylor has written a number of others, all successful.

**The Night Before Christmas**
Brandon Press pb £5.95
0863221904
**To School Through the Fields**
Brandon Press pb £5.95
0863220991

## NIALL TOIBIN

**Smile And Be A Villain**
Town House pb £8.99
1860590500

This book consists of Toibin's reflections on his life.
Born in Cork in 1929, he writes about his time working in the civil service, his varied stage and cinema career and his special relationship with the works of Brendan Behan in whose *Borstal Boy* he has appeared nine times.

## PAOLO TULLIO

**North of Naples, South of Rome**
Lilliput Press pb £6.99
1874675821

This is a beautifully written evocation of the Comino Valley, literally 'north of Naples, south of Rome', which has been home to the author and his family for the last six hundred years.
The author now divides his time between Italy and Co. Wicklow. Part travel book, memoir and history this book very skillfully weaves all its different elements together to create an originally rich and impressionistic portrait of people and place without falling into the trap of sentimentality.

## MICHAEL VINEY

**A Year's Turning**
Blackstaff Press hb £14.99
0856405620

This is the record of a year in Viney's life in Co. Mayo. Having lived on the beautifully wild west coast for over thirty years, Viney knows the land intimately and the book provides the privileged reader a glimpse into a typical year's growing, gathering and observing nature at work around him. Set out month by month, *A Year's Turning* is compelling, engaging, informative and one of those books that no reader will forget.

# Childrens

by Sarah Webb & Mary Rogers, Waterstone's, Dawson Street, Dublin

## Fiction Aged 2-8

**Irish Legends for Children Retold by Yvonne Carroll**
Gill & MacMillan 0717122239 £7.99
*Irish Legends for Children* filled a huge gap in the market when first published in 1994. In picture book format it retells six of the best known legends in clear, simple prose. Aimed at young children it has proved immensely popular both with Irish parents and as a gift for children of Irish descent living abroad.
*Recommended Age 4-8*
The book is also available in: –

| | | | |
|---|---|---|---|
| French | 0717123502 | £7.99 | |
| German | 0717123510 | £7.99 | |
| Video | 0717125424 | £9.99 | (VHS/PAL) |
| Video | 0717125432 | £9.99 | (NTSC) |

**Miniature Edition** 0717125513 £3.99
**Audio Pack** 071712603X £ 6.99 (Miniature edition plus C45 cassette)

# DON CONROY

Don Conroy is both a writer and an artist and is well known in Ireland as a television personality. He is a keen naturalist and environmentalist and his love of animals and the natural world permeates his work. The humorous, quirky illustrations that accompany his stories for young children endow each animal, however small, with his own distinct characteristics.

Don Conroy has written many books of illustrated fiction for young readers. His Wings Trilogy, an intriguing mix of closely observed wildlife and fantasy in which birds and rats act as champions of the forces of good and evil, is for older readers. Most recently he has written a Wildlife Colouring and Activity book to encourage young people to observe more closely the animals and birds of Ireland.

**Great Irish Legends for Children**
**Retold by Yvonne Carroll**
Gill & MacMillan 0717124673
£7.99

*Great Irish Legends* continues the good work of Yvonne Carroll's earlier book. She adapts more favourite stories for her young audience, including this time The King with Donkey's Ears and The Brown Bull of Cooley. The lively illustrations addenormously to children's enjoyment of some of the oldest of Ireland's traditional tales.
*Recommended Age 4-8*

The book is also available as:
**Video 0717127230 £9.99 (VHS)**
**Video 0717127249 £9.99 (NTSC)**

**The Tiger who was a Roaring Success**
O'Brien 0862783712 £3.99

When Barny Owl and his woodland friends hear the tiger's sad story of circus life they unite to help him return to India. How do you disguise a tiger? Cover him in flour and pretend he's a big dog! Zany humour for young readers.
*Recommended age 6-8*

**The Bookworm who Turned Over a New Leaf**
Poolbeg 1853718181 £3.99

Clive is a worm who lives happily among the books in a library. Now he must find a new home. Follow his adventures in words and humorous black and white line drawings.
*Recommended age 6-8*

**Elephant at the Door**
Poolbeg 1853718815 £3.99
Sophie makes a wish and her wish comes true. Sounds great until you know that Sophie wished for a big pink elephant. Now he's at the door! There are plenty of funny incidents to keep young readers absorbed.
*Recommended age 6-8*

## ANNA DONOVAN

**Fireman Sinead**
O'Brien 0862785294 £3.99
Sinéad definitely wants to be a fireman. The grown-ups try to discourage her but when a real fire breaks out Sinead discovers that it is, of course, perfectly possible for a girl to be a fireman.
*Recommended age 5-7*

## MARIE-LOUISE FITZPATRICK

**The Sleeping Giant**
Wolfhound 0863276431 £4.99
The gentle giant has been sleeping off the coast of Dingle for hundreds of years. He looks just like an island. One day the giant wakes up. This is a distinctively Irish tale of giants and druids in a contemporary setting. Written and illustrated by Marie-Louise Fitzpatrick, words and pictures combine seamlessly and contribute equally to our enjoyment of the story.
*Recommended age 4-7*

## ADRIENNE GEOGHEGAN

**Dogs Don't Wear Glasses**
Blackwater 0861218523 £4.99
Does Seymour need glasses or would it be better if his owner wore them? This is an unusual and engaging story for young readers with a sense of humour.
*Recommended age 4-7*

## ANNE MARIE HERRON

**Ribbit, Ribbit**
O'Brien 0862785278 £3.99
Freddy loves pretending to be a frog, hopping around and saying Ribbit, Ribbit. But how can he be persuaded to be a little boy again? Only Polly has the answer... An amusing story aimed at beginner readers.
*Recommended age 5-7*

## TOM HICKEY

**Granny Learns to Fly**
Children's Press 0947962964 £2.95
Granny Green's little red car breaks down and she discovers an unusual solution to her transport problems. To the amazement of her grandchildren, she learns to fly. So does Spit, the cat! The birds don't like all this activity in the air at all. This is an amusing, whimsical tale for young readers.
*Recommended age 5-8*

## TONY HICKEY

**The Matchless Mice**
Children's Press 0947962166 £2.95
The Matchless Mice live in Mangold Mansion. The series
revolves around stories of rivalry and friendship between
generations of cats and mice. Small children will delight in
the shifting relationships between animals often portrayed
as enemies.
Recommended age 5-8

Other books about the Matchless Mice also available from the
Children's Press: –
**The Matchless Mice's Adventure**
0900068817 £2.50
**The Matchless Mice in Space**
0947962107 £2.75

## LUCINDA JACOB

Lucinda Jacob always loved drawing and painting and as a child
created her own books. She studied English at Trinity College,
Dublin and then worked as a librarian. Her own children's
interest in stories and pictures inspired her to produce her first
professional books. Her illustrations are drawn using a soft
pencil and watercolours, the shades of colour carefully chosen
to capture the mood of her stories. Part of the immense charm
of her books is that the illustrations contain elements never
mentioned in the text. It is as important to look closely at the
pictures as it is to read the words which accompany them.
Lucinda Jacob's six published books are for young children.
She is presently working on a book for older readers. Her dual
language picture books are small masterpieces. The series
explores the ordinary events in children's lives weaving stories
from familiar activities. This type of storytelling is very
reassuring to a toddler trying to make sense of his or her
expanding world. The very young can 'read' the action in the
pictures, while an adult reads the words. The limited text is
attractive also to an older child beginning to read, in Irish or
in English, and eager to do so without too much adult help.
*Recommended age 2-6*

## FAVORITE IRISH FAIRY TALES

**Soinbhe Lally illustrated by
Finbarr O'Connor**
Poolbeg 1853717770 £9.99
Soinbhe Lally's storytelling
is fresh and imaginative.
She captures the emotions
within the old stories and
presents them to her young
readers. But what makes this
book really special is the
marvellous illustrations.
Finbarr O'Connor uses Celtic
motifs but the style is
absolutely modern.
The double page, full colour
picture of the Brown Bull of
Cooley, head to head with his
opponent the White Bull of
Connacht is particularly
striking.
*Recommended age 5-10*

**Emma's Hat**
Poolbeg pb £2.99 1853715131
**Emma and Julia in the Kitchen**
Poolbeg pb £2.99 185371514X
**Good Morning**
Poolbeg pb £2.99 1853717525
**Julia in the Garden**
Poolbeg pb £2.99 1853715158
**Lily and Ted**
Poolbeg pb £2.99 1853717479
**Molly is a Good Dog**
Poolbeg pb £2.99 1853717428

## UNA LEAVY

**No Shoes For Tom**
O'Brien 086278526X £3.99
Tom won't wear his shoes
and who can blame him
when it's such fun kicking
leaves or squelching through
mud? But when winter comes
he's glad of his cosy red
boots. A cheery story with
lively illustrations of the
determined Tom.
*Recommended age 5-7*

## FERGUS LYONS

**Muckeen the Pig**
O'Brien 0862785286 £3.99
Being a pig is great fun but
Muckeen doesn't like the
market. Can a clever pig find
a way out? Appealing and
funny with great illustrations
of Muckeen, this book is
perfect for early readers.
*Recommended age 5-7*

## SAM MCBRATNEY

**Illustrated by Anita Jeram**
**Guess How Much I Love You**
O'Brien 0862783909 £9.99
Small Nutbrown Hare and his
Daddy compete in describing
their love for each other. It's
not easy to find a measure-
ment for love; to the moon
and back will probably satisfy
most small readers.
A delightful, simple story in
which the illustrations as
much as the words convey the
tenderness and love between
Little and Big Hare.
*Recommended age 3-6*

## ARTHUR MCKEOWN

**Titanic**
Poolbeg 1853715166 £3.99
In this book we have an
account of the Titanic
disaster as seen through the
eyes of a child. Mary and her
mother survive, her father
goes down with the ship. It is
a clear and straightforward
retelling of the tragedy of the
great 'unsinkable' ship.
Very suitable for children fascinated by the story but too
young for the film versions.
*Recommended age 5-8*

## ARTHUR MCKEOWN

**Famine**
Poolbeg 1853715050 £3.99
All over Ireland people died
as the potato crop failed.
Joe and his daughter Maggie
are among those lucky
enough to be able to afford
passage across the Atlantic
and the chance of a new life
in America.
*Recommended age 5-8*

## ED MILIANO

**It's a Jungle Out There**
Wolfhound 0863275702 £8.99
The beautiful green eyed cat rules the garden. Or is it a jungle? Gorgeous, colourful pictures give us a cat's eye view of the world.
*Recommended age 2-6*

## JANE MITCHELL

**Olivia's Collection**
Poolbeg 1853727029 £3.99
When Olivia and her family move house, shyness prevents Olivia from joining the children playing in the sunshine. She decides to gather sunshine for herself but comes to realise that to have friends she must share the precious substance. Underlying the story is an explanation of the importance of sunshine in all our lives.
*Recommended age 5-8*

## MARY MURPHY

**I Like it When**
Mammoth 0749731192 £4.99
Baby Penguin loves his Mum. Each page shows just one action, 'I like it when you hold my hand' or 'I like it when you hug me tight'. The simple yet striking illustrations convey the warmth of a loving relationship. This is the perfect book for very small children.
*Recommended age 2-4*

## LARRY O'LOUGHLIN

**Fionn and the Scots Giant**
Blackwater 0861218779 £3.99
The Scots giant is coming to take Fionn's head. Can his clever wife Oonagh save Fionn and preserve his ferocious reputation?
The story is told cartoon style with lots of humour, perfect for young children especially if read aloud with plenty of emphasis.
*Recommended age 3-7*

## NIAMH SHARKEY

**Irish Legends for the Very Young**
Mercier 1856351440 £4.99
The stories of Setanta, Oisín and the Children of Lir are told here in simple versions suitable for beginner readers or to be read aloud by an adult. The graphic, unusual illustrations are immediately attractive to both age groups.
*Recommended age 4-7*

## GORDON SNELL

**Amy's Wonderful Nest**
O'Brien 0862785308 £3.99
Amy, a baby robin has fallen
from the nest and must build
a new one for herself. She is
not quite sure how to go
about the task and ends up
with a truly amazing nest.
This delightful story will
appeal to the hoarding
instinct in every small child.
*Recommended age 5-7*

## MARTIN WADDELL

**Owl Babies**
O'Brien 0862783925 £4.50
*Owl Babies* is a wonderful
picture story book for young
children. Three baby
owls wake up to find their
mother is gone. They try to
be patient and to believe the
eldest when she says that
Mummy will be back soon.
But little Bill will only say
'I want my Mummy'.
*Recommended age 2-6*

## MARTIN WADDELL

**The Pig in the Pond**
O'Brien 0862783739 £4.50
Another classic picture
book from Martin Waddell.
Pigs don't swim but one very
hot day the most unexpected
gathering takes place in
Farmer Neligan's pond.
*Recommended age 2-6*

## OSCAR WILDE

**The Happy Prince**
(Illustrated by Jane Ray)
O'Brien 0862784289 £5.50
World-renowned illustrator
Jane Ray brings her own
distinctive style to Oscar
Wilde's classic fairytale.
Special gold leaf printing
creates rich, sumptuous
illustrations ideally suited to
this story of the prince and
the little swallow.
*Recommended age 6-9*

**Irish Legends the Boyne Valley
Book and Tape**
O'Brien 086278140X £6.95
Six stories from Ireland's
distant past presented in a
book with the accompanying
tape narrated by well known
Irish personalities. The stories are written to be read
aloud to quite small children
who can, of course, listen
independently to the tape.
*Recommended age 5-10*

**The Second Boyne Valley
Honey Book and Tape of Irish
Legends**
Boyne Valley Honey Company
095178232 £5.95
Six more stories are brought
to life by well known readers.
An attractive paperback with
black and white or full colour
illustrations on almost every
page accompanied by a tape
over one hour long makes
this pack great value.
*Recommended age 5-10*

"So they pulled down the statue of the Happy
Prince. 'As he is no longer beautiful he is no
longer useful,' said the Art Professor at the
University."
Oscar Wilde – The Happy Prince

# ANN CARROLL

### Rosie's Quest
Poolbeg, 1853712817 £3.99

The first in the popular historical fiction series by Dublin based teacher Ann Carroll. Rosie McGrath travels back in time to Dublin in 1956, where she becomes her Mum's twin sister, also called Rose. But can she change the events of Friday the 13th, the day when her Mum and her Aunt were split up forever? An entertaining and thoughtful book for young readers.

### Rosie's Troubles
Poolbeg, 1853716812, £3.99

Rosie once again travels back in time, on this occasion to her Gran's childhood tenement days. Can she reunite her Gran and her Gran's best friend Catherine, who vanished in mysterious circumstances on Bloody Sunday in Croke Park, over three quarters of a century ago?

### Rosie's Gift
Poolbeg, 1853718750, £3.99

Rosie is on another quest, this time to 1870 where she meets her ancestor Joseph, a young servant boy in the rich de Courcy household. Together they face many dangers before ultimately overcoming evil and hatred, to change the past forever.

# MARITA CONLON-MCKENNA

Marita Conlon-McKenna is Ireland's best-selling children's author. Famous for her 'Famine Trilogy' – *Under the Hawthorne Tree, Wildflower Girl* and *Fields of Home'* Marita was born in Dublin in 1956 and now lives in Stillorgan, County Dublin. She is married and has four children. While listening to a radio programme about an unmarked children's grave from the Irish Famine which had been found under a hawthorne tree, she decided to write her first award winning book *Under the Hawthorne Tree*. Published in 1990, this book remained in the Irish best-seller list for over two years. It is now available in countries all over the world from Britain (Puffin edition), to Japan, Sweden and Germany. *Under the Hawthorne Tree* has also been filmed and will be shown on RTE and Channel 4 in 1998.

### Under the Hawthorne Tree
O'Brien Press, 0862782066, £3.99

The Irish Famine of the 1840s is dramatically brought to life in this epic tale. Three brave children undertake the treacherous journey to Castle Taggert and the safety of their fabled great-aunts. A heart-rending saga of courage, strength and survival against the odds. A classic and highly recommended historic page-turner.

### Wildflower Girl
O'Brien Press, 086278283X, £4.50

The second book in the 'Famine Trilogy' follows the life of the children as they grow up, dealing with issues of emigration from Ireland, poverty and the importance of family. Voted Bisto Book of the Year in 1992, *Wildflower Girl* is available all over the world.

### Fields of Home
O'Brien Press, 086278509X, £4.99

In the final book in the 'Famine Trilogy' Eily, Michael and Peggy are older and wiser. Each character's tale is recounted in rich detail, building up to a fitting climax for this epic trilogy. Michael starts work in the stables of a stately home, looking after the horses. When the home is burned to the ground, Michael loses his job and his family and the village suffer.

### The Blue Horse
Poolbeg, 0862783084, £3.99

Katie and her family are travellers. Their lives change when they move to a house in a strange area. Will the family ever fit in ?

### Safe Harbour
O'Brien Press, 0862784220, £4.50

Sophie and Hugh are sent to Ireland during the London Blitz. They find it difficult to adapt to life in another country with their grumpy and strict Grandfather. A moving and convincing story.

### No Goodbye
O'Brien Press, 0862783623, £3.99

Greg, Lucy, Conor and Grace are confused and scared when their mother leaves home. In a letter she says she wants 'time to be herself again', but what does that mean ? The enterprising children never lose hope and plot to bring their mother back home. An honest and brave book which explores theheartache, hope and determination of a family in crisis.

## DON CONROY

### On Silent Wings
O'Brien, 0862783690, £4.99

The first novel in the 'Wings' wildlife fantasy series. Kos, a young barn owl, is left alone and scared when his mother is killed by a hunter's trap. This begins his epic fight for survival, helped by kindly woodland animals. When the evil rat Fericul and his army arrive and begin to terrorise the animals someone has to take a stand. A gripping tale of danger, courage and adventure.

### Sky Wings
O'Brien, 0862784190, £4.50

The Feather of Light held at the Sacred Cliffs is the protector of the light of the world. A brave young falcon, Sacer, must bring this magical feather to the darkness of Ratland. Only then may the forces of evil and hatred be overcome forever in this exciting adventure story.

### Wild Wings
O'Brien, 0862784182, £4.50

Vega, a daring kestrel, escapes from the falconry, encouraged by his friend the owl. But an evil band of rats have broken loose from a laboratory. Can Vega and his animal friends save the world from these wicked rodents? Another gripping yarn from wildlife expert and broadcaster Don Conroy.

## MARGRIT CRUICKSHANK

### Skunk and the Ozone Conspiracy
Poolbeg, 1853712124, £3.99

When the SKUNK gang hold the world to ransom, Aishling and her eccentric godfather, Seamus decide to save the day. They travel to Switzerland with an amazing invention that can save the ozone layer. Joining them on their exciting adventure is the mad orange cat, Mulligan. A fun read from a popular author. (See also the 11+ section for other Cruickshank books)

### Skunk and the Bride of Dracula
Poolbeg, 1853717665, £3.99

Aishling, Seamus and Florence are invited to Antonia Browne's wedding in Transylvania but nothing is quite what it seems. The bridegroom is a Romanian Count and SKUNK are once more rearing their heads, this time in Budapest. Another exciting adventure story.

## PAULINE DEVINE

### Best Friends
Children's Press, 0947962794, £3.95

Sarah loves her pony Bluebell and looks forward to showing off her riding skills to her friends Babs and Trevor. She experiences the joys and disappointments of friendship in the world of Pony Club and Pony Camp. A fun and thoughtful read for all horse lovers.

## PAULINE DEVINE

**Riders by the Grey Lake**
Children's Press, 0947962999,
£3.95
Described by her cousin
Maeve as 'weird', Eithne has
problems both at home and
in school. When a strange
boy on a white charger comes
riding out of the lake towards
her, she finds herself torn
between two worlds.
A compelling read from this
popular author.

## ÉILIS DILLON

Éilis Dillon was born in
Galway in 1920. She is known
internationally as a fine writer
for adults and children.
Her novels for adults include
*Blood Relations* and *Across the
Bitter Sea* and the book *Cats
Opera* was adapted for the
stage. She died in 1994.

**Lucky Bag**
O'Brien Press, 0862781353,
£4.95
A delightful collection of folk
tales and short stories by Irish
authors, from Jonathan Swift
to Frank O'Connor. Each
excerpt is preceded by a
short biography of the
author. An excellent
introduction to Irish writing
for children, entitled *The
Lucky Bag* 'because it contains
a variety of surprises', according to one of its authors Éilis
Dillon.

**Cruise of the Santa Maria**
O'Brien, 0862782635, £4.50
Maggie takes over the building of the most perfect
Hooker in the world when
her grandfather dies. When
it is finished she takes to the
high seas and a great sailing
adventure begins. A wonderful seafaring yarn, rich in
surprises.

**Lost Island**
O'Brien Press, 08627811837,
£3.95
According to legend there is
a great reward hidden on the
'lost island', but who is brave
enough to find it? Michael's
father set out to find the
island, never to return. Now
the boy bravely decides to set
sail for the mysterious shores
of the fabled island.
A gripping adventure story.
Striking, atmospheric black
and white illustrations by
David Rooney.

**The Sea Wall**
Poolbeg, 185371304X £2.99
Inisharcain is threatened by
'a great wave', which could
destroy the island. Only Old
Sally and her grandson Pat
recognise the impending
danger. Together they plan
to re-build the sea wall and
save the island.

***Also by this author***
**San Sebastian**
Poolbeg, 1853716669, £3.99

## ROBERT DUNBAR

**Enchanted Journeys**
O'Brien, 0862785189, £8.99
The editor of this beautifully produced and far reaching collection is one of the most respected voices in the field of Irish children's literature. A lecturer, broadcaster and reviewer who edited the magazine 'Children's Books in Ireland' for eight years, Dunbar has cleverly brought together a feast of Irish children's writing from the last fifty years. Authors included are Maeve Friel, Patricia Lynch, Walter Macken and John Quinn. An excellent introduction to fine Irish children's writing for any reader of eight to eighty!

## MARIE-LOUISE FITZPATRICK

**The Long March**
Wolfhound 086327644X £9.99
In 1847 a group of desperately poor Choctaw Indians donated $170 towards the relief of famine in Ireland. Inspired by the generosity of this gift Marie-Louise Fitzpatrick has brought together the tragedies of two nations. The Choctaw Indians were forced to leave their own lands. On their Long March more than half their number perished. In Ireland, famished people wandered in search of food. Those who could, fled across the Atlantic. There are powerful images in both words and artwork as 14 year old Choona struggles to make sense of the story his elders tell. This book is an excellent introduction to history. It does not mask the realities of famine and dispossession and yet it carries a message of faith in the human spirit.

## AUBREY FLEGG

**Katie's War**
O'Brien, 0862785251, £4.50
Set in the time of the Irish Civil War, *Katie's War* is an exciting tale of loyalty and friendship in dangerous times. The author is a geologist and much of the meticulously researched story is set around areas he knows well, including the Killaloe slate quarries. Katie and her Welsh friend Dafydd conspire to protect the village from danger, but with a brother in the Rebels, she is faced with a difficult decision which could change the lives of all those she loves. An intelligent and satisfying read.

## CORA HARRISON

**Nuala and her Secret Wolf**
Wolfhound Press pb
0863275850, £3.99

Set in the Iron Age, *Nuala and Her Secret Wolf* is the story of a young girl who finds and takes care of an orphaned wolf cub. Will Fergus the tiny wolf survive in a world that hates and fears wolves? The first book in the Drumshee Timeline series, historic fiction for young readers.

***Also in this series***
**The Secret of the Seven Crosses**
Wolfhound Press, 0863276164, £3.99 and
**The Secret of 1798**
Wolfhound Press 0863276164, £3.99.

## DAN KISSANE

**The Eagle Tree**
O'Brien, 0862784867, £3.99

The wizard Lucifer John McCracken turns the horrible Prince Pugnaz of Porzana into a giant cockroach, after a disagreement! But now the Prince's evil nephew Bembex, Baron of Bellonia will take over the kingdom. So begins this wacky tale of villains, sorcery and ancient wisdom.

**The King of Wisdom's Daughter**
O'Brien, 0862784115, £4.50

The King of Wisdom, desperate to be the wisest man in the world, wants to get his hands on the famed Book of Riddles. But there is one little problem – the nasty prince of Porzana, Pugnax has the book. The King takes drastic action and decides to give his daughter's hand in marriage to the villain. Then along comes Agamemnon, who falls in love with the Princess and sets out to rescue her. A deftly plotted traditional tale, full of humour and old fashioned adventure.

**Jimmy's Leprechaun Trap**
O'Brien, 086278512X £3.99

Young Jimmy meets a nasty little leprechaun and strange things start to happen. With the help of his grandfather, he sets out to trap the little fellow and outwit him. A clever and funny story setting the story straight about the wee green men!

**The O'Brien Book of Irish Fairy Tales and Legends**
**retold by Una Leavy illustrated by Susan Field**
O'Brien 0862734824 £12.99

This lovely book with its beautiful and apposite illustrations contains an interesting and varied collection. It has the tragic story of The Children of Lir and the tale of Oisin in Tir na nOg but it includes also The Pot ofGold, a story that encapsulates the trickery and mischievousness of Leprechauns, the 'little people'.

## ELIZABETH LUTZEIER

**The Coldest Winter**
Wolfhound, 0862375575, £3.99
When British soldiers destroy
Eamonn Kennedy's home he
decides to move his family to
America. But will they survive
the coldest winter Ireland has
ever known and the terrible
Famine? A well written story,
set in the midlands town of
Tullamore.

## PATRICIA LYNCH

Patricia Lynch is renowned as one of the greatest Irish children's writers ever. Born in Cork in 1898, Patricia was educated in Ireland, Britain and Belgium. She worked as a journalist on the 'Christian Commonwealth' from 1918-1920 and also wrote an eye-witness account of the 1916 Rising for newspapers of the time. Her first published children's book was *The Green Dragon* in 1925 and she went on to write many well loved books. In 1947 she published *A Story-Teller's Childhood*, an autobiography. Patricia Lynch died in 1972. Patricia Craig in *Twentieth Century Children's Writers* wrote 'Lynch's reputation rests on her assured evocations of fairground and bog and fairy rath, the racy outspoken quality of her dialogue, and her ability to amalgamate the traditional folk tale with the present day children's story.'

### The Dark Sailor of Youghal
Poolbeg, 1853715174, £3.99
A young man dreams of a eerie ship and a terrible shipwreck. The next morning his father is lured away to sea by a strange 'Dark Sailor', a phantom who is doomed to roam the seas forever. A mystical ghost story by one of Ireland's greatest children's writers.

### The Grey Goose of Kilnevin
Poolbeg, 1853714062, £3.99
The Grey Goose meets some strange and unusual friends on her way home from the market such as the Apple Woman and the Swan Children. Together they have some incredible adventures. A magical fairy tale.

**The Turf Cutter's Donkey**
Poolbeg, 1853718084, £3.99
Patricia Lynch's best-loved
story is an Irish children's
classic. 'Eileen and Seamus
lived in a cabin just beyond
the cross-roads at the edge of
the great bog. The cabin was
so low and the thatch so covered with grass and daisies,
that a stranger would never
have found it only that the
walls were whitewashed'.
So begins one of the most
magical Irish fantasies.
When the brother and sister
team become the owners of
an extraordinary donkey,
strange things begin to
happen. Populated by a host
of wonderfully inventive characters, this book, first published in 1968, will delight
any modern young reader.

Also by this author **Back of
Beyond** – Poolbeg £1.99
185371206X, **The Bookshop
on the Quay** – Poolbeg £3.50
1853714437 and **Sally From
Cork** – Poolbeg £3.99
1853710709 all published by
Poolbeg Press.

## CORMAC MACRAOIS

**The Battle Below Giltspur**
Wolfhound, 0863273564, £3.99
The ancient, enchanted May
Day or 'Bealtaine' winds blow
and bring the scarecrow near
Niamh and Daire Durkan's
house alive. But the winds
have also awakened 'The
Black One' and the two brave
youngsters find themselves
caught up in a whirlwind of
danger and adventure.
A gripping fantasy adventure
tale, with expressive black
and white line drawings
throughout by Jeanette
Dunne.

Also in this series – **Dance of
the Midnight Fire** –
Wolfhound £3.99 0863273572
and **Lightning Over Giltspur**
– Wolfhound £3.99
0863273327.

## YVONNE MCRORY

**The Secret of the Ruby Ring**
Children's Press, 0947962646,
£3.95
Lucy is given a ruby ring for
her birthday, a gift with the
power to grant wishes. Lucy
finds herself in the Ireland of
1885, as a nursery maid in a
large house. The winner of
the Bisto Award for First
Children's Novel in 1992.

**Martha and the Ruby Ring**
Children's Press, 0947962778,
£3.95
Another spell binding time-
slip tale. Lucy's grandmother
recalls the time that she used
the ruby ring and found
herself in Dublin at the time
of the 1798 Rebellion.

**The Ghost of Susannah Parry**
Children's Press, 0947962905,
£3.95
Brian is dared to spend the
night in a haunted house,
one dark October night.
After two hours he leaves,
terrified of what he has seen
and heard. Who was
Susannah Parry, the lady who
haunts the house? And how
can he help her?

## WALTER MACKEN

**The Flight of the Doves**
Pan, 0330026550, £3.99

Finn Dove and his little sister Derval decide to run away from their cruel 'Uncle' Toby, across the sea to relations in Ireland. They are pursued by the police, reporters and Toby, who alone knows about their mysterious legacy.

An exciting adventure story with wonderfully expressive line drawings by Charles Keeping.

## GREGORY MAGUIRE

**Six Haunted Hairdos**
O'Brien, 0862785421, £3.99

The Tattletales girls club and the Copycats boys club are for-ever trying to outwit each oth-er. The two gangs become embroiled in a crazy adven-ture and unwittingly bring the local ghost to life, along with some modern ghosts with very strange hair-dos!

A fast moving and madcap adventure story from this Irish American author.

**The Good Liar**
O'Brien, 086278395X, £3.99

Three brothers, Pierre, Rene and Marcel live in a small village in Occupied France during the Second World War. Strange things begin to hap-pen in the village and the boys watch Jewish guests arrive and disappear, and learn that in war time only the 'good liar' will survive. A beautifully written historic novel for older readers of ten plus.

## BAIRBRE MCCARTHY

**Favourite Irish Legends Dual Language Book**
Mercier 1856351866 £4.99

Irish/English dual language books are quite rare though useful for a child not fluent in the second language. Bairbre McCarthy recounts three legends. She keeps her vocabulary simple but her language is poetic.

## TOM MCCAUGHREN

Tom McCaughren is widely regarded as one of Ireland's leading children's writers. He has won many awards includ-ing the Bisto Book of the Decade 1980-1990 Award. Tom was born in Ballymena, Northern Ireland and now lives in Dublin with his family. He works as the security correspondent for RTE and has a great interest in wildlife and the countryside. The 'Fox' books are Tom's best known works, **Run with the Wind** and its (at present) four sequels. The Fox series and other works have been translated into many lan-guages including Japanese, Latvian and Swedish!

## The Fox Series

### Run with the Wind

Wolfhound Press, 0863275680,
£3.99

'Don't forget,' said the old
fox, 'If danger threatens, run
with the wind.' Originally
published in 1983, this book
has become a modern
children's classic. In the Land
of Sinna the foxes Black Tip,
Vickey, Sage Brush, She-La
and Scavenger must fight for
their lives when the fur com-
panies arrive, looking for
fresh supplies of fur pelts.
The animals must rediscover
their age-old qualities of
cunning and slyness in order
to save their species from
extinction. An award winning
book full of adventure and
suspense, a must for all young
nature lovers. With delightful
line drawings by the talented
Jeanette Dunne.

Also in this series **Run to
Earth** – 0863271162 £3.95,
**Run Swift Run Free** –
0863275931 £3.95, **Run to the
Ark** – 0863273424 £3.95, and
**Run to the Wild Wood** –
0863275710 £3.95 all pub-
lished by Wolfhound Press.

### The Children of the Forge

Children's Press, 0947962687,
£3.95

The exotic world of the
Lebanon is linked with the
quiet hills of Wicklow in this
compelling mystery tale.

### The Silent Sea

Children's Press, 0947962204,
£3.95

A thrilling sea faring
adventure and mystery tale
from this popular author.
The black yacht the Magic
Dragon has the symbol of a
golden dragon emblazoned
on its sails. What strange
secret dies this yacht hide?
Charming black and white
line drawings by Terry Myler
enhance the text.

Also by this author **The
Legend of the Phantom
Highwayman** – 0947962581
£3.95, **The Legend of the
Corrib King** – 0947962603
£3.95 and **The Legend of the
Golden Key** – 0947962360
£3.95

## MCDONALD'S COLLECTIONS

Every year McDonald's hold a
young writers competition,
where children from all over
Ireland are asked to write a
story or a poem on a particular theme. The winning
entries are collected together
in a book and published by
O'Brien Press. The royalties
are donated to a children's
charity such as Children's
Books Ireland, the national
organisation for children's
books and reading. These
imaginative collections are
excellent for 'dipping into'
and make a great gift for any
prospective young authors.

### The Bee's Knees

O'Brien Press, 0862783801,
£4.50

### The Cat's Pyjamas

O'Brien Press, 0862782899,
£4.50

### The Top Dog

O'Brien Press, 0862784387,
£4.50

# MÍCHEÁL MAC LIAMMÓIR

**Fairy Nights/Oicheanta Sí**
O'Brien 0862781337 £3.95

Mícheál Mac Liammóir is remembered to-day for his contribution to Irish Theatre. He and his partner Hilton Edwards founded the Gate Theatre in Dublin in 1928. But as a very young man Mac Liammóir wrote Fairy Nights/Oicheanta Sí. The stories are set on the nights of four important ancient Irish festivals. Mac Liammóir's original illustrations are reproduced to charm a new generation of readers.

# KATE MCMAHON

**Timber Twig**
Children's Press, 0901737012, £3.95

Clare is horse crazy. Her first show goes terribly wrong but then Nick offers to school her and her beloved pony, Timber Twig. But can she defeat her arch rival Kelly and her champion Moonstepper? A compelling read for all horse lovers.

# ORLA MELLING

**Hunter's Moon**
O'Brien, 0862783550, £3.99

Gwen and Findabhair set out to enter the 'other world' at Tara, the ancient seat of the High Kings of Ireland. But unwittingly they break a sacred law and Findabhair is abducted by the Fairies. Gwen then sets out to challenge the King of the Fairies and to save her cousin. An exciting Celtic fantasy adventure story for readers of nine plus.

**The Druid's Tune**
O'Brien, 0862782856, £4.50

When two Canadian teenagers visit Ireland they come under the influence of a mysterious stranger and are transported back to ancient times. There they meet the young hero Cuchulainn and are caught up in a terrible battle against the warrior Queen Maeve. An action packed tale for readers of nine plus.

# FRANK MURPHY

**Charlie Harte and His Two Wheeled Tiger**
O'Brien, 0862785324, £3.99

Charlie Harte constructs a weird and wonderful bike from odds and ends. But strange things begin to happen when the bike develops a life of its own. A fast moving adventure tale featuring Charlie and his 'two wheeled tiger'.

**Lockie and Dadge**
O'Brien, 0862784247, £3.99

Lockie is an orphan, labelled as a 'troublemaker' who runs away from his latest foster home. On his travels he meets up with some strange characters, Pasha and Mammy Tallon and they become friends. Lockie, for the first time in his life, feels that he belongs. But soon his new found happiness is threatened. A touching story about the search for identity.

## AISLINN O'LOUGHLIN

**Cinderella's Fella**
Illustrated by Marie-Louise
Fitzpatrick
Wolfhound 0863274935 £3.99
Snappy, amusing retelling of
the Cinderella story for
modern readers. Prince Fred
and his friends sort out their
marriage prospects. If you
enjoy *Cinderella's Fella,* try
Aislinn O'Loughlin's other
books also available from
Wolfhound:
**A Right Royal Pain**
0863275141 £3.99
**Shak and the Beanstalk**
0863276745 £3.99
**The Emperor's Birthday Suit**
0863275974 £3.99

## SIOBHÁN PARKINSON

**The Leprechaun Who Wished He Wasn't**
O'Brien, 0862783348, £3.99
Laurence the leprechaun has
been a tiny green man for
over 1100 years and he now
wants to be tall, a real
'human bean'. Phoebe is a
girl with the opposite
problem, she is much too tall.
The unlikely pair become
friends and learn to come to
terms with themselves – tall
or small! A humorous tale for
young readers of eight plus.

## JOHN QUINN

**Duck and Swan**
Poolbeg, 1853713171, £3.99
Emer Healy finds 'Duck',
Martin Oduki, on a school
bus bound for Galway. 'Duck'
has run away from a
children's home after being
abandoned in Dublin by a
Nigerian doctor father and
an Irish mother. The two
young people become friends
and help each other come to
terms with the difficulties of
life. Described by Nicole
Jussek, Children's Editor of
Poolbeg Press as 'a moving
and often funny story of
friendship and acceptance set
against a background of intol-
erance and high adventure.'

## JOHN QUINN

**The Summer of Lily and Esme**
Poolbeg, 1853712086
Winner of the Bisto Book of
the year award 1990-1991,
*The Summer of Lily and Esme*
has become a modern classic
of Irish children's literature.
The story of Alan, who with
his family has recently moved
to the country from Dublin.
When he meets his elderly
neighbours, Lily and Esme,
and becomes 'Albert' in their
mysterious past world, he
decides to unearth the story
of one summer over seventy
years ago. The author,
John Quinn writes
'When...Alan moves into
Glebe House and comes
across the two old ladies, they
see him as Albert ... He is
initially repelled by them but
is gradually drawn to them,
and the book is about their
relationship and Alan's
growth during the summer...'

## PETER REGAN
## The Riverside Series

A fun and easy to read series about the under 14 'Riverside Boys' soccer team. Designed to interest even the most reluctant reader with large type, short chapters, limited but carefully chosen vocabulary, and lots of witty illustrations to break up the text.

### The Street League
Children's Press, 0947962468, £2.95

The lads from Riverside are on summer holidays and they decide to start a street league. And with Chippy, Jimmy and Mad Victor involved, things are bound to a little crazy. But when Chippy's Granny, who has been dead for years appears in the graveyard drinking Guinness life becomes even more complicated. Read it and laugh!

### The Croke Park Conspiracy
Children's Press, 1901727047, £2.95

The Riverside boys go 'Gaelic' and almost make it to Croke Park! The second in this fun soccer series.

## MICHAEL SCOTT

Described as the 'Master of Mystery', Michael Scott is the renowned author of over sixty books for adults and children. He has a special interest in Celtic mythology, horror and the supernatural and is best known for his 'Earthlord' series for children. Born in Dublin, Michael worked as an antiquarian bookseller before turning to writing full time. Orson Scott Card described *October Moon* as: 'A compelling story of dread. Scott is the master of the naturally unfolding mystery, and the tension never lets up'.

### Windlord
Wolfhound Press, 0863272967, £3.99

Ken and his sister Ally are catapulted into the ancient world of De Danann while descending the 670 steps at Skellig Michael. In this strange world they meet Paedur, a wise young bard and Faolan the son of the Windlord. Together this band of intrepid heroes must protect the secret of the wind. The first of the De Danann Tales, a highly original fantasy series, populated by dragons, sorcerers and reptilian warriors. Highly recommended.

Also in this series **Earthlord,** Wolfhound Press, 0863173432, £3.99 and **Firelord,** Wolfhound Press, 0863273858, £3.99.

# GORDON SNELL

Gordon Snell was born in Singapore and spent his childhood there and in Australia. He wrote his first play, a war saga, at the tender age of eight. Gordon writes for children and adults and also works as a broadcaster for BBC and RTE radio and television. He is married to author and journalist Maeve Binchy and divides his time between London and Dalkey, Co. Dublin. His books are much loved by children and have received much critical acclaim – 'Gordon Snell has a delightfully light touch, a rare understanding of children, and a sense of humour that will keep his readers chuckling to the final page' The Irish Times.

**The Curse of Werewolf Castle**
Poolbeg Press, 1853716243,
£3.99
The crew of a horror movie, called 'The Curse of Werewolf Castle' arrive in Ballygandon and Molly, Brendan and Dessie are chosen as extras. But when the filming is interrupted by bizarre accidents, ghostly apparitions and strange disappearances in the ruined castle, the three friends decide to solve the mystery and save the film and themselves from mortal danger. An exciting and authentic adventure story.

**The Mystery of Monk Island**
Poolbeg Press, 1853717657,
£3.50
Molly, Brendan and Dessie are reunited, this time on a week's boating holiday. Another excellent book, with all the ingredients of a good adventure story – a kidnapping, ghostly figures, a haunted island, and a brave dog.

**The Phantom Horseman**
Poolbeg Press, 1853717975,
£3.99
Brendan and Molly are worried when their grandfather Locky moves into the 'Horse Shoe' residential home. When the siblings find that the owners of the home intend to destroy a historic ruined castle and build an extension to cram more old people into the already crowded home, they decide to take the law into their own hands. With the help of some of the residents, they set out to frighten the owners by acting out an old legend to save the ruin, with unforeseen and eerie consequences.

Also by this author
**Dangerous Treasure,** Poolbeg Press, 1853716790, £3.50 and **The Tex and Sheelagh Omnibus** Poolbeg Press, 1853712706, £2.99.

## CAROLYN SWIFT

**The Mystery of the Mountain**
O'Brien, 0862784131, £3.99

Set in Peru, at the famous Inca site in Machu Picchu, this story combines an exciting plot and strong and likeable characters in the form of brother and sister team, Kevin and Nula. Accompanying their mother on an archaeological dig, the siblings find a lot more than old bones, and become enmeshed in a web of Peruvian political intrigue.

**The Secret City**
O'Brien, 0862783828, £3.99

Brother and sister team, Kevin and Nula travel to Petra, the famous secret city carved out of the rock cliffs in the Jordanian desert. While their mother works on an archaeological dig, the two teenagers find their own treasure. But they soon find themselves in mortal danger from the evil Hassan.
An exciting adventure story set in the magical land of the Bedouin.

## WILLIAM TREVOR

**Juliet's Story**
O'Brien, 0862784573, £3.99

Juliet is taken on a journey by her Grandmamma. As they travel, the old lady tells her stories which enable Juliet to make sense of her own life and all its difficulties. As their journey draws to its end, Juliet realises the importance of stories – 'having stories to tell makes all the difference'. A thoughtful and compelling tale from one of Ireland's master storytellers.

## GERARD WHELAN

**Dream Invader**
O'Brien, 0862785162, £3.99

Gerard Whelan's clever plot and fascinating characters combine to produce a readable modern horror story. Twelve year old Saskia is sent to stay with her Aunt and Uncle for the summer.
All appears normal until she learns the truth about her young cousin Simon's nightmares. As the story unravels the reader plunges into a world of white magic, childhood fears and the age old fight between good and evil. A terrific read for older children of nine plus.

## GERARD WHELAN

**The Guns of Easter**
O'Brien, 0862784492, £3.99

Set during the Easter Rising of 1916, this book tells the story of young Jimmy Conroy as he searches for food for his family, witnessing death and destruction all around him. Written in strong and direct language, *The Guns of Easter* tells of one family's suffering and courage and their ultimate will to survive. Winner of the Éilis Dillon Memorial Award for the outstanding first children's book – 1996-1997.

## MARY ARRIGAN

**Dead Monks and Shady Deals**
Children's Press, 0947962913,
£3.95

Maeve Morris, helped by her cousin Leo and her friend Jamie, save ancient artifacts from being stolen by the so-called 'respectable' auctioneer Rourke and his henchman Mossy. A funny and fast paced book, the first of a trilogy for older readers, combining clever plot and well rounded characters.

**Landscape With Cracked Sheep**
Children's Press, 0947962972,
£3.95

Maeve, Leo and Jamie are involved in another adventure when they set off in search of a lost family heirloom.

**Seascape With Barber's Harp**
Children's Press, 1901737020,
£3.95

The third book in the popular Maeve Morris series. On holiday in Baltimore, Maeve, Jamie and Leo get caught up in a hunt for buried Spanish treasure with their new friends Carla and Pedro. An old fashioned summer adventure story.

## MARGRIT CRUICKSHANK

**Circling the Triangle**
Poolbeg, 1853711373, £2.99

Stephen is a teenage boy suffering from unrequited love. In trouble at home and at school, he forms a strange friendship with the twelve year old sister of the beautiful but elusive Suzanne. *Circling the Triangle* is a wry and often touching novel which won a Reading Association of Ireland Special Merit Award in 1993.

**The Door**
Poolbeg, 1853716170, £3.99

Transition year brings the chance to explore different activities in and out of school. Rachel, Marie-Claire, Dave and Hugh start a school newspaper, but life begins to become difficult when Rachel accuses one of the teachers of sexual harassment in print. *The Door* is cleverly plotted, with plenty of tension and action to keep any teenager reading.

## ROSE DOYLE

**Good-bye Summer Good-bye**
Attic Press, 1855940434, £4.99

Martha is disgusted. She has been sent to her Grandmother's hotel, Lir House, to work for the summer. But things begin to look up when she meets the suave young French man Maurice and discovers a secret about her grandmother's distant past. An enjoyable and thoughtful title in the Bright Sparks series for readers of ten plus.

## ROBERT DUNBAR

**First Times**
Poolbeg, 1853717622, £4.99

A wide ranging collection of short stories for teenagers from some of Ireland's top writers such as Marita Conlon-McKenna and Siobhan Parkinson. Themes in the stories include first love, the war in Vietnam and lost innocence. A enjoyable collection of well-written stories.

## MAEVE FRIEL

Maeve Friel was born in Derry and educated in Dublin. She lived in Spain, Italy and England before. settling in Dublin with her husband and two children. Maeve was an avid reader as a child, devouring 'everything from *The Family From One-End Street* to all the Bobbsey Twins series to *Children of the New Forest* ...One winter when I was about 11, I had flu and feverishly read all of Dickens so that, to this day, I can't tell *Bleak House* from *The Old Curiosity Shop*. Maeve writes for adults and children and has been short listed for the Bisto Book of the Year Award on two occasions. She was awarded the Sunday Tribune/Hennessy Literary Award in 1990 for 'Irrational Developments', her first short story.

**Distant Voices**
Poolbeg, 1853714100, £3.99

Ellie is haunted by a ghostly figure in her dreams, Harald Olaafsson a young Viking from another world. 'Only you will know where to find me', he tells her, 'You have no need to fear me'. Ellie crosses the border from Derry to Donegal in search of this blonde stranger and makes a startling discovery on a deserted headland.

**The Lantern Moon**
Poolbeg Press, 1853716766, £3.99

Set during 1811 in Ludlow, England *The Lantern Moon* was described by Celia Keenan in *The Big Guide to Irish Children's Books* as 'one of the best works of historical fiction for children by a contemporary Irish writer'. The Spears family, Annie, a maid, William, a hat maker and little Libby, a glove maker have not heard from their father since he was transported to Australia. When their house is destroyed in a fire and the children are accused of theft, they take to the hills. But great danger lies ahead.

Also by this author **Charlie** and **The Deerstone,** both published by Poolbeg Press.

## PETER GUNNING

**Reaching the Heights**
Blackwater, 0861218108, £3.99

Set in 'McGillicuddy Heights' in inner city Cork, *Reaching the Heights* is a fast paced tale of courage and survival. Naylor's mother is viciously attacked and with the help of his friends 'posh' Aisling and Tosh, he sets out to find the culprit. The brave teenager is thrown into a world of money lending, drugs and violence, where he must battle for his very life.

**Kick the Can**
Blackwater, 0861219198, £3.99
Tanker has a 'jailbird' for a
father, Lucy is obsessed with
body piercing and reincarna-
tion and Yeoman has a
problem with drugs. In
'Terence McSwiney
Mansions' everyone has a
problem. A gritty, realistic
adventure tale set in inner
city gangland.

## SOINBHE LALLY

**The Hungry Wind**
Poolbeg Press, 1853717177,
£3.99
'It is the wind from the east
that blows you now. That was
a hungry wind and it has
done its worst with you.'
Maya and Breege find
themselves in a workhouse
during the Famine, after
being thrown out of their
homes by a unscrupulous
landlord. When the sisters
are offered places on a ship
bound for Australia they have
a difficult decision to make.

**A Hive for the Honey-bee**
Poolbeg Press, 1853716960,
£3.99
The lives of honey-bees are
examined in this clever and
beguiling tale. Thora is a
young worker, who ponders
the meaning of life. Alfred,
a male drone, is a poet who
questions the way the hive is
run. But can anything change
the ultimate destiny of the
drones and their 'servants',
the workers. 'It's quite a
challenge to set a novel in a
beehive with a cast of bees
and other insects, but Soinbe
Lally has risen to it brilliantly'
The Irish Times.

Also by this author: **Song of
the River,** Poolbeg Press,
1853714577, £2.99

## BERNADETTE LEACH

**I'm a Vegetarian**
Cork University Press,
185594040X, £4.99
One of the first in the excellent Bright Sparks series for
readers of ten plus, originally
published by Attic Press.
Vanessa Carter is horrified
when her parents decide to
move to Ireland. 'You'll love
Cork', her mother says.
'Cork, what's Cork', retorts
Vanessa, 'It's a bottle stopper.
It's a bathroom mat'. A realistic and funny story of modern
family life.

**Anna Who?**
Cork University Press,
1855940922
Anna is fourteen, she knows
she's adopted and has
recently begun to question
her own identity and her
place in the family. She is
tired of looking after her
baby sister and putting up
with her other bratty sister
and obnoxious brothers.
All Anna wants is to discover
herself by getting away from
her annoying family, until
tragedy strikes and she swiftly
changes her mind. Another
well written and moving
Bright Sparks title.

# JOAN LINGARD

Joan Lingard grew up in Belfast and decided to write for teenagers in 1970, soon after the start of 'the troubles'. She said in *Treasure Islands* 2 (BBC Books) 'It was one of those instances when I had a book in my head...It was really my strong desire to write something for young people which would be against prejudice and wouldn't be for one side or the other, but would be for both sides, seeing the good and the bad in both.' Married to a Canadian architect, whose Latvian family had to flee from the advancing Russian army, she deals with themes of displacement in many of her books such as *Tug of War* and *Between Two Worlds*. 'We inhabit only one body,' she says, 'but by reading and by writing we can live in many worlds!'

### The Kevin and Sadie Quintet

Set in Belfast, these five books follow the lives of Kevin and Sadie from their teenage years in Northern Ireland, to their young married lives in England and Wales. Written between 1970 and 1976 these books remain a lasting testament to Lingard's storytelling abilities.

### The Twelfth Day of July
Puffin, 0140371753, £3.99

The first in the Kevin and Sadie series. One night Kevin and his Catholic friends sneak into 'Protestant territory' and deface a mural, enraging Sadie and her friends. The incident sparks off a chain of events which culminate in tragedy on the 12th of July.

### Across the Barricades
Puffin, 0140371796, £4.50

Kevin McCoy is Catholic and Sadie Jackson is Protestant, and their relationship is condemned by families and friends on both sides. Intimidation and violence are used by each community to drive this message home. Kevin and Sadie want to continue their relationship, but at what cost?

Also in the series are **Into Exile** – 014037213X £4.99, **A Proper Place** – 0140371923 £4.99 and **Hostages to Fortune** – 0140374000 £4.99, all published by Puffin.

# MORGAN LLYWELYN

### Cold Places
Poolbeg Press, 1853715417

David McHugh has an extraordinary talent. He can find 'cold places', sites that have ancient power. When he finds a valuable artefact buried at one of the sites his father, a professor of archaeology, encourages his son towards more discoveries. But David and his girlfriend, Molly are worried and frightened with the influence that the 'spirit of the ice', a strange force unleashed from the cold places and linked to the Ice Age, is having on both the weather and on the young man himself.

**19 Railway Street**
Poolbeg Press, 1853716421,
£3.50
1776 – In her respectable
Dublin home Sophie is
terrorised by her bully of an
uncle. 1907 – In a Dublin
tenement house Mickser and
his family are threatened by
illness and hunger. A chilling
time-slip novel set in 19
Railway Street where nothing
is quite what it seems.

## CHRIS LYNCH

**Shadow Boxer**
Poolbeg, 1853715301, £2.99
A strong, realistic tale about
fourteen year old George and
his younger brother Monty.
George is the man of the family, his father died after a lifetime of boxing fights. Both
brothers have boxing in their
blood, but problems develop
when Monty tries to emulate
his late father in the ring.

## CHRIS LYNCH

**Slot Machine**
Poolbeg, 1853717908, £3.50
Elvin's school believes that
each boy should fit into a
suitable sport which will
define their place or 'slot' in
the class. But Elvin is fat.
Funny, warm, a good friend
with a strong will but not in
the least bit athletic. At the
sports summer school Elvin
proves that 'fitting in' is not
the most important thing in
life. A touching and funny
read.

## TOM MCCAUGHREN

**In Search of the Liberty Tree**
Children's Press, 0947962891,
£3.95
McCaughren's novel deals
with the 1798 Ulster
Rebellion and the United
Irishmen. The war is seen
through the eyes of two
friends Joshua and Sammy,
one a Presbyterian and the
other a member of the
Established Church. A deftly
constructed and superbly
written book.

## GERALDINE MITCHELL

**Escape to the West**
Attic Press, 185594085X, £4.99
Aoife is working for the
summer at Innisfree House,
an Old People's Home.
She befriends one of the
residents, Imogen O'Toole,
an intelligent independent
lady, and together they are
determined to unmask the
dishonest practices of the
bad-tempered Matron of the
Home. Aoife, Imogen and
their friend Jacko 'escape to
the West' of Ireland on an
unforgettable adventure. Part
of the Bright Sparks series.

Also by this author
**Welcoming the French,** Cork
University Press,
185594054X, £3.99

## JANE MITCHELL

**When Stars Stop Spinning**
Poolbeg, 1853718394, £3.99
Winner of the Bisto Book of
the Year award in 1993-1994,
*When Stars Stop Spinning* is a
story of courage and friendship, set in a Dublin rehabilitation centre. Tony is fifteen
and finds himself in
'Lismore' after a joy-riding
accident. He meets Stephen,
a gifted musician with a wast-
ing disease and they become
friends. Together they enter
a competition for new bands,
with far reaching conse-
quences. A compelling read
from a talented young
author.

**Making Waves**
Poolbeg Press, 1853718289,
£3.99
Ciara is determined to be
a world class swimmer.
Her family move home so
that she can be close to her
training pool but when her
sister Sorcha goes off the
rails, the young swimmer's
life is turned upside down.

## LUCY MITCHELL

**The King and I and the Rest of
the Class**
Attic Press, 1855941384, £4.99
St Mary's School for Girls are
staging 'The King and I' with
the boys from St Patrick's.
The girls in Transition year
are delighted and are all
determined to have
'boyfriends for Christmas'.
A light hearted and
humorous read.

## MICHAEL MULLEN

**Pillars of Fire**
Blackwater Press, 0861219090,
£4.99
Set in Paris in 1939, this book
tells the story of Celine, the
fourteen year old daughter
of a wealthy Jewish banker.
While travelling across Paris
to her music lesson, Celine
hears disturbing rumours of
the Nazi persecution of her
people. Before long her own
family are herded into the
east-bound train, on a
one-way journey to hell.
World War II is brought to
life in vivid and harrowing
detail by Michael Mullen's
skilled hand in this moving
book for older readers.
Through the courage and
tenacity of the young
heroine, we learn about the
Holocaust, the indefatigable
strength of the Jewish people
and their will to survive.

**Flight From Toledo**
Poolbeg, 1853716278, £3.99
'The three horseman reined
their horses and studied the
dry track across the hills.
It led up into the central
mountains of Spain. The
higher summits were capped
with snow and possessed a
lonesome grandeur.' From
the master of Irish children's
historical fiction comes an
exciting adventure story set
in Spain during the time of
the Spanish Inquisition. Well
written, with a real sense of
the atmosphere of the time.

Also by this author:
**Michelangelo,** Poolbeg Press,
1853714143, £3.99
and **The Long March,**
Poolbeg Press, 1853718904,
£3.50

## ULICK O'CONNOR

**illustrated by PAULINE BEWICK**
**Irish Tales and Sagas**
Town House 1860590381 £4.99
Most of the stories in this
book come from the heroic
age in Ireland.
Ulick O'Connor's fluent
storytelling combines
wonderfully with truly
beautiful illustrations by
artist Pauline Bewick.
Not specifically written for
children this book will
nevertheless attract artistic
or imaginative readers.

## ELIZABETH O'HARA

**The Hiring Fair**
Poolbeg, 1853712752, £3.99
In 1890 Sally Gallagher,
known as 'Scatterbrain Sally',
is forced to become a hired
servant after a tragedy in the
family. A moving story with
an unforgettable heroine.
Winner of the Bisto Book of
the Year Award for 1994-1995.

**Penny Farthing Sally**
Poolbeg Press, 1853716863,
£3.99
The third book in the trilogy
featuring Sally Gallagher,
the working girl from
Donegal. In this book Sally
is a servant girl in a Dublin
house. The lady of the house
is an independent woman,
interested in the Gaelic
League and giving women
the vote. Through Sally, the
reader comes into contact
with the fascinating world
of late nineteenth century
Dublin.

Also by this author: **Blaeberry
Sunday,** Poolbeg Press, £3.99

## MARK O'SULLIVAN

Mark O'Sullivan was born in
Nottingham, England of Irish
parents who returned to
Ireland some years later.
He now lives in Thurles, Co
Tipperary with his wife and
two teenage daughters. Mark
has been writing since his
early teens and has published
many poems, plays, short
stories and novels for both
adults and children. In 1995
he won the Éilis Dillon
Memorial Award for his first
children's book *Melody for
Nora*. Of *White Lies* he says
'there is always an element of
one self in the central characters ... (this book) was a
vehicle of examination of my
relationship with my uncle.'

**More Than a Match**
Wolfhound, 086327496X, £3.99
In Tipperary during the
summer of 1948 two girls
battle it out to be tennis
champion, Ginny Stannix
and the reigning champ,
Lida Hendel, a girl with
German parents. As the finals
loom, rumours and slander
are rife. But who is behind
the accusations against the
Hendel family? A gripping
tale of suspicion and
prejudice, and the journey
to friendship.

**Melody for Nora**
Wolfhound Press, 0863274250, £3.99

Set during the Irish Civil War, *Melody for Nora* tells the story of Nora, a Dublin teenager who has been sent to stay with her aunt and uncle following the death of her mother. The young heroine becomes mixed up in a dangerous adventure, but Nora is a survivor and has a lifeline in her love of music and her new found friend.

Also by this author: **Angels Without Wings,** Wolfhound Press, 0863275915, £3.95.

## SIOBHÁN PARKINSON

Siobhán Parkinson lives in Dublin with her husband, and their teenage son, Matthew, who she describes as her 'own personal proof-reader'. She studied English literature at college and now works as an editor in the publishing industry. *Amelia* was her first book for the ten plus age group, which became an immediate best-seller and was short listed for the 1994 Bisto Book of the year award. Siobhán writes for many different age groups, from early readers to teenagers but says that above all she writes 'for herself'. Her latest book, with the bizarre title *Four Kids, Three Cats, Two Cats, One Witch, Maybe* is a classic adventure story with a twist.

**White Lies**
Wolfhound Press, 0863275923, £3.99

Nance is adopted and wants to find her natural parents, her boyfriend OD has problems of his own. The two teenagers discover that everyone has secrets and that the truth is not as simple as it seems. A gritty, modern love story, full of tension. A satisfying read, highly recommended.

**Amelia**
O'Brien, 0862783526, £3.99

Amelia Pim will be thirteen in 1914, the year in which this story is set. Dublin is rife with the rumours of war and rebellion, but Amelia is only concerned with her imminent birthday party and what dress she will wear. When disaster strikes the Quaker family, Amelia must fight to keep the family together. An original and well plotted historical novel for readers of ten plus.

**Four Kids, Three Cats, Two Cows and One Witch (Maybe)**
O'Brien, 0862785154, £4.50

A group of friends visit an uninhabited island off the coast of Ireland and become stranded. Beverly and her 'city' friends Elisabeth and Gerard, join local teenager (and 'cool guy'), Kevin on an unforgettable adventure. A carefully crafted tale for readers of ten plus, with humour, mystery and a sack full of surprises!

**Sisters, No Way**
O'Brien, 0862784956, £4.50

Described by Children's Books in Ireland magazine as 'Irish teenage fiction at its most sophisticated', *Sisters, No Way* earned Siobhan Parkinson the Bisto Book of the Year award in 1997. A modern retelling of the Cinderella tale, this book combines high quality writing, with compelling characters and a fast moving and involving contemporary plot. Cindy and her reluctant step-sisters, Ashling and Orla, are thrown together when their parents decide to marry. Presented in a unique manner, with two back-to-back books each chronicling the sisters stories in diary entries, this story is sure to please even the most reluctant teenage reader. (A good choice for struggling parents of teens too!)

## JOHN QUINN

**One Fine Day**
Poolbeg, 185371612X, £3.99

Rossa and his family move to a mobile home in Co. Clare after his father is jailed for his part in an IRA bombing in Belfast and their lives have been threatened. The teenager meets Maggie, a local girl his own age with her own problems, and they establish a fragile friendship. A strong, well written book about growing up in difficult times.

## PETER REGAN

**Urban Heroes**
Children's Press, 094796262X, £3.95

*Urban Heroes* follows the lives and fortunes of a group of teenagers Gavin, Hammer, Elaine, Jake and Luke, who all share a love of soccer, pigeon racing, athletics and music. Fast moving and funny tale of modern life, the first book in a trilogy.

Also in this series: **Teen Glory,** Children's Press, 0947962786, £3.95 and **Young Champions,** Children's Press, 0947962921, £3.95.

## MICHAEL SCOTT

**Wolf Moon**
O'Brien Press, 0862784204, £3.99

'And in Ireland at that time there were men who wore the likeness of wolves' Geraldus Cambrensis, AD 1185.

Rachel has inherited the dreaded curse of the werewolf while staying in Ireland. She returns in an effort to rid herself of this dreadful fate. But an ancient tribe with secret powers need her for their own evil purposes. A chilling tale full of suspense and horror.

Also by this author: **October Moon** – 0862783003 , and **Gemini Game** – 0862783321 both O'Brien Press, £3.99.

## MICHAEL SMITH

### Boston Boston
Poolbeg Press, 1853718858, £4.99

When the Famine strikes in the Autumn of 1845 Kate, Liam and Tom decide to leave Connemara for America. The journey is long and hard and they arrive in Boston, penniless and yet determined to survive.
A spirited tale of the triumph of the spirit.

## MARILYN TAYLOR

### Could This Be Love, I Wondered ?
O'Brien, 0862783771, £3.99

Jackie spots the boy of her dreams from the bus. But Kevin is from the 'wrong side of the tracks', and their lives are worlds apart. Can love conquer all? The first in the Jackie trilogy, featuring this endearing and strong heroine.

### Could I Love a Stranger ?
O'Brien, 0862784425, £3.99

Jackie meets Daniel, a Jewish boy who is visiting Dublin and they become close friends. Interwoven with extracts from Daniel's mother's war diary, this book combines historical documentation with thoughtful insight into the minds and actions of teenagers.

### Call Yourself a Friend ?
O'Brien, 0862785006, £3.99

The third book in the Jackie trilogy. Jackie's friend Bernie is knocked down by a drunken driver and is in a critical condition. Kevin, Jackie's boyfriend and the victim's brother, decides to take the law into his own hands, with fatal results. A well-written and meticulously researched story, capturing contemporary teenage Dublin life in its gritty reality.

## MARIA QUIRK WALSH

### Searching For a Friend
Attic Press, 1855940884, £4.99

Aine's family are moving from Dublin to the West of Ireland, separating her from her closest friend Christina. Christina makes new acquaintances but realises that they are cowardly bullies and not worth calling friends. In her loneliness and desperation the teenager takes a drastic step. A tense and realistic contemporary tale.

Also by this author: **A Very Good Reason,** Cork University Press, £4.99

From Dorothea Lange's, Ireland

# Poetry for Children

## Collections

### The Poolbeg Book of Irish Poetry for Children
### edited by Shaun Traynor
Poolbeg 185717266, £4.99

A captivating collection of Irish verse, old and new, edited by the Northern Irish poet and children's author Shaun Traynor. Each poem was 'tested' on nine and ten year old pupils, their ultimate favourite being the irreverent and parent shocking 'How High' by Gabriel Fitzmaurice. This wide ranging anthology also features the poems of Oliver Goldsmith, James Joyce, Patrick Kavanagh, Brendan Kennelly, John Montague and others.

### The Poolbeg Book of Children's Verse edited by Sean McMahon
Poolbeg, 1853710806, £3.99

An anthology of verse for children from Ireland, Great Britain and all over the world. The poems are selected by the editor for their lasting and universal appeal and the book is divided into thematic 'chapters' on subjects such as humour, fantasy and childhood. Suitable for a reader of eight plus.

### The Wolfhound Book of Irish Poems for Young People edited by Bridie Quin and Seamus Cashman
Wolfhound, 0863270026, £4.95

Originally published in 1975, this collection edited by Quinn and the Wolfhound Press Publisher Cashman, has become the classic and standard book of Irish verse for young people.

The chosen works are all by Irish poets, ancient and modern, from the traditional William Allingham ('The Fairies' – 'Up the airy mountain, Down the rushy glen'), to Richard Murphy and Derek Mahon. Useful notes on the poems and their authors are included. An excellent introduction to Irish verse for any child of seven plus.

### Real Cool: Poems to Grow Up With edited by Niall MacMonagle,
Martello Press, 1860230024, £7.99

A ground-breaking collection of poems aimed directly at adolescents, covering all areas of 'teenage angst'. Divided into ten themed sections with evocative titles such as 'Pass Out the Moon', there is something for everyone in this book. From Roger McGough's 'Discretion' to Dorothy Parker's 'Valentine', McMonagle has chosen poems that above all 'strike straight...are streetwise and have street cred'.

### A Child's Book of Irish Rhymes edited by Alice Taylor
Gill and MacMillan, 0717124959, £6.99 hb

A collection of Irish poems and rhymes compiled by popular author Alice Taylor from her personal childhood favourites. Illustrated in full colour by Irish artist Nicola Emoe, this attractive book is ideal for sharing with younger children of three plus. Parents and grandparents will remember and enjoy reading old favourites such as 'The Old Woman of the Roads' to their offspring.

## PAUL MULDOON

Known to many as an 'adult' poet, Paul Muldon has produced two charming and quirky volumes of children's verse, *The Last Thesaurus and The Noctuary of Narcissus Bat*.

### The Last Thesaurus
Faber, 0571175805, £3.99

A pocket-sized book in verse with leading characters dear to all children's hearts – dinosaurs – in the form of 'Bert and Brunhilde Brontosaurus', Tyrannosaurus Rex and the baby Thesaurus 'who looks as if he's swallowed a dictionary'. Witty and clever, with a dazzling command of vocabulary and an array of wild and inventive characters, this book will delight any reader of eight to eighty.

### The Noctuary of Narcissus Bat
Faber, 0571190200, £8.99 hb

An A to Z with a difference. Each letter of the alphabet is represented by an animal, from an Ass to a Zebra who reveal themselves in alphabetical order from the chimney breast. Every animal's 'mini-story' in verse cleverly links on to the next, forming an ingenious, cryptic puzzle. Presiding over this Gothic madness is Narcissus Bat, wonderfully realised in Marketa Prachaticka's strong and distinctive line drawings. A book to bewitch any reader of eight plus.

## MATTHEW SWEENEY

Sweeney writes for both children and adults. A parent himself, his wide ranging verse for young readers has an innate sense of what it really feels like to be a child.

### The Flying Spring Onion
Faber, 0571161723, £3.99

A compelling collection of original poems on many different themes, from 'Bees' to a 'Ghost-Train'. Sweeney's poems capture many moods such the simple joy of being loved by the dogs in the park in 'All the Dogs' – in which dogs gather around the whistling youngster – 'To stare at the boy's/unmemorable face/which all the dogs found special'. Darker in mood is 'On the Stairs', where a young child waits for her absent mother, alone and scared on the stairs of her house – 'Why hadn't Mum phoned/if she wasn't going to be in?' Thoughtful and provocative verse for readers of seven plus.

**Fatso in the Red Suit**
Faber, 0571179037, £3.99
Another glimpse into the real
world of the child through
the eyes of Donegal-born
poet Matthew Sweeney.
Serious childhood concerns
such as 'ghost eyes' in the
attic and the inner thoughts
of the dog who was sent to
the moon – 'Did the dog
see,/through the
window/earth's blue ball?',
are carefully dissected and
recorded in verse.
These original poems never
fail to touch the heart and
prod the mind. Suitable for
readers of seven plus.

## Irish Language for Children

If you want your children to
grow up familiar with the
Irish language it is worthwhile starting while they are
very young. The following
books are all of interest: –

Ethel Agus and Harry
Wingfield **An Chéad Leabhar
Pictiúr** (An Gúm £1.60) Ethel
Agus and Harry Wingfield
**An Dara Leabhar Pictiúr**
(An Gúm £1.60)
Irish versions of Ladybird
First Picture books. The for-
mat looks old fashioned but
these books are still a good
start for the under threes.

## EDWINA RIDDLE
**Mo Chéad Leabhar Faoi
Ainmhithe**
(An Gúm 1857912632 £2.95)
A picture book/dictionary
for small children providing
the Irish words for the
animals, insects and birds
they are likely to see in the
garden, park or fields.

## EDWINA RIDDLE
**Mo Chéad Naíonra**
(An Gum 1857911962 £2.95)
A picture book/dictionary
with all the words a toddler
might need at play school
or nursery.

Gill and MacMillan publish
Irish language versions of
some of Usborne's best
selling titles: –

**Céad Focal**
(Gill and MacMillan
0717127133 £3.99)
The first hundred words in
Irish. Have fun finding the
little duck hiding on every
page.

**Buntús Foclóra**
(Gill and MacMillan
0717124193 £7.99)
Children's Irish picture dictionary designed to be both
attractive and really useful.
There is a picture for every
word and a complete vocabulary at the back of the book.

Also from Gill and
MacMillan/Usborne Na
Chéad Imachtaí or First
Experiences series. These little books aim to help very
small children cope with challenging events. Particularly
useful and often requested by
parents is An Leanbh
Nua/The New Baby: –

**An Leanbh Nua**
(Gill and MacMillan
0717118061 £2.60)
**Ag Aistriú Tí**
(Gill and MacMillan
0717118053 £2.50)
**Ag Dul Go Dtí An Chóisir**
(Gill and MacMillan
0717118908 £2.50)
**Ag Dul Go Dtí An Fiaclóir**
(Gill and MacMillan £2.50)
**Ag Dul Go Dti An Tospidéal**
(Gill and MacMillan
0717118894 £2.50)

## An Gúm

An Gúm is the publications branch of the department of Education. Since 1926 An Gúm has been a major publisher of books in the Irish language. Initially, the books published by An Gúm for children were translations of European classics. Over the past twenty years there has been a huge increase in the number of Gaelscoileanna (Irish medium schools) particularly at primary level. This created a demand for Irish language books for young children. An Gúm responded magnificently to this demand and currently publish a wide range of books for children, both original titles and co-editions.

**Déanann Bran Cáca**
(An Gúm 1857911016 £5.00)
Spot nó Bran, is cuma. Is madra álainn é.

Bran's everyday activities appeal to small children who can relate them to their own busy days. *Déanann Bran Cáca* is a particular favourite. Bran bakes the ultimate birthday cake for his Dad.
*Recommended age 2-5*

*Also available from An Gúm: –*
*Cá bhfuil Bran? No ISBN £4.95*
*Bran ar a lá breithe No ISBN £4.95*
*Bran ar scoil No ISBN £4.95*

## MARTIN WADDELL

**(translated by Máire Uí Mhaicín) Seáinín Agus An Chearc Mhór**
(An Gúm 1857911482 £4.95)
Tá cearc mhór ag leanúint Seáinín agus tá eagla an an mbuachaill bocht. Cad ba chóir dó a dhéanamh?

Seáinín thinks he is old enough to look after himself but face to face with a hen almost as big as himself he has second thoughts. A lovely story for small children who will identify with Seáinín.
*Recommended age 3-6*

**Pádraigin Ní Chionnaith Páid Agus An Scoil** (Illustrated by Wendy Shea) (An Gúm 185791113X £4.95)

Níl fonn ar Pháid dul ar scoil.

Páid doesn't want to go to school but he soon realises that having to play alone is no fun. The bright illustrations and simple story may well help to reconcile a reluctant school-goer to the inevitable.
*Recommended age 3-6*

# MARY ARRIGAN

Mary Arrigan was born in Newbridge, Co. Kildare. She grew up devoted to her local library and reading everything she or her friends could borrow. Now, she lives in Roscrea, Co. Tipperary and writes books in Irish for young children and in English for an older age group. The first Mamo book appeared in 1993. *Lá le Mamo* was so successful that Mamo became a character in her own right and now there are four books about her adventures. Mamo is a modern Irish granny whose lifestyle owes nothing to the traditional granny figure. She loves life. She goes looking for enjoyment. She is independent, no sign of a Daideo in her life. Above all she is happy. The Irish language is regarded by many as belonging only to our past. Mamo is definitely drawn from contemporary Irish life and gives hope that the language can belong to our future. In English Mary Arrigan writes adventure stories for the eight to twelve age group. Her novel *The Dwellers Beneath* is a scary story of religious fanaticism gone literally underground. It received a White Raven award in 1997.

## Lá Le Mamó
(An Gúm 1857910796 £4.95)
Is meidhreach an cailín í Mamó.

Mary Arrigan created Mamó in 1993 and this adventurous grandmother has been popular ever since. Her joyous approach to life is very attractive. This might not be what you expect from a granny but it's great fun
*Recommended age 3-7*

Also available from An Gúm:
**Mamó Cois Trá** 1857911024 £4.95 **Mamó ar an Fheirm** 1857911697 £4.95 **Mamó ag an Sorcas** 1857912365 £4.95

## An Scáth Báistí
(An Gúm 1857911350 £4.95)
Faigheann Daideo scáth báistí mar bhronntanas ón a chol ceathrar i Londain.

Daideo is delighted with his new umbrella. He has no idea of the chaos he leaves in his wake when he goes for a walk. Mary Arrigan's lively, cheerful drawings illustrate Daideo's essential innocence, to perfection.
*Recommended age 4-7*

# COLMAN O'RAGHALLAIGH

**Drochlá Ruairí**
**(Illustrated by Anne Marie Carroll)**
(Cló Mhaigh Eo 1899922016 £4.95)
Ruairí bocht!

We follow Ruairí through a school day when everything that can go wrong does. Anne Marie Carroll's choice of strong, vibrant colours, predominantly orange and blue brings her pictures alive. If you've ever had a bad day you'll love Ruairí.
*Recommended age 4-7*

# MARTIN WADDELL

**(Translated by Maire Ní Ici) An Lacha Feirmeora**
**Illustrated by Helen Oxenbury**
(An Gúm 1857910&21 £5.95)
Lacha bhocht! Caitheann an feirrneoir an lá sa leaba agus bíonn an lacha ag obair i rith an lae.

The lazy farmer thinks he can leave everything to the hard working duck. When the animals unite to drive the farmer away they discover that co-operation makes work easier.
*Recommended age 4-7*

## MARTIN WADDELL

**(Translated by Aoibheann Uí Chearbhaill) Bhí Fathaigh Ann Uair**
(Gill & MacMillan 0717119319 £4.50)

Dar leis an leanbh beag tá fathaigh ina gc6naí sa teach féin!

To the small baby the adults in the house and even her brother and sister are giants. As the story unfolds we watch the baby grow and develop until she becomes a giant with a baby of her own. A gentle tale of how life comes full circle.
*Recommended age 5-8*

## MURIEL O'CONNOR

**(Translated by Mairtín Beausang) Bándearg**
(An Gúm 1857911806 £4.95)

Níl aon airgead ag an lacha bheag Bándearg ach ba mhaith léi bronntanas a cheannach dá mháthair i gcomhair na Nollag.

The very fact that this baby duck is pink endears her to small children who will certainly enjoy the story of what happens when Bándearg goes in search of a Christmas present for her Mammy.
*Recommended age 5-8*

## GABRIEL ROSENSTOCK

**An Phéist Mhór
(Illustrated by Piet Sluis)**
(An Gúm 1857911520 £4.00)

Scéal béaloidis é seo mar gheall ar thriúr iascairí agus péist mhór.

Three fishermen go to sea taking with them a goat, a stool and an old woman. What do they do when they meet a sea monster? An old folktale retold for young children.
*Recommended age 5~8*

## UNA LEAVY

**(Translated by Gabriel Rosenstock) Oíche Na Stoirme**
(An Gúm 1857912454 £4.95)

Mar gheall ar an stoirm níl aon leictreachas i dteach Chóilín agus a chlann.

This is the Irish language version of *Harry's Stormy Night*. The story and illustrations evoke perfectly that lovely, cosy feeling when the wind howls outside but all is warm and safe within.
*Recommended age 5-8*

## MARIE-LOUISE FITZPATRICK

**(Translated by Bernadine Nic Giolla Phadraig An Chanáil)**
(An Gúm £3.90)

Tá Tiarnán in a chonaí i mBaile Átha Cliath in aice leis an gCanáil Mh6r. Lá amháin téann sé ag lorg a mhadra agus feiceann sé domhan nua.

Marie-Louise Fitzpatrick uses the device of a boy's search for his lost dog to take us on a journey along the banks of the Grand Canal. Her illustrations accurately portray the people and places of the city section of the canal and the wide skies and spaciousness of the countryside as the canal flows into Co. KiIdare. A beautiful book and a winner of the Reading Association of Ireland Childrens Book Award (1989).
*Recommended age 5-8*

## MARY ARRIGAN

**Agus Éilis Ní Anluain An Bhó Fhionn**
(An Gúm 1857912144 £4.95)

Tá Seán agus a shean-mháthair go sona sásta ina gcónaí le chéile. Ach lá amháin goideann duine éigin an bhó fhionn.

This reworking of an old folktale shows its origins in its casual description of a violent act. In the end good triumphs over evil but not before Sean and his grand-mother endure hard times. Mary Arrigan's illustrations are, as always, lively and attractive.
*Recommended age 8-10*

## VALERIE COUGHLAN & CELIA KEENAN (EDS.)

**The Big Guide to Irish Children's Books.**
Irish Children's Book Trust (Children's Books Ireland), 1872917011, £5.99

A comprehensive guide to the best Irish titles for children, from picture books to teenage novels. Hundreds of books are reviewed, in sections such as 'Poetry', 'Action and Adventure' and 'Myth and Legend'. Fully illustrated and indexed, this is an indispensable guide to the world of Irish children's literature for parents, teachers, librarians and all those interested in children's reading.

## DON CONROY

### Cartoon Fun
O'Brien, 0862783585, £4.95
A step by step guide to drawing cartoons for young people. Packed with diagrams, helpful tips and hints and lots of fun cartoon drawing ideas, from witches to dinosaurs and dolphins, this book will inspire any budding artist of seven plus.

### Wildlife Fun
O'Brien, 0862783852, £4.99
An easy to follow guide to drawing animals, birds, flowers and plants from this popular wildlife expert. This interesting book includes lots of facts about nature with clear diagrams and illustrations. A good choice for any animal lover of seven plus.

## ROBERT DUFFY

### Quiz Book 2000
Poolbeg, 1853712833, £3.99
A collection of questions and answers on all kinds of subjects from science and nature to music and literature. Good fun for all the family.

## MAIREAD ASHE FITZGERALD

### The World of Colmcille
O'Brien, 0862785049, £8.99 hb
Colmcille or Columba as he is also known, was born in the 6th century and founded the monastery of Iona. This book about him is written in an accessible style, with plenty of detailed facts for the curious. The text is accompanied by clear black and white line drawings. The small hardback volume is beautifully bound, with an attractive slip cover, making it an ideal present for an older child of ten plus.

## MORGAN LLYWELYN

Morgan Llwelyn was born in New York City but settled in Ireland, 'the land of her grandparents', in 1985. Her first book *The Wind From Hastings* was published in the US in 1978. Since then she has written many books for adults and children, including the best selling *Lion of Ireland – The Legend of Brian Boru*. Morgan won a Bisto Award in 1990 for first children's book for *Brian Boru* and won another Bisto Award for *Strongbow* in 1992.

### Strongbow
O'Brien Press, 0862782740, £3.99
The true tale of Strongbow, the Norman knight and Aoife, the Irish princess. A love story set at the time of the Norman conquest of Ireland, featuring the wilful and wild Irish princess and Richard de Clare (Strongbow), the greatest Norman knight.

### The Vikings in Ireland
O'Brien Press, 0862784212, £7.99
A fascinating account of the Vikings and their influence on all aspects of Irish life – from art and trade to the cities and towns. Llwelyn explores the customs and traditions of these famous warriors and provides fascinating cameos of the lives of original Vikings. Photographs and drawings enhance and support the text throughout.

## TERRY MYLER

**Drawing Made Very Easy**
Children's Press, 0947962984,
£3.95

'If you can write you can draw,' says artist Terry Myler. This large format book shows you how to draw in easy to follow stages, from the very beginning – holding your pencil to the more difficult areas of shading and perspective. Great value for money.

## SIOBHÁN PARKINSON

**All Shining in the Spring**
O'Brien, 0862783879, £4.99

Described as 'the story of a baby who died', *All Shining in the Spring* was written to help the author's son, Matthew, cope with the death of his new baby brother at birth. Siobhán deals with a difficult subject in a gentle, strong and uncompromising manner. Written in clear, simple language for younger children to understand, this is a moving yet comforting book.

## GEORGE OTTO SIMMS

George Otto Simms was one of the most outstanding Irish churchmen of the twentieth century. Born in 1910 in Lifford, Co Donegal, he was Bishop of Cork, Archbishop of Dublin and finally Archbishop of Armagh.
In a biography of Simms, Lesley Whiteside says this of his 'Kells' book – 'Much of the magic of his presentation lies in his realisation of the spiritual dimensions of the scribe's labour and his understanding of the details...his descriptions reflect the grandeur of the artistry'. In 1990 he won the Bisto Book of the Decade award for *Exploring the Book of Kells* and *Brendan the Navigator.*

**Brendan the Navigator**
O'Brien Press, 0862782414, £4.50

A beautifully produced book which explores the life and world of Brendan and his exciting journey across the sea. The ancient adventure story, complete with volcanoes, icebergs and all manners of sea monsters will charm any reader of nine plus. Photographs, maps and illustrations complement the text throughout.

**Exploring the Book of Kells**
O'Brien Press, 0862781795, £6.95 hb

Simms brings the Book of Kells to life in this exceptional book. He describes life in a monastery, detailing the daily toils and discomforts of the monks who he portrays as 'only human'. One monk complains,' I am cold and weary, ink is bad, vellum is rough and wrinkled and the day is dark'. A wonderful book, highly recommended for readers of ten plus.

Also by this author: **Saint Patrick** O'Brien, 086278347X, £4.95

## RICHARD TARRIES

**The History of Ireland**
Gill and MacMillan,
0717123251, £7.99
An attractive, large format
hardback book chronicling
the history of Ireland from
early times right up to the
present day. The major events
are fully illustrated in full
colour, with lots of detail and
a useful 'Timeline' running
along the bottom of each
page, highlighting inventions
and historic occasions
throughout the world.
Lively and interesting reading
for children of eight plus.

## SARAH WEBB

**Kids Can Cook**
Children's Press, 1901737039,
£3.95
*Kids Can Cook* is a collection
of easy fun recipes for children to cook for themselves,
written by a Dublin-based
Waterstone's Children's
Buyer. Included in the
recipes are Chocolate Biscuit
Cake, Barm Brac and
Strawberry Ice-cream. Each
recipe is preceded by a story
or poem and there is an
informative chapter on safety
in the kitchen. A must for any
aspiring chefs of seven plus.

## NICOLA WRIGHT

**First Irish Atlas**
Gill and MacMillan,
0717123243, £7.99
An attractive large format
atlas for younger children
of seven plus. Large, full page
maps in colour provide
fascinating information on
Ireland and other countries.
Also included are details of
each country's natural
resources, population and
native wildlife. The section
on Ireland provides a good
introduction to the country
for children all over the
world. A good choice for any
geography buffs.

## PJ LYNCH

P J Lynch was born in Belfast
in 1962, the youngest of five
children. He studied art at
Brighton college, where
Raymond Briggs was one of
his tutors. He says of his art
college days, 'The illustration
department was the one
place where people were still
drawing from life and good
draughtmanship considered
important'. *A Bag of
Moonshine*, PJ's first illustrated
book (1986) was awarded the
Mother Goose award. Since
then he has gone from
strength to strength, winning
both the Kate Greenaway
Award and the Bisto award in
1995 for *The Christmas Miracle
of Jonathon Twomey*. Working
in a studio in a large
Georgian house in Dublin,
he is very aware of his Irish
identity and says, 'I make the
most of living in Dublin, go
to the pub, listen to a lot of
music and play the fiddle'.
PJ has deservedly been
dubbed 'Ireland's national
treasure'.
**A Bag of Moonshine**
Harper Collins 0006741904
£3.50
**The Christmas Miracle of
Jonathan Twomey**
Poolbeg 185371870X £5.99

# Cookery

## DARINA ALLEN

**Simply Delicious**
Gill and Macmillan £7.99 0717116875

Darina Allen owns and runs the successful Ballymaloe Cookery School at Shanagarry, Co Cork. She presents the popular cookery series 'Simply Delicious' for RTE television and has written nine bestselling cookery books.

Darina Allen is a passionate advocate of using fresh and home-grown ingredients and has had a major influence on modern Irish cookery. Her first book is a collection of mouth-watering recipes that are easy to make. Each section, from 'Soups and Starters' to 'Breads and Jams', is introduced by this enthuastic cook, passing on her love of good food and useful cookery tips like how to choose the right chicken. The recipes are wide and varied, bringing out the best in the fresh Irish ingredients. 'Ballymaloe Chicken Liver Pate with Melba Toast', classic 'White Soda Bread and Scones' and 'Cod Baked with Cream and Bay-leaves, with Duchesse Potato' are just three of the 'simply delicious recipes'.

This book is highly recommended. There are a further eight books in the 'Simply Delicious' series including *A Simply Delicious Christmas*, *Simply Delicious Fish*, and *Simply Delicious Food for Family and Friends*.

## A Year at Ballymaloe Cookery School

Gill and Macmillan £19.99
0717126196

Described as 'a glorious celebration', this book is a must for any food enthusiast. Darina Allen has rejuvenated the Irish cookery scene with her fresh and down to earth approach and her sheer joy and enthusiasm for her work, all of which are reflected in this book. *A Year at Ballymaloe Cookery School* is laid out in four seasonal chapters - 'Spring', 'Summer', 'Autumn' and 'Winter'. Each chapter brings a new feast to the eye and a tingle to the tongue. 'Fraises des Bois Ice-cream with Strawberry and Rhubarb Compote' nestles beside the photograph of a glowing yellow sunflower on a perfect summer's day. A delightful addition to any foodie's bookshelf.

# MYRTLE ALLEN

## Cooking at Ballymaloe House

Gill and Macmillan £18.99
0717118126

Myrtle Allen and her husband bought the famous Ballymaloe House in 1948, a large house on a 400 acre farm. In 1964 Myrtle opened part of the house as a restaurant and this became a highly successful family business. Myrtle now oversees the running of two restaurants and has trained many skilled cooks in her kitchen including her daughter-in-law Darina. Over a hundred favourite recipes from Myrtle's kitchen are collected in this handsome book which captures the unique charm and atmosphere of Ballymaloe House. Classic Irish recipes from Champ to Brown Bread and Scones are included, along with Ballymaloe specials such as Ballymaloe Irish Stew and 'Balloons' (Sugared Doughnuts). Charming photographs accompany the well-written text.

# JENNY BRISTOW

## Country Cooking

Appletree Press £7.99
0862816459

Well known from her popular UTV television series, Jenny Bristow has written books that are an attractive mix of the everyday and the unusual. Her recipes give Irish ingredients like cod or potatoes an exotic twist: 'Soda Bread Pizza' for example. Full colour photographs of the finished food accompany the text.

Also by Jenny is: **Country Cooking** 2 Appletree Press £8.99 0862816971.

## GEORGINA CAMPBELL

**The Best of Irish Breads and Baking**
Wolfhound £9.99 0863275001
Ireland is famous for its home-baked breads and this book gathers together both traditional favourites and new recipes. Included are recipes for all sorts of delicious treats from 'Carrot Cake' and 'Gur Cake' to 'Barm Brac' and 'Dingle Pies'. Full colour photographs accompany the text.

## CLARE CONNERY

**Irish Cookery : Over 100 Classic Irish Recipes**
Hamlyn £12.99 0600585549
*Irish Cookery* is a handsome hardback, a stylish introduction to the world of Irish food. The author, a food critic and restaurateur from Belfast, has chosen recipes which use fresh, wholesome ingredients in a new or different manner. Classic 'Irish' dishes such as 'Oyster and Guinness' and 'Cockles and Mussels' are well represented, as are more earthy dishes such as 'Pig's Trotters' and 'Boiled Bacon and Cabbage'.

## CLARE CONNERY

**In An Irish Country Kitchen**
Weidenfeld and Nicolson
£10.99 0297836021
A lavish collection of recipes, complete with chapters on the history of food and cookery in Ireland: 'The Baking Tradition', 'The Farmhouse Tradition' and 'Living off the Land, Water and Wild'. The book contains over 150 classic Irish recipes from 'Soda Bread' to 'Dublin Bay Prawns'.

## BRENDA COSTIGAN

**Easy Does It Cookbook**
Crescent Press £7.99
0951411527
Brenda Costigan's attractive cookery book has a Mediterranean feel, with lots of Spanish and Italian influenced recipes such as 'Arroz Con Pollo' and 'Fillets of Trout with Pesto and Prawns'. The text is accompanied by full colour photographs of the recipes.

## PAT COTTER

**Irish Vegetarian Cookery**
Killeen £5.99 1873548346

## EVELEEN COYLE

**Irish Potato Cookbook**
Gill and Macmillan £3.99
0717125394
Eveleen Coyle's small book brings together 'Irish' potato recipes old and new. Divided into six chapters from 'Soups' to 'Potato Cakes', the book includes lots of delicious recipes for snacks, main meals and side dishes. Coyle, an editor and book publicist from Dublin, writes the chapter introductions and recipe asides in a thoughtful and accessible manner. A great book for anyone who has ever wanted to know the difference between Boxty and Potato Cakes, Champ and Colcannon.

## TAMASIN DAY-LEWIS

**West of Ireland Summers : A Cookbook**
Weidenfeld £9.99 0297818589
The author of this attractive hardback spent her childhood summers in the West of Ireland. This collection of anecdotes and recipes is illustrated with atmospheric photographs of the scenery and food of the West. Tamasin Day-Lewis has chosen a wide range of delicious recipes from both Irish and the broader world of cookery, such as 'Blackcurrant Fool' and 'Crabcakes with Herb Mayonnaise'. An entertaining and nostalgic book, perfect for browsing through on a cold winter's evening.

## THEODORA FITZGIBBON

**Irish Traditional Food**
Gill and Macmillan £8.99
071718673

The doyenne of Irish cookery writers was born in 1916, and after a short spell as an actress, turned her talent to gastromony and food journalism. She was the cookery correspondent for the Irish Times and wrote more than thirty cookery books in her lifetime. Her encyclopaedia of food won the Glenfiddich Special Award Gold Medal in 1976. Theodora Fitzgibbon died in 1991. *Irish Traditional Food* is an all -encompassing collection of traditional Irish recipes, from the sixteenth to the twentieth century. FitzGibbon's writing is clear and easy to read, her wide knowledge of Irish food is evident throughout the book. Recipes include unusual choices, 'Pigeons in Guinness' and 'Snipe cooked over turf', and old favourites, 'Red cabbage with bacon' and 'Porter cake'. Or you could try the 'Dublin lawyer'- lobster cooked with whiskey!

## THEODORA FITZGIBBON

**A Taste of Ireland**
Weidenfeld and Nicolson £8.99
0297833480

*A Taste of Ireland* combines traditional Irish recipes with fascinating black and white photographs of Ireland in the late nineteenth century. The recipe for 'Dublin Bay Prawns' is accompanied by a splendid photograph of the Pavillion in Kingstown (Dun Laoghaire) in 1904. Theodora Fitzgibbon also tells us that 'these succulent little creatures are not a prawn at all, but the Norway lobster (Nephrops norvegicus)'! Much more than just a cookbook.

## CONRAD GALLAGHER

**Conrad Gallagher's New Irish Cookery**
A and A Farmar £19.99
1899047298

Conrad Gallagher worked in top restaurants and hotels, such as Le Cirque in New York, before opening his own restaurant, Peacock Alley in Dublin at the tender age of 24. Each recipe in this book, all Peacock Alley favourites, was 'adjusted and refined so it could readily be cooked at home, and yet retain the bravura and kaleidoscope of the original'. Main dishes include suggested wines to serve. Recipes are not for the faint hearted cook - 'Crabmeat Salad with Lemon, Beetroot, Curried Creme Fraiche and Beetroot Chips' requires patience and a steady hand. A good choice for an experienced foodie.

## GERRY GALVIN

**Everyday Gourmet**
O'Brien Press £6.99 hb
0862785375
Gerry Galvin runs the Drimcong House Restaurant and has won both the Egon Ronay Chef of the Year (1994) and the Guinness Chef of the Year (1996). His philosophy of cookery is simple : the key is fresh ingredients used with flair and imagination. In *Everyday Gourmet* he brings his wide experience 'to book'. Divided into ten chapters including 'One Pot Dishes' and 'Children's Recipes', with glossy full colour photographs, this is a well-designed and accessible cook book. 'Smoked Salmon Scones', 'Stir-fried Cabbage with Mushroom, Onion and Bacon' and 'Baked Bananas' are just three of the simple but mouth watering dishes.

## LUCY MADDEN

**The Potato Year : 365 Ways of Cooking Potatoes**
Milu Press £9.99 0952534800
A potato recipe for every day of the year, with Christmas Pudding (using pureed potato) on Christmas Day and Colcannon on 31 October, Hallowe'en. An interesting book, great for browsing through, with some inventive and unusual potato recipes.

## PAUL AND JEANNE RANKIN

**Gourmet Ireland**
BBC Books £9.99 0563371552
Paul and Jeanne Rankin run the successful restaurant Roscoff in Belfast, which in 1991 was awarded a Michelin star. Their BBC television programme is very popular and this book, along with *Gourmet Ireland 2* (BBC Books £12.99 0563384018) accompanies the series. The Rankins insist on the freshest Irish ingredients, to which they add their own eclectic touch, influenced by their travels around the world. 'Irish Stew' rubs shoulders with 'Crispy Duck Confit with Chinese Spices' in this excellent cook book.

## REGINA SEXTON

**A Little History of Irish Food**
Kyle Cathie £9.99 185626243X
Written by Ireland's foremost food historian, *A Little History of Irish Food* is a must for anyone interested in cookery in Ireland past or present. Learn how to preserve eggs with lime, make a cure for coughs from seaweed and how to cook 'De Valera's Pie'. Irish food is set in its unique cultural context, making this much more than a cook book.

From Dorothea Lange's, Ireland

# Drama

## Anthologies

There are a number of valuable anthologies of Irish Drama available. John Harrington's **Modern Irish Drama** (Norton pb £8.95 0393960633) is a selection of twelve plays, including works from Lady Gregory, Brendan Behan and Brian Friel. Harrington provides both background and criticism of these plays which comfortably represent Irish Drama from the Literary Revival to Field Day. Christopher Fitzsimons has collected **Three New Plays From The Abbey Theatre** (Syracuse University Press pb £14.95 0815603452) which includes Donal O'Kelly's **Asylum, Asylum,** dealing with the contradictions in Irish Asylum Law. Niall Williams's **A Little Like Paradise** is set in a rural village, which hasn't been discovered by tourism or EU subsidy and Tom McIntyre's **Sheep's Milk on the Boil,** is set on a small island off the West Coast. In **A Brave & Violent Theatre: Monologues, Scenes & Historical Drama For The 20th Century** (Syracuse University Press pb £10.95 1880399717), Michael Dixon has put together a good range of dramatical excerpts from twentieth century plays, suitable for the student and general reader. **A Crack In The Emerald** published by Nick Hern Books (pb 9.99 1854592378) is a selection of work, concentrating on newer voices in Irish drama like Dermot Bolger, Marina Carr and Michael Harding. Frank McGuinness in **Dazzling Dark: New Irish Plays** (Faber pb 9.99 0571177700) has collected and illuminatingly introduced four recent Irish plays, **Portia Coughlan** by Marina Carr, **Danti-Dan** by Gina Moxley , **A Picture of Paradise** by Jimmy Murphy and **Good Evening Mr. Collins** by Tom McIntyre. Each play is also followed by an afterword, written for this volume, by the playwright.

## SEBASTIAN BARRY
### (b.1955)

Sebastian Barry was born in Dublin and educated at Trinity College. Between leaving university in 1977 and 1986 he wrote three novels (now out of print) and three collections of poetry. Since 1986, he has written exclusively for the theatre, producing what is now seen as a five part cycle written about his own family, culminating in the recent **The Steward of Christendom**. His most recent work is a return to prose, **The Whereabouts of Eneas McNulty**. In the novel the eponymous character joins the Royal Irish Constabulary having fought for the British in the Great War. In Sligo, he is seen as a traitor who fought for the enemy and is subsequently alienated and rejected from his family, friends and country. This novel contains many of the themes that Barry has dealt with in his plays.

**The Only True History of Lizzie Finn**
Methuen pb £8.99 0413698904
**Plays Vol 1**
Methuen pb £9.99 041371120X
**The Steward of Christendom**
Methuen pb £7.50 0413718204
**The Watercolourist**
Smythe pb £14.95 0851054129

## SAMUEL BECKETT (1906 – 1989)

After leaving Ireland in 1937 and finally settling in Paris, Beckett decided to write in French in order to disassociate himself from the literary tradition of the English language. In the late 1940s he began experimenting with drama. **Waiting for Godot**, written in 1948-49 and first produced in 1953, saw the transference of Beckett's philosophical ideas from the page to the stage. Beckett's sparseness is seen in the dialogue as well as in the stark staging he employs. With only five characters, a tree and a road Beckett created a play that spoke of the conflict between reality and how it is perceived, as well as the doubts uncovered by this conflict. His characters question, doubt and suffer, yet they stoically go on because that is all they can do.

In his later plays, Beckett focused his attention even more on language rather than action. In **Endgame** (1957) two of the characters are confined to dustbins, while in **Happy Days** (1961) one character is buried to the waist and then finally to the neck. In both cases the characters' movements are necessarily restricted and words are all that are left to them. **Krapp's Last Tape** (1958) explores the isolation of modern life through a monologue in which Krapp listens to a tape he made thirty years earlier and now viciously mocks the dreams and ideas of his younger self. Beckett continued to pare down his writing in both action and language in his later plays like **Breath** (1969) which lasts a mere thirty seconds and **Not I** (1973), a spewing forth of words by an illuminated mouth.

**Collected Shorter Plays**
Faber £6.99 0571130402
**Complete Dramatic Works**
Faber pb £9.99 0571144861
**Eleutheria**
Faber pb £6.99 057117826X
**Endgame**
Faber pb £5.99 0571070671
**Happy Days**
Faber pb £6.99 0571066534
**Krapp's Last Tape**
Faber pb £5.99 0571062091
**Theatrical Notebooks of Samuel Beckett**
Faber hb £50.00 0571145639
**Waiting For Godot**
Faber pb £5.99 0571058086

**Collected Poems in English and French**
Grove pb £6.99 0802130968

**(Beckett Criticism/Biography)**

*J. Acheson*
**Samuel Beckett's Artistic Theory**
Macmillan hb £35.00 0333565312

*Deirdre Bair*
**Samuel Beckett: A Biography**
Vintage pb £9.99 0099800705

*Ruby Cohn*
**Samuel Beckett's Waiting for Godot**
Macmillan pb £10.99 0333344898

*Anthony Cronin*
**Samuel Beckett: Last Modernist**
Flamingo pb £8.99 0586090762

*Lawrence Graver*
**Samuel Beckett: Waiting for Godot**
Cambridge University Press pb £6.99 0521357756

*Mel Gussow*
**Conversations with Beckett**
Nick Hern hb £13.99 1854593102

*Hugh Kenner*
**Readers Guide to Samuel Beckett**
Syracuse University Press pb £14.99 081560386X

*Vivian Mercier*
**Beckett/Beckett**
Souvenir pb £8.95 0285630105

*John Minihan*
**Samuel Beckett Photographs**
Secker pb £9.990436202522

*Pilling*
**Cambridge Companion to Samuel Beckett**
Cambridge pb £13.95 0521424135

*Christopher Ricks*
**Beckett's Dying Words**
Oxford University Press pb £7.99 0192824074
**Waiting for Godot Casebook**
Macmillan pb £9.99 0333546032
**Waiting for Godot York Notes**
Longman pb £2.99 0582023181

# BRENDAN BEHAN (1923–1964)

This Dublin born playwright and memoirist, who died from alcoholism at the age of forty one, has become part of the literary/folk legend of the capital city. At the age of sixteen, having joined the republican movement, he traveled to Liverpool on a bombing mission, was caught and imprisoned. He served two years in prison in England before being sent home. His experiences in prison became his brilliant memoir **Borstal Boy.** Shortly after arriving home, he was arrested and charged with shooting at a policeman and served five years of a fifteen year sentence. Over the eighteen years after his release and before his death he wrote stories and plays in English and Irish and went on a much publicized visit to New York, where he was much celebrated. In Dublin, he wrote a column for the Irish Press, which has been recently collected and published. He was associated with many pubs throughout Dublin city centre, probably nowhere as much as McDaids on Harry St.

**After the Wake**
O'Brien Press pb £4.950862780314 (Fiction)
**Borstal Boy**
Arrow pb £7.99 0099706504 (Memoir)
**Complete Plays**
Methuen pb £7.99 0413387801
**Confessions of Irish Rebel**
Arrow pb £6.99 0099365006 (Memoir)
**Poems & a Play in Irish**
Gallery Press pb £5.95 0904011151

**(Biography)**

*Ulick O'Connor*
**Brendan Behan**
Abacus pb £7.99 0349105146

*Michael O'Sullivan*
**Brendan Behan**
Blackwater Press hb £19.99 0861216989

## MARINA CARR (b.1964)

Marina Carr was born and grew up in Co. Offally. She now lives in Dublin and is a member of AosDána.
**The Mai** is a powerful family story revolving around seven women over two summers and enjoyed much critical and commercial success when produced in the Abbey Theatre. **Portia Couglan** was commissioned by the National Maternity hospital in its centenary year.

**The Mai**
Gallery Press pb £5.95
1852351616
**Portia Coughlan**
Faber pb £6.99 0571190235

## ANN DEVLIN

Born in Belfast, Anne Devlin has written two successful plays. **Ourselves Alone**, first staged in 1985, is a humorous but serious examination of the role of women in contemporary Northern Ireland. **After Easter**, first staged in 1994 by the RSC, concentrates on the feelings and emotions of Greta, self-exiled from Northern Ireland to escape her troubled background and identity. On returning home, she has to confront and deal with her denial.

**After Easter**
Faber pb £6.99 0571173942
**Ourselves Alone**
Faber pb £5.99 0571144578

## BERNARD FARRELL (b.1941)

Farrell is a hugely popular dramatist, who has ejoyed a long association and many revivals with both The Gate and Abbey Theatres in Dublin. Farrell's success is due to the fact that he is not afraid to place ordinary, credible characters on the stage to examine everyday human interaction. His play **Canaries** (1980) focuses on taking foreign holidays, while his **Last Apache Reunion** (1993) humorously portrays the difficulties and hang-ups experienced when a group of old friends meets after many years.

**All the Way Back**
Brophy pb £5.99 0907960995
**Canaries**
Campus pb £5.99 187322365X
**Forty-Four Sycamore Street & The Last Apache Reunion**
Mercier Press pb £7.99
1856351246
**Happy Birthday Dear Al & Stella**
Mercier Press pb £8.99
1856351807
**Say Cheese**
Campus pb £5.99 1873223315

Pat: He was an Anglo-Irishman.
Meg: In the blessed name of God, what's that?
Pat: A Protestant with a horse.
Brandan Behan – The Hostage

## BRIAN FRIEL (b.1929)

Born in Omagh, Co. Tyrone, and brought up in Derry, Brian Friel is, without doubt, Ireland's most important and prolific contemporary dramatist. Since 1964, and the success of **Philadelphia, Here I Come**, Friel has written over twenty original plays, a volume of short stories and a version of Anton Chekhov's **The Three Sisters. Philadelphia Here I Come!** rightly established Friel's reputation as a major dramatist. Performed first in theGaiety Theatre, Dublin and directed by Hilton Edwards, it very successfully portrays the private and public personae of Gar(eth) O'Donnell the night before he emigrates to Philadelpia, escaping the dreary life of Ballybeg in rural Donegal. Public Gar displays the usual bravado of the imminent emigrant while Private Gar provides the commentary of realistic misgivings and doubt.

In 1980, with the actor Stephen Rea, poets Seamus Heaney, Seamus Deane, Tom Paulin & singer/songwriter David Hammond, Friel founded the Field Day Theatre Company in Derry. The company was committed to touring annually with a dramatic production and to producing pamphlets that would examine different aspects of cultural debate on the island of Ireland. The first production from this new company was Friel's play **Translations** which was set in Donegal in the 1830s. The plot concerns the mapping of Donegal by the British Ordnance Survey, who anglicize all of the local place-names in an attempt to colonize the area linguistically. Openly encouraging debate about the British rule of Ireland, **Translations** is a very sophisticated presentation and summation of nationalist cultural thought of the time. International success came in the early 1990s with the production of **Dancing at Lughnasa**. The plot concerns an Irish missionary returning from Africa who sees the links between primitivism inherent in Irish harvest traditions and the African tribal customs he has experienced. The production transferred to Broadway and was recently made into a film with the screenplay written by Frank McGuinness. Friel's stories, recently reprinted by the Gallery Press, display a rare mix of pathos and anecdotal realism. Two generations of secondary schoolchildren from the early 1970s to the mid-1980s,were beguilingly returned to their earlier childhood when reading the short masterpiece 'Among the Ruins'. Depicting a family trip back to the father's ruined homestead, the story explores childhood memory and resultant grown-up misunderstanding with a truthful simplicity that has never been surpassed in contemporary Irish or indeed international short fiction.

**Crystal & Fox**
Gallery Press pb £5.95
0904011623
**The Enemy Within**
Gallery Press pb £5.95
0902996924
**The Freedom of the City**
Gallery Press pb £5.95
1852350881
**The Gentle Island**
Gallery Press pb £5.95
1852351101
**Living Quarters**
Gallery Press pb £5.95
1852350903
**Lovers**
Gallery Press pb £5.95
090401164X
**The Loves of Cass Mcguire**
Gallery Press pb £5.95
0904011607
**Philadelphia Here I Come**
Faber pb £6.99 0571085865
**Plays One**
Faber pb 9.99 0571177670
**Volunteers**
Gallery Press pb £5.95
1852350385
**Aristocrats**
Gallery Press pb £5.95
0904011119
**Faith Healer**
Gallery Press pb £5.95
1852350792
**Translations**
Faber pb £5.99 0571117422
**The Communication Cord**
Gallery Press pb 5.95
1852350369
**Making History**

Faber pb £5.99 0571154778
**The Three Sisters**
Gallery Press pb £6.95
0904011267
**Dancing at Lughnasa**
Faber pb £7.50 0571144799
**Give Me Your Answer Do**
Gallery Press pb £6.95
1852351993
**Molly Sweeney**
Gallery Press pb £5.95
1852351519
**Wonderful Tennessee**
Gallery Press pb £5.95
1852351144
**Fathers & Sons**
Faber pb £4.99 0571150799
**The London Vertigo:
After Macklin**
Gallery Press pb £4.95
185235058x
**Selected Stories**
Gallery Press pb £7.95
1852351497

*(Friel Criticism)*
**York Notes on Translations**
Longman pb £3.50 0582293480

*Alan Peacock*
**The Achievement of Brian Friel**
Smythe pb £6.99 0861403649

# OLIVER GOLDSMITH (1728–1774)

Born in Dublin Goldsmith was educated at Trinity College and then went to Edinburgh in 1752 to study medicine. Instead of taking a degree in Scotland, he went on a long walk around France, Holland, Italy and Switzerland. Although it has never been proven if he was ever awarded any medical degree, he returned to London and practiced as a physician from 1756. Soon becoming dissatisfied with the medical work he started to write poetry and plays. He is remembered mainly for his comedy, **She Stoops to Conquer**, the much anthologised poem **The Deserted Village** and a novel **The Vicar of Wakefield. The Vicar of Wakefield** narrates the story of George Primrose, whose idyllic life in a country parish is shattered by misfortune and adversity. After many trials and tribulations the fortunes of the vicar and his family are restored. **The Deserted Village** is based on Goldsmith's home village of Lissoy, Co. Westmeath and is an idealistic portrayal of the village that he loved. He was deeply worried about the agricultural revolution and the possible effects it could have on rural communities because small farms would be bought up and farmers like the previous four generations of his own family would have to leave the land. **She Stoops to Conquer** is one of the great comedies in English and recounts, in superbly plotted high farce, the misunderstandings that occur when a group of travellers mistake a private house for an inn.

**She Stoops to Conquer**
A & C Black pb £5.99 0713628944

## LADY GREGORY
### (1852–1932)

Born Isabella Augusta Persse at Roxborough, Co. Galway, she married Sir William Gregory of Coole, Co.Galway. This gave her the ideal introduction to the broader worlds of Victorian ideas. She became nationalist in her viewpoint and copperfastened her commitment by collecting as many folktales as she could from the villages and townlands in Co. Galway. She met W.B. Yeats in 1896 and thus started a life-long friendship. She invited Yeats and many other artists of the Literary Revival to her house in Coole Park where they could write and develop their ideas in quiet and comfort. It was while staying at Coole that Yeats, Edward Martyn and Lady Gregory thought up the idea for the Irish Literary Theatre, which would later become The Abbey and she went on then to write forty plays for the theatre, most of which were produced.

**Comedies**
Colin Smythe pb £6.95
086140016X
**Selected Writings**
Penguin pb £8.99 0140189556
**Tragedies and Tragicomedies**
Colin Smythe pb £7.95
0861400178
**Wonder and Supernatural Plays**
Colin Smythe pb £7.95
0861400186

## DOUGLAS HYDE
### (1860–1949)

Unusual for a lifelong champion of the Irish language Douglas Hyde was born into a Protestant clerical family in Frenchpark, Co. Roscommon. When he went to Trinity to study law, he was already writing poetry and collecting folk-songs and tales. In 1893, he became the president of the Gaelic League, which was dedicated to creating a modern Irish literature without involving politics. He resigned after 1915, when the league's constitution was changed to include political aims. In 1938, he became the first president of Ireland and remained in office until 1944. His main claim to fame must be his great collection of stories and his firm belief that a national literature could be created.

**Selected Plays**
Colin Smythe pb £5.95
0861400968

## DENIS JOHNSTON
### (1901–1984)

Born in Dublin, Denis Johnston was educated in Dublin, Cambridge and Harvard. He was called to the Irish bar in 1926. His first play **The Old Lady Says No** (the title refers to the response of Lady Gregory when the work was originally submitted to the Abbey) was performed in the Gate Theatre in 1929 and was very successful. So too was was his second play, **The Moon in the Yellow River**. In 1938, he joined the BBC in Belfast and moved to London in 1939. He became a war correspondent in 1942 and was made Director of Programmes in 1946. In 1948, he went to America and until the late 1960s taught at various universities. He returned to Dublin in 1969, where he died in 1984. His first play, which has Robert Emmet as its protagonist, compares late 18th Century patriotic idealism, with the realities of the Irish Free State, while **The Moon in the Yellow River** examines the reaction to modernisation in Ireland, using the Shannon hydro-electric scheme as its focus.

**Selected Plays**
Colin Smythe pb £7.95
0861400860

## JOHN B. KEANE
### (b.1928 )

Born in Listowel, Co. Kerry, where he has lived ever since except for a couple of years working in England. He runs a pub in Listowel and is regarded as one of the central figures in Kerry literary life. He was one of the prime-movers in setting up Listowel Writers Week. His plays have been incredibly successful and skillfully explore the darker side of the human psyche. His work has enjoyed many revivals in the Abbey Theatre and **The Field** has been made into a very successful film by Jim Sheridan.

**The Field**
Mercier Press pb £5.99
0853429766
**The Highest House on the Mountain**
Mercier pb £5.99 1898175012
**Sive In Two Acts**
Mercier Press pb £3.50
1898175004
**Three Plays (Sive, The Field, Big Maggie)**
Mercier Press pb £9.99
0853429073

## THOMAS KILROY (b.1934 )

Born in Callan, Co. Kilkenny and now living in Mayo, Tom Kilroy has enjoyed long and varied success with drama, fiction and his career as an academic. Having taught in the USA, he taught in University College Dublin. Following a six year sabbatical he became Professor of English at University College Galway. His novel **The Big Chapel** (now out of print) was shortlisted for the Booker prize in 1971. However, undoubtedly his greatest success has been in the theatre, from the acclaim given to **The Death & Resurrection of Mr. Roche** in the 1968 Dublin Theatre Festival to the enthusiastic reception of **The Secret Fall of Constance Wilde** in the same festival in 1997. He adapted Anton Chekhov's **The Seagull** for the Royal Court in London in 1981 and the Field Day Theatre Company produced his **Double Cross** in 1986. **Talbot's Box**, recently republished by the Gallery Press, was first produced in the Peacock Theatre in 1977. The play is based on the life of late 19th century Dublin steel worker Matt Talbot, venerated by the Catholic Church for his conversion from a life of alcoholism to one of daily prayer and penance.

**Double Cross**
Gallery Press pb £5.95 1852351470
**Madame Macadam's Travelling Theatre**
Methuen pb £6.99 0413663108
**The O'Neill**
Gallery Press pb £5.95 1852351632
**The Seagull**
Gallery Press pb £5.95 1852351209
**The Secret Fall of Constance Wilde**
Gallery Press pb £6.95 1852351934
**Talbot's Box**
Gallery Press pb £5.95 1852351985

## HUGH LEONARD
### (b.1926)

Dublin-born dramatist and memoirist, Hugh Leonard has enjoyed a long and successful career both on the stage and on television through various literary adaptions. His first huge success came in 1978, when his play **Da** was performed on Broadway. The play portrayed life in the Dalkey where Leonard grew up in the 1930s and 40s and in 1987 was made into a film starring Martin Sheen. He famously adapted *The Irish RM* stories by Somerville and Ross for Granada Television in the 1980s. He returned to Dalkey in his very charming and effective memoirs, **Home Before Night** and **Out After Dark,** both of which were very successful. He also wrote a column for the Sunday Independent and now regularly writes book reviews for the Irish Times.

**Da/A Life/Timewas**
Penguin pb £6.99 0140148094
**A Life**
French pb £4.95 0573112444
**Moving**
French pb £5.50 0573018375
**Selected Plays**
Smythe pb £9.95 0861401417
**Home Before Night (memoir)**
Penguin pb £6.99 0140055401
**Out After Dark (memoir)**
Penguin pb £6.99 0140129332

## MARTIN LYNCH
### (b.1950)

Lynch's drama is firmly set in the working class city Belfast of his birth and is a great combination of storytelling and humour. In his **Three Plays, Dockers** examines Belfast working class life, **The Interrogation of Ambrose Fogarty,** looks at police detention and **Pictures of Tomorrow,** which is set in the context of the Spanish Civil War describes the fading of left wing ideals in the age of Free State capitalism.

**Three Plays**
Lagan Press pb £4.95
1873687605

## MICHEAL MAC LIAMMÓIR
### (1899–1978)

Though born in London, Mac Liammóir, changed his name from Alfred Willmore, when he joined the Gaelic League. He founded the Gate Theatre in Dublin in 1928, with his partner Hilton Edwards. He played many roles in this theatre and also wrote many plays. His most famous, **The Importance of Being Oscar,** which is a one-man show based on the life and works of Oscar Wilde, made him world famous.

His selected plays, with an introduction by John Barrett was published this year and a biography is available from Brandon Press.

**The Importance of Being Oscar**
Smythe pb £5.95 0851055109
**Selected Plays**
Smythe pb £5.95 1813208890
*Micheal O'Haodha*
**The Importance of Being Micheal: A Portrait of Mac Liammóir**
Brandon Press pb £9.95
0863221068

## AIDAN MATHEWS

**Exit/Entrance**
Gallery Press pb £5.95
1852350547

This is a two act play, the first act of which introduces the two main characters and lets them look back on their lives together. The second act shows them starting off together and serves as good dramatic and emotional counterpoint.

# RUTHERFORD MAYNE

**(1878–1967)**

Mayne was born Samuel Waddell in Japan and was educated in Belfast. His **Selected Plays** were recently published, edited and introduced by John Killen. This volume includes **The Drone** (1908), a rural comedy, **Peter** (1930), a farce based in an upmarket hotel and **The Bridgehead** (1934) which is based on his experiences working for the Land Commission. The last two plays were written for the Abbey theatre.

**Selected Plays**
Institute of Irish Studies pb
£8.50 0853896674

# MARTIN MCDONAGH

*Katherine Gallagher of Waterstone's in Dawson Street, Dublin looks at the extraordinary achievements of the young Irish playwright.*

At just twenty seven years of age, Martin McDonagh has already earned the praise most playwrights only dream of attaining. In 1996, his play **The Beauty Queen of Leenane** won for him the Evening Standard Award for the Most Promising Playwright. In the same year he was awarded the George Devine Award for the Most Promising Playwright. For a man who claims he was bored by theatre and was more interested in cinema as a child this is quite an achievement. McDonagh uses the pacing of films coupled with the storytelling nature of drama in order to examine Irish life. Born of Irish parents and raised in London, McDonagh has returned to his roots through his plays. Just as Synge endeavoured to do, McDonagh takes stage-Irish rural Ireland and puts the stereotypes on their heads. He uses dark humour and precision-timing to expose the hidden pain and suffering of his characters, thus making them more well-rounded than the stereotypes they appear to be. In **The Cripple of Inishmaan** the action is set in typical Synge country on a remote island off the west coast of Ireland in 1934, but his characters are distinctly unlike those of Synge. The story revolves around Cripple Billy and his dream of leaving Inishman, where he is seen only for his disability, and of making it big in Hollywood in the film *Man of Aran* which is filming on a neighboring island. McDonagh uses comedy to examine difficult and typically 'unmentionable' subjects. When Billy asks the village gossip to stop calling him Cripple Billy he is told simply that is what he is, a cripple. Billy replies 'Well, do I go calling you 'Johnnypateenmike with news that's so boring it'd bore the head off a dead bee?" McDonagh is able to expose the undersides of this potentially romantic rural life with characters such as Slippy Helen, a brash girl who says exactly what she means.

Her name derives from her continual 'dropping' of the eggs she is meant to be delivering. She casually reveals she is not dropping them, but is actually throwing them at the local priest. When she is told this is a sin against God, her matter-of-fact response is, 'Oh, maybe it is, but if God went touching me arse in choir practice I'd peg eggs at that fecker, too.'

Despite the humour of his plays the audience is left feeling slightly uneasy about laughing at unfortunate events and at people that we are taught it is impolite to make fun of. Instead of conceding to the current vogue of political correctness and softening his tone, McDonagh continues to strike unflinchingly at the heart of the issues. Even the ending of the play is a tragic reversal of expectation. Despite his failure in Hollywood, Billy seems to have finally found the thing he most sought, acceptance from his family and neighbours, but fate steps in and issues a final blow against him. All will not end happily ever after in McDonagh's plays.

After a successful run of **The Leenane Trilogy** in Galway's Druid Theatre, the trilogy went on the receive equally high praise in London's Royal Court, the Dublin Theatre Festival, and the Sydney Festival. In early 1998 it moved to New York's Atlantic Theatre where it proved so popular it moved to the Walter Kerr Theatre and was nominated for six Tony Awards. While McDonagh will certainly continue to achieve acclaim in drama, he is also eyeing opportunities to work in his first love, cinema. He is reportedly engaged in talks about writing a screenplay, and like Cripple Billy he looks set to head for Hollywood. We can be sure that he will be more successful there than Billy.

**The Beauty Queen of Leenane**
Methuen pb £7.70 041370730X
**The Cripple of Inishmaan**
Methuen pb £8.99 0413715906
**The Lonesome West**
Methuen pb £7.70 0413719804
**Skull of Connemara**
Mthuen pb £6.99 0413719707

# FRANK MCGUINNESS (b.1956)

Born in Buncrana, Co. Donegal, McGuinness has combined a life as an academic teacher with writing plays and poetry. His first play **Factory Girls,** was staged in the Peacock Theatre in 1982 and deals with the awful wait for redundancy experienced by five women working in a Co. Donegal shirt factory.

His hugely successful **Observe the Sons of Ulster Marching Towards the Somme** was produced in the Peacock in 1985 and later moved to the Hampstead Theatre in London. Based on the Ulster Protestant experience in the Great War, it has recently been revived by the Abbey Theatre. **Innocence,** based on the life of Caravaggio, was produced in the Gate Theatre in 1986 and caused some controversy in Dublin of the 1980s with its explicitly sexual themes. His play **Carthaginians** was performed in the Abbey in 1988. Set in Derry in the aftermath of Bloody Sunday, 1972, it is the playwright's elegy to the living and dead of that city. During the 1980s, he also successfully adapted Frederico Garcia Lorca's **Yerma** as well as **Rosmersholm** and **Peer Gynt** by Ibsen.

That decade concluded with **Mary & Lizzie** for the Royal Shakespeare Company in 1989. In the 1990s he has maintained his prolific output with adaptations of Bertolt Brecht's **The Threepenny Opera,** Ibsen's **Hedda Gabler** and Anton Chekhov's **The Three Sisters** and **Uncle Vanya.** His original dramatic work continued with **The Bread Man,** for the Gate Theatre in 1991, **Someone Who'll Watch Over Me,** which dealt very movingly with the Lebanese hostage crisis of the 1980s and **The Bird Sanctuary.** He lives in Dublin where he has recently been appointed Faculty of Arts Writer-in-Residence at University College, Dublin. His poetry collection, **Booterstown** combines a beautiful lyricism with a great evocation of place and time. His most recent play **Mutabilitie** is a political drama based on Edmund Spenser's relationship with Ireland.

**Booterstown**
Gallery pb £6.95 1852351357
(Poetry)
**Mary & Lizzie**
Faber pb £4.99 0571142680
**Mutabilities**
Faber pb £6.99 0571193420
**Observe the Sons of Ulster Marching Towards the Somme**
Faber pb £5.99 0571146112
**Plays One**
Faber pb £8.99 0571177409
**Someone Who'll Watch Over Me**
Faber pb £5.99 0571168043

## CONOR MCPHERSON
### (b.1971)

Conor McPherson was born in Dublin and now divides his time between Dublin and London, where he is Writer-in Residence at the Bush Theatre. His play **St. Nicholas,** is a one man play, originally premiered with Brian Cox in 1997 as the theatre critic telling the story of his infatuation/obsession with a young actress. **The Weir,** originally commisioned by the Royal Court, is set in an Irish rural pub and starts off with three local men telling ghost stories to a visiting Dublin woman. It becomes clear, later in the play that the tables are being turned. Both plays demonstrate McPherson's great story-telling gift. Other work includes **Three Plays: Rum & Vodka,The Good Thing & This Lime Tree Bower.** He has also written the screenplay for **I Went Down,** a crime comedy, directed by Paddy Breathnach and starring Brendan Gleeson and Peter McDonald as two hapless criminals having a hard time as a result of bad luck, inexperience and naiveté.

**I Went Down**
Nick Hern pb £9`99
1854593935
**St Nicholas & the Weir**
Nick Hern pb £7.99
1854593471
**Three Plays**
New Island Books pb £7.99
1854592998

## JIMMY MURPHY

**Brothers of the Brush**
Oberon pb £5.99 1870259424

Murphy's very successful play **Brothers of the Brush** revolves around a group of house painters and shows how personal interest and self-ambition can be rife, even among the closest of 'friends'.

## THOMAS MURPHY
### (b.1935)

Born in Tuam, Co. Galway where he started his working life teaching in a local school. For most of the 1960s, he lived in London and worked as a full-time writer. **A Whistle in the Dark,** his first play, was produced in the Royal Court Theatre in London by Joan Littlewood in 1961, having been rejected by the Abbey Theatre. He returned to Dublin in 1971, and served as a director on the board of the Abbey Theatre until 1983. He achieved moderate success in the 1970s with **The Morning after Optimism, The Sanctuary Lamp** and **The Blue Macushla.** However, it was his work in the 1980s, especially **The Gigli Concert** at the Abbey in 1983 and **Bailegangaire** in the Druid Theatre,Galway in 1985 that made sure that Murphy was recognised as the great talent that he is. **A Whistle in the Dark** depicts the life of the

Carneys, an Irish family in England, who are desperately trying to settle in. Michael Carney is anxious to reject the violence of his father and brothers and his internal family conflict leads to a tragic conclusion. **Bailegangaire,** literally translated as 'the town without laughter' is a powerful story narrated by the senile Mommo, about how the town came to have its name. Intertwined with the story of the town, is the story of her own life and that of her granddaughters. The Druid production in the Galway was one of Siobháin McKenna's last and most memorable roles. **The Gigli Concert** focuses on the dependence and interdependence between J.P.W. King, an English 'Dynamatologist' or healer, an unnamed Irish property developer and a woman, Mona all of whom are striving to find their own true selves.

As well as writing for TV he has also adapted Oliver Goldsmith's **She Stoops to Conquer** and **The Vicar of Wakefield.** He has also written a novel **The Seduction of Morality,** which was critically acclaimed.

**A Crucial Week in the Life of a Grocer's Assistant**
Gallery Press pb £5.95
0902996770
**The Gigli Concert**
Gallery Press pb £5.95
0904011526
**Plays Vol.**
Methuen pb £6.99 0413665704
**Plays Vol.2**
Methuen pb £8.99 0413675602
**Plays Vol.3**
Methuen pb £8.99 0413683508
**Plays Vol.4**
pb £9.99 0413714500
**The Seduction of Morality**
Abacus pb £6.99 0349106177
(Fiction)
**She Stoops to Folly**
Methuen pb £6.99 0413714004
**Too Late for Logic**
Methuen pb £5.35 0413632202

**(Murphy Criticism)**
*Fintan O'Toole*
**Tom Murphy: The Politics of Magic**
New Island pb £9.95
1874597758

# JIM NOLAN
**Moonshine**
Gallery Press pb £5.95
1852350962
This play is set in an Irish seaside town. In the background of the closing of the parish church, the local undertaker is determined to stage a production of Midsummer's Night Dream. The result is a gently rolling play that has great characterisation and evocation.

## SEAN O'CASEY
### (1880–1964)

Dublin-born O'Casey is, with Brendan Behan, probably the playwright most associated with the capital city. Born into a poor Protestant family, O'Casey was the youngest of thirteen children. His education was intermittent and he suffered from eye trouble all of his life. He was secretary of the Citizen Army, but broke politically in the aftermath of the 1916 rising. His Dublin trilogy (**The Shadow of a Gunman, Juno & the Paycock** and **The Plough & the Stars**) are his most famous plays and portray the grim poverty inherent in the life of Dublin's working classes. When riots followed the first production of **The Plough & the Stars** and **The Silver Tassie** was rejected by the Abbey, O'Casey became embittered toward Ireland and left, never to return. In London, he became friends with Shaw and Augustus John, and tried but never quite succeeded in repeating his earlier success and fame. In 1938, he moved to Devon. For the rest of his life he continued to write both plays and autobiographies but he seemed increasingly an isolated figure. He died in Torquay in 1964.

**Five One Act Plays**
Gill pb £4.99 0717117766
**Juno & the Paycock**
Samuel French pb £5.50 0573012148
**The Plough & the Stars**
Samuel French pb £5.50 0573013446
**Seven Plays**
Macmillan pb £3.50 0333364317
**Three Plays**
Macmillan pb £5.50 0333616162

(O'Casey Criticism)

*Sean Moffatt*
**O'Casey's 'Juno and the Paycock**
Gill pb £3.50 071711757X
**York Notes on Juno and the Paycock**
Longman pb £3.50 0582030897

Sean O'Casey

## JOHN O'KEEFE
### (1747–1833)

O'Keefe was born in Dublin and moved to London in the 1770s. His most famous play is **Wild Oats, or the Strolling Gentleman,** which was first produced at Covent Garden in 1791. The play is a comedy which centres on Jack Rover and the intrigues he initiates to win the hand of the beautiful Amelia. Gentle in its satire of sentimental comedy, **Wild Oats** was successfully revived in the 1970s in both London and Dublin.

**Wild Oats**
Nick Hern Books pb £6.99
1854592297

## DONAL O'KELLY

**Catalpa**
Nick Hern Books pb £6.99
1854593579
**Catalpa** is a serious, if humorous, play focussing on an insomniac screen writer, who, bitter about his work acts out a film with a large cast in his head. Strongly portrayed, the central character is one of the unforgettable characters in modern Irish Theatre.

## STEWART PARKER
### (1941–1988)

Stewart Parker was born in Belfast and educated at Queen's University. He wrote many plays for both radio and the stage and also published some poetry in the late 1960s. He enjoyed a popular and critical success due to his strong sense of theatricality and his large themes, dealing with both the historical and social aspects of Irish life. His **Three Plays for Ireland** include **Northern Star, Heavenly Bodies and Pentecost,** which deal respectively with the 1798 rebellion, the life of Dion Boucicault and the 1974 Ulster Worker's Strike.

**Three Plays For Ireland**
Oberon pb £8.99 1870259173

## LENNOX ROBINSON (1886–1958)

Born in Co. Cork, Lennox Robinson had his first play, **The Clancy Name,** premiered in the Abbey Theatre when he was twenty two. Over the next two years he wrote two more plays, **The Crossroads** and **Harvest,** both depicting life in rural Cork. He was appointed manager of the Abbey in 1909 and in 1912 and 1915, two further plays by him, **Patriots** and **The Dreamers** were produced. One of his most enduring and successful plays, **The Whiteheaded Boy** was produced in 1916. This comedy sends up the notions of respectability in contemporary Irish society. The hero, Denis Geoghan, is to be sent to Canada by his parents, after repeatedly failing his medical exams. But, he ends his engagement to Delia Duffy, thus disgracing his parents further, when Delia's father brings a law suit against the family. The problem is solved by the negotiation and skullduggery of Aunt Ellen. This play was brilliantly revived in 1998 by the Barrabas Theatre Co. in Dublin. In 1923, Robinson was elected to the Board of the Abbey and in 1935, his **Drama at Inish** was produced, which satirised a 'serious' drama group who arrive at a small town only to be eventually hunted out by the locals who can no longer bear the Strindbergian gloom and welcome instead a circus.

**Selected Plays**
Colin Smythe pb £6.95 0861400887

## BILLY ROCHE (b.1949)

Wexford-born Billy Roche has enjoyed a varied career as barman, singer , actor, novelist and now playwright. His best known work is his **Wexford Trilogy,** performed between 1988 and 1991 and consisting of **A Handful of Stars, Poor Beast in the Rain** and **Belfry.** All explore small town life and the closure, claustrophobia and mean spiritedness which can permeate all levels of a small community. Roche's plays never shirk from presenting very credible social unpleasantness in an unstilted natural argot. His other publications include **Cavalcaders** and the screenplay of his film **Trojan Eddie,** set in the contemporary travelling community.

**Cavalcaders**
Nick Hern pb £5.99
1854592912
**Poor Beast in the Rain**
Nick Hern pb £6.15
1854590537
**Trojan Eddie Screenplay**
Methuen pb £7.99 041371800X
**Wexford Trilogy**
Nick Hern pb £6.99
1854592653

## GEORGE BERNARD SHAW (1856–1950)

Born in Dublin to Protestant parents, George Carr Shaw and Lucinda Elizabeth Gurly. His father was a businessman and his mother a keen musician. After very little schooling, Shaw worked for an estate agent, often as a rent collector. He emigrated to London in 1876. He was heavily influenced by Marx's Das Kapital and was a committed socialist all of his life. He joined the Fabian Society in 1884 and also became a very successful music critic. It was his study of Ibsen which first led to him writing his own plays. His first play **Widowers Houses** was produced in 1892 and he became theatre critic of the Saturday Review. He married the heiress Charlotte Payne-Townsend in 1892. In 1906 the couple left London to live in Ayot St Lawrence, Hertfordshire. Shaw was by then the leading dramatist of his age. He supported pacifism during the First World War and was critical of British behavior in Ireland. He was awarded the Nobel Prize for literature in 1925 and continued writing up to his death. He bequeathed money to the National Gallery of Ireland. All of his plays dealt with political themes and class, nationalism and gender featured heavily as themes. **St Joan,** which followed the rise and inevitable fall of Joan of Arc, astutely commented on the difficulties of a woman literally 'becoming' a man in the 15th century France and pointed out the hypocrisy of the Church that burned her at the stake only to canonize her centuries later. **John Bull's Other Island,** his main Irish play, strongly satirizes both the patronizing English, romantic view of Ireland as portrayed by Jim Broadbent while also representing the negative, begrudging attitude of Irish men who have left to work in England in the character of Larry Doyle. **Pygmalion,** probably his most famous play because of its film adaptation **My Fair Lady,** skillfully lampoons the British class system that prioritizes appearance and 'propriety' at the expense of feeling and naturalness.

**Back to Methuselah**
Penguin pb £7.70 0140450149
**John Bull's Other Island**
Penguin pb £6.99 0140450440
**Last Plays**
Penguin pb £7.50 0140450424
**Major Barbara**
Penguin pb £5.99 0140450181
**Man & Superman**
Penguin pb £6.99 014045019x
**Plays Extravagant**
Penguin pb £7.75 0140450319
**Plays Pleasant**
Penguin pb £6.99 0140450203
**Plays Unpleasant**
Penguin pb £7.99 0140450211
**Pygmalion**
Penguin pb £5.99 014045022X
**St Joan George**
Penguin pb £5.99 0140450238
**Selected Short Plays**
Penguin pb £7.20 0140450246
**Three Plays for Puritans**
Penguin pb £4.01 40450289

**(Biography)**

*Michael Holroyd*
**Bernard Shaw**
Chatto & Windus hb £25.00
0701162791

George Bernard Shaw

## RICHARD BRINSLEY SHERIDAN (1751–1816)

Born in Dublin, Sheridan's father was actor-manager of Theatre Royal, Smock Alley. Educated in Dublin and Harrow before the Sheridan family moved to England in 1770. His first play **The Rivals** was performed in 1775. He was the owner and manager of the Theatre Royal in Drury Lane from 1776 until it was burned down in 1809. After he went into politics, he wrote very little for the stage. He is best remembered for his comedies **The Rivals and The School for Scandal,** both of which have enjoyed many revivals since.

**The Critic**
A & C Black pb £4.40 0713631880
**The Rivals**
Oxford pb £4.99 0198319088
**The Rivals**
Nick Hern pb £2.99 1854590995
**The School for Scandal**
Penguin pb £5.99 014043240X
**The School for Scandal**
Dover pb £0.99 0486266877

**(Biography)**

*Linda Kelly*
**Richard Brinsley Sheridan**
Pimlico pb £12.50 0712666931

*Fintan O'Toole*
**A Traitor's Kiss: Richard Brinsley Sheridan**
Granta pb £8.99 1862071187

## GERRY STEMBRIDGE

**The Gay Detective**
New Island Books pb £5.99 185459320X

This is a brilliantly tense, noirish play focussing on a homosexual policeman based in Dublin who is used by his superior officer to track down a notorious queer-basher. During his investigation, he meets his first gay love, Ginger. But then the investigation turns into a hunt for the killer of a gay T.D. and things start to go hopelessly awry for Pat.

# J.M. SYNGE (1871-1909)

Born in Rathfarnham, Co. Dublin, Synge was educated mainly by private tuition and attended Trinity College as well as the Royal Irish Academy of Music. He was proficient at playing flute, piano and violin. A lot of his life was spent rebelling against and rejecting his puritanical Protestant upbringing. In 1893, he went to Germany to continue with his musical education only to turn towards literature two years later and head for Paris. He attended lectures there on Medieval Literature and Old Irish at the Sorbonne and befriended W.B. Yeats and Maud Gonne. In 1898, he went on his first trip to the Aran Islands. He met Lady Gregory and Edward Martin and agreed to become involved with the Irish Literary Theatre. He left Paris for good in 1903 and became one of the leading lights in the new Abbey Theatre. He shot to fame and notoriety in 1907 with the first production of **The Playboy of the Western World.** After the first night, Dublin audiences rioted at the portrayal of their fellow nationals on the West Coast. The importance of the Playboy is that it was the first Irish play to use any idiomatic Hiberno-English dialect on stage. The play is satirical but this was completely lost on the angry nationalist audience, who just felt that they and their country had been seriously insulted. Most of Synge's six plays attracted some sort of negative reaction but he can now be recognised as one of the greatest dramatists the country has produced. Synge died of Hodgkin's disease in 1909.

**The Aran Islands**
Oxford Up pb £5.99
0192812580
**Collected Works Vol.1 Poems**
Smythe pb £4.95 0861400585
**Collected Works Vol.2 Prose**
Smythe pb £5.95 0861400593
**Collected Works Vol.3 Plays I**
Smythe pb £5.95 0861400607
**Collected Works Vol.4 Plays II**
Smythe pb £6.95 0861400615
**Complete Plays**
Methuen pb £6.99 041348520X
**The Playboy of the Western World**
Oxford Up pb £5.99
0192826115
**The Playboy of the Western World**
Methuen pb £4.99 0413519406
**The Playboy of the Western World**
Penguin pb £6.99 0140188789

**The Playboy of the Western World**
Penguin pb £5.99 0140482245
**The Playboy of the Western World**
Dover £0.95 0486275620
**The Playboy of the Western World**
Routledge pb £5.99
0415078954
**Plays, Poems and the Aran Islands**
Everyman pb £4.99
0460875116

**(Synge Criticism)**

*Ayling*
**Synge: Four Plays**
Macmillan pb £9.99
0333423844

*Declan Kiberd*
**Synge and the Irish Language**
Gill pb £12.99 071712116X

# ENDA WALSH

**Disco Pigs & Sucking Dublin**
Nick Hern pb £6.99
1854593986

**Disco Pigs** is a funny two hander play, in which both characters are disaffected seventeen year olds. The play very acutely presents the concerns and worries of late teen life. **Sucking Dublin** is a fairly dark play revolving around five individuals in an area of Dublin badly affected by hard drug abuse.

# OSCAR WILDE (1854–1900)

Oscar Wilde's great fame lies in the series of plays he wrote to huge acclaim in the early 1890s. **Lady Windermere's Fan** (1892), **A Woman of No Importance** (1894), **An Ideal Husband** (1895), and **The Importance of Being Earnest** (1895) form a body of work so impressive and memorable that it stands comparison with that of any of the great dramatists in literature. Most of these plays use humour and comedy to discuss the roles of men and women in their society, their relationships with each other, and how they are confined to playing certain roles, dictated by the mores of the day. There is also the recurrent theme of the relationships between parents and their children, and how the memories and events of one's youth can affect adulthood in different ways. Wilde's great period of dramatic production was eventually overshadowed by the infamous trial which led to his imprisonment and almost certainly cut short his life, but the plays have re-emerged, standing the test of time, as more than just social comedies of their time, and examples of dramatic writing at its most brilliant.

From Tom Lawlor, At the Gate

**(Criticism/Biography)**

*Richard Ellmann*
**Oscar Wilde**
Penguin pb £9.99 0140096612

*Sos Eltis*
**Revising Wilde**
Oxford Up hb £35.00
0198121830

*Michael Foldy*
**The Trials of Oscar Wilde**
Yale University Press hb £19.95
0300071124

*Philip Hoare*
**Wilde's Last Stand**
Duckworth pb £11.95
0715628283

*Merlin Holland*
**the Wilde Album**
Fourth Estate hb £12.99
1857027825

**The Ballad of Reading Gaol**
Pluto pb £4.95 0904526267
**The Ballad of Reading Gaol**
Dover pb £0.95 0486270726
**The Ballad of Reading Gaol**
Duckworth pb £8.95
0715628046
**Complete Plays**
Methuen pb £9.99 0413187608
**Complete Poetry**
Oxford pb £3.99 0192825089
**The Importance of
Being Earnest**
Oxford Up pb £4.99
0192822462
**The Importance of
Being Earnest**
Penguin pb £4.50 0140482091
**The Importance of
Being Earnest**
Methuen pb £5.25 0413396304
**Nothing... Except My Genius**
Penguin pb £2.99 0140436936
**Plays, Prose & Writings of
Oscar Wilde**
Everyman pb £6.99
0460876554
**Poetry**
Bloomsbury hb £9.95
0747522618
**The Sayings of Oscar Wilde**
Duckwworth pb £4.99
0715623052
**The Uncollected Oscar Wilde**
Fourth Estate pb £6.99
185702334X

# Fiction

## PATRICIA AVIS

**Playing the Harlot**
Virago pb £6.99 1860490042

This *roman a clef* was originally rejected by a leading publisher in 1963 because it insulted too many of his literary friends. It tells the story of Mary Gallen, a talented young woman drifting through the rarified ambience of Oxford's literary scene during the 1950s.

## KEITH BAKER

*Inheritance* is a fast paced thriller based in contemporary Northern Ireland, written by the current Editorial Advisor to the BBC. Starting with the accidental death of a retired RUC officer, it builds to uncover a web of treachery and corruption. Baker's next novel *Reckoning*, set almost entirely in Dublin, is a very convincing and realistic thriller featuring ex-FBI agent Tom Gallagher returning home to Ireland where the ghosts of his past are lying in wait.

**Inheritance**
Headline pb £5.99 0747255520
**Reckoning**
Headline (published Nov.)
pb £5.99 0747255539

## IVY BANNISTER

**Magician & Other Stories**
Poolbeg £5.99 pb 1853716758

The skewed world of these short stories centres on the wars people wage with their partners, the world, even themselves. Despite the seemingly familiar terrain, the reader will be constantly surprised by the destinations reached.

# JOHN BANVILLE (b.1945)

Born in Wexford and now living in Dublin, John Banville is literary editor of the Irish Times. He has written ten novels and a collection of short stories. He has also adapted **The Broken Jug** by Heinrich Von Kleist for the Peacock Theatre. His first book, **Long Lankin**, a collection of short stories, is a haunting and moving series of meditations on death, loss and guilt which are presented with a remarkable clarity of mood and character. **Dr Copernicus**, the first novel in what was to become a science tetralogy won the Whitbread prize in 1976 and is a fictional recreation of the life of the austere scientist who first proposed the idea of a heliocentric universe. This book was followed by **Kepler**, **The Newton Letter** and **Mefisto**, all of which established his literary style and thematic concerns. **The Book of Evidence,** which was shortlisted for the 1987 Booker prize, is a dark examination of the nature of murder and its results. Freddie Montgomery, gentleman, art collector and, as a result, thief is a fascinatingly remorseless creation. He appeared again in Banville's following novels **Ghosts** and **Athena**. 1997 saw the publication of **The Untouchable**, which is undoubtedly his masterpiece. Revolving around the Cambridge spies and focussing on a character based on Anthony Blunt, it skillfully weaves fact and fiction to produce a darkly relentless narrative which mirrors the intrigue and deception it sets out to examine. Banville is also an astute and incisive literary journalist and his work has appeared in many international newspapers and magazines.

**Athena**
Picador pb £6.99 033037186X
**Birchwood**
Minerva pb £4.99 0749398116
**The Book of Evidence**
Picador pb £6.99 0330371878
**Doctor Copernicus**
Minerva pb £6.99 074939076x
**Ghosts**
Picador pb £6.99 0330371851
**Kepler**
Minerva pb £6.99 0749390778
**Long Lankin**
Gallery Press pb £5.95
0904011720
**Mefisto**
Minerva pb £6.99 0749397160
**Nightspawn**
Gallery Press pb £7.95
1852351268
**The Newton Letter**
Minerva pb £6.99 0749398183
**The Untouchable**
Picador hb £15.99 0330339311
**The Broken Jug**
Gallery Press hb £6.95
1852351454 (Drama)

## VINCENT BANVILLE

Vincent Banville is the creator of John Blaine, Dublin's answer to Sam Spade. Blaine is a hard drinking, chain smoking, wisecracking private dick, who used to be a hurling star. In **Death by Design** he stumbles upon a murder spree directed against Dublin's homeless when he is hired by the wealthy Mrs. Walsh-Overman to find her son, Redmond, who is living rough. **Death the Pale Rider** sees Blaine reluctantly taking a case from Maxie Morgan, a former and thoroughly unreliable friend. As he sweats his way through the meaner streets of Dublin uncovering corpses, conmen, and chicanery, Blaine clings to just two things, his honesty and his integrity.

**Death the Pale Rider**
Poolbeg pb £4.99 185371528X
**Death by Design**
Wolfhound pb £4.99
0863273351

## LELAND BARDWELL

**There We Have Been** is a resonant work that charts the return of Dilligence Strong to the border farm in northern Ireland where she was born. The struggles, with the land and her brother, and the joys, a relationship with the dispossessed Cathy and the memory of her virtuous sister, are evoked through Bardwell's sparse economical prose. Bardwell is also a poet.

**There We Have Been**
Attic pb £3.99 0946211817
**Dostoevsky's Grave**
Dedalus pb £4.95 0948268913
(poetry)

## SHEILA BARRETT

**A View to Die For**
Poolbeg pb £5.99 1853716898
A taut and malevolent tale of murder and suspense, this novel follows Detective Aidan Cummings in his attempts to track down the elusive strangler, who leaves nothing but minuscule shards of evidence at the scene of each crime.

## COLIN BATEMAN
(b.1962)

Using a great mix of genres, all of Bateman's novels are sharply paced, ironic and paint a blackly humorous portrait of current sectarian relations. Using a range of contexts from the world of journalism to that of professional boxing, this novelist isn't afraid to take the risks involved in using labyrinthine plots mixed with a hard-boiled style to produce gripping narratives which are at times brutal and hard-hitting, but undercut with wit and poignancy.

**Cycle of Violence**
Harper Collins pb £5.99
0006479359
**Divorcing Jack**
Harper Collins pb £5.99
0006479030
**Empire State**
Harper Collins hb £6.99
0002254174
**Of Wee Sweetie Mice & Men**
Harper Collins pb £5.99
0006496121

# SAMUEL BECKETT (1906–1989)

Although he is best known as a playwright, Samuel Beckett began his literary career as a novelist. He was born into an upper middle class family in Foxrock, Co. Dublin and was educated in Enniskillen at Portora Royal School, followed by Trinity College, Dublin. He taught briefly in Belfast and then at the Ecole Normale Superieure in Paris. While in Paris he was introduced to James Joyce whom Beckett helped to transcribe his work as Joyce was quickly losing his sight. In 1930 Beckett returned to Dublin but left the following year after suffering a breakdown. Between 1932 and 1937 he lived in Germany, France, England and Ireland. In 1934 his first collection of short stories **More Pricks Than Kicks**, which revolved around student life in Dublin, was published. Also during this period Beckett began work on his first novel, **Dream of Fair to Middling Women**, which he never completed and which remained unpublished until 1992. In 1937 he returned to Paris where he wrote **Murphy** (1938). This novel showcases Beckett's philosophical ideas, specifically his fascination with the separateness of the mind and its physical surroundings, as well as his apathetic feeling towards Irish nationalism. In 1945 Beckett was awarded the Croix de Guerre for his assistance to the French Resistance during the war. It was around this time that Beckett began to write in French in order to disassociate himself from the literary tradition of the English language. The trilogy of novels **Molloy** (1951), **Malone Dies** (1951), and **The Unnameable** (1953) centre on the despair and suffering of the human condition. Their darkness is saved by an infusion of black humour. While writing the trilogy Beckett began to experiment with drama, returning briefly to the novel in 1961 with **How It Is** which reflects his movement towards minimalism. In 1969 Beckett was awarded the Nobel Prize for Literature thus cementing his place in literary history.

**Beckett Trilogy**
Calder pb £11.99 071451053X
**Company**
Calder pb £5.99 0714538574
**Complete Shorter Prose 1929-89**
Grove pb £ 9.99 0802134904
**Complete Shorter Prose**
Grove hb £15.99 0802115772
**Disjecta**
Calder pb £6.99 0714540161
**Dream of Fair to Middling Women**
Calder pb £9.99 071454213X
**Expelled & Other Novels**
Penguin £4.99 0140180117
**First Love & Other Shorts**
Grove pb £7.99 0802151310
**How It Is**
Calder pb £4.95 0714509523
**I Can't Go On**
Grove pb £11.99 0802132871
**Lost Ones**
Grove pb £7.99 0802130925
**Mercier & Camier**
Picador pb £4.99 0330300369
**More Pricks than Kicks**
Calder pb £4.99 0714507059
**Murphy**
Calder pb £6.99 171450042X
**Murphy**
Calder pb £6.99 0714500429
**Nohow On**
Calder pb £6.99 0714541117
**Stories & a Text for Nothing**
Grove pb £9.99 0802150624
**Watt**
Calder pb £5.99 0714506109
**Worstward Ho!**
Calder pb £4.99 0714540064

Samuel Beckett

## SAM HANNA BELL
### (1909–1990)

Born in Scotland, Bell lived in Northern Ireland most of his life and was a radio producer with BBC Northern Ireland. His first novel **December Bride**, set in Northern Ireland in the early part of the century, is loosely based on one of his mother's family anecdotes. It narrates the story of Sarah Gomartin who has affairs with both Hamilton and Frank Echlin, sons of her employer. She gives birth to a baby Sarah, and after refusing to name the father of the child is shunned from her community. Adapted for the screen by Thaddeus O'Sullivan in 1990, **December Bride** vividly describes family, feeling and place of Ulster early this century. The Blackstaff Press have recently republished **Erin's Orange Lily**, a reflection on Ulster folklore, with **Summer Loanen**, his early stories.

**December Bride**
Blackstaff Press pb £5.95
0856400610
**Erin's Orange Lily & Summer Loanen**
Blackstaff Press pb £9.99
0856405892

## RONAN BENNETT

**The Catastrophist**
Headline hb £14.99
074722210X
Bennett's latest book tells the story of Gillespie, a writer who goes to the Congo to find his Italian lover. Gillespie just wants love to work and tries to deny the political terror unfolding around him until the awful moment that he has to.

## MAEVE BINCHY
### (b.1940)

One of the best known and best loved of contemporary Irish authors, Maeve Binchy has had the kind of successful career which puts her at the forefront of popular fiction throughout the world. Her novels deal mostly with Ireland, and with an Ireland of nostalgia and memory, often mixing contemporary settings with more traditional values and characters. Although her earlier work began with stories clearly set in contemporary London, such as **Central Line** in 1977, it was with her Irish novels that she began to find both her natural setting and loyal readership. **Light A Penny Candle** (1982) was the first in a string of bestselling novels, and was followed by, amongst others, **Firefly Summer** (1987) and **Silver Wedding** (1988). A successful and enjoyable film adaptation of **Circle of Friends** was made in 1994. In general, Binchy is an author full of warmth and humour, with a clear love for her characters and their settings, as well as of a time less hectic and troublesome than the one in which we live today. For readers interested in her views on that subject, her weekly column in The Irish Times presents a series of observations on modern life.

# DERMOT BOLGER (b.1959)

One of the many very powerful literary voices to emerge from Dublin in the 1980s, Bolger's work has an unsettling quality in that he offers no compromise or cosy platitudes in his realistic depiction of contemporary Dublin working-class life. Reacting strongly against the traditional Irish hierarchical figures of Teacher, Priest and Politician, his novels, plays and poetry combine gritty description with a rare lyricism which, though rich in imagery, never becomes overstated. Apart from his own literary work, he is also an important publisher who set up the Raven Arts press in the 1980s, a very important platform for new writers. He has since set up New Island books which publishes a brilliant diversity of authors from Nuala O'Faolain to Francis Stuart.

*Finbar's Hotel* conceived and edited by Dermot Bolger is a conglomerate work by Bolger himself with Roddy Doyle , Jennifer Johnston, Anne Enright, Hugo Hamilton, Colm Toibín, Joseph O'Connor. Set in the eponymous Finbar's Hotel over a single night, each chapter tells a new, richly inventive story without giving away who wrote it.

**Circle of Friends**
Coronet pb £6.99 034055133X
**Copper Beech**
Orion pb £6.99 1857979990
**Dear Maeve**
Poolbeg pb £4.99 185371531X
**Dublin 4**
Poolbeg pb £4.99 1853711020
**Echoes**
Arrow pb £5.99 0099485311
**Evening Class**
Orion pb £6.99 0752809636
**The Firefly Summer**
Arrow pb £5.99 0099485419
**The Glass Lake**
Orion pb £5.99 1857978013
**Light a Penny Candle**
Arrow pb £6.99 0099196514
**The Lilac Bus**
Poolbeg pb £5.99 1853711160
**Silver Wedding**
Arrow pb £4.99 0099604302
**Tara Road**
Orion 0752814478
**Victoria Line Central Line**
Arrow pb £4.99 0099218216

**April Bright/Blinded by the Light**
New Island pb £7.99 1854593625
**Dublin Bloom**
New Island Books pb £7.99 (Poems) 187459726X
**Dublin Quartet**
Penguin pb £6.99 0140482350
**Emily's Shoes**
Penguin pb £6.99 0140148728
**Father's Music**
Flamingo pb £9.99 000225655X
**Finbar's Hotel (with others)**
New Island pb £9.99 1874597634
**Journey Home**
Penguin pb £6.99 0140131590
**Night Shift**
Penguin pb £5.99 0140148736
**Second Life**
Penguin pb £6.99 0140238794

## ANGELA BOURKE

**By Salt Water**
New Island pb £5.99 1874597391

Angela Bourke has written a moving collection of stories in **By Salt Water**. Followwing the lives of women narrators from Dublin to America, Bourke has spun together a series of haunting stories that will engage and entice any reader.

## ELIZABETH BOWEN (1899–1973)

Though she was born in Dublin, Bowen's family moved to London in 1907, where she lived mostly for the next thirty three years. After her father's death in 1930, she inherited Bowen's Court, the family home in Co. Cork. She lived in between Ireland and London for most of World War II, reporting to the English Government on the Irish feeling towards the War. She died in London in 1973 and is buried on the land where the beautiful Bowen's Court once stood. (The next owner demolished the house in 1960). As a writer she occupies that rare place in Irish and English letters, being one of the few women who can obviously fit in both canons. As well as her novels she wrote short stories and was a gifted memoirist, perfectly capturing the Anglo-Irish moment she experienced. Her main Irish novel is **The Last September** which deals with the fall of a big house during the Black & Tan war of the 1920s. Her style, falling in between that of Jane Austen and Henry James, beautifully combines the lyricism of the latter with the very effective quotidian description of the former.

**Collected Stories**
Penguin pb £12.00 0140182977
**The Death of the Heart**
Penguin pb £6.99 0140183000
**Eva Trout**
Penguin pb £6.99 0140182985
**The Heat of the Day**
Penguin pb £7.99 0140183019
**The Hotel**
Penguin pb £6.99 0140183027

**The House in Paris**
Penguin pb £6.99 0140183035
**The Last September**
Penguin pb £6.99 0140183043
**The Little Girls**
Penguin pb £6.17 pb
0140183051
**To the North**
Penguin pb £6.99 014018306x
**A World of Love**
Penguin pb £6.99 0140182969
(Biography)

*Victoria Glendinning*
**Elizabeth Bowen**
Phoenix pb £7.99 1857990722

## CLARE BOYLAN
(b.1948 )

Born in Dublin, Clare Boylan has been writing good-natured but serious fiction since 1993, when she published **Holy Pictures** which introduced the character of Nan Cantwell, teenager and recent movie fan. The novel records a family life complicated by the introduction of cinema. Boylan returned to the Cantwell family in **Home Rule** in which she tells the story of Nan's grandparents in the latter years of the 19th Century. Her latest novel, **Room for a Single Lady**, is a beautifully evoked story of loneliness, loss and friendship.

**Home Rule**
Abacus pb £6.99 0349109672
**Pandora's Christmas Box**
Poolbeg pb £7.99 1853717851
**Room for a Single Lady**
Abacus pb £6.99 034910901X
**That Bad Woman**
Abacus pb £5.99 0349107378

## PAULINE BRACKEN

**Indian Summer**
Collins pb £5.99 1898256225

A passionate and life changing affair between Vera Nolan, fifty-three and married, and Dan Devereux, the younger man she chances upon at an evening class, is delicately portrayed in this heartwarming and superbly readable romance.

## DAVID BRETT

**All these are Memories of my Voyage**
Blackstaff Press pb £9.95
095292630X

David Brett, a reader in the History of Design at the University of Ulster, treats the reader to a tale of art, fashion, mathematics, medicine and unrequited love against the backdrop of the melting pot of immigrant experience. The graphic fragments were provided by Graham Gingles, and the whole forms a worthy conclusion to the series of stories and scripts which David has produced.

## EANNA BROPHY

**Jesus Letters**
Blackwater Press pb £7.99
0861217187

This a skillfully constructed set of letters to Spain from Jesus, a student staying in Dublin for a summer. Remarkably well mimicked, the letters very successfully satirise the attitude of many Dubliners to the 'invasion' of over 400,000 European students every year.

## KEVIN BROPHY

**Almost Heaven**
Marino pb £7.99 1860230512

Kevin Brophy, himself recently returned to his native Galway after much time in Dublin and London, charts the return of Michael O'Hara, a man who has lost both his accent and his past, to the Ireland which stole from him the love of his life. This touching voyage is both a quest for love lost and for understanding of the past.

## DECLAN BURKE KENNEDY

**Leonie**
Poolbeg pb £6.99 1853715425

The fascinating tale of the friendship between two boys whose families are stationed at the Curragh army base during the 1960s. Cormac, the Commandant's nephew, is devoted to Leonie, the Commandant's maid, and helps her to carry on an affair with Corporal Bill Dwyer. This situation changes as Cormac develops a friendship with Eddie, the Corporal's son.

## BILLY BYRNE

**Foolish Notions**
Mather pb £7.99 0953133605

This is the wildly subversive tale of Jeremy Brightside, a failed English actor, who decides to take his talents out of the theatre and into the courts and medical establishments of the land. By studying an array of medical texts Jeremy convinces judges, psychiatrists, and possibly readers that he has experienced the A to Z of psychological conditions.

## MATTHEW BYRNE

**Heaven Looked Upwards**
Townhouse hb £14.99
1860590268

This clever retelling of the birth of Jesus concentrates on the earthy human elements of the story, focusing on the ordinary townsfolk who were involved in these momentous events in their own small ways. The book also depicts the political intrigue and paranoid bloodletting which surrounded the conspiracy-ridden court of Herod.

## MARY ROSE CALLAGHAN

**Emigrant Dreams**
Poolbeg pb £5.99 1853716200

The central character in Callaghan's fifth novel is the troubled but resourceful Anne O'Brien. Set in the United States, this is a compelling tale of murder, deceit and cultural identity.

## PAUL CARSON

**Scalpel**
Mandarin pb £5.99
0749324473

Carson, a general practitioner working in Dublin, has written a gripping medical thriller. Set in Dublin, it concerns a kidnapping ring set up in and around the capital's main maternity hospital. As the story unfolds shadowy government ministers loom in the background and add to the page-turning panache of the narrative.

## PHILIP CASEY

**The Fabulists**
Lilliput Press pb £5.99
1874675309

Casey's beautifully truthful novel is set in Dublin and recounts the relationship between Tess and Mungo and the way it develops (after a chance meeting) through the recounting of fantastical and erotic tales set in Berlin and Barcelona. The author has a great gift of making the ordinary seem rare.

## ANNE CHAMBERS

**The Geraldine Conspiracy**
Marino pb £7.99 1860230342
Set in Tudor Ireland and most aptly described by the Irish Times as 'a colourful and dashing chronicle', **The Geraldine Conspiracy** is a highly acclaimed and wonderfully evocative novel of epic proportions from novelist, scriptwriter and best-selling biographer Anne Chambers.

## PAUL CHARLES

**I Love the Sound of Breaking Glass**
Do-Not Press pb £5.99
1899344160

Part crime story, part love story, this accomplished debut novel from music promoter Paul Charles introduces us to the memorable Detective Inspector Christy Kennedy and his trusty team. The explosive characters and riveting plot amount to a truly enjoyable and worthwhile read.

## SIGERSON CLIFFORD

**The Red Haired Woman & Other Stories**
Mercier pb £4.99 0853428824
In this well received collection, Clifford employs his considerable talents as a playwright to create strong characters within atmospheric and fluent pieces of writing. At times brief but always lively and natural, these tales entertain and charm the reader effortlessly.

## TOM COFFEY

**Don't Get Mad Get Even**
Marino pb £7.99 1860230407
This impressive debut novel
by award-winning playwright
Tom Coffey contains a colony
of colourful characters within
a comic and quirky storyline
by the end of which life in
one small Irish town will
never be the same again.

## MICHAEL COLLINS
(b.1964)

Born in Limerick and now
living in Chicago, Michael
Collins has written two darkly
funny collections of short
stories and one novel. Writing
from America, his observation
is always acute and his distance
from home makes possible a
quite serious examination of
Irish stereotypes. Collins'
writing comfortably mixes the
everyday with the surreal
which compounds and
reinforces his darkly comic
vision.

**The Feminists go Swimming**
Phoenix pb £5.99 1857999789
**The Life & Times of a Teaboy**
Phoenix £5.99 1857993322
**The Meat Eaters**
Phoenix £5.99 1857990714

## SHANE CONNAUGHTON
(b.1946)

Screenwriter and actor
Connaughton has written
two novels, **The Run of the
Country** and **A Border
Station,** both set in the
border counties of Northern
Ireland and the Irish
Republic. Dealing with
themes of ostracism,
both moral and sectarian,
Connaughton has mixed
family history, humour and
pathos to produce fine stories
told with great enthusiasm.

**A Border Station**
Penguin pb £5.99 0140178562
**The Run of the Country**
Penguin pb £5.99 0140242503

## BEATRICE COOGAN

**The Big Wind**
Arrow pb £6.99 0099246422
This epic novel of 19th
Century Ireland is set in the
time between the famous
'Big wind' of 1839 and the
time of the Great Famine.
It was originally published in
1969 and reprinted recently.
Former journalist Coogan
skillfully weaves fact and
fiction together to produce
a great tale of love, loss
and destiny.

## LOUISE COUPER

On the publication of
**Philippa's Farm** in 1995,
Louise Couper established
herself as a storytelling force
to be reckoned with. **Philippa's
Folly** (1996) and **Philippa's
Flight** (1997) follows the
eponymous heroine on an
energetic journey of self-
discovery and growth.
Combining humour, warmth,
insight and a dose of good
old-fashioned romance,
these beguiling tales are
testimony to Cooper's notable
writing talent.

**Philippa's Farm**
Poolbeg pb £4.99 1853712809
**Philippa's Flight**
Poolbeg pb £4.99 1853716944
**Philippa's Folly**
Poolbeg pb £4.99 1853715433

## KATHLEEN COYLE

**A Flock of Birds**
Wolfhound Press pb £5.99
0863274714
Originally published in the
1930s, this tells the poignant
tale of Christy Munster,
innocent yet sentenced to
hang for murder. It simply
and successfully interweaves
themes of family love, gallows
humour, despair and
indomitable spirit in the
face of injustice.

## ROBERT CREMINS

**A Sort of Homecoming**
Sceptre pb £10.00 034071722X
Robert Cremins' debut novel
follows the adventures of
Tom Iremonger as he
comes home to Dublin for
Christmas following a six
month 'transcontinental
lost weekend' funded by
an inheritance. Skilfully
describing the emotions
involved in both coming
home and coming down,
Cremins' novel is a suitable
testimony to the emotional
lives of Irish twenty-
something exiles.

## ERIC CROSS

**(1905–1980)**

**The Tailor & Ansty** is the
hilarious story of tailor
Tim Buckley and his wife
Ansty who narrate many of
traditional Irish folk customs
to a third person in the book.
These uncensored accounts
of the Irish folk tradition led
the book to be banned after
its re-publication in 1942.

**The Tailor & Ansty**
Mercier Press pb £6.99
0853420505

## ELAINE CROWLEY

This hugely successful
popular novelist was born
in Dublin and has lived in
Germany and Egypt and Port
Talbot, her present home.
Her novels, set in 19th and
20th century Ireland describe
dramatic events unfolding
in a historical context and
are praised for their
unforgettable characters
and page-turning quality.

**Dreams of Other Days**
Orion pb £5.99 0752804030
**A Family Cursed**
Orion pb £5.99 075280409X
**The Ways of Women**
Orion £5.99 1857974387

## LEO CULLEN

**Clocking Ninety on the Road
to Cloughjordan**
Blackstaff Press pb £5.99
085640537X
Born in Tipperary in 1948
and now living in Dublin, Leo
Cullen has written a brilliant
collection of short stories,
celebrating Irish small town
life in the 1950s. Focussing
on the young character of
Lally Connaughton and his
father, these interconnected
stories explore the familiar
but sometimes strange world
of local farmers, teachers and
other pillars of the
community.

## PETER CUNNINGHAM

This writer and journalist,
based in Co. Kildare, while
working as a commodities
broker, wrote a number of
thrillers which are now out of
print. He has written two fine
literary novels since. The first
novel **Tapes of the River
Delta,** narrated by Theo
Shortcourse, former customs
officer and at present prison
escapee, is a wonderful
meditation on growing up,
family history and political
skullduggery.
Peter Cunningham's next
novel, **Consequences of the
Hart** returns to the town of
Monument, where we meet
Chud Conduit and Jack
Santry, both of whom are
from different sides of the
tracks and both of whom are
in live with Rosa.
Cunningham, as with is
literary debœt, weaves a story
of intrigue, well drawn
characters and engagement
with landscape which is not
often matched in
contemporary fiction.

**Consequences of the Heart**
Harvill Press hb £15.99
186046498X
**Tapes of the River Delta**
Harvill pb £5.99 0099227312

## MICHAEL CURTIN

Limerick-born Michael Curtin has a great talent for pointing out the absurd and comic quality of human life and this is reflected in his novels. **The Cove Shivering** Club acutely portrays the rules and regulations that children create just to play a game. **The Plastic Tomato Cutter** demonstrates the author's ability to highlight the unbelievable but true nature of adult life and demonstrates once again Curtin's great comic gift. **The League Against Christmas** is a hilarious farce involving five social misfits deciding to spend the festive season robbing the diddly club funds in rural Co. Mayo.

**The Cove Shivering Club**
Fourth Estate pb £6.99
1857025709
**The League against Christmas**
Fourth Estate pb £9.99
185702740X
**The Plastic Tomato Cutter**
Fourth Estate pb £6.99
1857024729

## ITA DALY

Ita Daly first came to prominence when she won a Hennessy Literary Award in the 1970s for her early short stories. These and others were collected together in the volume **The Lady With The Red Shoes** (1980). Her first novel **Ellen** (1986) concerned the growing pains of an unambitious young Dublin girl, while **A Singular Attraction** (1987) deals with the sudden release from a self-imposed exile of a middle aged woman whose long-delayed hopes for her own life are released upon the death of her mother. Witty and good humoured and laced with a gentle sensitivity, her latest novel is **Unholy Ghosts** (1996) which is the powerful story of Belle who looks back on her troubled and painful life.

**Ellen**
Poolbeg pb £5.99 pb
1853714607
**The Lady with Red Shoes**
Poolbeg pb £5.99 1853714569
**A Singular Attraction**
Poolbeg pb £5.99 1853714550
**Unholy Ghosts**
Bloomsbury pb £6.99
0747529418

## PHILIP DAVISON (b.1957)

Dublin-born Phillip Davison has written scripts for television as well as a number of novels and a play, **The Invisible Mending Company**. Most recently he has written **The Crooked Man**, a highly entertaining thriller concerning the life and times of one Harry Fielding, gin-swigger, unofficial MI5 odd-jobber but basically decent sort. Set in London, Ireland and Bosnia, this highly entertaining narrative has many twists and turns and involves murder, corruption, and political intrigue, all combined with a wry but bleak vision.

**The Crooked Man**
Vintage pb £5.99 0099735415

## ÉILIS NÍ DHUIBHNE

**Eating Women is not Recommended** (1991) is a collection of short stories that combine comedy, black humour and the macabre, many of which were previously published in anthologies and newspapers, while **The Inland Ice and Other Stories** (1997) presents a series of characters who confront emotions which have the power to wreck their lives. Eilis Ni Dhuibhne is a scholar of Old & Middle English and Irish Folklore and has also written novels, childrens' books and television scripts.

**Blood & Water**
Attic pb £4.95 094621154X
**Eating Women is not Recommended**
Attic pb £6.99 1855940299
**The Inland Ice and Other Stories**
Blackstaff pb £7.99
0856405965

## EAMON DELANEY (b.1967)

This Dublin-born novelist has produced a humorous look at student life, Irish politics and especially historical revisionism. Its great strength is its accurate portrayal of Dublin student life in the mid-1980s and it provides a rare look into young cultural life at the time that is neither nostalgic nor sentimental.

**The Casting of Mr O'Shaughnessy**
Bloomsbury hb £14.99
074752002X

## SEAMUS DEANE (b.1940)

Poet, academic, and novelist Seamus Deane was born in Derry and was educated in Belfast and the University of Cambridge. He now lives in Dublin and Indiana. He has published three collections of poetry (**History Lessons**, **Gradual Wars** and **Rumours**) to great critical acclaim. His **Selected Poems** appeared in 1987. His academic works include **Celtic Revivals**, **A Short History of Irish Literature**, **The French Revolution and Enlightenment in England** and most recently **Strange Country**. He was professor of Modern English & American Literature in University College, Dublin from 1986 to 1993 when he was appointed the first Keogh Professor of Irish Studies at the University of Notre Dame, Indiana. He was one of the founding members of the Field Day threatre group and was General Editor of the **Field Day Anthology of Irish Writing**, published in 1991. He shot to international fame in 1996 with the publication of his first novel **Reading in the Dark**. The novel had a long gestation, first advertised in the early 1990s, and it revolves around the life of a young boy in Derry and his experiences growing up in that city. Fragmented in structure, the novel combines history, myth, fable and ghost story narrated in a style that appropriately (and beautifully) matches the different nuances of a troubled life.

**Field Day Anthology of Irish Writing**
Field Day hb £100.00 0946755205
**Reading in the Dark**
Vintage pb £5.99 0099744414

## FRANK DELANEY
### (b.1942)

Acclaimed critic, broadcaster and biographer, Delaney published his first novella **Dark Rosaleen** in 1988. His gift for great narrative sweep which had been demonstrated in his books on Boswell, Joyce and the Celts was put to great use in his loose trilogy, **Sins of the Mother**, **Telling the Pictures** and **Stranger in Their Midst**. These novels chronicle the lives of mid-century Ulster and combine drama, suspense and epic story-telling to great effect. His latest novel **The Amethysts** changes territory and genre and tells a story of Nazi war crimes in a pronounced noir-ish style.

**The Amethysts**
Harper Collins hb £16.99
0002255634
**The Sins of the Mothers**
Harper Collins pb £5.99
0586214895
**A Stranger in their Midst**
Harper Collins pb £5.99
0006493181
**Telling the Pictures**
Harper Collins pb £4.99
0006479243

## MARGARET DOLAN
**Wire Me to the Moon**
Poolbeg pb £7.99 185371772X

Following the publication of her first novel **Nessa** in 1994, Margaret Dolan released **Wire Me To The Moon** in 1997, a collection of stories set around the world from Dublin to New York. These stories are humorous and sharp, with a well tuned ear for dialogue.

## J.P. DONLEAVY (b.1926)

Donleavy is an American of Irish descent who studied at Trinity College, Dublin shortly after the end of the Second World War. There he befriended fellow American Gainor Crist who became the model for Sebastian Dangerfield, the hero of Donleavy's first and best-selling novel **The Ginger Man** (1955). 'A study of drift, desperation, of dark-caveism, of youth thrown upon the world as upon a strange planet', as Arland Ussher called it, it caused a stir among the Irish clerical establishment because of its bawdy tone and storyline and a stage version was duly banned in 1959. Donleavy has published prolifically in the decades since but none of his later works has equalled his debut novel in either critical or commercial impact. Most are portraits of American life, although **The Beastly Beatitudes of Balthazar B** is also set in Ireland. Latterly he has turned more directly to his own life as the source of his books, **A Singular Country** and **A History of the Ginger Man**. At the outset of his career Donleavy was compared with Joyce and Flann O'Brien. As the years have passed a truer, and more modest, assessment of his literary value has become possible.

**Are You Listening, Rabbi Low?**
Penguin pb £6.99 0140098216
**The Beastly Beatitudes of Balthazar B**
Penguin pb £6.99 0140030565
**The Destinies of Darcy Dancer, Gentleman**
Penguin pb £6.99 0140049002
**The Ginger Man**
Abacus pb £6.99 0349108757
**The Lady who liked Clean Restrooms**
Abacus pb £5.99 0349108501

## EMMA DONOGHUE (b.1969)

Born in Dublin Emma Donoghue, at the precocious age of twenty two and despite a rigid convent education, became the first openly gay Irish woman writer to gain popularity with a general audience. Her first novel, **Stir Fry** (1994), a classic tale of coming out and coming of age at university, was published while she was completing studies at Cambridge and her first play was produced at the same time. Her subsequent novels **Hood** (1995) and **Kissing the Witch** (1997) have broached similarly weighty subjects but have done so with a deft lightness of touch. Emma Donoghue has also published academic works, including **Passions Between Women: British Lesbian Culture 1668-1801** and **We Are Michael Field**, a biography of two Victorian women poets.

**Hood**
Penguin pb £6.99   014023084X
**Kissing the Witch**
Penguin pb £6.99 0140258027
**Stir Fry**
Penguin pb £6.99 0140230831

## MARY DORCEY

Mary Dorcey has enjoyed a varied writing career, winning prizes for her short story collection **A Noise From The Woodshed** (1989) and her poetry. She has been published in many anthologies around the world and in 1997 published the novel **Biography of Desire** which took as its theme the lives of two women who meet by chance in a city hospital and whose lives become inextricably linked as their relationship is tested through the conflicting themes of loyalty and desire. A prolific writer, Mary Dorcey is currently a lecturer at Trinity College, Dublin.

**Biography of Desire**
Poolbeg Press pb £7.99 185371707X
**A Noise from the Wood Shed**
Onlywomen Press pb £4.95 0906500303

## RODDY DOYLE (b.1958)

One of the most famous success stories of contemporary Irish fiction, Roddy Doyle came to prominence with the Barrytown trilogy: **The Commitments** (1989), **The Snapper** (1990) and **The Van** (1991). The books represent one of the best views of working class Dublin today, mixing social commentary with hilarious situations and highly believable characters. In Jimmy Rabbite Sr., who finally comes into his own in **The Van**, Doyle has created a character full of contradictions – troubled but easy-going, warm but emotionally stunted – who, nevertheless, rises off the page as a great comic individual with whom the reader cannot help but empathise. While the film version of **The Commitments** in 1991 brought Doyle to a wider readership and established his reputation, it was with **Paddy Clarke Ha Ha Ha** (1993) that the Dubliner reaped his richest rewards. The novel, a memoir of a boy growing up in working class Dublin, was less reliant on the almost cinematic dialogue of the earlier books, concerning itself with a child's observations and memories of a difficult but happy time. It went on to win the Booker Prize. Subsequent work has included the novel **The Woman Who Walked Into Doors** and **Family**, a tough, uncompromising drama for television.

**Barrytown Trilogy**
Minerva pb £8.99 0749397365
**The Commitments**
Minerva pb £6.99 0749391685
**Paddy Clarke Ha Ha Ha**
Minerva pb £6.99 0749397357
**The Snapper**
Minerva pb £6.99 0749391251
**The Van**
Minerva pb £6.99 0749399902
**The Woman who Walked into Doors**
Minerva pb £6.99 0749395990

## ROSE DOYLE

Rose Doyle published her first novel **Images** in 1993, which was followed by **Alva** (1996) and **Perfectly Natural** (1997). Already a prolific writer of childrens' books, Rose Doyle has enjoyed popular success with her novels, which are set in Ireland and combine a sensitive warmth of character with a realistic view on modern Ireland and how an independent soul can approach it.

**Alva**
Town House pb £5.99
1860590357
**Kimbay**
Town House pb £4.99
0948524685
**Perfectly Natural**
Town House pb £5.99
186059039X

> "The Irish are the blacks of Europe; Dubliners are the blacks of Ireland, and on our side, we're the blacks of Dublin. So say it: I'm black and I'm proud."
> Jimmy Rabbitte in the film of The Commitments

## ANNE DUNLOP

Anne Dunlop has published four novels in the 1990s, achieving most success with her latest work **Kissing The Frog** in 1996. Her first **The Pineapple Tart** (1992), published when she was only twenty four, dealt comically with a young girl's first experiences of life when she leaves her sheltered upbringing for a university education. This was followed by **A Soft Touch** and **The Dolly Holiday**. Her popularity is growing with each successive entertaining and witty novel.

**The Dolly Holiday**
Poolbeg pb £4.99 1853713252
**Kissing the Frog**
Poolbeg pb £5.99 1853714402
**The Pineapple Tart**
Poolbeg pb £5.99 1853714054
**A Soft Touch**
Poolbeg pb £4.99 1853714046

## CATHERINE DUNNE

Catherine Dunne's first novel **In The Beginning** (1997) saw the emergence of one of the best new Irish writers of recent years. An unusual tale of post-marriage despair, it was quickly followed by **A Name For Himself** in 1998. With her literary style, insightful characterisation and realistic plotting, Catherine Dunne is a name to watch out for.

**In the Beginning**
Vintage pb £5.99 009976041X
**A Name for Himself**
Cape pb £9.99 0224050907

## LEE DUNNE
**Goodbye to the Hill**
Wolfhound Press pb £3.50
0863271618
First published in 1965, **Goodbye to the Hill** is a great story which powerfully evokes and celebrates Dublin working class life. Set in Ranelagh, about a mile from St. Stephen's Green, the sexual and social adventures of the central protagonist are recounted with wit and good humour. It has also enjoyed great success as a stage play since 1978.

## MIRIAM DUNNE
**Blessed Art Thou a Monk Swimming**
Headline pb £6.99 0747258473
This is a fine first novel concerning the coming of age of Marian, desperate to find out about the facts of life. Set in Dublin in the 1960s, the novel beautifully evokes the wide-eyed wonder of a girl reaching adulthood.

## MARIA EDGEWORTH
### (1767–1849)

Although Maria Edgeworth was born in England, the Edgeworth family seat was in Ireland and the family moved back permanently in the 1780s. Rightly seen as one of the Protestant Ascendancy with a sense of responsibility to her tenants, she published four Irish novels, the most famous being **Castle Rackrent**. This is narrated by the ironic Thady Quirk, one of the most brilliant creations in Irish writing, who quietly castigates the irresponsibility of the squirearchical Rackrent family and in the second half of the novel is implicit in its downfall. **Ormond** is the story of an aristocratic orphan struggling to make his way in Anglo-Irish society.

**The Absentee**
Oxford UP pb £6.99
0192816829
**Castle Rackrent**
Oxford UP pb £2.50
0192823949
**Ormond**
Gill & Macmillan pb £4.95
0717117774

## ANNE ENRIGHT
### (b.1962)

Anne Enright was born in Dublin and educated at TCD. She has written a collection of short stories, **The Portable Virgin,** and a novel **The Wig My Father Wore.** Her stories display a quirkiness of subject-matter (clocks, death, angels), written in a jaunty style that is captivating and often funny. Her novel tells the story of Grace as her life is changed forever when Stephen, former suicidal builder, now angel, comes to stay. The magic of the sections between these two is brilliantly counterpointed by descriptions of life behind the scenes running a tacky TV show, 'Love Quiz'. Displaying a rare mix of humour and poignancy, **The Wig My Father Wore** is one of the most impressive debut novels of recent years.

**The Portable Virgin**
Vintage pb £5.99 0749399473
**The Wig my Father Wore**
Minerva pb £6.99 0749397152

## MARTINA EVANS

Martina Evans was originally known as a poet but published her first novel **Midnight Feast** in 1996 and followed it with **The Glass Mountain** in 1997. Evans takes a humorous look at the maturing of girls in modern Ireland while maintaining a lyrical and readable style.

**The Glass Mountain**
Secker hb £14.99 1856196925
**Midnight Feast**
Minerva pb £5.99 0749322500

"It was a tough, wiry wig with plenty of personality. It rode around on his head like an animal. It was a vigorous brown. I was very fond of it as a child. I thought it liked me back."
Anne Enright – The Wig My Father Wore

## SHERIDAN LE FANU
### (1814–1873)

Related distantly to Sheridan, Le Fanu was born in Dublin and, after studying at Trinity College, was called to the bar in 1839. By this time he was already publishing short stories and had begun a long involvement with publishing and journalism in the city. He produced numerous short stories and a dozen novels, writing in a variety of styles, but the work that has survived consists of the ghost stories and tales of the macabre at which he was particularly adept. His best-known novel is probably **Uncle Silas** which is a skillfully constructed tale of suspense, rather than the supernatural.

**Ghost Stories & Mysteries**
Dover pb £8.95 0486207153
**In a Glass Darkly**
Gill & Macmillan pb £4.95
0717117790
**Madam Crowl's Ghost & Other Stories**
Wordsworth pb £0.99
1853262188
**The Rose & the Key**
Sutton £5.99 0750906707
**Uncle Silas**
Dover pb £8.95 0486217159
**The Wyvern Mystery**
Sutton pb £5.99 0750906871

## KATHLEEN FERGUSON
**The Maid's Tale**
Poolbeg pb £5.99 1853712620
Kathleen Ferguson burst onto the scene in 1994 with her debut novel **The Maid's Tale**. She explores the changes in the Catholic Church over the past fifty years, and specifically one woman's fight for self-expression within the confines of the church. Ferguson went on to win The Irish Times Literature Prize for Fiction 1995 and was shortlisted for the Whitbread First Novel Award.

## THOMAS FLANAGAN
### (b.1923)
**The End of the Hunt**
Mandarin pb £6.99
0749319836
This powerful historical epic by the Irish-American critic and novelist concludes the trilogy that began with **The Year of the French** and continued with **The Tenants of Time.** This novel is set during the Troubles of the 1920's and displays Flanagan's talent for finely balancing period description with a great narrative.

## DORIS FLOOD-LADD
**The Irish**
Virgin pb £6.99 0352316977
This romantic novel, first published in the U.S.A (and aimed largely at that market) tells the story of immigrant siblings Sean & Nora O'Sullivan who leave Ireland at the turn of the century to seek their fortunes in New York.

## CIARÁN FOLAN

**Freak Nights**
New Island pb £5.99
1874597413

In this collection of stories that move from Ireland to Italy and Spain, Folan explores the conflicts found in various types of relationships. He exposes the secrets and lies between lovers, families and friends. Folan's talent as a short story writer was confirmed by his winning the RTE Francis MacManus Short Story Award.

## TOM FOOT

**Undertow**
Salmon pb £5.99 1897648936
**Undertow** tells the story of the mysterious sinking of a ship off the West coast of Ireland. The sole survivor of the wreck finds himself embroiled in a case of international intrigue when MI6 becomes involved. They believe the accident to be part of an IRA plot. The action builds to a tense climax of revenge carried out at sea.

## CARLO GEBLER

Born in Dublin, raised in London and now a resident of Enniskillen Carlo Gebler has established himself as a writer, of fiction and non-fiction, as well as a documentary director. In **The Cure** Gebler brings the traditional art of storytelling to the genre of the modern novel. He explores the myth of a village's attempt to overcome the supernatural elements believed to be causing a woman's barrenness. In **How to Murder a Man**, Gebler moves to post-Famine Monaghan where he exposes the fear and terror of the people as a new land agent arrives to deal with his embittered tenants. In the stories of **W9 and Other Lives**, Gebler examines modern life, but instead of the emptiness and loneliness that are often focused on, he revels in the positive aspects of living.

**How to Murder a Man**
Little Brown hb £16.99
0316643890
**W9 & Other Lives**
Lagan pb £5.95 1873687958
**The Cure**
Abacus pb £6.99 0349106487

## MAGGIE GIBSON

Maggie Gibson entered into the male-dominated genre of crime fiction in 1996 with her first Grace de Rossa detective novel **The Longest Fraud**. This was quickly followed by her hugely popular second novel **Deadly Serious**. Here the female Sleuths detectives take on the case of an ageing hippy who claims her sister has been murdered. After the initial problem of no body is overcome, a once simple case takes a number of interesting twists.

**Deadly Serious**
Poolbeg pb £4.99 1853717754
**The Longest Fraud**
Poolbeg pb £4.99 1853715492

## ANTHONY GLAVIN

**Night Hawk Alley**
New Island pb £5.99
1874597685

This is an acutely observed novel by Boston-born Glavin, who uses his native city as setting to tell the story of Mickey McKenna, Irish born mechanic and garage owner. Having been in the U.S. for thirty years, McKenna reflects on the pains and pleasures of his life as he approaches retirement. This is a truly Irish-American novel concentrating on everyday detail with a melancholy charm.

## GERALD GRIFFIN
### (1803–1840)

First published in 1829, Griffin's most lasting work, **The Collegians**, tells the story of the murder of Eily O'Connor by her husband's friend Danny Mann. Her husband Hardress Gregan is wracked by remorse, and is eventually found out and deported. His friend, Kyrle Daly (the other collegian) then marries heiress Anne Schute, who had earlier rejected Gregan. Although melodramatic, the novel very successfully portrays the background turbulence of early to mid 19th century Ireland.

**The Collegians**
Appletree Press pb £6.99
086281443X

## HUGO HAMILTON

Hamilton is one of the most interesting novelists of his generation whose recent books combine the plots of thrillers with the language and in-depth characterisation of literary fiction. **The Love Test** is a tale of blackmail and betrayal in divided Germany. **Headbanger** is the story of an obsessive Dublin policeman and his crusade against a notorious gangleader.

**Dublin Where the Palm Trees Grow**
Faber pb £8.99 0571176933
**Headbanger**
Vintage pb £5.99 0099268086
**The Love Test**
Faber pb £5.99 0571171842
**Sad Bastard**
Secker & Warburg pb £9.99

## GERARD HANNAN

**Ashes**
Treaty pb £6.99 190207100X
Following the success of Frank McCourt's **Angela's Ashes**, Gerard Hannan responded with his fictionalised memoir, based on interviews with Limerick residents. He details what he feels to be a more accurate portrayal of life in post war Limerick. He sees it as not just a dreary existence, but as poverty and pain coupled with hope for a brighter future. **Ashes** is the first part of the 'Penance' trilogy.

## W.A. HARBINSON

**Departures**
Poolbeg pb £5.99 1853716405
**Departures** is a novel narrating three damaged lives from the Second World War to the present. Mixing romance, humour and sadness with poignancy and readability, Harbinson has created a memorable and ultimately moving novel.

## JOSEPHINE HART

Josephine Hart was born in Dublin and has lived in London since the 1960s. Author of four novels, the most famous of which is *Damage,* first published in 1991. This is a darkly tragic tale of obsessive lust which displays Hart's gift for combining readability with a cool, detached prose style. This novel was later adapted for the cinema by Louis Malle.

**Damage**
Vintage pb £5.99 0099592312
**Oblivion**
Vintage pb £5.99 0099592118
**Sin**
Vintage pb £5.99 0099592215

## LARA HARTE (b.1976)

**First Time**
Phoenix pb £5.99 1857998367
This first novel from a young,
Dublin-born writer describes
the coming-of-age trials and
tribulations of Cassandra and
Emma, two very different
teenage girls. Movingly
realistic and well observed,
the novel beautifully
illustrates the difficulties of
teenage life and social reality.

## ANNE HAVERTY

**One Day As A Tiger**
Vintage pb £5.99 0099756218
Winner of the 1997 Rooney
Prize for Literature, this
unique debut novel combines
the unlikely topics of cloning
and rural life in Ireland.
Haverty brilliantly uses black
comedy to tell the story of
Marty who returns to his
family's farm after the death
of his parents. He begins an
unusual friendship with Missy,
a cloned sheep. The novel
was received to great acclaim
and was also shortlisted for
the 1997 Whitbread First
Novel Award and won the
Rooney award.

## KATY HAYES (b.1965)

Dublin-born Hayes has
published a collection of
short stories and a novel.
**Curtains**, set in contemporary
Dublin, takes a witty and
well-observed look at the
theatrical scene and astutely
draws over-the-top characters
who, nonetheless, never fall
into caricature or stereotype.

**Curtains**
Phoenix hb £12.99 1861590415
**Forecourt RUC**
Poolbeg pb £4.99 185371500X
**Opening Nights**
Phoenix £5.99 0753805189

## DERMOT HEALY
### (b.1947)

Born in Finea, Co. Westmeath,
Dermot Healy has written
short stories, novels, plays,
poetry and most recently a
memoir. He has also edited
two literary journals, Force
10 & Drumlin. His last novel
**A Goat's Song** is without
doubt, one of the finest
Irish novels of recent years,
combining love story, tragedy
and some of the greatest
evocations of the Irish
landscape ever written.
His memoir **The Bend for
Home** is a lyrical retelling
of the main events in the life
of the author's family, from
the death of his father when
he was a young boy to the
recent death of his mother.
Often hilarious, it perfectly
combines humorous
incidental anecdote with
heart-breaking sadness.

**A Goat's Song**
Harvill pb £6.99 1860463096
**The Bend for Home**
Harvill Press pb £6.99
1860463541

## SHAY HEALY

**Green Card Blues**
O'Brien Press pb £5.99
0862783860

Shay Healy, renowned songwriter, Eurovision winner and journalist, put his knowledge of the music business to use in his first novel, **The Stunt**. With great personal insight he delves into all aspects of the Dublin music scene. Healy followed this novel with **Green Card Blues**.

## CHRISTINA HICKEY

In her planned trilogy, Hickey sets out to examine the changes in a family from the First World War onwards. Beginning with **The Dancer**, she explores the lives of two sisters and their younger brother, the dancer, against the backdrop of the Dublin of World War I. The second part of the trilogy, **The Gambler**, moves to Dublin between the wars and tells of the family's decline as it moves on to the next generation. The third part of the trilogy, not yet published, is eagerly awaited.

**The Dancer**
Marino pb £9.99 1860230113
**The Gambler**
Mercier Press pb £9.99
1860230377

## AIDAN HIGGINS
### (b.1927)

Born in Celbridge, Co. Kildare and educated in Clongowes Wood College. He has lived in England, Spain, Germany and South Africa. He won the James Tait Black Memorial Award in 1961. His novel **Langrishe, Go Down**, first published in 1966 has become a modern classic. Recording the demise of the Langrishe family who were big house Catholics, the novel is striking in that it focuses on the undramatic but nevertheless permanent decay of the family. His stories were recently collected in the volume **Flotsam and Jetsam**. He has published two volumes of memoirs, **Donkey's Years** and **Dog Days** which both record the incidents of his youth and adulthood with remarkably moving candour and style.

**Flotsam & Jetsam**
Minerva pb £7.99 0749396962
**Langrishe, Go Down**
Minerva 5.99 0749397322
**The Lions of the Grunewald**
Minerva pb £6.99 0749397187
**Donkey's Years**
Minerva pb £7.99 0749396946
**Dog Days**
Secker hb £15.99 0436204843

## DESMOND HOGAN
### (b.1951)

Born in Galway, this sadly underrated writer has written novels and short stories of great originality. His first novel **The Ikon Maker** explores the relationship between an estranged son and mother who rediscover their relationship when she comes to accept his homosexuality and the difference between their generations. His short stories display a rare use of language, form and narrative while exploring strong themes of loneliness, grief and exile.

**Farewell to Prague**
Faber pb £7.99 0571174280
**The Ikon Maker**
Faber pb £5.99 0571167683

## SEAN HUGHES

**The Detainees**
Simon & Schuster pb £6.99
0671516671

John Palmer is not the sort of man to upset as Alan 'Redser' Bulger finds to his cost in this potent and gritty black thriller from best-selling writer and performer Sean Hughes, gloriously presented in his usual inimitable comic style.

## JENNIFER JOHNSTON (b.1930)

Born in Dublin and now living in Northern Ireland, Jennifer Johnston has written ten fine novels since 1972. Her great strength lies in her insightful and acute portrayal of the inner lives of her characters. She was interested in the Big House theme in her early fiction but in later years has concentrated on singular characterisation. Nowhere is this more apparent than in **The Illusionist**, the story of Stella who meets the mysterious Martyn and then maybe wishes that she hadn't. Never afraid to take risks in her plotting to put her characters through the traumas she wishes to explore, Johnston's is a singular voice in Irish fiction.

**How Many Miles to Babylon?**
Penguin pb £5.99 0140119515
**The Illusionist**
Minerva pb £6.99 0749395826
**The Invisible Worm**
Penguin pb £6.99 0140152571
**Shadows on our Skin**
Penguin pb £5.99 0140139796
**Desert Lullaby**
Lagan Press pb £4.95 1873687265 (Drama)
**Three Monologues**
Lagan Press pb £4.95 1873687702 (Drama)

## HEATHER INGMAN

**Survival**
Poolbeg pb £5.99 1853715441
From the author of popular novels **Sara** and **Anna**, this skilfully woven tale depicts realistic characters and an absorbing storyline set in modern day Ireland, England and Germany. In essence, this is an emotional, humorous and thought-provoking read.

## NEIL JORDAN (b.1950)

Born in 1950 and educated at University College, Dublin, award-winning film director Neil Jordan has written three novels and a collection of short stories. His early fiction **Night in Tunisia** is set in 1960s Ireland and is a good examination of social mores. He went on to write **Dream of a Beast** and **The Past**. His last novel **Sunrise with Seamonster** is mainly set in Bray, a town on the Wicklow coast. Although set in the context of the Spanish Civil War and the Anglo-Irish War, it is not an overtly political novel, but displays Jordan's strength in poetically describing internal emotion and place. His published film scripts include **The Crying Game**, for which he won an Oscar, and his recent film about the political career and death of Michael Collins. The latter also includes a fascinating diary of the making of the film, describing the project from its beginnings to the final take.

**Collected Fiction**
Vintage pb £7.99 0099753618
**Dream of a Beast**
Vintage pb £6.99 0099327317
**Night in Tunisia**
Vintage pb £5.99 0099327414
**The Past**
Vintage pb £5.99 009932721x
**Sunrise with Seamonster**
Vintage pb £5.99 0099585510

## Screenplays
**The Crying Game**
Vintage pb £5.99 0099327112
**Michael Collins Filmscript**
Vintage pb £7.99 0099737515

## The much-acclaimed novelist Colm Tóibín writes about Joyce's masterpiece, Ulysses

During the years when James Joyce was writing *Ulysses,* the Catalan Painter Joan Miró was becoming increasingly uneasy about inherited ideas of perspective. Just as Joyce viewed the traditional novel as a way of glossing over the random nature of experience, Miró viewed perspective as a great lie, and he sought to find a system for his art which would deal with the true shape of things. 'With the exception of the primitives and the Japanese,' he wrote, 'everyone has painted only the great masses of trees and mountains... that which interests me above all else is the calligraphy of a tree or the tiles of a roof, and I mean leaf by leaf, branch by branch, blade by blade of grass'.

Joyce was concerned also to find a language, a form and a style which would remain close to the shape of life in Dublin at the turn of the century and which would allow certain characters to thrive, to live on the page without forcing them into a plot-line where they got married or went bankrupt or lived happily. He tried to find a system which would capture the strange beauty of consciousness, just as Miró developed a dream-iconography for his paintings.

We grow to love Leopold Bloom not because of the story in which he plays a part, nor for his adventures in the plot, but because of the rich way he notices things, because of the way he remembers and then becomes distracted, then is reminded of something, and then watches, notices again, wishes and makes calculations. Some of his observations are desperately funny, as when he agrees with himself that wine in the chalice is better than Guinness maybe or ginger ale. But he is always burdened with other matters such as his father's death, his son's death, and his marriage, and then once more he is distracted.

What is so fascinating in the book besides Bloom's mind is Joyce's sense of Irish society, which, as we know from *Dubliners,* was acute and vivid. In the years between the rise of Parnell and the rise of De Valera there was a peculiar and intense aura around politics and religion in Ireland and the possibilities surrounding this aura gave Joyce his great subject, which was language.

The language of Ulysses moves from the plain, clipped, almost throwaway style for solitary moments – shitting, masturbating, thinking – to the cross-talk of friends, associates and colleagues in which speaking is half clap-trap or small-talk, full of witticism, quotations and half-baked opinion, laced like all of the book with snatches of songs. The style is always fluid. Blooms's stream-of-consciousness can be broken by clear description of what is going on around him. The pub talk can be broken, as in Barney Kiernans, by Bloom's efforts to be serious and almost solemn. Other scenes and situations are described in a language which is playfully baroque. Molly Bloom's soliloquy is direct and passionate.

But throughout the book there is a game being played between public and private discourse. The language of provincial (or indeed cosmopolitan) journalism, the language of nationalism and religion, and public rhetoric of all sorts are parodied, thrown up in the air and let float back down, all the more to tease them and humiliate them. Ireland, in the years after Parnell, had suddenly become "Ireland" with its Gaelic League, its Sinn Féin, its Abbey Theatre, its urgent need to de-anglicise. The supposed ancientness of Ireland is the source of much laughter and many jokes in *Ulysses,* so too Ireland's natural resources which both the Citizen and Skin the Goat (assuming it was he) extol in different sections of the book: 'And our wool that was sold in Rome in the time of Juvenal and our flax and our damask from the looms of Antrim and our Limerick lace, our tanneries and our white flint glass down there by Ballybough' Joyce loved lists, the longer and more incongruous the better. He loved the aura around proper names. There is a sense in *Ulysses* that anything which is held sacred in Ireland, especially respectability, history, nationalism and Catholicism, will be ridiculed; instead, sanctity will be offered to ordinary experience, to memory, love and sex, to companionship, long shapeless days and city life, to men half down on their luck, to song.

To that extent, *Ulysses* is a deeply political book in which Joyce sets his masterpiece against the idea that a nation is anything more than motley people in much the same place. But *Ulysses* is also, in an odd and admirable way a deeply patriotic and liberating book. Most of the Irish fiction written before Joyce was written for an English audience; much of it sought to describe Ireland's history and landscape and people as peculiar and alarmingly dramatic. Some of the most talented writers from Oliver Goldsmith to George Moore had set their novels in England. But Joyce's work is almost hermetically sealed in Ireland.

*Ulysses* is full of local references – names of people, streets, places, figures of speech, lines of songs. Nothing is ever explained in the book but Irish readers get most of the references. The book depends on the idea that the city being described is not a centre of paralysis, but rather the centre of the world. Local reference and proper names are not there to add colour to the book; most of the time their effect is entirely natural and often poetic. When names appear which have also appeared in *Dubliners* (and this happens throughout the book) there is a double pleasure in knowing what a name like Gretta Conroy means and then in meeting her briefly once more.

To understand the idea that this book was written first for an Irish audience, all one has to do is imagine Virginia Woolf reading the book and coming across the many proper names and missing the resonance which each one has in Ireland. Take the list of clergy, for example, who appear in the Cyclops section at an imagined meeting to discuss the revival of Irish sport: "the Rev. T.Brangan, O.S.A.; the Rev. J. Flavin C.C. the Rev, M.A. Hackett C.C, the Rev. W Hurley C.C., then Rev. Mgr McManus, V.G.; the Rev. B R. Slattery O.M.I., the Very Rev. M.D. Scally P.P., the Rev. F.T. Purcell, O.P.; the Very Rev. Timothy Canon Gorman, P.P.; the Rev. J. Flanagan C.C." The list is, first of all, funny, because it is based on the lists you still read in Irish provincial and indeed daily newspapers, and because it plays with titles and hierarchy but it is also graphic – it is easy to imagine these priests in a group photo, strong farmers' sons. All of the names signify a certain class and status. None of this is explained in the book and most of it could not be felt by a non-Irish reader. This is merely one example of the ways in which Joyce handed Ireland back to Irish readers in his book, how he made Ireland the centre of the known world. The Citizen would have been proud of him.

Joan Miró, throughout his long career, tried to return painting to two dimensions, to the making of marks on a surface. He wanted to erase the pretense of depth. He loved the flatness of the Romanesque tradition, it was like the blood in his veins, he said. Joyce, too, found in the Odyssey a map which he could follow so that his use of detail (and his creation of structure) in *Ulysses* was not simply a matter of establishing verisimilitude, but of unleashing irony – making clear that words and sentences are marks on a page, arid sounds we make, rhetorical systems and ways for us to perform, a long time before they come near disclosing or approaching the truth. This idea offered Joyce a new beginning in the creation of fiction and gave us this masterpiece. We are, to some extent, still getting over the shock.

## JAMES JOYCE (1882–1941)

"I fear those big words, Stephen said, which make us so unhappy."
James Joyce – Ulysses

The one writer most often associated with modernist Irish literature is James Joyce and, through his writing, Joyce memorialised his birthplace of Dublin. His childhood was marred by his family's loss of fortune and their movement down the social ladder. Joyce's education was overseen by the Jesuits which accounts for their treatment in his fiction. He began first at Clongowes Wood College in 1882 followed by Belvedere College where he attended as a non-paying student when his father was unable to pay the fees. During his time at University College, Dublin Joyce became interested in writing poetry, the majority of which has been lost. After graduating he went twice to Paris, returning the second time after his mother's death from cancer in 1903. While in Dublin he worked as a schoolmaster and famously lived for a short time with Oliver St. John Gogarty in the Martello Tower in Sandycove. Joyce left after an argument which led to his unflattering immortalisation of Gogarty as 'stately, plump Buck Mulligan' in the opening of **Ulysses.** In June of 1904 he met Nora Barnacle and on 16 June 1904 they went out together for the first time, thus making that such an important date that Joyce later chose it as the day in which the action of **Ulysses** takes place. On 8 October 1904 Joyce and Nora eloped to Pola. After stays in Trieste and Zurich they moved to Paris in 1920 where Joyce became firmly ensconced in the literary scene. After the Second World War they returned to Zurich where they remained until Joyce's death in 1941.

Although he lived most of his life in a self-imposed exile, Joyce's writing revolves around life in Ireland, most specifically in Dublin. Before leaving Ireland Joyce began **Stephen Hero,** an autobiographical novel that shows the beginning of the views that he would expand upon in later works. He abandoned this novel and it was left unpublished until 1944. Joyce later adapted **Stephen Hero** into **A Portrait of the Artist as a Young Man** (1916). Here Joyce produced a study of growing up as he charts the life of Stephen through childhood to the beginnings of adulthood. Joyce used epiphanies, moments of self-awareness, to show Stephen's spiritual, sexual and political awakenings. As early as 1905 Joyce had sent the stories that would comprise **Dubliners** to publishers, but it was not until 1914 that it was published. In these fifteen stories Joyce examines various aspects of Dublin life, chosen as he said 'because that city seemed to me the centre of paralysis.' Here Joyce used realism to portray the factors that hold his characters unable to act. **Ulysses,** Joyce's masterpiece, was published in 1922 on his fortieth birthday. Joyce used Homer's Odyssey as his model, but he moved the story to

Dublin on 16 June 1904. He experimented with a number of literary forms in order to examine various types of love – sexual, paternal, filial and national – through the story of Leopold Bloom, his adulterous wife Molly and Stephen. Dedalus, a student Bloom befriends. The changing styles and densely written prose make **Ulysses** a daunting read, but it can still be enjoyed for its musical quality even if every reference isn't understood. In 1997, Danis Rose published **Ulysses: A Reader's Edition** to much controversy. Rose attempted to make **Ulysses** more readable by correcting textual faults resulting from errors in proof-reading and printing of previous editions. By blending various texts and original documents into one isotext he wanted to produce 'Ulysses as James Joyce wrote it.' Joyce's most ambitious work is **Finnegans Wake** (1939) in which he uses stream of consciousness to explore the dream world of H C Earwicker. While it is considered Joyce's most difficult work to understand fully, it can also be appreciated for its humour and its lyrical quality.

**Anna Livia Plurabelle**
Faber pb £8.95 0571192955
**Dubliners**
Penguin pb £4.99 0140185542
**Dubliners**
Harper Collins pb £5.99
0586087850
**Dubliners**
Wordsworth pb £1.00
1853260487
**Dubliners**
Everyman hb £7.99
185715049X
**Dubliners**
Gill & Macmillan hb £14.99
0717119017
**Dubliners**
Lilliput Press pb £12.95
**Dubliners Repr. Of 1914 ed**
Dover pb £1.00 0486268705
**Essential James Joyce**
Harper Collins pb £8.99
0586090932

**Finnegans Wake**
Faber pb £6.99 0571108075
**Finnegans Wake**
Penguin pb £7.99 0140185569
**Poems & Exiles**
Penguin pb £7.99 0140185550
**Poetical Works**
Wordsworth pb £1.99
185326427X
**Portrait of the Artist as a Young Man**
Gill & Macmillan pb £6.99
0717120481
**Portrait of the Artist as a Young Man**
Everyman hb £11.99
1857150090
**Portrait of the Artist as a Young Man**
Penguin pb £4.99 0140185534
**Portrait of the Artist as a Young Man**
Harper Collins pb £5.99
0586087869

**Portrait of the Artist as a Young Man**
Dover pb £1.00 0486280500
**Portrait of the Artist as a Young Man**
Wordsworth pb £1.00
1853260061
**Ulysses**
Oxford University Press pb
£6.99 0192828665
**Ulysses**
Harper Collins pb £7.99
0586091491
**Ulysses**
Penguin pb £6.99 0140185585
**Ulysses**
Everyman hb £12.99
1857151003
**Ulysses**
Penguin pb £17.50 0140185593
**Ulysses-Readers' Edition Danis Rose (Ed)**
Picador hb £20.00 0330352296
**Ulysses Special Edition**
Lilliput Press hb £75.00
1874675996

## Joyce Biography

The standard biography of Joyce is Richard Ellmann's magisterial **James Joyce** (Oxford University Press pb £15.00 0195033817). Originally published in 1959 and revised in 1982, this exhaustive work contains everything one needs to know about the life of Ireland's most famous novelist. Ellman also edited the **Selected Letters of James Joyce** (Faber pb £17.50 0571107346) which is a fascinating fund of information about his relationships with the people who most affected his life. **The Critical Writings** (Cornell pb £11.99 0801495873) edited by Ellmann with Ellsworth Mason contain reviews, essays and articles written over Joyce's lifetime and illuminate the author's views on various writers including Mangan, Wilde and Shaw.

Any biographical reading of Joyce and his works has to be augmented by the lives of his wife and his father. **Nora: A Biography of Nora Joyce** by Brenda Maddox (Minerva pb £9.99 074939014X) is an extremely informative work which justly highlights the powerful influence that this complex, strong and long suffering woman had on her husband and also illustrates her constant support. **John Stanislaus Joyce** by John Wyse Jackson (Fourth Estate hb £20.00 1857024176) provides a hugely entertaining portrait of this larger that life patriarch as well as providing great background to the early life of James Joyce. Immortally characterised by his son in *Portrait of the Artist as a Young Man,* John Joyce lived life to the full and Wyse Jackson expands on the description given by his son James.

## Joyce Criticism – General

**Cambridge Companion to James Joyce**
Cambridge pb £12.95 0521376734
*Vincent Cheng* **Joyce, Race and Empire**
Cambridge pb £13.95 0521478596
*James Fairhall* **James Joyce and the Question of History**
Cambridge pb £13.95 052155876x
*David Norris* **Joyce for Beginners**
Icon pb £7.99 1874166196
*Vincent Sherry* **James Joyce**
Cambridge pb £7.95 0521421365

## Joyce Criticism – Ulysses

Any study of Ulysses is helped enormously by Don Gifford's great scholarship in **Ulysses Annotated** (California University Press pb £19.99 0520067452) which provides a clear gloss for many references, sources and background throughout the novel, whether quotidian or recondite. **James Joyce's Ulysses: Critical Essays** Edited By Clive Hart & Don Hayman (California University Press pb £12.95 0520032756) is a book of essays, one for each section of the novel. Written by leading Joyce scholars, all writing within different theoretical and cultural frameworks, the book displays the rich diversity of *Ulysses* as well as the diversity of Joyce criticism. **The Irish Ulysses** by Maria Tymoczko (California Universtiy Press pb £14.95 0520209060) examines *Ulysses* in its Irish context and argues persuasively for a reading that concentrates on sources in the Irish rather than the European literary tradition. **The New Bloomsday Book** by Harry Blamires (Routledge pb £11.99 0415138582) is a very useful tool, providing section by section summary and line by line glossary. Now in its third edition, it is still extremely popular.

## Joyce Criticism – Finnegans Wake

There are two books available which are invaluable aids to a reader grappling with the complexities, allusiveness and density of Finnegans Wake. **Readers Guide To Finnegans Wake** by Tindall (Syracuse University Press pb £14.99 0815603851) aims to provide precisely what its title suggests and even more thorough is **Annotations To Finnegans Wake** by Roland McHugh (Cornell pb £22.50 0801841909).

## Joyce Criticism – Others

**Portrait of the Artist as a Young Man/Dubliners**
**Joyce Annotated by Don Gifford**
California University Press pb £14.95 0520046102
**Dubliners**
Cambridge pb £3.75 0521485444
**Dubliners and Portrait of the Artist Casebook**
Macmillan pb £9.99 0333140338
**The Dead**
Nautica pb £8.550333618491
**York Notes on 'Dubliners'**
Longman pb £3.00 0582782155

# JOHN B. KEANE

As well as his highly acclaimed work for the stage, John B. Keane has also been writing many works of fiction since the late 1960s. His very successful series of fictional letters are satirical and often hilarious. Keane has invented letters from, among others, a match maker, and a country postman both of which poke gentle fun at rural Irish mores. His most successful novel The Bodhrán Makers is based in the fictional Co. Kerry town of Dirrabeg, and focuses on the conflict between the parish priest and the Wrenboys, the men who carry out the traditional pagan ceremony of carrying a dead wren around the town while singing and beating their bodhráns on St. Stephens Day. The priest is eventually driven insane by the noise. In the meantime, the bodhrán maker himself is practicing his nearly magic gift for seduction on the local women. Combining the usual John B. Keane qualities of good humour, strong evocation of place and clever satire, this novel is the ideal introduction to his fiction.

**The Bodhrán Makers**
Brandon Press pb £5.95
0863220851
**Celebrated Letters**
Mercier Press pb £9.99
1856351564
**The Contractors**
Mercier Press pb £6.99
1856350584
**Durango**
Mercier Press pb £6.99
1856350010
**A High Meadow**
Mercier Press pb £6.99
1856350908
**Innocent Bystanders & Other Stories**
Mercier pb £5.99 1856350843
**Irish Short Stories**
Mercier Press pb £4.99
0853428190
**John B Keane's Christmas**
Mercier Press pb £6.99
185635198X
**Letters of a Civic Guard**
Mercier pb £4.99 0853429251

**Letters of a Country Postman**
Mercier pb £4.99 1856350509
**Letters of a Matchmaker**
Mercier Press pb £5.99
0853429227
**Letters to the Brain**
Brandon Press pb £5.95
0863221572
**Man of the Triple Name**
Brandon pb £4.95 0863220614
**More Irish Short Stories**
Mercier pb £4.99 0853428182
**Owl Sandwiches**
Brandon Gill pb £5.99 pb
0863220754
**Power of Words**
Brandon pb £3.95 0863221084
**Under the Sycamore Tree & Other Stories**
Mercier Press pb £6.99
185635170X
**A Warm Bed on a Cold Night**
Mercier Press pb £6.99
185635184X

# MOLLY KEANE (b.1905)

Born in Co. Kildare, Molly Keane grew up in Co. Wexford and published her first novel in 1926 under the name M.J. Farrell, the pen-name she was to use until the 1980s. Her earlier novels **(Mad Puppetstown, Taking Chances)** in the main were concerned with the day to day affairs and activities of the Anglo-Irish big house while also examining the difficult relationship between social classes. Her later novels **(Good Behaviour, Time After Time)**, published after a gap of some 20 years are slightly darker, introspective explorations of character.

**Conversation Piece**
Virago pb £6.99 1853813478
**Good Behaviour**
Abacus pb £6.99 0349120757
**Loving & Giving**
Abacus pb £6.99 0349100888
**Time After Time**
Abacus pb £6.99 0349120765
**Young Entry**
Virago pb £6.99 0860686817

**(as M.J. Farrell)**
**Mad Puppetstown**
Virago pb £5.99 0860685888
**Treasure Hunt**
Virago pb £6.99 0860688003

## RICHARD KEARNEY

**(b.1954)**

Philosopher, cultural critic and novelist, Richard Kearney was born in Cork and is currently associate professor of philosophy at UCD. He has written 2 novels of a proposed trilogy. The first Sam's Fall introduces the Toland twins, Sam & Jack, both educated at at the Columbanus Abbey School. Sam stays on to become a monk but soon discovers that even a life devoted to God can be subject to temptation. Walking at Sea Level continues the story of Jack Toland, now estranged form his Swiss wife and living in Montreal. When summoned to Geneva to look after his daughter, his wife disappears. The resultant quest forms the body of the narrative. Both books are marked with an elliptic style that is extremely effective.

**Sam's Fall**
Hodder pb £5.99 0340660821
**Walking at Sea Level**
Hodder hb £14.99 0340689757

## CATHY KELLY

**Woman to Woman**
Poolbeg pb £5.99 1853717967
**Woman to Woman** tells the blockbusting and cleverly written story of two nineties women as they both contend with modern-day life, love and lots more besides. A courageous, forceful and most enjoyable first novel from Cathy Kelly.

## EAMON KELLY

**According to Custom**
Mercier pb £5.99 1856351122
Widely regarded as the Prince of Irish storytelling, Kelly continues the great oral tradition of the seanchai in this volume form of his acclaimed one-man show, a sharply humorous and wildly entertaining collection of yarns on the theme of custom.

## JOHN KELLY

**Grace Notes & Bad Thoughts**
Mercier Press pb £7.99
1860230032
This witty and well-paced debut offering by radio presenter John Kelly charts the moral decline of one young man during his relentless pursuit of pleasure in its multifarious forms and his obsession with uilleann pipes and their enchanting music.

## JAMES KENNEDY

**Armed & Dangerous**
Mandarin pb £5.99
074932242X
James Kennedy's contemporary thriller **Armed and Dangerous** begins with an IRA jailbreak and keeps up a cracking pace throughout, dealing with a renegade IRA unit's attempt to destroy the ceasefire in Northern Ireland by mounting an attack on the Queen.

## MARIAN KEYES
### (b.1965)

After graduating in Law, Marian Keyes spent ten years working in London before returning to Ireland to pursue her writing career. In this she was greatly encouraged by the talented editor and writer at Poolbeg Press, the late Kate Cruise O'Brien. Keyes's books were originally published by Poolbeg but Penguin were quick to see the potential and bought the British rights. She is now published simultaneously by both publishing houses. All three of Keyes's books have been phenomenal bestsellers. Arguably **Rachel's Holiday** is her best work to date and its central character the best drawn and developed. The book is engaging and funny yet deals tenderly with the subjects of addiction and obsession.

**Lucy Sullivan is getting Married**
Poolbeg pb £6.99 1853716154
**Rachel's Holiday**
Poolbeg pb £6.99 1853718963
**Water Melon**
Poolbeg pb £6.99 1853716235

## BENEDICT KIELY
### (b.1919)

One of Ireland's most respected men of letters, Benedict Kiely was born on Co. Tyrone and was educated at UCD. He has worked as a journalist and as a university lecturer but since the early 1970s has concentrated on writing and broadcasting. In 1996, he was elected a Saoi of Aos D‡na. His novels enjoy a huge thematic range from the pastoral to seduction and to the political violence of his later work. His early novel, In a Harbour Green is a study of the lives led by people living in a quiet valley in Northern Ireland. His Poor Scholar is a study of the 19th Century novelist William Carleton while his As I Walked down by Granard's Moat is a mix of memoir and local history, song and folklore.

**And as I Rode By Granard Moat**
Lilliput Press pb £7.99
0946640785
**The Cards of the Gambler**
Wolfhound pb £6.99
0863274773
**Dogs Enjoy the Morning**
Wolfhound pb £6.99
0863275281
**God's Own Country**
Mandarin £7.50 074939708x
**The Poor Scholar**
Wolfhound Press pb £2.99
0863276067
**There was an Ancient House**
Wolfhound Press pb £6.99
0863275761

## DAVID M KIELY
**Angel Tapes**
Blackstaff Press pb £6.99
0856406163
David Kiely's first novel **Angel Tapes** is a thriller which pits canny but dissolute Detective Superintendent Blade Macken against a psychopathic bomber who threatens an American presidential visit. Pacy and colourful, the novel races through the city of Dublin to an explosive conclusion.

## WILLIAM KING
**Strangled Impulse**
Falcon Books pb £5.99
0952980002
William King's first novel, **Strangled Impulse**, follows the story of a young priest on his appointment as curate to the parish of Melrose. In parti-cular, its theme is celibacy and the pressure which this injunction places on the clergy.

## MAURA LAVERTY
### (1907–1967)

Born in Co. Kildare, this autobiographical novelist has two books currently in print. **Never No More,** first published in 1942 is a gentle novel about her early life spent in her grandmother's home Derrymore House while **No More Than Human** is a thinly fictionalised account of her not altogether happy experiences living and working in Spain as a governess in the 1920s.

**Never No More**
Virago pb £6.15 pb 0860684849
**No More Than Human**
Virago pb £4.99 pb 0860684792

## MARY LAVIN (1912–1996)

Born in Massachusetts of Irish parentage, she came to Ireland for her formal education, culminating in an MA thesis at UCD on Jane Austen, an author who was to inform much of her later writing. Her prolific writing career spanned more than forty years and embraced many genres. She wrote two novels, **The House on Clew Street** (1945) and **Mary O'Grady** (1950), and regularly contributed short stories to *The New Yorker.* Lavin was considered by many to be Dublin's 'grande dame of letters' and 'the mistress of the Irish short story', a reputation earned not only by her publication of twelve volumes of short stories, beginning with **Tales from Bective Bridge** (1943), but also by her encouragement of younger writers in the often oppressive atmosphere of Ireland in the forties, fifties and sixties. The drama of her work is derived from deceptively simple, domestic and quotidian things. Yet her apparent guilelessness enabled her to be one of the first writers to deal with the role of women in Irish society and not be censored and reviled, unlike later writers (McGahern, Edna O'Brien) whose greater explicitness was condemned by church and state.

**In a Café & Other Stories**
Town House pb £8.99 1860590012
**Tales from Bective Bridge**
Town House pb £6.95 1860590411

## MAURICE LEITCH
### (b.1933)

Antrim-born Maurice Leitch has written a fine body of novels concerned with the political reality of Northern Ireland. **Silver's City** is set in a grim Belfast which is rapidly falling into anarchy where two men fight out their own private war of vengeance. **Gilchrist** is the story of the eponymous crooked evangelist set in Antrim and Spain. His latest book **The Smoke King** is set in Northern Ireland during World War II. A murder has just taken place but Lawlor the drunken, disillusioned police sergeant doesn't believe that the motive was sectarian but that the murderer came from the nearby U.S. army barracks. What follows is a murder hunt between two very different cultures.

**Silver's City**
Minerva pb £6.99 0749396571
**Gilchrist**
Minerva pb £6.99 0749396555
**The Smoke King**
Secker & Warburg pb £9.99 0436205068
**Poor Lazarus**
Minerva pb £6.99 074939658X

## BRIAN LEYDEN

**Departures**
Brandon pb £6.99 0863221548
The stories in **Departures**
explore the changes in Irish
life from the 1960s to the
1990s. Leyden writes in the
first person in order to
describe the modernisation
of Ireland and how ordinary
people's lives are affected.
Leyden is the winner of the
1988 RTE Francis MacManus
Short Story Award and the
Ireland's Own short story
competition in 1989.

## FERGUS LINEHAN

**Under The Durian Tree**
Town House pb £5.99
1860590322
Fergus Linehan's first novel
**Under the Durian Tree** tells
the story of Tim O'Hara, who
has retired to Ireland after a
lifetime in the civil service in
Malaya. The novel intertwines
the histories of the two
countries in a narrative both
poignant and powerful.

## MORGAN LLYWELYN

Originally published by Forge,
New York (1996), in **Pride of
Lions** Morgan Llywelyn's deft
mix of tragedy and history is
applied to the account of
Brian Boru's brood in her
thoroughly researched
treatment of ancient Irish
history. **On Raven's Wing**
(1990), the story of
Cuchulain, Hound of Ulster,
interprets age-old myth,
subtly recreating the heroic
legends of the warrior elite
of northern Ireland.

**On Raven's Wing**
Minerva pb £5.99 0749302054
**Pride of Lions**
Poolbeg pb £6.99 1853717606

## GENEVIEVE LYONS

Genevieve Lyons writes
romances with an Irish
flavour. Her three novels,
**Summer in Dranmore**,
**The Lovely American** and
**Demara's Dream**, are all
ultimately concerned with
the conflicts which exist
within families and the
unifying effects of love,
both romantic and familial.
Collisions of class in the
historical novel **Demara's
Dream** and of generation
in **Summer in Dranmore**
generate both passion and
disaster, in narratives which
see the modification of
ambition and the slow
gaining of wisdom as their
young protagonists are led
towards adulthood and love.

**Demara's Dream**
Warner pb £5.99 0751511684
**The Lovely American**
Warner pb £5.99 0751517704
**Summer in Dranmore**
Warner pb £4.99 0751503819

# FERDIA MACANNA

**The Last of the High Kings** is a delightfully warm and humorous coming of age novel set in 1977, first published in 1991. The film of the same name appeared in 1996. In a vivid, turbulent and amusing tale, Howth-born MacAnna adroitly weaves Frankie Griffin's search for independence amidst his family's struggles, setting it in a suspiciously familiar-sounding small seaside town outside Dublin, showing that even the most dysfunctional family can make it, if there's love there.

**The Last of the High Kings**
Penguin pb £5.99 014024770X
**The Ship Inspector**
Penguin pb £5.99 0140232079

# WALTER MACKEN
## (1915–1967)

This Galway-born novelist and short story writer was a prolific author for most of his life but is most remembered for three historical novels which describe the misery of the ordinary Irish people under British Rule. **Seek the Fair Land** describes the awful injustice and savagery of Cromwell's campaign in Ireland. **The Silent People** is set in the time of the Great Famine and **The Scorching Wind** is set against the backdrop of the Anglo-Irish war of 1919-1921. All three novels are rich in detail, description and drama.

**Brown Lord of the Mountain**
Brandon Press pb £5.95
0863222013
**City of the Tribes**
Brandon Press pb £2.99
0863222285
**God Made Sunday & Other Stories**
Brandon Press pb £5.95
086322217X
**Green Hills & Other Stories**
Brandon Press pb £5.95
0863222161
**Quench the Moon**
Brandon Press pb £5.95
0863222021
**Rain on the Wind**
Brandon pb £5.95 0863221858
**The Scorching Wind**
Pan pb £5.99 0330303260
**Seek the Fair Land**
Pan pb £5.99 0330303279
**The Silent People**
Pan pb £5.99 0330303287

# JOHN MACKENNA
## (b.1952)

This fine short story writer and novelist was born in Co. Kildare and is now a producer in RTE. His story collections **The Fallen and Other Stories** & **A Year of Our Lives**, although set in, and engaging with, the landscape and mood of South Co. Kildare are fascinating because of their distinctively 'unIrish' feel, which makes MacKenna one of the most interesting contemporary prose writers. His first novel **Clare**, about the Northampton poet John Clare is now out of print. His latest novel, **The Last Fine Summer**, returns to Kildare and is a beautifully moving meditation on sex, death and memory, focused through the recollections of Kevin, the central character, who looks back on the last fine summer just before he left home.

**The Fallen & Other Stories**
Blackstaff Press pb £6.95
0856404950
**The Last Fine Summer**
Picador hb £15.99 033035213X
**A Year of our Lives**
Picador pb £5.99 0330339575

# BERNARD MACLAVERTY (b.1942)

Born in Belfast and now living in Scotland, Bernard MacLaverty has written three volumes of short stories and three novels. Over the last twenty years, MacLaverty has displayed his gift for writing beautiful, poignant prose and is undoubtedly one of the current masters of the short story form. His great strength lies in his truthful portraits of human relations. All of MacLaverty's stories engage with characters who are on the margins of society, friendship and death and range in subject matter from the stigmatic shame of a young boy with psoriasis to the sudden realization that a distant friendship is now non-existent. His novel **Cal** is a haunting story set in mid-1980s Northern Ireland and explores a tender but doomed love affair between Catholic Cal and Protestant Marcella, bravely examining the complexities of a socially and religiously divided society. **Lamb** chronicles the relationship between a priest at a reform school and one of his pupils, and builds slowly to a redemptive but ultimately tragic finale. **Grace Notes**, his latest novel, nominated for the 1997 Booker prize, explores, through the character of pianist Catherine McKenna, the human ability to transcend difficulty for the sake of pursuing a single dream.

**Cal**
Vintage p £6.99 0099767112
**Grace Note**
Vintage pb £5.99 0099778017
**The Great Profundo & Other Stories**
Vintage pb £5.99 0099773716
**Lamb**
Penguin pb £5.99 0140108114
**Secrets & Other Stories**
Penguin pb £5.99 0099773619
**Walking the Dog**
Penguin pb £6.99 0140236368

# BRYAN MACMAHON (1909–1997)

Born in Listowel, Co. Kerry, where he was to live most of his life, Bryan MacMahon produced work suffused with a deep understanding, love and engagement with the Kerry people, landscape and folklore. He was also one of the few members of the settled community to have a thorough grasp of Shelta, the language spoken by many Irish Travellers. Teaching in Listowel for most of his working life, his genius and knowledge quickly earned him the title of 'The Master' (the title of his bestselling memoir). His play **The Honey Spike** was inspired by his knowledge of the Traveller's way of life and is now available as a novel.

**Children of the Rainbow**
Poolbeg pb £5.99 1853713112
**The Honey Spike (Drama)**
Poolbeg pb £5.99 1853713104
**The Sound of Hooves**
Poolbeg pb £5.99 1853714666
**The Tallystick**
Poolbeg pb £5.99 185371447X

## BRINSLEY MACNAMARA
### (1890–1963)

Born in the village of Delvin, Co. Westmeath, MacNamara is best known for his first novel, **The Valley of the Squinting Windows**, published in 1918. Based on his own native village, the novel points out all the hypocrisy, back-stabbing and small-mindedness which he felt was inherent in small village life. The novel revolves around the vengeful murder of Ulick Shannon, by his nephew John Brennan after Shannon has an affair with a school teacher, Rebecca Kerr, which leads to her expulsion from the village. The book caused outcry at the time and led to litigation and the boycotting of MacNamara's father's school. MacNamara also produced other fiction and had a lifelong connection with the Abbey theatre.

**The Clanking of Chains**
Anvil pb £2.95 0900068485
**The Valley of the Squinting Windows**
Anvil pb £5.95 0947962018
**The Various Lives of Marcus Igoe**
Anvil pb £6.95 0947962956

## DEIRDRE MADDEN
### (b.1960)

Born in Co. Antrim and educated at Trinity College, Dublin, Deirdre Madden has produced a very impressive body of work since the publication of her first novel **Hidden Symptoms** in 1988. This novel explores the aftermath of murder in the North of Ireland but her work since has been by no means confined to that locale. **Remembering Light and Stone** is set in Italy and perfectly records the minutiae of daily life focussed through the response of the central character to her new surroundings. Her latest novel **One by One in the Darkness** returns to Northern Ireland and is a moving and tragic account of three sisters' reactions to the current troubles.

**Birds of the Innocent Wood**
Faber pb £5.99 0571152813
**Hidden Symptoms**
Faber pb £5.99 0571150748
**Nothing is Black**
Faber pb £5.99 0571172474
**One By One in the Darkness**
Faber pb £6.99 0571175511
**Remembering Light and Stone**
Faber pb £6.99 0571169465

## AISLING MAGUIRE
**Breaking Out**
Blackstaff Press pb £6.99
0856405744

**Breaking Out** tells the story of Eleanor Leyden, orphaned and forced to conform by her middle-class Catholic foster-parents. Spurred on by her aunt and her schoolfriend Louise, she 'breaks out' and lives her life as she wants to, but realises that she must, ultimately, face the world alone.

## MAURICE MANNING
**Betrayal**
Blackwater Press pb £7.99
0861219708

Senator Maurice Manning has written a sharp political novel in **Betrayal**. Revolving around a new Taoiseach, Jack Mulcahy, who realises that he is not paranoid but that people really are out to get him, this intriguing political thriller has a cute insider's eye for detail.

## EMER MARTIN
**Breakfast In Babylon**
Wolfhound Press pb £6.99
0863274838

Emer Martin's debut novel introduces readers to Isolt and Christopher, two young hedonists on the run from their former lives and, in the latter's case, from the police and Detroit bikers. Martin has written an arresting debut that never lets up its pace.

# EUGENE MCCABE
## (b.1930)

Though born in Glasgow, McCabe has lived in Co. Monoghan since he was ten years old where he still runs his family's farm. As well as farming and writing, he has also wrtten for RTE television. Dramatic success came in 1964 with his play *King of the Castle*, a tour de force which centres on the character of ÔScober' MacAdam, recent acquisitor of a big house on Co. Leitrim. He is literally Ôking of the castle', but is undermined by his sexual impotence. McCabe's most recent novel, *Death & Nightingales*, thankfully recently reissued, is set in the Irish border counties in the early 1880s at the height of the political and agrarian unrest. Using this turbulence as background, McCabe weaves a chilling fable of deception around the central character Elizabeth, who is besotted with the mysterious Liam Ward and as a result puts herself in terrible danger. With its plot, characterisation and pastoral description, McCabe's novel is undoubtedly a modern masterpiece.

**King of the Castle**
Gallery Press pb £6.95
1852351926
**Death & Nightingales**
Vintage pb £6.99 074939868X

# PATRICK MCCABE (b.1955)

In the last ten years Patrick McCabe has established himself as one of the most original writers in Ireland. He was born in Clones, Co. Monaghan, a border town McCabe has fictionalised in several novels. His novels are set in the recent past, a period in which Ireland is trying to come to terms with its modern identity. He describes the tension between the old Catholic Ireland and the permissive influences of British and American culture. This is expressed through the distinctive voice of the oppressed and the isolated. His first two novels were **Music on Clinton Street** (1986) and **Carn** (1989) but it was with **The Butcher Boy** (1992) that he received widespread recognition. Based on a real case, it describes the horrific murder committed by Francie Brady, the paranoid yet inventive, and increasingly unreliable, narrator. This was also the first in a loose trilogy of novels, completed by **The Dead School** (1995) and **Breakfast on Pluto** (1998). **The Dead School** tells the stories of two schoolteachers representing the inflexible past and the confused present, a conflict which results in a typically macabre conclusion. **Breakfast on Pluto** explores the complex relationship betweeen Ireland and Britain, through the period of the beginning of the Troubles. It is narrated by McCabe's most extraordinary character, transvestite prostitute and embarrassment to small town Ireland, Patrick 'Pussy' Braden. Mc Cabe's descriptions of the troubled development of post-war Ireland, through its most confused and borderline inhabitants, have made his voice a unique addition to contemporary Irish writing.

**Breakfast on Pluto**
Picador hb £15.99 0330352938
**The Butcher Boy**
Picador pb £6.99 0330328743
**Carn**
Picador pb £5.99 0330328085
**The Dead School**
Picador pb £6.99 0330339451

## COLUM MCCANN

### (b.1965)

Dublin born Colum McCann is one of the rising literary stars of his generation whose work skillfully combines a learned style with a raw power. His time in America marks him apart from his contemporaries and he exploits the distance between himself and his native land to great effect as he explores the way that exile works. **Songdogs,** his first novel, explores the poignant relationship between a father and son. **This Side of Brightness** moves away from Ireland altogether and chronicles the rise of New York City through the eyes of the immigrants who helped to built the early city. All of his work is marked by his fastidious eye for detail.

**Fishing the Sloe Black River**
Phoenix pb £5.99 1857992156
**Songdogs**
Phoenix pb £5.99 1857995090
**This Side of Brightness**
Orion hb £14.99 1857780193

## MARY MCCARTHY

Dublin-born Mary McCarthy's first novel, the bestselling **Remember Me** (1996) sensitively tackles the issue of adoption from all sides in a story assessing the precarious balance between love and loss, family and ambition. **And No Bird Sang** (1997) reveals a tale of betrayal, rumour, revenge and murder with harsh personal truth learned in the process in an intriguing second novel.

**And No Bird Sang**
Poolbeg pb £5.99 1853717037
**Remember Me**
Poolbeg pb £5.99 1853716103

## MOLLY MCCLOSKEY

**Solomon's Seal**
Phoenix House pb £8.99 1861590237
This brave collection of sixteen stories returns repeatedly to the brittle frailty of human relationships, sexual grief and family disintegration. Philadelphia-born McCloskey moved to Sligo during the 1980s, and was subsequently awarded the RTE Francis MacManus Award in 1995.

## MIKE MCCORMACK

**Getting It In The Head**
Vintage pb £5.99 0099743213
This is a wonderfully macabre first collection of stories, which although quietly terrifying and sometimes brutally shocking are always suffused with a rare humour. 'A is for Axe' coldly (and alphabetically) recounts the plans for and details of a brutal patricide. 'Thomas Crumlesh: a Retrospective', comprises of the catalogue notes for an exhibition of amputated body parts of the eponymous sculptor. With these stories, McCormack paints a unforgettably quirky world of sad brutality.

## EUGENE MCELDOWNEY

Eugene McEldowney's Megarry Mysteries are marvellous additions to the crime genre, imbued with a sense of realism and tight direct prose. Born in Belfast, now living in Howth, north Dublin, McEldowney uses his own roots to construct authentic backdrops against which strong characters play out the chilling intricacies and ingenious plots of his sparkling thrillers. Eugene McEldowney has been a journalist for over twenty five years and is currently assistant editor at the Irish Times.

**Murder at Piper's Gut**
Minerva pb £5.99 0749323442
**The Sad Case of Harpo Higgins**
Minerva pb £5.99 0749322284
**A Stone in the Heart**
Mandarin pb £4.99 0749321741

## JOHN MCGAHERN (b.1934)

Born in Dublin and now living in Co. Leitrim, McGahern is one of the finest living writers in the world. From his first novel **The Barracks** to his most recent **Amongst Women**, McGahern has consistently demonstrated the power and simple beauty of his prose. The language of his books is pared right down and not a word is out of place or unnecessary. His characters inhabit a world that manages to be both familiar and menacing and constantly battle with forces of intransigence and alienation. **The Barracks** centres on the life of Kathleen Regan who marries a widowed policeman and spends the rest of her short life trying to fit in with him and his children in the barracks of the title. His second novel **The Dark**, is the story of a boy growing up with his widowed father and skillfully creates the adolescent psyche where confusion and mistrust of adults is exemplified by the character's bitter, drunken teacher and frustrated, brutal father. This novel was banned on its publication. He went on to write the novels **The Pornographer** and **The Leavetaking** and three collections of short stories – **Nightlines**, **Getting Through** and **High Ground**.

His **Collected Stories** appeared in 1992. His most recent novel **Amongst Women**, is the story of Michael Moran, a bitter veteran of the War of Independence, who runs a farm with his wife and family in Sligo. Although the women surrounding him all love him, they are wary of his aggression and old-fashioned values. This novel beautifully describes the difficulties inherent in changing with new social and political values in the wider world, and the awful intransigence that results when adults have to grow up with, and adapt to their children.

**Amongst Women**
Faber pb £6.99
**The Barracks**
Faber pb £5.99 0571119905
**Collected Stories**
Faber pb £6.99 0571169481
**The Dark**
Faber pb £6.99 0571119913
**Getting Through**
Faber pb £5.99 0571149979
**High Ground**
Faber pb £6.99 057114571x
**The Leavetaking**
Faber pb £6.99 0571132804
**The Pornographer**
Faber pb £5.99 0571161618

## EAMONN MCGRATH

**Fish in the Stone** by Eamonn McGrath is a haunting novel revolving around Mary Ennis, coming to terms with her parents' loveless marriage and the way she has been abused by her father. Mary's parents, both pillars of their community are trapped in a loveless marriage. McGrath has also written **The Charnel House**.

**The Charnel House**
Blackstaff pb £5.95 0856404470
**The Fish in the Stone**
Blackstaff pb £6.99 0856405248

## EOIN MACNAMEE (b.1960)

Born in Co. Down, educated at TCD, and now living in Co. Sligo, Eoin MacNamee rose to fame in 1994 with the publication of **Resurrection Man**, a brutal story of Loyalist paramilitaries on the rampage in Belfast. Using a tight structure, appropriately reminiscent of traditional crime narratives, the novel describes brute savagery and tribal hatred in stark, clinical language. MacNamee has also written two novellas, **Last of the Deeds** and **Love in History**.

**The Last Of Deeds & Love In History**
Picador pb £5.99 0330333429
**Resurrection Man**
Picador pb £5.99 0330332759

# GLENN MEADE

Glenn Meade, an ex-journalist and now writer and pilot trainer has written two fast-paced thrillers set in Europe. **Brandenburg** is set in the new Germany and focuses on Joseph Volkmann who is an agent with the new EC security force. **Snow Wolf** is the story of American journalist Bill Massey's investigation into his father's death in 1953. He finds out that his father was involved in a high level CIA assassination attempt on Joseph Stalin.

**Brandenburg**
Hodder pb £4.99 0340601043
**Snow Wolf**
Hodder & Stoughton pb £5.99
0340602910

# LIA MILLS

**Another Alice**
Poolbeg pb £5.99 185371562X
This is an important first novel from Dublin-born Lia Mills, which unflinchingly examines the cause and effect of child abuse through the memories of Alice, its central character. The book is particularly strong when it evokes universal childhood emotions. It is difficult reading at times but it haunts and moves the reader long after it has been put down.

# BRIAN MOORE (b.1921)

Born in Belfast and now living in Malibu, Brian Moore has lived in Europe and Canada. He served in North Africa, Italy and Germany during the latter end of the Second World War for the British Ministry of War Transport. He emigrated to Canada in 1948. Since 1955 he has published nineteen novels, all of which have received great critical acclaim. The tableau of his work stretches from Belfast to London, Canada, Eastern Europe and the Caribbean. His great gift is to draw characters whose emotions are instantly recognisable even if the settings or scenes are not. His prose is spare and detached but never unsympathetic. His first novel **The Lonely Passion of Judith Hearne**, published in 1955, describes the grey of 1950s Belfast like no other. It looks at the life of Judith Hearne, who in early middle age, slowly realises that her delusions of grandeur, popularity and happiness are being replaced by the reality of poverty, alcoholism and loneliness. **The Luck of Ginger Coffey**, published in 1960 is set in Montreal and revolves around the days that everything goes wrong for the eponymous character. Newly emigrated from Dublin, Coffey is one of the few realistic 'Walter Mitty' characters in modern fiction. Constantly making promises to his wife and friends that he cannot keep, Coffey is never happy with his lot until he realises how much he has. **Catholics**, which was published in 1970, is an elegant novella describing a lonely monastery island off the south west coast of Ireland which has to face up to the modern world. The book questions the wisdom of enforcing modern religious practice on church members who seem quite happy practising their faith as they are. **Black Robe**, published in 1980, is a historical novel set in the harsh world of rural Canada in the 18th Century. Focussing on a journey upriver by French Jesuit (Black Robe) Fr Paul Laforgue, the novel examines the nature of religious faith and the barbarism that results from a clash of diametrically opposite cultures. Although sometimes savage in its descriptions, the book has a rare beauty in its prosaic and meticulous portrait of life at the frontier of 'civilisation'. **Lies of Silence**, published in 1990, sees Moore returning to his native Belfast to examine the Troubles that started in the late 1960s. The central character, Michael Dillon is forced by the IRA to leave a bomb outside the hotel where he works or else his wife will be shot. Bravely using troubled Belfast as a setting, Moore weaves the plot of a contemporary thriller around a quiet castigation of all sides of the modern society that has come to tolerate such violence and hypocrisy.

# GEORGE MOORE
## (1852–1933)

**Answer From Limbo**
Flamingo pb £5.99 0586091459
**Black Robe**
Flamingo pb £5.99 0586086153
**Catholics**
Vintage pb £5.99 009985760X
**Cold Heaven**
Flamingo pb £5.99 0006548318
**Colour of Blood**
Flamingo pb £5.99 0586087370
**The Doctor's Wife**
Flamingo pb £5.99 0586087397
**The Emperor of Icecream**
Flamingo pb £5.99 0586087036
**The Feast of Lupercal**
Flamingo pb £5.99 0586090444
**The Great Victorian Collection**
Flamingo pb £5.99 0586087389
**I Am Mary Dunne**
Vintage pb £5.99 0099102218
**Lies of Silence**
Vintage pb £6.99 0099998106
**The Lonely Passion of Judith Hearne**
Flamingo pb £5.99 0586087583
**The Luck of Ginger Coffey**
Flamingo pb £5.99 0586087028
**The Magician's Wife**
Bloomsbury hb £15.99
0747537186
**The Mangan Inheritance**
Flamingo pb £5.99 0006548334
**No Other Life**
Flamingo pb £5.99 0006546927
**The Statement**
Flamingo pb £6.99 0006550231
**The Temptation Of Eileen Hughes**
Flamingo pb £5.99 0006548326

Born in Co. Mayo, George Moore attended school in Birmingham and moved to London in 1869. In 1873, he moved to Paris, where he tried to establish himself as a painter. Failing at this, he then decided to write. While in Paris he spent time with artists like Manet, Zola and Picasso. Possibly his most famous work set in Ireland, **A Drama in Muslin**, explores the world of the decaying ascendancy, by using the Vice-regal ball (which, in the novel, is a glorified marriage market), to point out the jaded cynicism of this class. In addition to such once well-known novels as **Esther Waters** and **The Brook Kerith**, Moore wrote three volumes of memoirs, collected as **Hail & Farewell**, which chart his involvement with the Irish Literary Revival and include comments on and criticisms of Lady Gregory, Synge, Douglas Hyde and Yeats among others. His short story collection, **The Untilled Field**, set in Mayo and Dublin in the 1880s, was written to be translated into Irish for the Gaelic League. With its recording of both rural and urban realism, it served as a precursor for Joyce's **Dubliners**.

**A Drama In Muslin**
Smythe pb £4.95 0861400569
**Esther Waters**
Everyman £4.99 pb 0460873261
**Hail & Farewell**
Smythe pb £9.95 0861401980
**The Untilled Field**
Gill & Macmillan pb £4.95 0717117804

George Moore

## DANNY MORRISON

Former Republican activist, Danny Morrison has written three books, **West Belfast**, **The Wrong Man** and **On the Back of a Swallow**, which is an exploration of love through the eyes of Nicky Smith whose best friend dies. He is embittered until he meets Gareth Williams, who is from a different community. Their friendship provokes great anger in both of their communities.

**On The Back Of A Swallow**
Mercier Press pb £7.99
1856350967
**The Wrong Man**
Mercier Press pb £7.99
1856351645
**West Belfast**
Mercier pb £6.99 0853429103

## MARY MORRISSEY
### (b.1957)

Born in Dublin, Mary Morrissey has written a collection of short stories and one novel. **A Lazy Eye** displays the author's great skill in describing emotions, the title story being a near perfect description of an emotional range from embarrassment through humiliation to final elation. **Mother of Pearl** is a haunting novel which centres on the kidnapping of a baby. Told through the experiences of the kidnapper, the mother and the baby, the novel questions what constitutes a family with great compassion.

**A Lazy Eye**
Vintage pb £5.99 0099701413
**Mother Of Pearl**
Vintage pb £5.99 0099582511

## MICHAEL MULLEN

Popular novelist Michael Mullen has been praised for his fine storytelling and well drawn characters. These qualities are clearly displayed in his novel **Midnight Country**, a big family saga which travels from Vienna to St. Petersburg and Berlin in the fading light of the last days of the Hapsburg Empire.
**The Hungry Land**
Poolbeg pb £5.99 185371240X
**The Midnight Country**
HarperCollins pb £4.99
0006479111

## IRIS MURDOCH
### (b.1919)

Dublin-born novelist and philosopher Iris Murdoch has written two novels set in Ireland. **The Unicorn,** first published in 1963, is set in a big house in the West of Ireland and is the story of Marian Taylor, a polite governess who is marked out as an outsider in the frenetic society surrounding her. **The Red and the Green,** set during the 1916 Easter Rising, explores the relationship between the sympathetic but law-abiding Anglo-Irish and the republican rebels.

**The Red And The Green**
Penguin pb £6.99 0140027564
**The Unicorn**
Penguin pb £6.99 014002476X

## HENRY MURPHY

**An Eye On The Whiplash And Other Stories**
Ashfield pb £9.99 1901658104
Henry Murphy, a barrister practicing in Dublin, has written a collection of humourous stories which look at life at the Irish Bar. His central character Dermot McNamara BL, is a young barrister just starting out in his career.

## GERARD MURPHY

**Once In A New Moon**
The Collins Press pb £6.99
189825611X

This is a moving novel dealing with the passing of country ways of life in the technological 20th Century. The novel unfolds over twenty four hours in the lives of the narrator, his father and his brothers as they reap and gather wheat and American astronauts land on the moon.

## CLARE NÍ AONGHUSA

**Four Houses And A Marriage**
Poolbeg pb £6.99 1853717703

This is a well-crafted novel which focusses on the troubled life of its central character Sinead. Her marriage and her relationship with her parents are falling apart, her employment is threatened and her aunt, to whom she was close, dies. She tries to escape to London but is forced to realise that she has to face problems rather than running away from them.

## EDNA O'BRIEN

Edna O'Brien was born in Co. Clare and moved to London in 1957. Between 1960 and 1963, she established her literary career with the publication of what now has become known as the Country Girls Trilogy (**The Country Girls**, **The Girl with Green Eyes** and **Girls in their Married Bliss**). All three were banned in Ireland on first publication. Over thirty years later, these novels are still incredibly fresh and provide an acute and important insight into the lives of women in Ireland of the 1950s. O'Brien's main themes concern women in Ireland having to deal with the oppressive forces of chauvinism, loneliness and despair. She also has a great gift for the short story and has written very successfully in that genre. She has also published a critical, documentary journey around Ireland with photographs by Fergus Bourke, **Mother Ireland**. In the 1990s, her themes have become more overtly political; **The House of Splendid Isolation** is the story of a republican terrorist who commandeers a house and the relationship that develops between him and the woman who owns the house. Her last novel, **Down by the River,** deals with the emotional and psychological horror of incestuous abuse.

**August Is A Wicked Month**
Penguin pb £4.99 0140027203
**The Country Girls**
Penguin pb £5.99 0140018514
**The Country Girls Trilogy**
Penguin pb £9.99 0140109846
**Down By The River**
Phoenix House pb £5.99
1857998731
**The Girl With Green Eyes**
Penguin pb £6.99 0140021086
**Girls In Their Married Bliss**
Penguin pb £5.99 0140026495

**The High Road**
Penguin pb £5.99 0140113266
**The House of Splendid Isolation**
Phoenix House pb £5.99
1857992091
**Lantern Slides**
Penguin pb £6.99 0140130179
**Mrs Reinhardt & Other Stories**
Penguin pb £4.99 0140051287
**Some Irish Loving: A Selection**
Penguin pb £6.30 0140049827
**Time & Tide**
Penguin pb £5.99 014017107X

"My father coughed a little to let them know that he was there, and he passed them cigarettes two or three times, but they did not include him in the conversation because he was in the habit of saying stupid things. Finally he played ludo with Declan, and I was sorry for him."
Edna O'Brien – The Country Girls

Anne Enright author of The Wig My Father Wore, writes about Flann O'Brien's novel The Third Policeman and what it means to her

If the devil were a civil servant, his name would be Flann O'Brien. I come from several hundred generations of civil servants, and he is like a disreputable uncle to me – I don't want to talk about him to people outside the family. I don't want to wonder at his brilliance, or regret that it was so stained by drink. I cannot lionise him or his life and I only love him, simply and entirely, when I open his books.

Flann O'Brien has done a lot of damage to Irish writers. After him, we are all expected to be drunk. After him, drunkenness is a witty, heroic and deeply literary state. Of course there are many drunks, but there is only one Flann O'Brien.

His influence is everywhere. An American teacher complained to me that every time his Irish students wanted to be funny, they did this thing. It was hard to describe – a kind of complicated prose, full of ludicrous precision; tortured by inversions, asides and mock lyricism. I realised that, for us, 'funny' means 'like Flann O'Brien' – for many years Flann O'Brien was what funny is for the Irish. Except of course, no one is as funny as he was.

I first read *The Third Policeman* on a beach in Crete. My copy is smudged with suntan oil, and sand falls out of the creases. I discovered while reading it that there is nothing so foolish as laughing out loud while surrounded by topless German families. There is nothing so stupid as failing to go for a swim and getting sunburned, because you can't do anything until after the last page. This is not a beach book.

*The Third Policeman* is my favourite Flann O'Brien novel probably because it was rejected by every publisher he sent it to. He later claimed that it had been blown, page by page, from the back seat of his car on a journey from Donegal to Dublin. In those days, it has to be said, there were many reasons for a writer to resort to the porter.

His first book *At-Swim-Two-Birds* is crammed full of everything he had in his head: all his ideas and hopes; all his brilliance, and not a little showing off. It has three different openings and more endings. Written in several different styles, and parodies of styles, it has a structure as complicated as a snail shell inside a Russian doll inside a Chinese box. It sank like a stone.

But out of this generous, wonderful, confusion came the simple thing that is *The Third Policeman;* a distilled, more essential version of what Flann O'Brien was all about. His obsessions and affections are all there, for the pettiness of the bureaucrat, the pedant, and the policeman; for the large, helpless thoughts of small men in the face of the universe.

The narrator is a harmless sort of murderer, who enters strange territory when he tries to put his hands on the corpse's money. It is a country where time and weather can be arbitrarily adjusted, roads are either with you or against you. In it he meets the mysterious Sergeant Pluck who wears, over the tight collar of his tunic 'a red ring of fat fresh and decorative as if it had come directly from the laundry.' His constable MacCruiskeen invents, in his spare time, rooms full of eternity and colours that make you mad just to look at them. Both policemen have decided, fairly cheerfully, to hang our friend, when they get round to it.

O'Brien parodies various styles, from academic footnotes to lyrical Irish descriptions of landscape. The problem is that the parodies are better than the originals, his sentences are just too well made. His aversion to cliché makes what he describes always new and therefore moving. You could say he had his pint and drank it: the book is full of the kind of truth that comes out of really good writing.

*The Third Policeman* is among other things a love letter to the bicycle. Due to the exchange of atoms with their owners' backsides, the bicycles in this book are half human and the men are on their way to being bicycles. How can you tell how far gone a man might be? 'He will lean against the wall with his elbow out and stay like that all night in his kitchen instead of going to bed. If he walks too slowly or stops in the middle of the road he will fall down in a heap and will have to be lifted and set in motions again by some extraneous party.'

The only female character in the book is also a bicycle, for which, much thanks. O'Brien could never do women, perhaps because they were not allowed in the back room of his local, the Palace Bar. But it is too easy to get uppity – a more tender description of a bicycle would be hard to find as it rests on its 'prim flawless tyres with irreproachable precision, two tiny points of clean contact with the level floor.' Her two handlebars 'float finely with the wild grace of alighting wings', her saddle is 'hard with a noble hardness'. It sounds quite male to me, especially the bit about the pump, but anyone who has ever ridden a bike will recognise how 'she' moves beneath him 'with an agile sympathy in a swift, airy stride, finding smooth ways among the stony tracks, swaying and bending skillfully to match (my) changing attitudes.'

There is such an ache in all this – in the bad joke of a woman as bicycle; in the fond joke of a man falling in love with a Raleigh three-speed – it makes me wish that this disreputable uncle had a better life. *The Third Policeman* is an innocent book, or a kind book. O'Brien later plundered it for *The Dalkey Archive,* which did get published in his lifetime, but by then, you feel, he wasn't so simply delighted by the contents of his head.

An untransmitted interview in the RTE archives shows him later in life, blithered, pompous and stupid with drink; the kind of drunk you avoid even when you are boiling over with insight and porter. The person who showed it to me wanted to transmit it for a laugh. They wanted to show up the marvellous Irish Literary tradition for that it really was. I was so saddened; because they hated books, because they could not see, through all the slurring, that he was a better man nor any of us.

## FLANN O' BRIEN (1911–1966)

Born in Co. Tyrone, Flann O'Brien (real name Brian O'Nolan) was educated at Blackrock College and at UCD, where he was very active in the college debating society. In 1935, he joined the Civil Service, and in 1939 published his first novel **At Swim Two Birds**. Although critically well received, including notice by James Joyce, it was a commercial failure. In 1940, he started writing his Cruiskeen Lawn column for the Irish Times, thus inventing the character, Myles na gCopaleen. This column started out written in Irish but gradually became English through a series of linguistic metamorphoses. These pieces are collected in **The Best of Myles**. For the next twenty years, most of his fame grew out of this column, and then in 1964, **At Swim Two Birds** was republished to great success. A novel he had written in Irish, An Béal Bocht was published in translation in 1964 as **The Poor Mouth**. **The Dalkey Archive** was published in 1964. O'Brien died of cancer in 1966. A posthumous publication of **The Third Policeman** followed, a novel which had failed to find a publisher in the 1940s when it had first been written. All of O'Brien's work displays his satiric and inventive genius. He satirised the Catholic Church, the Irish government and most other figures of authority that he felt should be targeted. He is one of the few figures in Irish writing that has matched huge popularity with a very sophisticated literary output.

**At Swim Two Birds**
Penguin pb £6.99 0140181725
**Best of Myles Na Gopaleen**
Harper Collins pb £6.99
0586089500
**The Dalkey Archive**
Harper Collins pb £5.99
0586089535
**The Hard Life**
Harper Collins pb £5.99
0586089519
**The Third Policeman**
Harper Collins pb £5.99
0586087494
**The Poor Mouth**
Harper Collins pb £4.99
0586087486
**Rhapsody In Stephens Green:
The Insect Play**
Lilliput Press pb £5.99
1874675279

## Flann O'Brien
## Criticism

**Conjuring Complexities: Essays On Flann O'Brien**
**Anne Clune/Tess Hurson**
Institute Of Irish Studies pb
£12.50 0853896755

## KATE O'BRIEN (1897–1974)

Kate O'Brien was born in Cork and educated at UCD. Her first novel, **Without My Cloak**, was published in 1931. Her fame came in 1934 with the publication of **The Ante-Room** and in 1936 with the publication of **Mary Lavelle**. Both novels examine women's sexuality and the choices that different women have to make. The central character of **The Ante-Room** chooses abstinence, while in **Mary Lavelle**, the eponymous heroine explores her own sexuality. The latter was banned. In 1941 she published **The Land of Spices**, which is the story of a nun who has to deal with finding out about her father's homosexuality, thus reflecting on her life and faith. This was also banned. In 1943 **The Last of Summer** was published and **That Lady** in 1946. This novel is set in Spain and is the story of the relationship between Anna de Mendoza and Phillip II. It demonstrates O'Brien's comfort in looking outside Ireland for inspiration.

**The Ante-Room**
Virago pb £6.99 0860688259
**The Land Of Spices**
Virago pb £6.99 0860688267
**Mary Lavelle**
Virago pb £5.99 0860684288
**That Lady**
Virago pb £7.99 0860684334
**Without My Cloak**
Virago pb £5.99 0860687600

Kate O'Brien

## GARETH O'CALLAGHAN

**Dare To Die**
Poolbeg pb £5.99 1853716359

Popular RTE radio presenter O'Callaghan has written this very effective thriller. Set in London it explores the life of Jamie Carroll, a life that is about to get very complicated. As her relationship with her policeman boyfriend is fizzling out, a chance finding makes her realise that she is very much alone in a big dangerous city.

## BRENDAN O'CARROLL

Hugely popular comedian and actor Brendan O'Carroll has written a trilogy revolving around his finely drawn and good humoured character Agnes Brown. In **The Mammy**, we meet Agnes recovering from the death of her husband and wondering how she is going to make ends meet. **The Chisellers**, set three years later, sees her moved out of Dublin city to the new suburb of Finglas, and concentrates on the lives of her six children. In the final part of the trilogy, **The Granny**, Agnes has to deal with her French lover, her new grandchildren and the gradual dispersal of their family. These three novels are written with great compassion and humour. He has recently written a thriller, **Sparrow's Trap**, whose central character, Sparrow McCabe, an ex-boxer who never made it to the World Title, is now working for gangster Simon Williams.

**The Chisellers**
O'Brien Press pb £5.99
086278414X
**The Granny**
O'Brien Press pb £5.99
0862784891
**The Mammy**
O'Brien Press pb £5.99
0862783720
**Sparrow's Trap**
O'Brien Press pb £5.99
0862785383

## FRANK O'CONNOR (1903–1966)

Throughout his career, Frank O'Connor worked as a novelist, a translator, and a lecturer, but it is his over thirty collections of stories that have cemented his reputation as a masterful short story writer. O'Connor's childhood was dominated by his mother, as his soldier father was often absent. This situation is reflected in many of his stories where he uses the innocence of a child narrator to examine the hardships of adult life. In **My Oedipus Complex**, O'Connor humorously explores a boy's readjustment when his father returns after a long absence at war. While at first viewing the father as a rival for his mother's affection, the boy begins to realise the difficulty they all are having adjusting to this new life. Having left school at an early age, O'Connor came under the guidance of Daniel Corkery, who was responsible for encouraging his strong nationalist beliefs. O'Connor's republican politics led to his internment in 1923. In his first collection of stories, **Guests of the Nation** (1931), O'Connor's disillusionment with the unquestioning obedience of soldiers is examined. Here he tells the story of two IRA soldiers guarding British prisoners the night before the prisoners' executions. This gripping story uncovers the underlying humanity of people which crosses political divides. **The Collected Stories of Frank O'Connor** provides the best overview of his works and displays why O'Connor is so highly regarded in the short story genre.

**Collected Stories**
Henry Holt pb £14.99 0394710487
**Guests of the Nation**
Poolbeg pb £4.95 0905169891
**My Oedipus Complex & Other Stories**
Penguin pb £6.99 0140188193
**An Only Child**
Blackstaff Presspb £6.95 1850856405213 (memoir)

Frank O'Connor

## CLAIRE O'CONNOR

**Love In Another Room**
Marino pb £8.99 1860230199
This is a well-drawn novel, involving many characters and different locations including London, Crete and St. Petersburg. Exploring the problems of love, the novel's many characters include Billie, the Irish landlady who is having an affair with her best friend's son, and Susan, the recently jilted Cockney nurse.

## GEMMA O'CONNOR

Gemma O'Connor writes very well-told thrillers and murder mysteries. **Sins of Omission** is set in Dublin and London and revolves around the character of Brid Lacey. Her **Farewell to the Flesh** explores the consequences of the unveiling of a convent secret as a lead casket is uncovered during the exhumations of the cemetery. Tess Callaway, the lawyer leading the investigation suddenly finds herself in great danger.

**Falls The Shadow**
Poolbeg pb £5.99 1853716057
**Sins of Omission**
Poolbeg pb £4.99 1853715344

## JOSEPH O'CONNOR (b.1963)

Born in South Dublin Joseph O'Connor was educated at Blackrock College and at University College, Dublin. Since 1991, he has written three novels, a collection of short stories, four works of non-fiction, two plays and three screenplays. He wrote a weekly column for the Sunday Tribune in Dublin for three years. **Cowboys and Indians**, his first novel centres around Eddie Virago, who we meet as he is on his way to London from Dublin to make it big as a rock star. Wisely describing the experiences of the immigrant Irish in London but never lapsing into cliché, O'Connor created one of the most memorable Irish heroes of the decade. **Desperadoes**, is set in Dublin and Nicaragua and tells the story of estranged parents going to bring back the body of their son killed in the Contra War. As always, the author's gift for ironic comment on everyday situations comes to the fore. **The Salesman** tells the story of Billy Sweeney, TV salesman turned vigilante after his daughter is attacked in the garage where she works and ends up in a coma. He stalks his daughter's attacker but his plans for vengeance go horribly wrong. This violent story is very effectively intercut with the tender and poignant story of Sweeney's courtship, marriage and eventual separation from his wife.

### Fiction
**Cowboys & Indians**
Harper Collins pb £5.99 0006544584
**Desperadoes**
Flamingo pb £5.99 0006546978
**The Salesman**
Secker pb £9.99 0436202654
**True Believers**
Harper Collins pb £5.99 0006544754

### Drama
**Red Roses & Petrol**
Methuen pb £6.99 0413699900

## MARY O'DONNELL

**The Virgin & The Boy**
Poolbeg pb £6.99 1853715573
Poet and broadcaster O'Donnell's most recent novel is a rock 'n' roll story which centres on Virgin (Ginnie Maloney) an up and coming singer, who falls passionately in love with Luke O'Regan, a boy fourteen years her junior. Well drawn characters and vivid description mark this engaging novel.

## Non-Fiction

**The Secret World of the Irish Male** is a satiric examination of contemporary Irish life, culminating in O'Connor's hilarious 1994 World Cup diary which skillfully recreates the dream/nightmare of an Irish soccer fan-infested Orlando (New Island pb £6.99 1874597146). It was followed by **The Irish Male at Home and Abroad** (New Island pb £6.99 1874597421) which, as the title suggests, is a look at Irish behaviour overseas and includes wry accounts of trips to London, Australia, Nicaragua and Italy. His travel book **Sweet Liberty: Travels In Irish America** (Picador pb £5.99 0330333232) is the result of a mission to visit all of the towns called Dublin in America. The author realised quickly that many of the places in between the 'Dublins' were a lot more Irish and interesting but he soldiered on and the result is a fun trip through Irish-American history and culture.

## PEADAR O'DONNELL
### (1893–1986)

Born in Co. Donegal, Peadar O'Donnell was one of the founding editors of *The Bell*. His book **The Big Windows** is a moving novel which explores the difficulties faced by Tom Manus as he brings his new wife from her island home to his small community on the mainland.

**The Big Windows**
O'Brien Press pb £3.95
086278090X
**Proud Island**
O'Brien Press pb £3.95
0862780934

## GERALD O'DONOVAN
**Father Ralph**
Brandon pb £6.95 0863221742
Gerald O' Donovan was born in 1871 and became a priest. In 1904, he left the priesthood and went toLondon. He was closely involved with the Irish Literary Revival. His novel **Father Ralph** first published in 1913, tells the story of the life and difficulties of a young priest in Ireland at the turn of the century and is a valuable insight into the Catholic psyche of the time.

## SEAN O'FAOLAIN
### (1900–1991)

Sean O'Faolain was born in Cork and educated at UCC. Following the British treatment of the Republican leaders, he joined the republican side in the Civil War. Within a few years, he had become dissatisfied with the movement and left. This time in his life is recorded in his memoir **Vive Moi** and in his short stories **Midsummer Night Madness & Other Stories**. He will probably be most remembered for his founding and editing of *The Bell*, the literary and cultural monthly magazine, which ran from 1940 to the mid 1950s. He was editor for the first six years, and published many writers such as Brendan Behan, Patrick Kavanagh and Frank O'Connor. *The Bell* was also a great centre for progressive literary and cultural debate.

Sean O'Faolain

**Heat of The Sun**
Penguin pb £7.99 014018340X
**Midsummer Night Madness**
Penguin pb £7.99 0140183396

## KATHLEEN O'FARRELL
**The Fiddler of Kilbroney**
Brandon pb £7.95 0863221777
This is a well-researched and stylishly written novel about the ordinary people of Ireland in the run up to the 1798 rebellion.

# LIAM O'FLAHERTY (1896–1984)

Born on Inishmore, the largest of the Aran Islands, Liam O'Flaherty was educated at Rockwell College in Cashel, Co. Tipperary, where he completed some of his studies to join the Holy Ghost Fathers. He left however, in 1915, to join the Irish Guards and was wounded in 1917 in France. His experience of shell shock was used for his novel **Black Soul**, in which the shell shocked central character seduces a married woman on the island of Inverara (Inishmore), whose husband then goes mad. O'Flaherty's most famous works was a trilogy of historical novels **Famine**, **Land** and **Insurrection**, which deal respectively with the Great Famine, the Land Wars and the 1916 Rising.

**The Assassin**
Wolfhound Press pb £4.99
0863273688
**Black Soul**
Wolfhound Press pb £6.99
0863274781
**Famine**
Wolfhound Press pb £6.99
0863270433
**Insurrection**
Wolfhound Press pb £4.99
0863273750
**Mr Gilhooley**
Wolfhound Press pb £4.99
0863272894
**Thy Neighbour's Wife**
Wolfhound Press pb £5.99
0863273289
**Short Stories**
Wolfhound Press pb £6.99
0863275362
**Wilderness**
Wolfhound Press pb £6.99
0863275346

# VICTOR O'REILLY

**Games of the Hangman** is a well crafted and exciting thriller set in Ireland and Switzerland. Retired soldier Hugo Fitzduane, finds a hanged body on his island home. His search to uncover the mystery leads him to Switzerland and a deadly game of cat and mouse with 'The Hangman' a ruthless terrorist. O'Reilly's other equally stylish thriller is **Games of Vengeance**.

**Games of The Hangman**
Headline pb £5.99 0747238677
**Games of Vengeance**
Headline pb £5.99 0747242224

# SHEILA O'FLANAGAN

**Dreaming of a Stranger**
Poolbeg pb £5.99 1853716847
**Dreaming of a Stranger** is a well-told romantic novel revolving around Jane O'Sullivan, whose dreams of love and marriage are shattered by reality.

# TIMOTHY O'GRADY

**I Could Read The Sky**
Harvill pb £14.99 1860463185
This is a powerfully elliptical novel which illustrates with snatches of memory the harsh, bleak lives of many Irish emigrants to England this century. What could have been a 500 page family saga, has been beautifully and deftly pared down to a poetic meditation on love, loss, death and family. The haunting monochrome images by photographer Steve Pyke, form a second narrative woven through the text and serve to counter-point and complement the spare beauty of the prose.

## JOAN O'NEILL

**Leaving Home**
Hodder pb £5.99 0340694963
Joan O'Neill, well known author of the 'Daisy Chain' books for teenagers has written an engaging romantic novel for adults. **Leaving Home** tells the story of three friends, born in a Co. Wicklow village who leave to go to the city, and how their lives pan out.

## DAVID PARK (b.1954)

This Belfast born novelist and short story writer has skilfully managed to write novels set in contemporary Northern Ireland which don't deal explicitly with sectarian violence, but examine closely the feelings and mood of his characters, who have grown up with this background strife.

**Oranges From Spain**
Phoenix £5.99 pb 1857990013
**The Healing**
Phoenix £4.99 pb 0857990951
**Rye Man**
Phoenix £5.99 pb 1857993551
**Stone Kingdoms**
Phoenix £5.99 pb 1857998820

## GLENN PATTERSON

Patterson has written three novels. **Burning Your Own** revolves around the Northern Irish troubles but from a Protestant point of view. **Fat Lad** is set mainly in a Belfast bookshop and is a very accurate portrayal of family lives and tensions. The Fat Lad of the title is the family goldfish whose name is made up from the initial letters of the counties of Northern Ireland. His last novel **Black Night at Big Thunder Mountain** is set in Euro-Disney in Paris and revolves around a kidnapping and bomb threat on the mountain ride of the title.

**Black Night At Big Thunder Mountain**
Minerva pb £6.99 074939563X
**Burning Your Own**
Minerva pb £6.99 0749398914
**Fat Lad**
Minerva pb £5.99 0749398906

## KATE O'RIORDAN

Born in West of Ireland and now living in London, Kate O'Riordan has written two novels. **Involved** is a fascinating love story-cum-thriller which describes the love between Kitty Fitzgerald and Danny O'Neill and how it changes when Kitty meets Danny's Northern Irish family and realises how intimately 'involved' the O'Neills are in the Northern troubles. **The Boy in the Moon** is a frighteningly disturbing novel of hidden family history. Julia, having left her husband Brian following an accident caused by his awful negligence, goes to live at Brian's family home. She slowly uncovers his family's repressed past from his hostile father and his schoolfriend Cathal.

**The Boy In The Moon**
HarperCollins pb £5.99
0006550533
**Involved**
HarperCollins pb £5.99
0006547613

# TERRY PRONE

Well known communications consultant Terry Prone has written a book of short stories, **Blood Brothers, Soul Sisters**, and more recently a novel, **Racing the Moon**. The latter is the racy story of two sisters, both enjoying successful international careers, both falling for the charms of the same man and ultimately united by family tragedy.

**Blood Brothers, Soul Sisters**
Poolbeg pb £6.99 185371402X
**Racing The Moon**
Marino pb £7.99 1860230628

# DEIRDRE PURCELL

Immensely popular both at home and abroad, Deirdre Purcell has written six novels. Her debut, **A Place of Stones,** is the story of Molly O'Brien, rescued from an aircrash as a baby and brought up on the island of Inisheer. Now a successful actress, she explores her family's past and finds a dark secret she should have left alone. **That Childhood Country** is the story of separated lovers, heiress Rose O'Brien Moffat and John Flynn whose poverty forces him to emigrate to Canada. **Falling for a Dancer** is the story of Elizabeth O'Sullivan, stuck in an arranged marriage on the Béara peninsula, who falls for the charm of the dancer George. The story is continued in **Francey**, where the eponymous hero, son to Elizabeth and George goes in search of his father and finds more that he bargained for. **Sky** sees Purcell setting her writing farther afield and offers a change of style. Sky McPherson is a newspaper reporter in Montana. An obituary she writes leads to a murder investigation. The novel makes great use of suspense. Purcell's latest novel **Love, Like, Hate, Adore** is more serious as it tackles the difficult theme of incest head on. The main character Angela Devine has to deal with the fact that her brother has been accused and has to ask herself the impossible question of whether he could be guilty or not.

**Falling For A Dancer**
Town House pb £5.99
0948524855
**Francey**
Town House pb £5.99
0948524987
**Love Like Hate Adore**
Town House hb £5.99
1860590454

**A Place of Stones**
Town House pb £4.99
0948524340
**Sky**
Town House pb £5.99
1860590225
**That Childhood Country**
Town House pb £5.99
0948524634

# PATRICK QUIGLEY
**Borderland**
Brandon pb £7.95 0863221793
**Borderland** is a moving novel whose main theme is sectarianism in the border counties of Ireland. Quigley is a great stylist, employing a very clever imagistic motif of memory in which a mantle-piece photo of a boy soldier is replaced by one of John F. Kennedy.

# JOHN QUINN
**Generations of the Moon**
Poolbeg pb £4.99 1853715522
John Quinn in his **Generations of the Moon** traces the lives of twins, Brian and Hannah Johnston, separated at birth after the death of their mother in 1926. Brian is raised a Catholic by his mother's family while Hannah is raised as a Protestant by her father and her aunt. Quinn's powerful story is told in light of the emergence of two states on the island of Ireland.

## KEITH RIDGEWAY

**The Long Falling**
Faber pb £9.99 0571191711
Dublin-based writer
Ridgeway's acclaimed debut
is the story of Grace Quinn,
forced to choose between her
brutal husband and another
man, following the death of
her son. Set in Dublin in the
early 1990s, Ridgeway's book
also provides sharp political
and historical context.

## MOYA RODDY

**Long Way Home**
Attic pb £5.99 1855940396
**Long Way Home** is the story
of Jo Nowd, a working class
girl determined to be
successful as a dress designer
in 1960s Ireland. The novel
explores the difficulties faced
by people trying to fit into
parts of society where they
feel they don't belong.

## FRANK RONAN
### (b.1963)

Born in Ireland in 1963,
Frank Ronan now lives in
England. He has written five
novels and a collection of
short stories. Like many
writers of his generation he
has found inspiration and
subject matter far away from
the Ireland in which he grew
up. His last novel **Lovely** is
based in London and Goa
where the author has spent a
lot of time and tells the story
of Aaron Gunn, who falls
hopelessly in love at a rave.
The ensuing relationship is a
disaster and Ronan, as in
other work, is not shy about
describing the squalor of love
and lust.

**Dixie Chicken**
Sceptre pb £6.99 0340632445
**Handsome Men Are Slightly
Sunburnt**
Sceptre pb £5.99 0340660759
**Lovely**
Sceptre pb £6.99 0340660767

## JAMES RYAN

Born in Co. Laois and
educated in Trinity College,
Dublin, James Ryan is now a
teacher. He has written two
novels which have been very
well received. **Home from
England** is a warm look at the
awful experience of coming
home and expecting to pick
up pieces of a previous life.
Written from the perspective
of a young boy growing up in
1960s rural Ireland, the novel
is poignant, funny and
compassionate. **Dismantling
Mr Doyle** is a wry portrait of a
conservative patriarch
realising that the moral and
social values for which he has
lived have not been accepted
by his family in a modern
world very different to the
one he knows.

**Dismantling Mr Doyle**
Phoenix House pb
£9.991861590857
**Home From England**
Phoenix House pb £5.99
1857998006

## LIZ RYAN

Well-known features editor and columnist with the Dublin Evening Herald, Liz Ryan has written three very successful novels. Although all three have been praised for their escapist quality and easy readability, Ryan does deal with many serious themes and, with her journalist's eye for detail, examines many issues which face young people in contemporary Irish society. **Blood Lines** is the story of Kerry Laraghy who has no interest in the life that her family have planned for her. **A Note of Parting** describes the experiences of Aran Campion, a young woman who has to escape from the rural Irish fishing village where she was born and go to London.

**Blood Lines**
Coronet pb £5.99 0340624566
**A Note of Parting**
Coronet pb £5.99 0340624582
**A Taste of Freedom**
Coronet pb £9.99 0340716983

## MARY RYAN

Popular novelist Mary Ryan has written a number of well-crafted romantic novels. **The Promise** is a novel of self-realisation which starts in Florence where Colm meets Robin, an elusive and mysterious American girl, during his student days who makes him promise to meet her in Florence on his 50th birthday. **Shadows from the Fire** revolves around the life of Polly Caine, Fine Art graduate and dissatisfied housewife. After placing an ad in a lonely hearts column, she rejects all of the many offers but one. She goes to London to explore this option and discovers a whole new life.

**Mask of the Night**
Headline pb £5.99 0747245215
**The Promise**
Headline pb £6.99 0747220476
**The Seduction of Mrs Caine**
Headline pb £5.99 0747251304
**Shadows From The Fire**
Headline pb £5.99 0747246823
**Summer's End**
Headline pb £5.99 0747251290
**Whispers In The Wind**
Basement pb £4.99
1855941864

## PATRICIA SCANLAN

Highly successful Dublin born novelist, who has been at the forefront of Irish popular fiction since the publication of **City Girls** in 1990. While all of her novels are unashamedly romantic in theme, Scanlan does mix in real life issues to which many people can relate. For example, **Foreign Affairs** looks at a beach holiday taken by four women together who realise during the time spent together how unhappy they have been before and also come to understand how much their lives will change.

**Apartment 3b**
Poolbeg pb £5.99 1853711365
**City Girl**
Poolbeg pb £5.99 1853710725
**City Woman**
Poolbeg pb £5.99 1853712760
**Finishing Touches**
Poolbeg pb £5.99 1853711861
**Foreign Affairs**
Poolbeg pb £5.99 1853714461
**Mirror Mirror**
Poolbeg hb £6.99 1853717673
**Promises Promises**
Poolbeg pb £5.99 1853717363

## ANNE SCHULMAN

Anne Schulman's **Chapter & Hearse** is a well plotted, page turning murder mystery set behind the scenes in the publishing industry. Her next novel, **Intrigue**, is a globe trotting mystery which takes the reader from Las Vegas to Paris, tying up the mysterious links between five strangers.

**Chapter & Hearse**
Poolbeg pb £5.99 1853717800
**Encounters**
Poolbeg pb £5.99 1853714585
**Intrigue**
Poolbeg pb £4.99 1853713368

## GAYE SHORTLAND

Cork-born Gaye Shortland has spent many years living in Africa. Her latest novel **Polygamy** is set in French Niger and is a story of betrayal and the inherent difficulties in the mixing of totally foreign cultures. Her first novel, **Mind That Is My Brother** is narrated by Tony, the spirit of a man who died of AIDS. Both humorous and magical but dealing candidly with gay sexuality, Tony's story is continued in **Turtles All the Way Down** which is also a mix of gender exploration and celebration of life.

**Mind That Is My Brother**
Poolbeg pb £5.99 1853714216
**Polygamy**
Poolbeg pb £6.99 1853718521
**Turtles All The Way Down**
Poolbeg pb £6.99 1853716995

## SOMERVILLE & ROSS

Edith Somerville and her cousin 'Martin Ross' (Violet Martin) founded a literary partnership in 1889 with the publication of their first book **An Irish Cousin**. Their most famous and successful books however, were **The Real Charlotte** (1894) and **The Irish RM** [first published as two volumes, **Some Experiences of an Irish R.M** (1899) & **Further Experiences of an Irish R.M** (1908)] which explore late 19th Century Anglo-Irish relations with great irony and humour. **The Irish RM** chronicles the experiences of Major Sinclair Yeates, the Resident Magistrate (RM) in the village of Skebawn. The stories charmingly and astutely illustrate the nuances between the different strata of Anglo-Irish life.

**The Irish RM**
Abacus pb £7.99 0349101469

## BREDA SPAIGHT

**God On The Wall**
Collins pb £6.99 1898256233
**God on the Wall** is a lively look at the hypocrisies of supposedly 'normal' family life seen through the eyes of Elizabeth Wallace, a working class woman who decides to have a child on her own.

James Stephens

## JAMES STEPHENS (1882–1950)

Born in Dublin, James Stephens was educated at an industrial school and was 'discovered' by George Russell (AE) while he was working in a solicitor's office in the city. Russell had read one of Stephens' poems in *Sinn Féin,* Arthur Griffith's paper. Feted by Russell and other writers, he published **The Charwoman's Daughter** and **The Crock of Gold** in 1912. Probably his most famous book, **The Charwoman's Daughter**, chronicles the life of the Dublin slums, with which, while growing up, Stephens would have had intimate acquaintance. Although grim in its description and tone, it is an ultimately uplifting story with great charm. Stephens lived in Paris from 1912 to 1915 where he met James Joyce with whom he became great friends. (Later Joyce proposed that Stephens finish **Finnegans Wake**, a project which Joyce was thinking of relinquishing due to his failing eyesight.) Stephens returned from Paris to Dublin to become the Registrar of the National Gallery and wrote a chronicle of the Easter rising in 1916. Before he left for London in 1922, he translated many Irish folk tales and much Irish poetry. In London, Stephens worked for the BBC where he became a much-admired broadcaster on a wide variety of topics. He died in London.

**The Crock of Gold**
Gill & Macmillan pb £7.99 0717122972
**Irish Fairy Tales**
Gill & Macmillan pb £8.99 0717122980

## BRAM STOKER (1847–1912)

Bram Stoker was born in Dublin and moved to London after a short spell in the Dublin Civil Service. He managed Henry Irving's Lyceum Theatre from 1878 to 1905 and married Florence Balcombe, an early love of Oscar Wilde. His most famous work **Dracula** divides critics as to whether it should fit into the category of 'literature' or 'horror' but it has undoubtedly had a lasting influence on many cultural works (both popular and artistic) since its publication. Many interpretations have been made of Stoker's work. One convincingly clever, if contentious, argument has been put forward that Count Dracula was the first 'absentee landlord' in Irish fiction.

**Dracula**
Orion pb £2.99 0460875981
**Dracula**
Oxford University Press pb £4.99 0192815989
**Dracula**
Brandon Press pb £5.99 0863221432
**Dracula's Guest**
Brandon Press pb £5.99 0863221203
**The Lady of the Shroud**
Sutton pb £5.99 0750906898
**The Lair of the White Worm**
Brandon pb £5.99 0863221246

# FRANCIS STUART (b.1902)

Born in Australia to Irish parents, Francis Stuart's father died just after he was born. His mother returned to Ireland that year and they lived Louth and then in Dublin. He attended various secondary boarding schools in England. He married Iseult Gonne (daughter of Maud Gonne and Major John McBride) in 1920. He fought on the republican side in the Irish Civil War and was imprisoned by the Free State forces only to be released in 1923. He wrote eleven novels in the 1930s and at the end of that decade moved to Berlin to teach English Literature at Berlin Universtity.

He stayed in Berlin for the duration of the Second World War and wrote broadcasts for Nazi propaganda radio. As a result of his sympathies, he was imprisoned by the French after the war. After his release, he lived in Germany and England, only returning to Ireland in 1958. His most famous novel **Black List, Section H** was published in 1971 and was based on his Berlin experience. He was elected to high office of Aosdána in 1997, which caused outcry among certain members of the organisation because of his previous Nazi involvement.

**Black List Section H**
Penguin pb £8.99 0140189262
**Blacklist Section H**
Lilliput Press pb £9.99
1874675414
**Compendium of Lovers**
New Island pb £6.95
1851860770
**Fallandia**
New Island pb £5.95
1851860061
**King David Dances**
New Island pb £5.99
1874597448
**Pillar of Cloud**
New Island pb £5.95
187459709X
**Redemption**
New Island pb £5.95
1874597081

## Poet Paul Durcan looks at Francis Stuart's extraordinary, controversial masterpiece.

**Even unto Mount Sion, which is Hermon.**
**Deut: 4. 48.**

**Behold how good and how pleasant it is for brethren to dwell together in unity! As the dew of Hermon falling on the heights of Sion.**
**Ps. 133: 1,3.**

Two of the greatest Irish novels of the century, *Ulysses* and *Black List, Section H*, share specific, fundamental affinities. Each has for the central character an individual who is preoccupied with the Jewish imagination; and each is devoted to the minutiae of quotidian existence. It is, however, when we acknowledge their dissimilarities that we recognise the surprising but perhaps inevitably austerer gravitas and quietude of *Black List, Section H* in terms of style and content.

Aesthetically magical as are the rhetorical and lyrical devices of *Ulysses,* these lack the rectitude of the more wrought, conscience-driven prose of *Black List, Section H.* The awkward, angular prose of *Black List, Section H* is an achieved style that took a lifetime of mining in the real world to arrive at; an indispensable tool for the open-cast truthtelling that its author engaged in. The content of *Ulysses* is constrained by its literary apparatus whereas *Black List, Section H* extends our awareness of human nature and attempts a reconciliation between the new man of the New Testament and the old man of the Old Testament.

Narratively *Black List, Section H* is the story of an Irish youth who goes out into the savage wilderness of the 20th century in search of his soul. Interiorly the novel is a microscopically-observed vision in which the archetypal soul-struggle between Jew and Gentile is delineated in unorthodox, super-Bloom mode against the background of the Second World War. The difference between *Black List, Section H* and *Ulysses* is one of technique. Joyce avoids fiction by adhering to the documentary; Stuart utilises fiction in order to transform the documentary.

Stuart's later alter ego, Simeon Grimes, explains his technique: 'I paint what I see, and then only I see what I paint. A point comes when, if all goes well, I no longer look at the sitter, still life or whatever is there, but, concentrating on the canvas, distort what I've done to give it a chance to reflect some of the truth about the subject that I'd missed by direct observation'.

Before they embarked on their Himalayan observations, both Joyce and Stuart would know lifelong ostracism. Since its first publication in 1971 *Black List, Section H* has been blacklisted. In my own life I have met only five people who have read it. Its confrontation with truth is regarded as being too close to the bone; too many taboos get broken. It is seen as being politically and culturally incorrect. Only when the hegemony of Europe and North America passes to Africa and Asia will *Black List, Section H* come into its own and become the best-seller it ought to have become in the year of its original publication. We in Europe and North America seem to have become too genteel for moral, prophetic fiction. Stuart is a hybrid of Blake and Camus: a plant too exotic for cold speleological climes.

The narrative of *Black List, Section H* is circular as well as linear. The book begins with a gilt edged, Rembrandt-like image of a boy seeking sexual consolation from a mattress in an attic in Co. Antrim and it concludes with a similar evocation of a mattress in a prison garden in Austria. In the Jewish-Gentile struggle in *Black List, Section H,* it is the Jewish imagination that supervenes; and in the final pages the promise of the psalmist is fulfilled. Mount Hermon is glimpsed and the two Chagall-like lovers (the woman is surnamed Vitebsk, after the painter's birthplace) have no more need of coition; having gone beyond the ecstasy of copulation into the tranquility of salvation in affection.

In the literature of Europe *Black List, Section H's* kindred novel is *Dr Zhivago*. Both novels became casualties of propaganda. Pasternak, 'most wonderful of lyric poets', produced an embarrassingly awful novel which western critics for propaganda purposes hailed as a masterpiece. Stuart, 'a poet in prose', produced a genuine masterpiece which for propaganda purposes was condemned.

Stuart's project was almost identical to Pasternak's: to demonstrate the primacy, first, of the individual over history in the person of Christ; and, secondly, of the Jewishness of Christ. Stuart restored Mount Hermon as man's ultimate destiny and he recreated Christ's mentors as the old prophets in the guise of displaced twentieth century Jews: Dr. Weiss, Julia Jenners, Mr Davis, Mogadori, Gollancz, and the English diamond smuggler in Vienna, Mr Isaacs: 'Mr Isaacs revealed just those kinds of intimate things H was concerned to discover'. In the end 'in his resolution of the patricidal conflict between Jew and Gentile' Stuart reveals the feminine as the source of reconciliation with the murdered father. Like Zhivago, Stuart's central character H, transpires to be Hamlet: 'to live your life is not as simple as to cross a field.'

Stuart's twentieth century testament is founded on the ancient Jewish belief in the preeminence of the Word: the unspoken epigraph is Holderlin's, ' Linguistically, man dwelleth on earth' or the psalmist's, 'In God I will praise the word'

Now that Penguin Books and The Lilliput Press have had the good sense to re-issue *Black List, Section H,* albeit in editions that are in need of punctilious editing, new generations may read it. One of the fascinating aspects of the blacklisting of *Black List, Section H* has been that few of its defenders, and fewer of its detractors have ever themselves had the nerve to read the novel.

Having conquered his Mount Everest with *Black List, Section H* Stuart went on to write his classic trilogy of love, war and art in the 1970s: *Memorial, A Hole in the Head* and *The High Consistory*. It is to be hoped that Penguin will now have the extra good sense to re-issue the trilogy to keep its rightful company on the bookshelves with *Black List, Section H.*

## BARRY SWAN

**The Deserted Village**
Valley pb £4.99 0953076806
Barry Swan's novel, **The Deserted Village** is set in 1967, in a changing Dublin and examines the difficulties faced by rural communities settling in the new city.

## EAMON SWEENEY (b.1968)

Sligo-born Sweeney, now living and working in Dublin has written an important first novel **Waiting for the Healer**. The novel details the difficulties that Paul Kelly (now living in London) experiences in trying to solve the mystery of his brother's death in his hometown in Ireland. This is also probably the first Irish novel that deals with working class urban life outside Dublin. The realistically harsh world of drink, drugs, and fights in both settled and travelling communities is a far cry from postcard towns normally associated with the West of Ireland. This is no political tract however, and Sweeney has written a powerful story about familial and social relationships which also manages to capture a side of Irish life which has been ignored by many parts of our society. **There's Only One Red Army** is the story of Sweeney's own obsession with and love for Sligo Rovers and wittily narrates how he went to his first football match while still in his mother's womb. The memoir also movingly pictures the life of despair which goes with following a constantly losing team coupled with the despair of a life racked with alcohol abuse.

**Waiting For The Healer**
Picador pb £6.99 0330350307
**There's Only One Red Army**
New Island pb £7.99 1874597480

## JONATHAN SWIFT
### (1667–1745)

**Gulliver's Travels**, after **Ulysses,** is probably the most famous Irish novel, written when Swift was serving as dean to St. Patrick's Cathedral in Dublin and published in 1726. It is narrated in the first person, by the eponymous surgeon, Lemuel Gulliver, who travelled to fantastical places such as Lilliput (inhabited by tiny people), Brobdingnag (a land of giants) and the land of the Houyhnhnms (a society ruled by horses). Because of the element of fantasy throughout the book, it has been retold for children throughout the years although it was clearly written as a political and moral satire, by the acerbic and acute pen of a man who was highly critical of both Irish and English society.

**Gulliver's Travels**
Penguin pb £2.50 0140430229

## NEVILLE THOMPSON

**Jackie Loves Johnser OK?**
Poolbeg pb £5.99 1853718807
In **Jackie Loves Johnser O.K.?,** Neville Thompson has written a believable thriller set in Ballyfermot and revolving around the lives of Johnser Kelly and Jackie Clark, a couple who should have got together but didn't.

## COLM TÓIBÍN (b.1955)

Born in Enniscorthy, Colm Tóibín has become a significant novelist, journalist and cultural commentator. His non-fiction work prefigures and complements much of the fiction dealing with Irish politics (**Walking along the Border** 1987), European cultural identity (**Homage to Barcelona**, 1989), wide-ranging journalistic concerns (**The Trial of the Generals**, 1990) and the state and contemporary meaning of Catholicism (**Sign of the Cross**, 1994). These works indicate the breadth of interests which inform the fiction. Far more than any other contemporary Irish writer, Toibin looks outwards too, to Europe and beyond. His debut novel, **The South** (1990), tells the story of an Anglo-Irish painter, Katherine Proctor, who discovers her creative fulfilment through her experiences during the Spanish Civil War. **The South** gives one of the most convincing of descriptions of what it is to create a work of art. It introduces the reader to Toibin's sparse yet lyrical style, in which the horror of an unnnecessary adjective is matched by a quiet serenity of descriptive tone. His second novel, **The Heather Blazing** (1993) explored the political history of Ireland through the character of Eamon Redmond, a High Court judge forced to reassess his life. What is particularly effective is Toibin's sense of landscape. He describes in minute detail the beauty and power of his own Wexford coastline. His most ambitious novel to date is **The Story of the Night** (1996). The novel tackles questions of national identity and sexual awakening through Richard Garay's upbringing in Argentina during the time of the generals. As Garay comes to terms with his homosexuality, Argentina goes to war with Britain and AIDS afflicts a generation. It, too, is written in the cool, exact voice which brings a quiet resonance to all of Toibin's work.

## Fiction

**The Heather Blazing**
Picador pb £5.99 0330321250
**The South**
Picador pb £5.99 0330323334
**The Story of the Night**
Picador pb £6.99 0330340182

## Non-Fiction

**Bad Blood**
Vintage pb £6.99 0099301202
**The Sign of the Cross**
Vintage pb £6.99 0099883007

## WILLIAM TREVOR (b.1928)

Born in Mitchelstown, Co. Cork and now living in Devon, William Trevor is one of the most esteemed and respected living Irish novelists and short story writers. Brought up in Co. Cork and educated at Trinity College, Dublin, he has also written plays for television, many of which are based on his short stories. His 1983 novel, **Fools of Fortune** has been made into a feature film. Since the publication of his first novel **The Old Boys** in 1964, each of his books have received great critical praise and have won many awards including the Whitbread prize for fiction. His novella **Reading Turgenev** (in **Two Lives**) was shortlisted for the Booker Prize in 1991. His **Collected Stories** was published in 1992. His non-fictional prose, containing book reviews and some pieces of memoir, **Excursions in the Real World**, was published in 1995. Trevor's great strength is his poignantly accurate portraits of characters on the outside of their society. Whether it is the more extreme outsider like the paedophile of **The Old Boys** or the despairing wife in a loveless, claustrophobic marriage of **Reading Turgenev**, Trevor can describe and dissect feeling, emotion and situation like few others in contemporary fiction.

## Novels

**After Rain**
Penguin pb £6.99 0140258345
**The Boarding House**
Penguin pb £6.99 0140107495
**Children Of Dynmouth**
Penguin pb £5.99 0140047182
**Elizabeth Alone**
Penguin pb £7.50 0140097562
**Felicia's Journey**
Penguin pb £6.99 0140240241
**Fools Of Fortune**
Penguin pb £5.99 0140111816
**Ireland: Selected Stories**
Penguin pb £6.99 0140242635
**The Love Department**
Penguin pb £6.99 0140031308
**Miss Gomez & The Brethren**
Penguin pb £6.99 0140252649
**Mrs Eckdorf In O'neill's Hotel**
Penguin pb £6.15 0140107487
**The Old Boys**
Penguin pb £6.99 014002428X
**Other People's Worlds**
Penguin pb £6.99 0140106693
**Outside Ireland**
Penguin pb £6.99 0140242627
**Short Stories**
Penguin pb £12.00 014015857X
**Silence In The Garden**
Penguin pb £5.99 0140120653
**Two Lives**
Penguin pb £6.99 0140153721

## Non-fiction
**Excursions In The Real World**
Penguin £5.99 014023845X

## LEON URIS

Leon Uris, who writes epic novels in the style of Jame Michener, has written two political thrillers based around the Irish 'Troubles' in the early 20th Century. Although written for the American market, both are well researched and provide some insight into both sides of the Civil War and War of Independence.

**Redemption**
Harper Collins pb £6.99
0006498957
**Trinity**
Corgi pb £6.99 0552105651

## ELIZABETH WASSELL

**Honey Plain**
Wolfhound Press pb £6.99
0863275958
Probably the first 'Summer School' novel to be written. It tells the story of a poet and the American woman he falls for while teaching at one of the many summer schools that have proliferated in Ireland since the early 1980s. Using the framework of the myth of Diarmuid and Grinne, the lovers race to the Honey Plain followed by the poet's jealous wife.

## ROBERT WELCH

Robert Welch, currently professor of English at the university of Ulster at Coleraine and editor of the magisterial **Oxford Companion to Irish Literature,** has written two novels. **The Kilcolman Notebook** is based on a spirited interlude in the life of the poet Edmund Spenser and his relationship with Ireland. **Groundwork** focusses on two families, the Condons and the O'Dwyers in the province of Munster. In taking the lives of these two families from Elizabethan times to the early twentieth century, Welch has written a moving reflection on the past and the history within every family.

**The Kilcolman Notebook**
Brandon Press £6.99
1863221807
**Groundwork**
Blackstaff Press pb £8.99
0856406082

## OSCAR WILDE

While most of Oscar Wilde's fame rests on his achievements in the field of drama, his fictional work should not be overlooked. **The Happy Prince** (1888) is a collection of five fairy tales (including 'The Selfish Giant). Fable-like in their telling, they mark the point where Aesop meets Hans Christian Anderson through funny, meaningful, and yet suspiciously dark story-telling. In **Lord Arthur Savile's Crime and Other Stories** (1891), Wilde published a collection of stories which had been previously published individually a few years earlier, while **The Picture of Dorian Gray**, Wilde's only novel, was published a year before. The novel is a short, tragic piece about vanity, beauty, and growing old. Its central motif of a painting growing old has passed into everyday speech. Wilde's work always has the ability to amuse, but while the drama often has a basis in social commentary, the fiction deals in more troubling areas – the human soul, the mind – and as such is just as interesting as anything else Wilde has written.

**Complete Shorter Fiction**
Oxford University Press pb
£2.50 0192815008
**Complete Works**
Harper Collins pb £9.99
0004704738
**Complete Works**
Harper Collins hb £14.99
000470472X
**De Profundis & Other Writings**
Penguin pb £4.99 014043089X
**The Picture of Dorian Gray**
Penguin pb £1.99 014043187X
**The Wit & Humour of Oscar Wilde**
Dover pb £4.95 0486206025
**The Portable Oscar Wilde**
Penguin pb £7.99 0140150935

# NIALL WILLIAMS
**Four Letters Of Love**
Picador hb £12.99 0330352687
This book marks an astonishing debut from Niall Williams, a Dublin-born teacher now living in Co. Clare. The novel tells the parallel stories of Isobel Gore and Nicholas Coghlan, two young people destined to meet and fall in love. Throughout the novel, there is also an incredible evocation of the Irish countryside, better than anything similar in recent fiction. Combining love story, myth and a formidably confident stylistic voice, Williams has written a hauntingly beautiful novel which stays with the reader long after it has been read.

# ROBERT MCLIAM WILSON

Born in Belfast in 1964 where he now lives, McLiam Wilson burst on the literary scene in 1989 with the publication of **Ripley Bogle**, whose eponymous hero is a tramp hailing from West Belfast and now living on the streets of London. But Ripley Bogle is nothing like the tramps of other fictions but a spinner and weaver of lyrical observations intercut with haunting memories of his life growing up. The research for the novel led to McLiam Wilson's study of homelessness **The Dispossessed** ( with Donovan Wylie). His latest novel **Eureka Street** is possibly the first 'ceasefire' novel to come out of Northern Ireland.

**Eureka Street**
Minerva pb £6.99 0749396725
**Ripley Bogle**
Minerva pb £6.99 074939465X

# GRACE WYNNE-JONES

Both of Grace Wynne-Jones's novels have well-drawn characters and tell of very believable emotions. In **Ordinary Miracles** we meet Jasmine Smith who is dissatisfied in her marriage and feels she needs a miracle to get her life going again. **Wise Follies** examines the decision that Alice Evans faces. She is thirty eight years old, well settled with all mod cons but still unhappily single. Can she spend her life with the dull and mediocre Eamon or will she strike out to find someone different?

**Ordinary Miracles**
Simon & Schuster pb £5.99
0671855174
**Wise Follies**
Simon & Schuster pb £5.99
068481725X

# Folklore & Mythology

## Folklore and Mythology

The origins of Irish folklore and mythology are almost certainly oral, dating back to the ancient tradition of storytelling. Many of the fairy-tales we know and love from childhood were originally not meant for children, but for adults; told to pass the evening sitting around the hearth, long after the youngsters had gone to bed. The first evidence of these stories being written down dates back to the eighth century A.D., when the early Christian monks composed manuscripts containing versions of stories and sagas of heroes such as Cú Chulainn and Fionn Mac Cumhail. Many stories also come to us through an unbroken line of oral tradition, where stories were handed down from generation to generation through the storytellers themselves.

The wealth of material in print on Irish folklore and mythology ranges from short, introductory collections of stories to academic translations of early manuscripts. For a general overview, **Kennedy's Dictionary of Irish Mythology** (Goldsmith, £3.95 187049105X) or **Smyth's Guide to Irish Mythology** (Irish Academic Press, £5.95 0716526123) are good reference points. As for the stories themselves, some titles well worth reading are **Over Nine Waves** (Faber £8.99 057117518X) by Marie Heaney; **Early Irish Literature** (Four Courts Press, £9.95 1851821775) by Miles Dillon; **A Celtic Miscellany** (Penguin, £6.99 0140442472) by Kenneth Jackson; **Irish Tales and Sagas** (Townhouse, £7.95 0948524596) by Ulick O'Connor; **Myths and Folklore of Ireland** (Roberts, £6.99) by Jeremiah Curtin; and **Early Irish Myths and Sagas** (Penguin, £7.99 0140443975) by Jeffrey Gantz. These books contain famous tales about characters such as Cú Chulainn, the Children of Lir and Deirdre of the Sorrows, and also others less familiar to the general reader, including stories of Irish saints, local legends, and traditional customs. Many are retellings or translations from the original manuscripts, dating back to the twelfth century A.D.

Stories based on collections from the oral souces of the Irish people can be found in William Carleton's books **Traits and Stories of the Irish Peasantry** (Two Volumes Smythe, £6.95 0861401727 and 0861401735), and also Joseph Jacobs' **Celtic Fairy Tales** (Roberts, £2.99 0752902091), which includes popular tales from other Celtic countries, with informative notes and references; as do P.W. Joyce's **Ancient Celtic Romances** (Parkgate, £3.99 1855853906) and **Old Celtic Romances** (New Orchard, £7.99 1860790054). These stories would have been collected from traditional storytellers, or Seanchaí, and then written down or translated in order to be published.

Other more famous collectors of stories were, of course, Lady Gregory and the poet William Butler Yeats, who based many of their works on stories they heard in and around Lady Gregory's Coole Park Estate in County Galway. Lady Gregory's book, **Complete Irish Mythology** (Slaney, £16.00 076519824X), **Gods and Fighting Men** (Smythe, £5.99 0901072370) and **Selected Writings** (Penguin £8.99 0140189556) are fairly comprehensive collections covering all aspects of folklore, including stories about the Tuatha De Danann, the people of Danu, who appear in what is known as the Mythological cycle of tales, Fionn Mac Cumhail and his band of Fenians and also material relating to traditional remedies and cures. **Cúchulainn of Muirthemne** (Smythe, £5.95 0900675853) are a group of well-known tales relating to this famous hero of Ulster such as his boyhood deeds, the wooing of Emer his wife, and his adventures in Scotland where he went to train in arms.

W.B. Yeats, too, having spent a great deal of time in Coole Park, developed his interest in reviving the old Celtic traditions (discussed in his book **The Celtic**

**Twilight** (Smythe, £4.50 0861400704) also adapted many of the stories he heard from the locals of Kiltartan near Coole Park to his own literary style. The finished product can be seen in his famous books **Fairytales of Ireland** (HarperCollins, £3.99 0261667904); **Irish Fairy and Folk Tales** (Hippocrene Press £7.99 0880290730); and **Fairy and Folk Tales of the Irish Peasantry** (0468269418 Constable, £7.95 / 0861403924 Constable, £6.95). The fairies, of course, play a huge role in the beliefs and customs of the Irish people. Legends are told of attempted abductions, changelings (fairies substituted for human babies), and narrow escapes from fairy kingdoms. Many stories are featured in the titles mentioned above, but for something more specific see the beautifully illustrated **Field Guide to the Irish Fairies** (Appletree, £6.99 0862816343).

Witches, too, were something to be wary of; they could turn themselves into hares, or cause a storm at sea, or curse the livestock of their neighbours. One book that deals with these tales is Patrick Kennedy's **Legends of Irish Witches and Fairies** (Mercier, £5.95 0853429715). Another famous character in Irish Folklore is, of course, the Devil, who appears during card games and is only discovered when someone drops a card under the table and spots his cloven hoof. **The Devil is an Irishman** (Mercier, £6.99 1856350169) contains four stories of such comical encounters. Ghosts, too, in a land of mist and rain, are often sighted, and some of the better books dealing with stories of hauntings and eerie happenings are **Irish Ghost Stories** by Bob Curran (Appletree, £6.99 0862815533), **Irish Ghosts and Hauntings** by Michael Scott (Warner, £5.99 0751501549) and **True Irish Ghost Stories** by John Seymour (Senate Books, £2.99 1859580505). But perhaps the most famous figure of all in Irish tradition is the wailing Banshee, the harbinger of death. The Banshee (meaning bean sidhe, fairy woman), was traditionally supposed to follow old Irish families, characterised by having an 'O' or a 'Mac' at the beginning of a surname. She would be heard, and occasionally seen, wailing and combing her long hair as a sign that someone in a family would die soon afterwards. Dr. Patricia Lysaght, in her book, **The Banshee** (O'Brien, £12.99 0862784905), methodically outlines the criteria for the Banshee's appearance, and discusses possibilities for her origins in the most comprehensive work ever done on this enigmatic character.

Another book to give an academic insight into a well-known personage in Irish customs and folklore is Séamas Ó Catháin's **The Festival of Brigit: Celtic Goddess and Holy Woman** (ADBA, £17.50 0951969226). Saint Brigit is second only to Saint Patrick as Ireland's Patron Saint, but there are many customs practised on St Brigit's Day (1st February) that hark back to the times when Brigit was worshipped as a goddess in Ireland. Professor Ó Catháin looks at many of these arcane traditions, and explores evidence in the wider context of Europe and Scandinavia, linking Brigit to what may be the remnants of a bear-cult in a country where the bear died out 25,000 years ago. For anyone interested specifically in customs, particularly those relating to certain times of the year, Kevin Danaher's book **The Year in Ireland** (Mercier, £9.99 1856350932) gives a detailed account of the calendar festivals, including saints' days, Quarterly festivals, and the activities and rituals associated with them.

*Jean Kavanagh of Waterstone's, Dawson Street, Dublin looks at Thomas Kinsella's version of one of the greatest stories in Irish literature.*

The Táin Cuailnge or The Cattle-raid of Cooley, is one of the greatest narratives of Early Irish Literature, forming the main body of a group of stories known as The Ulster Cycle, as they take place for the main part in the province of Ulster in the North of Ireland. It is also the oldest prose epic in the Western world. It tells the story of King Conchobhar Mac Neasa of Ulster and his hero-warrior Cú Chulainn, who defend Ulster and the Cooley Peninsula in Louth against a cattle-raid by Queen Medbh of Connacht. She is in search of the great bull, the Donn Cuailngne, in order to win a bet with her husband King Aillil.

The story as we know it exists in three separate manuscript sources dating from the twelfth to the sixteenth centuries, and contains some archaic passages which are older again, possibly from an eighth century source. The Táin itself dates back further again in oral tradition, although it is almost impossible to say how long it was in existence before the monastic scribes of Early Christian Ireland saw fit to write it down. Kinsella amalgamates two of the older versions of the Táin for his translation. The first was compiled in the twelfth Century in a manuscript known as Lebor na hUidre, the Book of the Dun Cow. The second is the Yellow Book of Lacan, which dates from the Fourteenth century. The third, and latest translation, and probably the most cohesive, is to be found in the Book of Leinster, which, being the most complete, has received more attention from translators, notably Cecille O'Rahilly and, to a lesser extent, Lady Gregory. Kinsella also includes what are known as remscela, or 'pre-stories', which were added to the text later to explain the background to some of the action in the narrative.

For example, the actual motive for the raid is not included in the main body of the older texts. It begins with what is known as the 'pillow talk' of Queen Medb and King Aillil, who compare their wealth in a bid to outdo each other, and it is discovered that Aillil has a bull in his herd, Finnbennach (the white-horned), that Medb has no equal of. There is only one bull in Ireland who can match Aillil's, and that is Donn Cuailnge, the Brown Bull of Cuailnge, owned by Daire mac Fiachna on the Cooley peninsula. Medbhattempts to borrow the bull, but due to the bragging of one of her men Daire refuses, and she resolves to take it by force, therefore declaring war on Ulster. Also explained in the remscela is the reason why Fergus mac Roich, an Ulsterman, has defected to the army of Connacht and fights against Conchobhar (the story of Deirdre and the sons of Uisliu); the legendary curse of Macha which left the Ulstermen as weak as a woman in labour in the first few days of the battle, and ensured that Cúchulainn had to stand alone against Medbh's armies; and indeed the origins of the two bulls themselves. The main text itself has all the ingredients one would expect of an epic narrative - strong characters, heroic and violent battles, love triangles, tales of honour and betrayal - and includes perhaps the most poignant scene of all in which Cúchulainn is forced to fight his foster-brother Ferdia, who had defected with Fergus to Connacht's army. Although Kinsella's translation remains true to a difficult, sometimes contradictory text, part prose, part verse, the narrative is perhaps surprisingly coherent and intensely readable, and offset beautifully by the brush drawings of Irish artist Louis le Brocquy.

**The Táin (translated Thomas Kinsella)**
Oxford UP pb £8.99 0192810901

# Gaeilge

## Dictionaries

There is a variety of dictionaries on the market. **Foclóir Gaeilge Agus Béarla: An Irish-English Dictionary** by Pádraig Ó'Duinnín (Áis hb £25.00 1870166000) was first published in 1904 and remains an incredibly valuable work. A Celtic scholar, O'Duinnín drew from his vast knowledge of folklore, song, stories and studies of the language to prepare his dictionary which is thus an important and valuable source of Gaelic culture. Other standard dictionaries of modern Irish include **Focloir Gaeilge Béarla** edited by Niall O'Donaill (Áis pb £14.00 1857910370), **Irish-English/English-Irish** edited by Mairtín Ó'Siochfhradha (Talbot hb £9.95 0861675231) and **English/Irish Dictionary** edited Séamus De Bhaldraithe (Áis pb £12.00 1857910354) There are also a number of concise, handily sized dictionaries ideal for the student/beginner such as **Foclóir Póca/Pocket Dictionary** (An Gúm pb £4.75 1857910478), **Collins Pocket Irish Dictionary** (Harpercollins pb £7.99 0004707656) and **Collins Gem Irish**

**Dictionary** (Harpercollins pb £3.50 0004707532). A couple of more specialised dictionaries are worth mentioning. **Slanguage Dictionary of Irish Slang** (Gill & Macmillan pb £10.99 0717126838) by Bernard Share is a recently published dictionary of modern Irish slang, which records the contemporary argot heard in Ireland. **Concise Ulster Dictionary** (Oxford University Press pb £9.99 0198600593) edited by Caroline Macafee is a short dictionary explaining words and phrases that are particular to the province of Ulster.

## Learning Irish

There are many books and tapes available for learning the Irish language. One of the most popular is the **Buntús Cainte** (literally 'basic conversation'). It comes in three parts, with both booklets and tape and covers all aspects of rudimentary conversation. (Part One Book Ais pb £2.90 1857910656. Parts 2 & 3 no ISBN £2.90 each. All three tapes £9.99). The Teach Yourself series published by Hodder have been very popular in all modern languages for many years. The course in Irish is designed and presented by Diarmuid O'Sé and comes with both book and tape. The course is presented in graded units and the book includes a grammar and pronunciation guide with a good summary of grammatical terms. The concentration is on pronunciation and dialogue with exercises for both. **Teach Yourself Irish** (Hodder & Stoughton pb £7.99 0340564903) **Teach Yourself Irish Tape** (Hodder & Stoughton pb £7.99 0340564911) **Teach Yourself Irish Book & Tape** (Hodder & Stoughton pb £15.65 034056492X). The **Now You're Talking** series, which is based on a TV programme of the same name is a very comprehensive beginner's guide which starts off with the basics but also goes on to cover more complex conversational and grammatical constructions. Thus it is very suitable for anyone who wants to brush up on the Irish they learnt at school. All five tapes are ninety six minutes long. **Now You're Talking Book** (Gaelmedia pb £9.99 0717123448) **Now You're Talking Book And Tape** (Gaelmedia pb £29.99 0717123499) **Now You're Talking Tapes 3vol** (Gaelmedia £19.99 0717123901) **Now You're Talking Tapes 4&5** (Gaelmedia 0717124177 £13.00). Also suitable for anyone returning to Irish or the beginner is Mairéad Ní Ghrada's **Progress In Irish** (Áis pb £5.20 0861671597) which is a graded course for beginners but also has revision for the more competent student. Noel McGonagle's **Irish Grammar Basic Handbook** (Ais pb £3.00 0907775217) is a good starting point for the general learner and it cover all aspects of basic grammar. The **Pocket Irish Phrase Book** (Appletree

Press pb £3.99 0862810108) by Paul Dorris, although designed for the tourist market is still useful for the beginner. The acclaimed poet Micheál Ó'Siadhail, who writes in both Irish and English has prepared an excellent language course. **Learning Irish** (Yale University Press £14.95 0300064624) and **Learning Irish Tapes** (Yale University Press pb £15.50 0300064632) are based on years of teaching experience. The course adopts a conversational approach and includes phonetic spelling. It can be used by both the individual and in a classroom situation. The author has also written a very comprehensive and lucid study of modern Irish, **Modern Irish** (Cambridge pb £17.95 0521425190), highlighting the development and changes in the contemporary language.

## Language Studies

Michael Cronin's **Translating Ireland** (Cork University Press pb £14.95 1859180191) is an illuminating study of the importance of translation in Irish Literature. Starting with the translations made by monks during the middle ages and continuing to the Celtic revivals of the late 19th and early 20th centuries, Cronin's signal study is an essential book for anyone interested in the history of Irish literature.

  **English As We Speak It In Ireland** (Wolfhound pb £7.95 0863271227) by P.W. Joyce is the classic study of Hiberno-English which has developed in Ireland over the last four centuries, making the English spoken in Ireland quite unique and often untranslatable. Introduced by Terence Dolan, who is currently preparing a standard dictionary of Hiberno-English, Joyce's book includes countless examples of expressions and proverbs that are only spoken in Ireland. It also includes a 142 page glossary of Hiberno-English words. A more up to date companion volume is **How The Irish Speak English** by Padraig O'Farrell (Mercier pb £5.99 185635055X).
 For many years , Diarmuid O'Muirithe has written a weekly column for the Irish Times explaining the background to many of the words and phrases that have slipped into modern parlance from many sources. These columns have been collected in two volumes **The Words We Use** (Four Courts Press pb £6.95 1851822208) and **A Word In Your Ear** (Four Courts Press pb £6.95 1851823395). O'Muirithe has also prepared a dictionary of the Irish words and phrases which are commonly used in the English of Ireland. The **Dictionary of Anglo-Irish** (hb £35.00 185182197X) is also published by Four Courts Press.

## MICHAEL DAVITT
### (b.1950)

Michael Davitt was born in Cork and educated at UCC. He was the founder of the innovative Innti group of poets in 1970. He is currently a television producer for RTE. His poetry has a powerful lyricism, like in his elegy for his father (An Scáthán/ The Mirror) but can also provide strong political imagery such as that in his poem written in response to the Palestinian massacre in Beirut in 1982 (Ó Mo Bheirt Phailistíneach/ O My Two Palestinians).

**Srúth Na Maoile** (£20.00 Coiscéim 0862413567)
**An Tost A Scagaidh** (Coiscéim £4.00 pb No Isbn)

## MICHAEL HARTNETT
### (See Poetry)

## NUALA NÍ DHOMHNAILL
### (See Poetry)

## THOMAS O CROHAN
### (See Biography)

## MÁIRE MHAC AN TSAOI (b.1922)

Though born in Dublin, Máire Mhac an tSaoi spent much of her younger life in the gaeltacht area of Co. Kerry. She was educated at University College, Dublin and at the Sorbonne. She worked in the Dublin Institute of Advanced Studies until she joined the Department of External Affairs. Her poetry is influenced by her deep rooted knowledge of the Gaelic tradition and history. She has recently published a book of translations of European poetry.

**Transladáil** (Lagan Press pb £4.95 1873687273)

## MÁIRTÍN Ó CADHAIN

Máirtín Ó Cadhain was born in Connemara in 1906 and qualified as a teacher. He later joined the IRA and was interned in the Curragh during World War II. Throughout his life he collected folklore from the Connemara Gaeltacht region. He was appointed lecturer in Irish at Trinity College, Dublin in 1956 and was appointed professor in 1960. He died in Dublin in 1970. His most famous work,the novel **Cré na Cille,** first published in 1948 has recently been republished. The literal translation of the title is 'Graveyard Clay'. Set in a graveyard, the action concentrates on each new arrival brought to be buried and the news they bring from the world of the living. Vividly critical of and rejecting the image of the pastoral West of Ireland, Ó Cadhain's novel marks an important turning point in twentieth century Irish writing.

**Cré Na Cille** (Sáirséal pb £8.95 0862890721)

## PHÁDRAIC Ó CONAIRE (1882–1928)

O Conaire was born in Galway and orphaned by the age of eleven. After his parents died he went to live with his relations in the Irish speaking area of Ros Muc Co. Galway. He was educated at Rockwell and Blackrock colleges. In 1889, he went to London and joined the Civil Service. He started drinking heavily in London and returned to Ireland in 1914. On his return he made a meagre income from writing articles for journals and newspapers. He died penniless at the Richmond Hospital in Dublin. His most famous work **Deoraíocht** (Exile) is a bleak novel which begins in London and finishes in Galway. It follows the unfortunate life of Galwayman Micheál Ó Maoláin, who is maimed in an accident and becomes a freak in Alf Trott's circus. When the circus goes to Galway, Micheál sees one of his former lovers in the audience. He plans with some of the locals to destroy the circus and is then stabbed to death by Alf Trott. The novel deals with Micheál's physical and emotional exile and, though bleak, is one of the most remarkable Irish novels this century.

**Deoraíocht**
(Educational Company pb £4.99 0861673638)

## MÁIRTÍN Ó DIREÁN

Máirtín Ó Direán was born into the Irish speaking community on Inishmore, the largest of the Aran Islands in 1910. He was educated locally and worked for the Post Office in Galway city for ten years from 1928. In 1938, he went to Dublin, and joined the Civil Service where he worked until he retired in 1975. He died in Dublin in 1978. He is respected as one of the major Irish language poets this century and has very effectively used the island where he grew up as his subject matter. **Árainn 1947** (Aran 1947) evokes a stark, unwelcoming Aran which has failed to progress into the modern world while **Ómos do John Millington Synge** (Homage to John Millington Synge) celebrates the playwright whose writings brought the language of the islands to the outside world.

## MICHEAL O'GUIHEEN
**(See Biography)**

## LIAM Ó MUIRTHILE

Born in Cork and educated at UCC where he was taught by Seán Ó Tuama and Seán Ó Riordáin. He has written the popular An Peann Coitianta column in Irish for the Irish Times which have been collected. The themes of his poetry are varied, from the jaunty evocation of youth in Portráid Óige (Portrait of Youth I) to the haunting elegy for an elderly friend, Do Chara Liom (For My friend). His latest collection is Diallan Bóthair.

**Diallan Bóthair**
(Gallery Press pb £5.95 1852351568)
**An Peann Coitianta**
(ÁIS £4.50 No Isbn)

## SEÁN Ó RIORDÁIN
### (1916–1977)

Born in West Cork and educated at UCC where he met Daniel Corkery and Seán Ó Tuama. He worked for Cork Corporation all his life, but was left in poor health, having suffered from TB in his youth. This strongly affected his poetry and he has written movingly about illness, especially in his Fiabhras (Fever). The death of his mother also affected him hugely as reflected in his haunting poem Adhlacadh Mo Mháthar (My Mother's Burial).

## CATHAL Ó SEARCAIGH

Born in the Donegal gaeltacht area and graduated from the Celtic Studies program in St. Patrick's College, Maynooth. He has lived in London and in Dublin, working as a producer for RTE. In recent years, he has returned to his native Donegal and has farmed. His poetry sensually evokes the landscape that he knows best and his most recent book is a collection of beautiful gay love poems **Na Buachaillí Bána.**

**Homecoming: Selected Poems**
(Áis pb £9.00 1874700559)
**Out In The Open**
(Clo-Iar hb £4.00 1900693747)
**Na Buachailli Bana**
(Áis pb £9.00 1874700990)

## MICEAL O SÍADHAIL
### (See Poetry)

## MAURICE O SULLIVAN
### (See biography)

## SEÁN Ó TÚAMA
### (b.1926)

Born in Cork and educated at UCC where he was influenced by Daniel Corkery. He has taught in the USA on a regular basis since the late 1960s. His **Rogha Dánta/ Death in the Land of Youth** (Selected Poems) have recently been published which display his poetic insight and a body of work firmly founded in, but augmentative of, the Irish literary tradition. A gifted linguist and literary critic, he has also written many articles on Irish literature which have been recently collected as **Repossessions: Selected Essays on the Irish Literary Heritage.**

**Rogha Dánta/ Death in the Land of Youth Selected Poems**
(Cork University Press pb £7.95 1859181589)
**Repossessions: Selected Essays on the Irish Literary Heritage**
(Cork University Press pb £14.95 1859180450)

## PEIG SAYERS
### (See Biography)

# Genealogy

## General Names

There is a huge interest in Irish genealogy and every summer countless American and European tourists visit Ireland to try and find out about their families of many generations ago. Many books have been written specifically about Irish families. John Grenham's **Clans And Families of Ireland** (Gill & Macmillan Hb £12.99 0717120325) provides a very good introduction to the main Irish families. More comprehensive however are Edward Lysaght's two volumes of informative family history, **Irish Families: Their Names, Arms & Origins** (Irish Academic Press Hb £25.00 0716523647) and his **More Irish Families** (Irish Academic Press pb £12.95 0716526042). He has also published the shorter **Surnames of Ireland** (Irish Academic Press pb £5.95 0716523663). **From Family Tree to Family History** by Ruth Finnegan (Cambridge University Press pb £10.99 052146577X) is part of the Studying Family and Community History series which aims to place individual families within their social context.

## Surnames

**Irish Family Names** by John Grenham (Armada pb £6.99 0004720709) gives the histories of over a hundred and twenty family names, tracing their roots and development. It also has a colour list of family crests with maps showing where each family is from. The book has introductory essays focussing on the way names evolved through the years, through Viking, Norman and Tudor influence.

## First Names

There are a number of books which explain and elaborate on Irish first names which are very popular with new parents and tourists. Ronan Coghlan has written a **Pocket Guide to Irish First Names** (Appletree Press pb £3.99 0862811538). There is also a Collins Gem guide by Julia Cresswell on **Irish First Names** (Harper Collins pb £3.50 000470942X) which also features anglicised versions of Irish names that have become popular in the US and Australia. Lauren Flanagan's **Favourite Irish Names For Children** (Gill & Macmillan pb £3.99 071712021X) concentrates on the Irish first names that are more popular at the moment while **Irish Names For Children** by Patrick Woulfe (Gill & Macmillan pb £12.99 0717106977) provides useful historical information on the origins of many first names, as does Donncha O'Corrain's **Irish Names** (Lilliput Press pb £5.95 0946640661).

## Tracing Ancestors

Four books which detail the practical ways of tracing Irish ancestors and which also give details of family history are particularly useful. John Grenham's **Tracing Your Irish Ancestors** (Gill & Macmillan pb £10.99 0717118983) and Christine Kinnealy's **Pocket Guide to Tracing Your Irish Ancestors** (Appletree Press pb £3.99 086281278X) provide good advice and information on social and government sources while **The Irish Roots Guide** by Tony McCarthy (Lilliput Press pb £4.990946640777) shows how to use valuable sources like Census figures and the Registration of Births, Deaths and Marriages. Tony McCarthy has also produced **The Ancestor Album** (Lilliput Press pb £5.99 1874675457) which is a practical album that you fill in with information to complete and present your family tree.

## Regional

**The Book of Ulster Surnames** by Robert Bell (Blackstaff Press pb £9.99 0856406023) is a valuable book that provides the history and origins of many prominent Ulster families. **Family Names of County Cork** by Diarmuid O'Murchadha (Collins Press pb £11.99 1898256136) puts all of the main names of both Cork city and county into their historical context. Flyleaf have produced a very good series of local family guides for Kerry, Donegal & Mayo, **Tracing Your Kerry Ancestors** by James Ryan (Flyleaf pb £7.00 0950846651), **Tracing Your Donegal Ancestors** by Godrey F Duffy (Flyleaf pb £7.00 095084666X) and **Tracing Your Mayo Ancestors** by Brian Smith (Flyleaf pb £7.00 0950846678). All three of these books describe all the practicalities of how to build your family tree in these counties.

# History & Archaeology

## Archaeology

### General Archaeology

The richness of Ireland's archaeological inheritance is reflected in the richness of books available on the subject. A number of titles look at the forces which have shaped the Irish landscape. **The Atlas of the Irish Rural Landscape** (Cork University Press hb £35.00 1859180957) edited by Kevin Whelan, F.H.A. Aalen & Matthew Stout is one of the most ambitious publishing projects to have taken place in Ireland. Richly illustrated it shows how the Irish landscape has been developed over the centuries and the current state of its development. Combining history, archaeology and geography, the book starts with general essays on the landscape and continues with examinations of different factors that profoundly affect the landscape, e.g. bogs, forests, buildings, towns and mining. The conclusion of the book consists of a number of regional case studies including Hook Head in Co. Wexford and The Burren in Co. Clare. Also included is a chapter on the management of the landscape. This is the definitive guide to all aspects of the way that Ireland looks today. **The Historical Geography of Ireland** edited by Brian Graham & Lindsay Proudfoot (Academic Press pb £24.95 0122948815) provides an illuminating range of essays covering the historical geography and economic history of Ireland from Medieval times up to the Irish diaspora in 20th Century Britain. **Reading the Irish Landscape by** Frank Mitchell (Town House pb £16.99 094617254) is a new edition of what has now become a modern classic. Frank Mitchell, with Michael Ryan, tells the story of how archaeology, tourism, and industry have shaped the landscape that we know today. Beautifully illustrated and combining archaeology, history and social study, this is an indispensable book. Frank Mitchell has also written **Where Has Ireland Come From?** (Town House pb £6.95 0946172439) which he calls a 'magic carpet ride' through the geological history of Ireland. Light-hearted, but very informative, Mitchell's book provides 'eyewitness' accounts of the various geological events which resulted in the formation of the island of Ireland.

Lauren Flanagan's **Dictionary of Irish Archaeology** (Gill & MacMillan pb£12.99 0717119289) lists all of the major excavated sites in Ireland and also provides illustrations. As well as being an informative reference tool, this book is also a useful guide as to how to find these sites. **The Antiquities of the Irish Countryside** by Sean O'Riordan (Routledge pb £12.99 0415065895) discusses in some detail the origin, purpose, date and distribution of many of the antiquities spread around the country. Valuable to the general reader and the student, this is one of the best introductions to the history of crannógs, forts, tombs and stone circles. **Irish Archaeology Illustrated** by Michael Ryan (Country House pb £14.99 0946172331) is a very interesting series of essays in which thirty seven authors discuss various aspects of Irish archaeology from the Stone and Bronze Ages right up to the 17th Century. **Irish Prehistory: A Social Perspective** by Gabriel Cooney & Eoin Grogan (Wordwell hb £25.00 1869857119) is a study in social archaeology, taking as its premise that all excavated artefacts must be in some way a reflection of the people and society where they were found. Although academic in tone, the book is also useful to the general reader as it provides valuable sociological background to Irish prehistory. **Ireland in Prehistory** by Michael Herity (Routledge pb £15.99 0415048893) places Irish Prehistory squarely in the context of recent archaeological work. Examining the period from the Stone Age to the Celts, Herity looks at how many recent excavations have greatly improved our understanding of these times. The peatlands of Ireland have played a huge part in Ireland's history, both as a source for fuel and as an area of preservation for archeological finds. In **The Bogs of Ireland** (Royal Irish Academy hb £48.00 1898473404), Feehan and O'Donovan provide a comprehensive introduction to the natural, cultural and industrial heritage of the Irish Bog. In **The Construction of Heritage** (Cork University Press pb £14.95 1859180531), David Brett examines this term that has become such an important one in contemporary culture. He looks at the relationship of heritage to tourism and explores the ideas, sometimes spurious ones, behind interpretive centres and heritage attractions.

Other general archaeology titles include Peter Harbison's **Pre-Christian Ireland** (Thames & Hudson pb £8.95 0500278091) which is a general account of civilisation in Ireland from 8000 B.C. to the arrival of Christianity with St. Patrick in the fifth century A.D, and two books on the archaeology of Ireland in Medieval times, **The Archaeology of Medieval Ireland** by Terence Barry (Routledge pb £15.99 0415011043), which discusses both military and rural medieval settlements and Nancy Edwards's **Archaeology of Early Medieval Ireland** (Batsford pb £25.00 0713479957) which is a comprehensive and lucid discussion of the richness of medieval artefacts that remain around the country. She also explores the impact of the Viking invasion on medieval Ireland. There are two good books on Ogham, the ancient Irish system of writing. This system has been discovered on several hundred stones in Ireland and is made up of a series of slashes, varied in number, length and concentration. Thought to date from the 4th to the 7th century, most of the Ogham stones found have been in the Munster area. **Ogham Irish Alphabet** (AIS pb £4.99 1874700435) is by MacFhearaigh and **Guide To Ogham** (AIS pb £12.00 1870684753) is by McManus.

# Monuments

Ireland is littered with the archaeological monuments of its past and there are many books which describe them. **The Guide to the National & Historic Monuments** by Peter Harbison (Gill & MacMillan pb £12.99 0717119564) is the classic and comprehensive practical guide to the monuments of Ireland, providing plans, maps, illustrations and re-constructions. **The Irish Ringfort** by Michael Stout (Four Courts Press pb £19.95 185182300X) comprehensively shows the general and academic reader the shape, size, date and functions of many of the ringforts built around Ireland in the first centuries A.D. By basing his evidence on material remains, Stout also provides a great insight into the lives of the people who built, lived in and died in these forts. **High Crosses of Ireland: Early Christian Symbolism In Great Britain & Ireland** by J. Allen (Llanerch pb £4.95 0947992901) is a clear and descriptive introduction to these very important symbols of early Christianity. The author makes great use of reproductive drawings which give the modern reader a very good insight to the original state of the crosses. **Irish High Crosses with the Figure Symbols Explained** by Peter Harbison (Boyne Valley pb £7.95 0951782371) is a very good field guide with maps showing locations of the high crosses. The author also explains all of the symbols carved on the crosses. **Symbolism of the Celtic Cross** by Derek Bryce (Llanerch pb £5.99 1897853335) argues that the Wheel cross inherent to the form of the high cross derives from the Chi-Rho monogram, i.e. is made from the first two letters of the name of Christ in the Greek alphabet Chi and Rho, thus suggesting that the origins of the form were not based on conventional Christianity. **An Introduction to Irish High Crosses** by Hilary Richardson & John Scarry (Mercier Press pb £9.99 0853429545) gives a very clear account of the history and development of the Cross in Ireland. Short and concise chapters on the interpretation and sites of the crosses around the country, give way to 199 black & white plates of crosses, giving alternate views of the many inscriptions on over thirty crosses in Ireland. Roger Stalley's **Irish High Crosses** (Town House pb £5.99 0946172560) is a well-illustrated book discussing the form, function and mystery of many of the 200 crosses that remain intact. **Sheela Na Gigs: Origins & Functions** by Eamon Kelly (Town House pb £4.99 094617251X) explains the background and function of these curious stone carvings of naked women emphasising and displaying their genitalia. Useful to the general reader as well as the scholar, the book also functions as a field guide to the locations of many of the carvings. Kelly also describes how they have been viewed over the centuries, discussing the changes from the idea of them as sinister, negative icons to the modern interpretation which views Sheel-Na-Gigs as a positive affirmation of female sexuality. **Stone Circles in Ireland** by Sean O'Nuallain (Town House pb £5.95 0946172455) shows how Stone Circles were built in Great Britain and Ireland from 2000 to 800 B.C. Of the 1000 or so built, around 250 were built in Ireland and this is the first book to discuss exclusively the Irish examples.

Detailing the layout and purpose of many of these circles the author also draws conclusions about the lives of the people who built them. A useful companion volume is Aubrey Burl's **Guide to Stone Circles of Britain, Ireland & Brittany** (Yale University Press pb £9.95 0300063318) which is a practical and comprehensive handbook, showing locations of the monuments. Kenneth McNally, in his **Standing Stones & Other Monuments of Early Ireland** (Appletree pb £6.99 0862812011) discusses the background to many monuments from tombs to the early monasteries using very good photos and illustrations as well as concise, informative text. And stone walls may not, strictly speaking, be monuments but they are central to the landscape. **Irish Stone Walls** by Pat McAfee (O'Brien Press hb £14.99 0862784786) is a brilliant study, of and guide to the 250,000 miles of stone walls that have become such an integral part of the Irish landscape. McAfee points out the differing regional styles and also includes a practical guide to building, using drystone or lime processes.

From Beautiful History of Ireland

**The Archaeology of Ulster: From Colonization to Plantation** by J.P. Mallory & T.E. McNeill (Institute of Irish Studies pb £9.50 0853893535) illustrates the development of Ulster society by studying the archaeological remains that are extant. Tracing remains from 7000 B.C. to the 18th Century, Mallory and MacNeill provide the general reader with a fundamental understanding of the development of Ulster society. Michael Slavin's **Book of Tara** (Wolfhound hb £19.99 0863275079) mixes archaeology and anthropology with history, myth and legend to lay bare the story of the Hill of Tara in Co. Meath. Well-illustrated, the book also includes a 'walkabout guide', displaying clearly the entire area. Chapters range in subject from the legends surrounding the hill, to details of the Norman invasion to the geography of the current landscape and give the general reader a great insight into this famous site. Two very good academic reference books to accompany Slavin's work are published by the Royal Irish Academy. **Tara: A Select Bibliography** (Royal Irish Academy hb £9.95 1874045356) is the most comprehensive bibliography of publications concerning the Hill of Tara, while Conor Newman's **Tara: An Archaeological Survey** (Royal Irish Academy £28.00 187404547X) is the most up-to-date survey of the archaeological remains of the area. Michael Poynder's **Pi in the Sky** (Collins Press pb £14.99 1898256330) is a study of the mathematical and astronomical basis for the positioning, shape and size of many archaeological sites and artefacts. Using many ancient examples that survive today like Newgrange, the Tara brooch and the Pyramids, Poynder shows how Stone Age cultures manipulated their knowledge of the life force of the Sun and stars. An interesting companion volume relating only to Newgrange is **The Age of Newgrange: Astronomy & Mythology** by William Battersby (Battersby pb £5.00 0951865137) which focuses on the astronomical importance of the passage tomb and its alignment with the stars. **Knowth & the Passage Tombs of Ireland** by George Eogan (Thames & Hudson pb 12.95 0500275939) is based on a fifteen year excavation of this 5000 year old tomb. It gives the full background and history of the area surrounding the archaeological site. The Royal Irish Academy have also published a two volume inventory/catalogue of Eogan's findings at Newgrange, which is a reference tool for the general reader and archaeologist (Vol 1 0901714348/ Vol2 1874045496). **Loughcrew: The Cairns** (After Hours Books pb £4.95 0952198703) by Jean McMann is a short but concise and definitive study of the 5000 year old passage tombs that survive in the Loughcrew area of north Co. Meath. Useful both as a study and practical guide, the book also focuses on the excavation of the sites from the 19th century to the 1970s and discusses the folklore surrounding the site.

South Kerry is heavily populated with archaeological artefacts and monuments. Over the last ten years Ann O'Sullivan and John Sheehan have explored the area to try to record and catalogue as many of the sites as possible. The resulting book, **The Iveragh Peninsula: An Archaeological Survey of South Kerry** (Cork University Press pb £25.00 0902561847) is a richly illustrated guide and reference work to this region. Charting the heritage from the Stone Age to Medieval times, this book is both a record and testament to the people who lived, worked and survived in this region. A very useful companion volume is **Past Perceptions: The Prehistoric Archaeology of South West Ireland** (Cork University Press pb £17.95 0902561898) edited by Elizabeth Shee Twohig & Margaret Ronayne which is a collection of original essays discussing the archaeology of the same region. **Inishmurray** by Patrick Heraughty (O'Brien Press pb £9.99 0862784735) examines the history and archaeology of this island of the Sligo coast. Murray, who lived on the island until he was twelve years old, takes as his starting point the monastic community on the island which existed from 520-1170 A.D. and finishes in 1948 when the last inhabitants left the island forever. Combining both modern history and illustrated archaeological study, Murray gives us a unique perspective on this island and community.

Lastly, the Office of Public works in Ireland have produced a series of inventories of many of the Irish counties. At the end of the project, it is hoped that all of Ireland's achaeological sites will have been recorded. Beautifully printed with illustrations and line drawings showing location, size and importance of all the monuments within a particular county, they are the ultimate archaeological reference. Titles available so far are: –

**Carlow Archaeological Inventory**
Office of Public Works hb £11.00 0707603242
**Cavan Archaeological Inventory**
Office of Public Works hb £23.00 0707616948
**Cork Archaeological Inventory**
Office of Public Works hb £20.00 0707601754
**Meath Archaeological Inventory**
Office of Public Works hb £18.50 0707600316
**Wexford Archaeological Inventory**
Office of Public Works hb £22.00 070762326X

# History

## General History

J.C. Beckett's **The Making of Modern Ireland** 1603-1923 (Faber pb £16.99 0571180361) although first published in 1966 is still one of the best narrative histories of the three centuries which started with the Ulster Plantation and ended with the Anglo-Irish war of the 1920s. Lucid and scholarly, but without being overbearing with facts, Beckett's book is an ideal introduction to the period. Another very good starting point for a general recent history of Ireland is F.S.L. Lyons's **Ireland since the Famine** (Harper Collins pb £10.99 0006860052) which is an exhaustive exploration and examination of the period from the 1850s up to the early 1970s. In 1988, R.F. Foster's **Modern Ireland 1600-1972** (Penguin pb £10.99 0140132503) was published to great acclaim. Dealing with roughly the same period as Beckett's book (although covering more of this century), Foster re-examines the notion of Irishness using these three centuries as context. This book is a brilliant synthesis of narrative history, revisionist examination and personal opinion and with its biographical footnotes, which detail the lives of all of the major figures mentioned is also a brilliant reference book. Many of R.F. Foster's essays have been collected and published as **Paddy & Mr Punch: Connections in Irish & English History** (Penguin pb £9.99 0140171703). These essays provide both historical and literary insight into many figures in Anglo-Irish history such as Charles Stewart Parnell, W.B. Yeats, J.M. Synge & Elizabeth Bowen. Foster has also edited the **Oxford History of Ireland** (Oxford University Press pb £8.99 019285271X) which is a set of six illuminating essays, which between them cover the history of Ireland from earliest times to the 20th Century. The book closes with a fascinating essay on Irish Literature by Declan Kiberd, that is one of the best short summaries of Irish literary achievement in print. It is also available in an illustrated edition (Oxford University Press pb £13.99 0192852450) which provides illuminating portraits, maps and drawings.

There are three other illustrated histories available, **Ireland: A Graphic History** by Morgan Llywelyn & Michael Scott (Gill & MacMillan pb £9.99 0717122999) sets out Irish history as a graphic novel. Although not fully comprehensive, it has a very strong story-telling style which makes its information easy to assimilate. The same could be said for **Ireland for Beginners** (Icon Books pb £5.99 1897784163) edited by Rupert Besley. One of the very successful graphic-based 'Beginners' series, this book presents Irish history in a quirky and sometimes irreverent fashion. John Grenham has also put together the more serious **Illustrated History of Ireland** (Gill & MacMillan pb £5.99 071712553X) which combines text with illustrative pictures and drawings.

Robert Kee has made a huge contribution to the writing of Irish history. His three volume study **The Green Flag** (first published in one volume in 1972) is still one of the most accessible accounts of Irish history in print. Vol 1 **The Most Distressful Country** (Penguin pb £7.99 0140147608) covers the period from early Ireland to the Great Famine of 1845 and discusses the origins of the Irish people. Vol 2 **Bold Fenian Men** (Penguin pb £8.99 0140147586) starts in 1858 and the beginnings of the Fenian movement and finishes at the Easter Rising of 1916. The final volume **Ourselves Alone** (Penguin pb £7.99 014014756X) focuses on the aftermath of the Rising and the period that led to the War of Independence up to 1923. In the late 1970s, Kee went on to write the enormously successful **Ireland: A Television History,** which educated a generation of young Irish people. The series covered Irish history up to the 1970s and the accompanying book has been recently republished as **Ireland: A Concise History** (Abacus pb £14.99 0349106789).

First published in 1966 to tie in with a very successful TV series of the same name **The Course of Irish History by** T.W. Moody & F.X. Martin (Mercier Press pb £13.99 1856351084) was republished in an expanded form in 1994. The book is a very good survey of Irish history, with a geographical introduction, from the earliest times to the 1994 IRA ceasefire. The bibliography has also been updated to include modern studies. **The Atlas of Irish History** by Sean Duffy (Gill & MacMillan pb £9.99 0717124797) is an illuminating map-based survey from prehistory to the present. With clear text and high quality maps, diagrams and drawings, this is an ideal reference book and introduction. **The Military History of Ireland** by Thomas Bartlett (Cambridge University Press £17.95 0521629896) is a collection of essays focussing on the various military activities in Ireland over the last thousand years. Starting with a chapter on warfare in Ireland before 1100 and continuing with chapters on the Middle Ages, the Williamite wars of the late 17th century, and finishing with a brilliant account of British army activity in Ireland since 1922, this book effectively tells a new history of Ireland from a military perspective. **Irish Battles: A Military History of Ireland** by Gerard McCoy (Appletree pb £9.99 086281250X) provides a detailed account of the most important Irish battles from Brian Boru's battle against the Vikings in Clontarf 1014 to the Battle of Arcklow during the 1798 Rebellion. Brian Walker in his **Dancing to History's Tune: History, Myth and Politics in Ireland** (Institute of Irish Studies pbk£8.50 0853896194) considers Irish history in the context of Europe and questions whether the study of history is more or less important in Ireland than anywhere else. He also looks at the commemorative practices of history, looking at the way the celebrations of St.Patrick's Day and the 12th of July have changed.

**Ireland: A Concise History** by Conor & Maire Cruise O'Brien (Thames & Hudson pb £7.95 0500273790) is a clear introduction to Irish history from prehistory to self-government, well-illustrated with black-and-white photographs and diagrams. Edmund Curtis has written a very thoroughly researched work in **The History of Ireland** (Routledge pb £14.99 0415027861) which is a very good mix of religious, social, cultural and economic history and includes both a clear chronology and a guide to pronunciation of proper names. E. Estyn Evans's classsic study **The Personality of Ireland: Habitat, Heritage and History** (Lilliput Press pb £6.95 0946640815) has been recently republished with a thoughtful preface by Paul Durcan. This book, applying French historiography to Irish history, thus blending studies of landscape and folklore with document-based history, is one of the few books about Ireland that have a genuinely 'European' feel.

**Harvest: A History of Grain-Growing in Ireland** (Heritage House pbk£17.99 0952970708) by Majella Flynn is a study for the general reader of the importance of grain to Irish society and economy. Describing the whole process, from soil separation to milling, Flynn also highlights recent technical developments and discusses the dietary and socio-economic implications of the annual grain crop in Ireland. **Women and Irish History** (Wolfhound Press pbk£17.99 0863275796) edited by Mary O'Dowd and Mary Ann Gianella Valiulis explores the public role of Irish women from the 18th century to the present day, in a series of essays written in honour of the pioneering historian Margaret MacCurtain. Included are essays by prominent historians, Mary E. Daly, Mary Cullen and Maria Luddy. The volume also addresses the issues involved in women writing history. **The Cause of Ireland: From the United Irishmen to Partition** by Liz Curtis (Beyond the Pale pb £12.95 0951422960) is a history of the English colonisation in Ireland from the late 17th century to the 1920s. **The History of the Irish Working Class** by Peter Beresford Ellis (Pluto Press pb £12.99 074530009X) is a well documented study and demonstrates the relationship between labour and nationalism through the last four centuries.

Finally, there are many short histories of Ireland available, which are ideal for the visitor or student who wish to glean the facts, without having to sift through historical interpretation. These include John Ranelagh's **A Short History of Ireland** (Cambridge pb £12.99 0521469449); Sean McMahon's **A Short History of Ireland** (Mercier Press pb £18.99 1856351378) & Richard Killeen's **A Short History of Ireland** (Gill & MacMillan pb £3.99 0717121569). There are also two very concise but accurate histories aimed squarely at the tourist market, although many Irish people would benefit greatly from their clear and concise overviews. These are Breandain O'Heithir's **Pocket History of Ireland** (O'Brien Press pb £4.99 0862781884) and Martin Wallace's **Little History of Ireland** (Appletree Press hb £3.99 0862814553).

Interest in Celtic culture has rarely been higher than it is now and there are a number of fascinating, general studies of the subject. **The Celts** by T.G.E. Powell (Thames & Hudson pb £6.99 0500272751) brilliantly portrays Celtic life around Europe based on historical, archeological & linguistic evidence. **The Celts: An Illustrated History** by Helen Litton (Wolfhound pb £6.99 086327577X) is a concise and informative introduction focussing on Celtic Europe between the 8th and 5th Centuries B.C. It also concentrates on Ireland and is the ideal starting point for a study of the period. **The Celts** by Frank Delaney (Harper Collins pb £7.99 0586203494) is a witty and informative introduction and general history of Celtic life and times and can be read in tandem with Delaney's **Legends of the Celts** (Harper Collins pb £6.99 0586211519) which is a good modern retelling of the tales which were to become such an important part of Irish culture. **The Celts** by Nora Chadwick (Penguin pb £8.99 0140250743) has long been recognised as one of the classic histories of the Celts, covering all aspects of Celtic life, lore and history. **Ancient Celts** by Barry Cunliffe (Oxford University Press hb £25.00 0198150105) is a detailed archeological study concentrating on the origins and history of the Celts in Europe and shows how they differed dramatically from region to region, thus dispelling the notion of a homogenous Celtic population in Europe.

Other books study particular aspects of Celtic life. **Celtic Sacred Landscapes** by Jennifer Pennick (Thames & Hudson hb £12.95 0500016666) is a study of the most important Celtic holy sites in Ireland, Britain and Europe, closely examining the mystery and lore behind these powerful sites and arguing for the importance of the Celtic tradition today. **Pagan Celtic Ireland: The Enigma of the Irish Iron Age** by Barry Raftery (Thames & Hudson pb £16.95 0500279837) is a very well illustrated study which tries to unravel the maze of information surrounding the Iron Age in Ireland using recent archeological research. **Celts and the Classical World** by David Rankin (Routledge pb £12.99 0415150906) fascinatingly reinterprets the Celts as they would have been seen by the Greeks and Romans. This book also concentrates on the Celts in Europe before they were assimilated into Roman society. **Celtic Heritage** by David Alwyn Rees (Thames & Hudson pb £9.95 0500270392) is an interesting, if contentious, reinterpretation of Celtic tradition from the perspective of new studies in religion, mythology and anthropology. **Celtic Book of Days** by Caitlin Matthews (Gill & MacMillan pb £12.99 071712326X) is a lavishly illustrated book of days which highlights the Celtic importance of each day set in the context of the four seasons. **Gods & Heroes of the Celts** by Marie Louise Sjoestedt (Four Courts Press pb £6.95 1851821791) surveys Celtic mythology and shows how the gods were seen to exist without hierarchy, a striking contrast to the classical view of deity. **Celtic Treasury** by Catriona Luke (Gill & MacMillan hb £ 9.99 0717124975) is a beautifully illustrated study of the intricate jewelry (gold, silver, bronze, enamel) and illuminated manucripts produced during the Celtic era. **Celtic Women** by Peter Beresford Ellis (Constable pb £9.95 009476560X) demonstrates the way that women were perceived and treated in Celtic society and shows how they were treated as individuals and not as servants appended to husband and family. **Celtic Sexuality** by Peter Cherici (Duckworth pb £9.95 0715627252) is an interesting short study concentrating on sexual relations in Celtic society and **Exploring the World of the Druids** (Thames & Hudson hb £17.95 050005083X) by Miranda Green is a cogent examination of Celtic religious life, placing this life in the context of Ireland as a whole.

## Early and Medieval Ireland

Early Irish Christianity remains central to the story of medieval Ireland and there are plenty of books available for the general reader. The founder of Irish Christianity was, of course, St. Patrick. David Dumville's **Saint Patrick, AD 493-1993.** (Boydell hb £40.00 0851153321) is a biography of the Irish patron saint which argues that the real date of his death was 493 and not 461 as has been previously agreed. This book was published to coincide with the 1500th anniversary of St. Patrick's death and also looks at the Patrick tradition and myth since his death. **St Patrick's World: The Christian Culture of Ireland's Apostolic Age** edited by Liam De Paor (Four Courts Press pb £12.50 1851821449) brings together a number of 4th and 5th Century Latin texts which show how Christianity spread from Ireland over Europe. Liam de Paor's lucid and informative introduction places the texts squarely in their own context. D. Howlett has edited **The Book of Letters of Saint Patrick the Bishop** (Four Courts Press pb £12.50 1851821376) in order to provide a reassessment of the view that St. Patrick was uneducated. The book presents two texts, with introduction and commentary, Letters to the Soldiers of Coroticusi and the Confession. The other great figure in Celtic Christianity is Columba. Written by Adamnán, the ninth abbot of Iona, which was founded by St. Columba in the 6th Century, **The Life of St Columba** (Llanerch pb £6.95 0947992197) is one of the earliest lives of this saint and was mainly based on manuscripts from Iona. **Studies in the Cult of St Columba** by Cormac Bourke (Four Courts Press pb £17.50 1851823131) uses archaeological, religious and literary studies to discuss the many different aspects of the Columba cult through the centuries. Máire Herbert's **Iona, Kells & Derry: History & Hagiography of the Monastic Familia of Columba** (Four Courts Press pb £19.95 1851822445) relates the story of Columba's settlements and legacy from the days when Iona was the centre of monastic activity, until the Viking invasion. She then discusses how the Familia moved to Kells in Co. Meath and became much more Irish-centred and eventually quite secular. She finishes with a description of the return to Columban monasticism with the foundation of the monastery in

Derry, and its eventual demise at the hands of the Normans. A good companion volume is Les Whiteside's **In Search of Columba** (Columba pb £5.99 1856071804) which gathers together the little documentary evidence that survives to tell the life of the saint.

Other books look at various aspects of early religious life. Two further saints have early lives readily available in new editions. **The Life of Colman** (Llanerch pb £7.95 1861430175), translated and edited by Kuno Meyer from a manuscript in the library of Rennes, is a short life of this little known Irish saint, supposed to have died towards the end of the 6th Century. **Irish Life of Saint Finian of Clonard** edited and introduced by Elizabeth Hickey (Meath Archaeological Society pb £5.00 0950033278) is a life from early Irish manuscripts, of Finian, who founded the monastery in Clonard, Co. Meath in the late 5th and early 6th Centuries B.C. **Isle of the Saints: Monastic Settlement & Christian Community in Early Ireland** by Lisa M. Bitel (Cork University Press pb £12.95 1859180175) is a brilliant recreation of the every day reality of life in Irish monasteries between 800 and 1200. It also shows how the monasteries interacted with the communities around them. **How the Irish Saved Civilisation** by Thomas Cahill (Hodder & Stoughton pb £6.99 0340637870) shows how in the 5th Century, while Rome was being overrun by the Visigoths, Ireland was fast becoming the 'isle of saints & scholars'. As a result of this, Irish monks transcribed and distributed many invaluable manuscripts that were being destroyed all over Europe. **Columcille & the Columban Tradition** by Brian Lacey (Four Courts Press pb £6.95 1851823212) examines the real, historical figure of Columcille and the spread of his influence from Iona to Ireland, Scotland and the North of England. **They Built on Rock: The Story of the Men and Women of the Early Celtic Church** by Diana Leeson (Llanerch pb £8.95 1861430248) provides a detailed narrative of the lives of the people who built the early monasteries, often literally on rocks like the Skelligs off the Co. Kerry coast. The book also examines the role of the early church in the community at large. **The Modern Traveller to the Early Irish Church** by Anne Hamiln & Kathleen Hughes (Four Courts Press pb £9.95 1851821945) is an informative guide to the early Christian sites of Ireland and as a result provides a very good reconstruction of the lives of 12th Century monks. Complementing this volume from the same publisher is A. Gwynn's **Irish Church in the 11th & 12th Centuries** (Four Courts Press pb £19.95 1851821171) which is a detailed study of the early church. Fr John Ryan's **Irish Monasticism** (Four Courts Press pb £19.95 1851821112), first published in 1931 and now reissued with a new introduction and updated bibliography, compares the Irish monastic tradition to that of the European tradition from the 5th to the 7th Centuries A.D. Ryan shows how the Irish experience of monasticism was totally different to that in the rest of Europe because of the role that monasteries played in the social and economic make up of the Irish community. Another book first published in 1931, Louis Gougaud's **Christianity in Celtic Lands** (Four Courts pb £19.95 1851821139) provides us with a detailed history of the church between the 4th and 12th Centuries. Jean Michel Picard's foreword to this new edition provides both context and explanation to this classic work.

A good general history of early Ireland is **Early Ireland: An Introduction** by Michael O'Kelly (Cambridge University Press pb £18.95 0521336872). This is a very usefully illustrated history of Ireland from the end of the Ice Age to the first centuries of Christianity. With its archaeological dimension it gives the modern reader great insight to the daily lives of the early Irish people. Other books examine particular facets of Early Ireland. Nerys Patterson's **Cattlelords & Clansmen: Social Structure of Early Ireland** (Eds pb £19.95 0268008000), concentrating on the Pre-Norman period, explores the agriculture, daily life, the role of hospitality and the relationship between the sexes in Irish Society. **Ireland & Early Europe: Essays & Occasional Writings on Irish Culture** by Liam Depaor (Four Courts Press pb £14.95 1851822984) is a brilliant collection of essays discussing Ireland's relationship with Great Britain and Europe and showing how the art and culture of Ireland interacted with the wider world. Gerald of Wales's twelfth century **History & Topography of Ireland** remains of interest and is available in a modern translation (Penguin pb £6.99 0140444238). **Celtic Leinster: Towards Historical Geography of Early Irish Civilization A.D. 500-1600,** (Irish Academic Press hb £14.95 0716500973) by Alfred Smyth discusses the importance of the Irish landscape in the formation of Irish society. Smyth brings out the fact that impassable bogs and mountains acted as very effective natural protection for both monasteries and kingdoms, thus ensuring their long life. Three books by Ian Adamson cover different aspects of early Ulster history. **Cruthin: The Ancient Kindred** (Pretani pb £6.99 0950346101) the history of these people, precursors to the Celts, and descended from the Picts. Adamson goes on to argue in his **Ulster People** (Pretani pb £5.99 0948868139) that the population of Ulster have a shared identity, despite the traditional, ethnic reading of Ulster history. His third book **Identity of Ulster: Land, Language & the People** (Pretani pb £6.99 094886804X) builds on his argument by discussing the shared native traditions of the Ulster people. **Sex & Marriage in Ancient Ireland** by Patrick Power (Mercier Press pb £5.99 1856350622) is an interesting study of early Irish attitudes towards sexuality and marriage. The book discusses the more liberal and humane view taken in Ireland at this time which tolerated divorce and remarriage unlike their Christian counterparts in Britain and Europe. **Women in Early Modern Ireland** by Margaret MacCurtain (Edinburgh Up pb £19.95 0748602410) is a scholarly but readable study of its subject. **Colonial Ireland 1169-1369** by Robin Frame (Educational Company pb £6.85 0861670574) is part of the Helicon History of Ireland series and illuminatingly deals with the Anglo-Norman invasion of Ireland and the effects of introducing English Law and administration to Ireland. A fascinating complementary volume is **Skryne & the Early Normans** edited by Elizabeth Hickey for the Meath Archeological & Historical Society (MAHS hb £21.00 095003326X). Skryne was a huge estate near the town of Navan in Co. Meath and a large number of related documents were found at St. Mary's Cistercian Abbey in Dublin. Presented and introduced by Hickey, these documents provide a rare insight to the Anglo-Norman invasion and to the interaction between the people of Ireand and Britain. Another important book on the subject is **The Norman Invasion of Ireland** by Richard Roche (Anvil pb £9.95 0947962816), a lively account which very effectively brings the period to life for the modern reader.

Finally a couple of books which cover the territory where history and myth cross over. **Cycles of the Kings** by Miles Dillon (Four Courts Press pb £6.95 1851821783) is a very good study of this, the last of the cycles in Irish mythology, which tells us the stories of high kings such as Brian Boru and Cormac MacAirt. Combining history and myth, this book will appeal to both the scholar and the general reader because of its inclusion of original documents and its informative introduction. **Brian Boru King of Ireland** by Roger Newman (Anvil Press pb £9.95 0900068655) is a biography of Brian Boru the first high king of Ireland, who extended his power very effectively from Munster to the North and East, over the 10th Century. He was killed at the battle of Clontarf in 1014, by the Leinster forces who had allied themselves with the Vikings, although the battle itself was a victory for Munster.

# 16th Century

There is a wealth of material available on Ireland in the sixteenth century. **Sixteenth Century** Ireland by Colm Lennon (Gill & MacMillan pb £14.99 0717116239) is a comprehensive history of this important century arguing very astutely that the most important social, political and economic change was the spread of the concentration of power from Dublin to include larger towns around the country. **Elizabeth's Irish Wars** by Cyril Falls (Constable pb £9.95 0094772207) discusses and documents how rebellion in Ireland was put down with ruthless military action by an English queen threatened by a network of Irish warrior chieftains. Also by Cyril Falls, **The Birth of Ulster** (Constable pb £9.99 0094784000) was first published in 1936 but is still the clearest account of the Elizabethan Plantation of Ulster, detailing Elizabeth's plans to colonise the North of Ireland and the ensuing struggle and development of the settlement. **Tudor Ireland: Crown, Community and the Conflict of Cultures 1470-1603** by Steven Ellis (Longman pb £17.99 0582493412) is a brilliant re-appraisal of the Tudor conquest of Ireland which examines the difficult but often mutually enhancing relationship between English and Irish Culture in Ireland. It also demonstrates how successful the Tudor government was in Ireland and that military conquest was only necessary when traditional methods of government were abandoned. **Reformations in Ireland: Tradition & Confessionalism 1400-1690** by S. Meig (Gill & MacMillan pb £12.99 0717126390) is an informative examination of the Irish Church and shows how the leaders in the secular community, chieftains and bards, gave Irish Catholicism great strength. It goes on to discuss how after 1600, many former exiles, home from Europe, brought back both European sensibility and experience and were able then to reform the Church to bring it in line with European Tridentinism. **Protestant Reformation in Ireland 1590-1641** by Alan Ford (Four Courts Press pb £14.95 1851822828) is an examination of the foundation of the Church of Ireland and the inherent founding of an Irish Protestant identity.

The important figures of the time have biographies devoted to them. **Shane O'Neill** by Ciaran Brady (Dundalgan Press pb £6.00 0852211295) is a short study of the life of this prominent and successful Ulster leader, son of Conn O'Neill, the 1st earl of Tyrone. By murdering his adoptive brother Matthew, Shane O'Neill took the role of head of the clan. He was given the 'O'Neillship' by the Crown in 1563. He was kept in check by the arrival of Sir Henry Sidney in the same year. Sidney weakened O'Neill's power base by setting up a garrison in Derry. O'Neill was defeated and killed in 1567 and was succeeded by Turlough O'Neill. However, Matthew's son Hugh, who had been brought up near Dublin, after the murder of his father, was set up by the British to curb Turlough's power and he defeated Turlough with his son-in-law Red Hugh O'Donnell in 1592. Hugh and O'Donnell were eventually defeated by the Crown forces at the Battle of Kinsale in December 1601. O'Neill left the country and died in Rome in 1616. Sean O'Faolain has written **The Great O'Neill: A Biography of Hugh O'Neill** (Mercier Press pb £9.99 0853427690) while M.K. Walsh's biography **Hugh O'Neill: Prince of Ulster** (Four Courts Press pb £7.95 1851822348) focuses on O'Neill's exile from Ireland between 1607 and 1616. **Granuaile: Life and Times of Grace O'Malley** by Anne Chambers (Wolfhound Press pb £5.95 0863272134) is a very exciting biography of Grace O'Malley (1530-1603), who because of her piracy and naval power in the west of Ireland has become both a nationalist and feminist icon. O'Malley ran a very successful operation out of Clew Bay and to an extent controlled maritime activity on the West coast. She was imprisoned by the British between 1577 and 1579 and went to London in 1593 to complain about the Bingham family and especially Sir Richard Bingham's government. Details of this family are to be found in Theresa B. Daly's **The Mayo Binghams** (Pentland pb £15.00 1858214378). This family led by Sir Richard Bingham, president of Connacht from 1584 to 1596, fought with many of the leading Connaught families of the time and his government collapsed in 1595. The collapse was blamed on him and he left in 1596 to defend his position in London. He was imprisoned for his over enthusiastic use of martial law but was reinstated as marshall of Ireland in 1598. One of the best-known of the English Elizabethan colonialists was the poet Edmund Spenser. Andrew Hadfield and Willy Maley have recently edited **The View of the State of Ireland** by Edmund Spenser (Blackwell pb £12.99 0631205357). This edition provides the full text, which outlines Spenser's view that a tough martial policy was the only way to deal with Ireland. It also provides very useful context, bibliographical information and details of its initial reception.

One of the most unusual books of sixteenth century history is **Irish Wrecks of the Spanish Armada** by Laurence Flanagan (Town House pb £5.95 0946172471), a fascinating account of the discovery and excavation of the twenty Spanish ships that sunk around the Irish coast. The details of artefacts found on board greatly enhance modern understanding of life aboard these 16th Century Spanish warships.

# Seventeenth Century

The best general history of the seventeenth century is **Seventeenth Century Ireland: The War of Religions** by Brendan Fitzpatrick (Gill & MacMillan pb £14.99 0717116263) one of the brilliant 'New Gill History of Ireland' series. This is a comprehensive survey which argues that real understanding of the period hinges on an understanding of the relationship between the differing religious groups. **Hell or Connaught: Cromwellian Colonisation of Ireland** 1652-1660 by Peter Beresford Ellis (Blackstaff Press pb £6.99 0856404047) is a detailed history of this brutal and savage period of Irish history in which unquestionably barbaric acts were committed by a superior and ruthless colonising force. A very good companion volume which both complements and contrasts with Ellis's point of view is **The Cromwellian Settlement of Ireland** by J.P. Prendergast (Constable hb £20.00 0094766207) which surveys the period after the colonisation. William Nolan's excellent study, **Fassadinin: Land, Settlement and society in Southeast Ireland 1600-1850** (Geography Publications hb £9.50 0906602009) is a history of this important Barony in Kilkenny, which was set up and maintained by the Swift and Webb families in this period. Nolan also focusses on the foundation and development of the town of Castlecomer. **Ulster 1641: Aspects of the Rising** edited by Brian MacCuarta (Institute of Irish Studies hb £ 9.50 0853895910), is an interesting collection of essays examining the social and religious division in Ulster at the time in the context of the 1641 Rising. **1690: William & the Boyne** by Ian Adamson (Pretani Press pb £6.99 0948868201) brilliantly reveals many of the complexities behind the Battle of the Boyne, a battle which has passed into the realm of myth. The book argues that there is a much larger and complex understanding of preceding events which challenges the consensual idea that the battle was just an evil annihilation of Catholics by marauding Protestants. **Siege of Derry in Ulster Protestant Mythology** by Ian MacBride (Four Courts Press pb £14.95 1851822992) is a comprehensive survey of the causes of this siege which has become the main political myth in Northern Protestantism. The book also examines the politics behind contemporary commemorative events. **Patrick Sarsfield & the Williamite War** by P.A.C Wauchope. (Gill & MacMillan pb £9.95 0716524961) is a biography of this fascinating figure, well documenting his life from his unpromising early military career to his brilliant negotiations and terms with the Williamites which led directly to the Treaty of Limerick.

Biographies of other seventeenth century figures are available. **Justin McCarthy** by Eugene J. Doyle (Dundalgan Press pb £6.00 0852211287) is a short but concise biographical study of McCarthy (1643-1694) detailing the major events in his life. He was employed by the French as a soldier and, in the pay of the English in 1689, defeated a Protestant revolt in Munster. He was defeated at Newtownbutler and escaped to France in 1690. In France he commanded 5,000 Irish troops which were exchanged by James II for French soldiers. He later commanded soldiers in France and Spain. Hector MacDonnell's **Wild Geese of the Antrim MacDonnells** (Irish Academic Press hb £25.00 0716526093) is a detailed examination of the exile of one of the more famous Irish families between 1650 and 1820. All of the characters discussed were direct descendants of the 16th Century warrior Sorley Boy MacDonnell and the book follows the family to The Netherlands, France and Spain.

Several works on religion in the period are worth mentioning. **As by Law Established: The Church of Ireland Since the Reformation** edited by Alan Ford/J. McGuire & K. Milne (Lilliput Press hb £25.00 1874675376) is a lively and diverse collection of essays, all first presented as papers at a 1993 conference in University College, Dublin. The book, covering much more than the seventeenth century, effectively traces the development of the Church of Ireland over five centuries but is particularly strong on this period. **The Irish Dissenting Tradition 1650-1750** by Jim Herlihy (Four Courts Press pb £11.95 1851822100) is a collection of essays providing definitions of Protestant dissent and studies of Baptist, Quaker, French Huguenot and Palatine communities placed in the context of Protestantism and 17th and 18th Century Irish society. **The Politics of Irish Dissent 1650-1800** edited by Kevin Herlihy (Four Courts Press pb £11.95 1851823026) traces the political aspect of the Irish dissenting tradition. The essays in this volume discuss the relationship between dissent and government authority as well as providing documentary evidence.

# 18th Century

A number of biographies exist of eighteenth century figures, both well-known and not so well-known. Stella Tillyard has vividly recreated the Irish 18th Century as well as the life of Edward Fitzgerald in her **Citizen Lord: Edward Fitzgerald 1763-1798** (Vintage pb £7.99 0099732114). Fitzgerald, who had served in the British Army in the American Revolution, became an admirer of the French Revolution. Having been dismissed by the British Army, he joined the United Irish movement in 1796 and passionately advocated military action. He was arrested in May 1798 and died from his wounds soon after. **Aristocrats: Caroline, Emily, Louisa & Sarah Lennox 1740-1832** (Vintage pb £8.99 0099477114), also by Stella Tillyard, is a fascinating and lively account of the four Lennox Sisters, who were great-grand daughters of Charles II and daughters of the Duke of Richmond. Caroline eloped with Henry Fox, the 1st Lord Holland; Emily married the Duke of Leinster, had nineteen children, the most famous of these being Edward Fitzgerald; Louisa married Thomas Connolly, the wealthiest man in Ireland and Sarah married a baronet, divorced him and then married George Napier. Tillyard has woven these four turbulent, adventurous lives into a wonderful story of 18th Century society, both in England and Ireland. Conor Cruise O'Brien's **Edmund Burke** (New Island pb £9.99 1874597626), doesn't just tell the life story of Edmund Burke, but, through a close examination of and commentary on Burke's writings, demonstrates how he supported the American Revolution but, after the excesses of the French Revolution, came strongly in favour of the existing order. Nicholas Robinson has collected and introduced many of the contemporary caricatures of Burke which make up **Edmund Burke: A Life in Caricature** (Yale University Press hb £30.00 0300068018). **John Fitzgibbon, Earl of Clare: A Study in Personality & Politics** by Ann Kavanaugh (Irish Academic Press hb £35.00 0716526050) is a fascinating biography of this brilliant but difficult figure. Between 1778 and 1795 he went from being Attorney General to succeeding to the Earldom of Clare, having been Lord Chancellor and Viscount of Limerick in the meantime. He had huge contempt for Irish Catholicism and happily supported and implemented English Government anti-Catholic policy. **Humanity Dick Martin 'King of Connemara' 1754-1834** by Shevawn Lynam (Lilliput Press pb £6.99 094664036X) is a lively biography of a colurful 18th century Galway figure. During his lifetime he was an environmentalist, founder of the animal protection society and lawyer and landlord. Lynam's book succinctly recreates the life and world of this great humanitarian of the west. **Mary Ann McCracken 1770-1866** by Mary McNeill (Blackstaff Press hb £19.99 0856406031) describes the life of this Belfast-based philanthropist, who also ran a successful textile factory from the 1780s to 1815.

More general books on the country in the eighteenth century are plentiful. **Endurance & Emergence: Catholic in Ireland in the 18th Century,** edited by T.

Power & K. Whelan (Irish Academic Press hb £27.50 0716524201), is a fascinatingly contentious book which challenges the consensual view of the catholic population living in persecution and servitude. It covers the period from the Williamite wars in the 1690s to Catholic Emancipation in the 1820s. **Graces Card: Irish Catholic Landlords 1690-1800** by Charles Trench (Mercier Press pb £12.99 1856351637) is a political history focussing on the Catholic landlords who lost part of their holdings in the time of Elizabeth I and lost it all during Cromwell's campaign. It also shows how badly effected these landlords were by the Penal Laws. **The Catholic Community in the 17th & 18th Centuries** by Patrick Corish (Educational Company pb £6.85 0861670639), one of the invaluable 'Helicon History of Ireland' series, discusses the two main social forces in Ireland at the time, penal legislation and Tridentine Catholicism and demonstrates the many regional and class divisions that were endemic to the Catholic community. **Catholicism in a Protestant Kingdom: A Study of the Irish Ancien Regime** by C.D.A Leighton (Gill & MacMillan pb £12.99 0717121240) is a study of what the people of Ireland thought about Catholicism and Protestantism and as a result is an illuminating essay on the attitudes of the 18th century Irish. **Parties, Patriots & Undertakers: Parliamentary Politics in Early Hanoverian Ireland** by Patrick McNally (Four Courts Press hb £30.00 1851822550) is a detailed commentary on the relationship between the Irish and English parliaments in the 17th and 18th centuries. Following the 1991 bicentenary of the United Irishmen and the resulting conference David Dickson and Daire Keogh and Kevin Whelan edited **The United Irishmen: Republicanism, Radicalism & Rebellion** (Lilliput Press pb £15.00 1874675198) which is a very interesting collection of papers relating to many aspects of the formation, policy and demise of the movement. **Partners In Revolution: United Irishmen & France** by Marianne Elliott (Yale University Press pb £14.50 0300043023) examines the intellectual background to the United Irishmen in the context of the French Revolution. **Rebels & Informers: Stirrings of Irish Independence** by Oliver Knox (John Murray hb £20.00 0719555736) is a study focussing on the issue of informants which plagued the United Irishmen movement. The book concentrates on the relationship between Wolfe Tone, Edward Fitzgerald, Hamilton Rowan and William Drennan. **'French Disease': Catholic Church & Radicalism in Ireland 1790-1800** by Daire Keogh (Four Courts Press hb £19.95 1851821325) is a fascinating account of the Catholic hierarchy's response to the French radical political thought which swept the country in the late 18th century. At the time, the church was in turmoil because of the many priests involved in the Rebellion and Keogh's book shows how the church exploited this unrest to found the church that exists today. **Dublin Hanged** by Brian Henry (Irish Academic Press pb £8.95 071652614X) is a lively account of crime and punishment in 18th century Dublin. It brings to life the atmosphere of the city and explains the sometimes cloudy system of legal retribution and punishment. **Dictionary of British & Irish Travellers in Italy 1701-1800** by John Amells (Yale University Press hb £50.00 0300071655), compiled from the Brinsley Ford archive, is a fascinating documentation of the social and cultural traffic between the British Isles and the

Mediterranean in the 18th Century. **Arctic Ireland Famine 1740-41: The Extraordinary Story of the Great Frost and Forgotten Famine of 1740-41** by David Dickson (White Row Press pb £4.95 1870132858) tells the story of this meteorological disaster when a freak frost descended on the country which was celebrated at first but resulted in a huge famine as proportionately damaging the Great Famine of the 1840s. **Irish Charter Schools 1730-1830** by K. Milne (Four Courts Press hb £ 35.00 1851822321) examines the reasons and beliefs behind the foundation of these schools, drawing heavily on contemporary manuscripts. From the end of the 17th century to the mid-19th Century, Hedge Schools were very popular around the country. Although little documentary evidence is available about the schools, **The Hedge Schools of Ireland** (Mercier Press pb £6.99 1856351815) discusses how the locals, protected and sheltered the travelling schoolmasters, who introduced many of the population to Mathematics and Classics for the first time and how the Hedge Schools were eventually replaced by the National School system in the mid 19th Century. **The History of the Church of Ireland: 1691-1996** (Columba hb £25.00 185607210X) by Alan Acheson covers the period from the Williamite Wars to the present and Acheson discusses such topics as the Church's role in the Famine and in contemporary Irish Society but it is particularly strong on the period.

## 1798 Rising

The most important event in eighteenth century Irish history came at its end and that was the 1798 Rising. The subject is well covered by the many books available. Recently revised to coincide with the 200th anniversary of 1798, with a new chronology and very useful glossary **The Year of Liberty** by Thomas Pakenham (Weidenfeld & Nicolson hb £20.00 0297819550) has become the standard one-volume study of the Rebellion. Combining history, biography and local study and using sources such as the National Archive Rebellion papers and local, contemporary accounts, Pakenham has woven all the threads of this story into a very readable, if complex, whole. The author also provides detailed background and context to the times thus demonstrating the inevitability of this brave revolt which turned into a horrific bloodbath. Weidenfeld & Nicolson have also issued a large format abridged and illustrated edition (hb £14.99 0297823868). Richard Musgrave's **Irish Rebellion of 1798** (Tower Books hb £34.95 096439250X) is the classic loyalist account of the rebellion. First published in 1802, it is encyclopaedic in scope, listing most of the people involved. This new edition comes with a new foreword by David Dickson which places the book in its historical perspective. **Eyewitness 1798** edited by Terence Folley (Mercier Press pb £5.99 185635153X) is a fascinating and valuable collection of contemporary accounts and greatly helps our understanding of 18th Century public opinion. **Wolfe Tone: Prophet of Irish Independence** by Marianne

Elliott (Yale University Press pb £12.95 0300051956) is the first major biography of the great rebel leader and comprehensively chronicles the life of this Dublin-born and Trinity College-educated barrister from his early life to his suicide in September 1798 after being captured and sentenced to death by the English. He was one of the founders of the United Irishmen in 1791 and in 1796 travelled to France to try and raise support for an armed rebellion. Other valuable and concise biographies are Henry Boylan's **Wolfe Tone** (Gill & MacMillan pb £6.99 0717126404) and Thomas Bartlett's short study Wolfe Tone (Dundalgan Press pb £6.00 0852211333).

A.T.Q. Stewart's **Summer Soldiers: The 1798 Rebellion in Antrim & Down** (Blackstaff Press pb £12.99 0856405582) is a comprehensive account of the rebellion in these Northern Irish counties. Kevin Whelan's study **The Tree of Liberty: Radicalism, Catholicism & the Construction of Irish Identity 1760-1830** (Cork University Press pb £14.95 1859180604) is a collection of four essays, which deal with the role of Catholic middlemen in the 1798 Rebellion, the United Irishmen, Sectarianism and the Irish collective memory of 1798. Combining historiography, geography and social study, these essays are a landmark in the contemporary understanding of the late 18th and early 19th centuries in Ireland. **The Tellicherry Five: The Transportation of Michael Dwyer and the Wicklow Rebels,** by Kieran Sheedy (Woodfield Press pb £9.99 0952845334) narrates the story of Dwyer and his partners in rebellion in 1798, who caused havoc for the Crown forces in Wicklow. They were transported to New South Wales on the ship Tellichery where they clashed with William Bligh (of Bounty fame), the then Governor General of this new colony. Sheedy describes the grim conditions in the colony and the Five's struggle to get the rights they deserved. **Protestant, Catholic & Dissenter: The Clergy & 1798** edited by Liam Swords (Columba Press hb £25.00 1856072096) is a collection of lucid essays, discussing the role of ministers, priests and preachers in the 1798 rebellion. The book includes an overview of the period by Daire Keogh, a chapter on Wexford priests by Kevin Whelan and a chapter on Fr. John Murphy of Boolavogue by Nicholas Furlong. **Wexford Rising in 1798** by Charles Dickson (Constable hb £16.95 0094772509) is a classic account. Dickson has also written **Revolt in the North** (Constable hb £16.95 0094772606) which is a detailed local study of the rebellion in Antrim and Down. **The People's Rising: Wexford, 1798** by Daniel Gahan (Gill & MacMillan pb £12.99 0717123235), though only recently published, has become an instant classic describing in great detail the events which led up to the appalling massacre on Vinegar Hill. To coincide with the bicentennial celebrations, Gahan published **Rebellion: Ireland in 1798** (O'Brien Press hb £14.99 0862785413) which is a general overview of the rebellion around the country and is the official bicentennial book. Local historian Nicholas Furlong, with Daire Keogh, has edited a collection of essays **The Mighty Wave: 1798 Rebellion in Wexford** (Four Courts Press pb £9.95 1851822542) which focuses on the Wexford battles. **The Decade of the United Irishmen** by John Killen (Blackstaff Press pb £12.99 0856406112) examines the contemporary accounts and reactions to the rebellion. **The French are in the Bay: The Expedition To Bantry Bay 1796** by John A. Murphy (Mercier Press pb £7.99 1856351718) examines the strategy involved in the organisation of a French 'armada' to land on the South East coast, and the role that Wolfe Tone played in this strategy. **On the Road to Rebellion: United Irishmen and Hamburg** by Paul Weber (Four Courts Press hb £30.00 1851823115) is an account of how important the German city was to the Irish radicals who used it as a place to liaise with the great figures of revolutionary Europe. Michael Kenny, curator of the National Museum of Ireland, has edited **1798 Rebellion: Photographs & Memorabilia from the National Museum of Ireland** (Town House pb £4.99 0946172501) which is a very interesting, illustrated catalogue of the 1798 artefacts in the museum's collection.

Finally, Art Kavanagh has published a fascinating and informative series of pamphlets which describe in detail many of the battles which took place around the country: –

**Battles of 1798: Carlow**
Kavanagh pb £2.50 0952478552
**Battles of 1798:Enniscorthy**
Kavanagh pb £2.50 0952478528
**Battles of 1798: Newtownbarry**
Kavanagh pb £2.50 0952478579
**Battles of 1798: Oulart**
Kavanagh pb £2.50 0952478560
**Battles of 1798: The Harrow**
Kavanagh pb £2.50 095247851X
**Battles of 1798**
Kavanagh pb £9.95 0952478587

The best general overview of the period is **Nineteenth Century Ireland** by P.W. Boyce (Gill & MacMillan pb £14.99 0717116212) There are many books available which deal exclusively with different aspects of 19th century Irish history. **Irish Peasant Society** by K.H. Connell (Irish Academic Press pb £14.95 0716526107) discusses the social fabric of Ireland as does **Ordinary Lives** by Tony Farmar (Farmar & Farmar pb £8.99 1899047107). Mark Bence-Jones's pioneering study **Life in an Irish Country House** (Constable hb £20.00 009474680X) clearly chronicles and illustrates the life and times of The Big House and all who lived therein. A book of essays, **Science & Society in Ireland: The Social Context of Science & Technology in Ireland 1800-1950** edited by Peter Bowler & Nicholas Whyte (Institute of Irish Studies pb £8.50 0853896690) is one of the few books which discusses and records the history of science in Ireland and is a valuable sourcebook. Other social studies include **Women, Power and Consciousness** by Mary Cullen & Maria Luddy (Attic Press pb £15.99 1855940787) and **Gender Perspectives in 19th Century Ireland: Public & Private Spheres** edited by Margaret Kelleher & James H. Murphy (Irish Academic Press hb £30.00 0716525909). One of the other fascinating books concerned with Women's History is **Women & Philanthropy in 19th Century Ireland** by Maria Luddy (Cambridge pb £12.95 0521483611). This discusses the great charity work carried out by many wealthy women in the last century. Political studies of the last century include **Local Government in 19th Century Ireland** by Virginia Crossman (Institute of Irish Studies pb £4.95 0853895090) which is a fascinating and informative explanation of the role of local government in 19th Century Irish Society; **Nationalism & Unionism** by Jonathan Bardon (Cambridge University Press pb £6.25 0521466059); **Colonialism, Religion & Nationalism in Ireland,** a book of essays by Liam Kennedy (Institute of Irish Studies pb £9.75 0853896216); **Government & Reform, 1815-19** by Robert Pearce (Silhouette pb £4.99 034059814X); **Ireland, 1828-1923: From Ascendancy to Democracy** by D.G.M Boyce (Blackwell pb £6.99 0631172831) **Ireland Since 1800: Conflict and Conformity** by Theodore Hoppen (Longman pb £14.99 058200473X). Gearóid O'Tuathaigh's **Ireland before the Famine, 1790-** (Gill & MacMillan pb £18.990717117839) provides a useful overview of pre-Famine Ireland. **Workhouses of Ireland: The Fate of Ireland's Poor** by John O'Connor (Anvil Press pb £9.95 0947962719) is a study demonstrating the opposition to the workhouses from both the clergy and politicians and how far they fell short of their expected role and contribution to society when they inevitably became disease ridden places for the Irish destitute to die. **The Night of the Big Wind: The Story of the Legendary Big Wind of 1839, Ireland's Greatest Natural Disaster** by Peter Carr (White Row Press pb £4.95 1870132505) is an entertaining study of this great disaster. **The Royal Irish Constabulary: A Short History & Genealogical Guide with a Select List of Medal Awards & Casualties** by Jim Herlihy (Four Courts Press pb £14.95 1851823433) is the only comprehensive history of the forerunners of the

Garda Síochána.

## The Famine

The Great Famine was the central historical experience for Ireland in the last century and was mainly caused by the repeated failure of the potato crop over the years 1845-49. There are many books available which detail various aspects of this disaster. The main general modern studies are **The Great Irish Famine** by Campbell (pb £5.95 095235411X), **The Famine in Ireland** by Mary E. Daly (Dundalgan Press pb £7.50 0852211082) and **'This Great Calamity': The Irish Famine** by Christine Kinealy (Gill & MacMillan pb £17.99 0717118819). Thames & Hudson's New Horizon series also has a very useful volume on the Famine. Entitled **The Irish Famine** and edited by Peter Gray, it contains many fascinating contemporary images (Thames & Hudson pb £6.95 0500300577). Helen Litton has written an illuminating history of the famine with her **Irish Famine: An Illustrated History** (Wolfhound Press pb £16.99 0863274277). Cormac Ó Gráda, one of the most important of the current generation of historians and teachers, has written two lucid and perceptive studies, **The Great Irish Famine** (Gill & MacMillan pb £5.99 0717117316) and his magisterial **Ireland Before and After the Famine** (Manchester University Press pb £12.99 0719040353).The two classic accounts that are still available are **The Great Famine** by Edwards and Williams (Lilliput Press pb £14.99 0946640947) and Cecil Woodham Smith's **The Great Hunger** (Penguin pb £9.99 014014515X). **Famine Decade** by John Killen (Blackstaff Press pb £10.99 0856405604) is a fascinating collection of contemporary reports and articles from the 19th century and brilliantly displays the different 19th century views. **Famine 150 – Commemorative Lectures** (Teagasc pb £6.99 1901138097) is a lucid collection of essays originally given as lectures by, among others, Joseph Lee, Mary Daly and Cormac O'Grada. The Thomas Davis Lectures, broadcast annually on RTE radio took the Famine as their subject in 1995. The lectures have been published with an introduction by Cathal Portéir as **The Great Irish Famine 1845-1852** (Mercier Press pb £8.99 1856351114). These offer fascinating insights into various aspects of famine studies. Particularly notable is Margaret Kelleher's piece on 19th Century literature. Kelleher went on to engage brilliantly with famine in world culture with her full-length **Feminization of Famine** (Cork University Press pb £16.95 1859180787). **Irish Famine Documents** published by the National Library of Ireland and edited by Noel Kissane provide rare contemporary documents concerning the Famine around the country (pb £9.95 0907328245). Another very valuable source is **Letters from Ireland during the Famine of 1847** by Alexander Somerville (Irish Academic Press pb £12.95 0716525453). This modern re-set edition by Keith Snell offers a uniquely contemporary account of the Famine from twenty three places around the country.

Of the many historical essays published over the last few years, the two most notable are **'Fearful Realities': New Perspectives on the Famine** edited by Chris

Morash & Richard Hayes (Irish Academic Press pb £14.95 0716525666) which is a valuable collection in that it offers fresh viewpoints of the Famine without getting bogged down in revisionist debate and **The Hungry Stream: Essays on Famine & Emigration,** edited by Margaret Crawford (Institute of Irish Studies pb £9.50 0853896747) which is a superbly diverse collection of essays dealing with the emigration caused by the Famine. The essays, first presented as papers at the sesquicentary anniversary conference at the Ulster American Folk Park examines the experience of emigrants to America, Australia and Britain as well as examining the effects that the Famine had on the people who didn't emigrate. Emigration is also examined exclusively in **The Famine Ships,** a recent study by Edward Laxton (Bloomsbury pb £6.99 0747535000). This wonderfully written book skillfully chronicles the nightmarish conditions experienced on the ships which brought many people away from starvation but managed to kill many due to overcrowding and disease. Some of these conditions are also narrated in Robert Whyte's **Famine Ship Diary** edited by J.J. Managan (Mercier Press pb £6.99 1856350916). The Post-Famine experience in Australia is brilliantly reconstructed by David Fitzpatrick in his **Oceans of Consolation: Personal Accounts of Irish Migration to Australia** (Cork University Press pb £19.95 1859180361). This massive book focuses on fourteen different sets of correspondences from 1843 to 1906 and is both wonderfully informative and moving. There is also a cassette available of readings from the letters (Cork University Press £5.95 1859180752). **The Irish Diaspora: A Primer** by Donald Harman Akenson (Institute for Irish Studies pb £9.50 0853896631) examines the phenomenon of the Irish Diaspora from the Famine to the present day and looks at the various Irish communities that have settled all over the world.

There are plenty of local studies available, which deal with how the Famine affected particularly the West and South of the country. In 1841, over 33,400 people lived in the West of Ireland. Ten years later, the population had reduced to 21,349. **Patient Endurance: The Great Famine in Connemara** by Kathleen Villiers-Tuthil (Connemara pb £9.95 0953045501) explores this statistic and explains that the main reason so many of the population died was that they were tenants, heavily reliant on the potato crop. Tim Robinson has edited a new edition of Thomas Conville Scott's Martin Estate journal **Connemara after the Famine: Journal of a Survey of the Martin Estate** (Lilliput Press pb £5.99 1874675694). **The Famine in Waterford** by Cowman/Brady offers an account of the affects of the famine on the South East of the Country (Geography Publications pb £9.95 0906602602). **The Great Famine in Killala** (pb £14.00) is a good account of the famine as it affected the west coast. Historian Ignatius Murphy has written two fascinating case studies about 19th Century life in West Clare, **Before the Famine Struck: Life in West Clare 1834-1845** (0716525860) and **A Starving People: Life & Death in West Clare 1845-1851** (Irish Academic Press pb £8.95 0716525828). The first book examines life before the Famine and traces many customs and folklore around the village of Kilkee. The second, drawing heavily on 19th Century sources, examines both the Famine and its aftermath on the same area. Probably the most impressive of all the local studies is Robert Scally's **The End of Hidden Ireland; Rebellion, Famine & Emigration** (Oxford University Press pb £12.99 0195106598) which painstakingly recreates the life of the community of Ballykilcline in Co. Roscommon that was wiped out in the 1840s. Combining archive research, archaeology and an uncommon narrative flair, Scally chronicles the gradual demise and eventual death of the townland in harrowing and heart-breaking detail. Concentrating on the North of Ireland, G. MacAtasney's **This Dreadful Visitation: The Famine in Lurgan & Portadown** (Beyond The Pale pb £6.95 1900960028) dispels the myth that the linen industry and the Northern work ethic protected this area from starvation and lays the blame for the number of people dying at the feet of the local gentry.

Finally **The Irish Hunger: Personal Reflections of the Legacy of the Famine** (Wolfhound hb £16.99 0863275532), edited by Tom Hayden, is a series of modern reactions in poetry, prose and interview by a range of artists and historians such as Seamus Heaney, Seamus Deane, Paul Durcan, Luke Gibbons and Luke Dodd.

## Post – Famine

The relationship between Nationalism and Unionism was a crucial issue in Ireland from the 1880s to the 1920s. In **Nationalism & Unionism: Conflict in Ireland 1885-1921** (Institute of Irish Studies pb £8.50 0853894957) edited by Peter Collins, a number of leading historians examine this relationship during these turbulent times. Among others, Brian Walker discusses the 1885-6 general elections, Catherine Shannon writes about Arthur Balfour and Alvin Jackson devotes a chapter to Irish Unionism. **The Irish Question & British Politics** by D.G. Boyce (MacMillan pb £9.99 0333665309) is a lucid and interesting discussion of how British Government policies since the early 19th century have had such a profound effect on the shaping of modern Ireland. Mark Bence Jones's by now classic study, **The Twilight of the Ascendancy** (Constable pb £11.50 0094723508) discusses in a lively and entertaining fashion how the Anglo-Irish Ascendancy lost their power in the 100 years from the 1870s to the 1970s, due to dwindling fortunes, both World Wars and the Irish Troubles of the 1920s. Bence-Jones presents portraits of various characters and the different conditions of their houses, some riddled with dry rot, some burnt to the ground, some convulsed by preparations for a Royal visit. **The Fenians: Photographs & Memorabilia from the National Museum of Ireland** (Town House pb £4.95 0946172420) by Michael Kenny contains valuable photographs and illustration as well as clear text, focusing on the artefacts concerning the Fenians housed in the Museum. Robert Kee's **The Laurel & the Ivy: The Story of Charles Stewart Parnell** (Penguin pb £9.99 0140239626) is the most recent biography of the great statesman and concentrates on the relationship between Parnell and Kitty O'Shea. Using his enormous knowledge of Irish history and experience of writing, Kee has not just written a biography, but a cogent introduction to late 19th and early 20th Century Irish politics and history.

Further biographical studies can be recommended. **The Parnell Split, 1890-91** by Frank Callanan (Cork University Press pb £15.95 0902561642) establishes the cause of the split between Charles Stewart Parnell and T.M. Healy. Callanan went onto write a wonderfully lucid biography of Healy, **T.M. Healy** (Cork University Press pb £15.95 1859181724). **Parnell: A Documentary History,** edited by Noel Kissane (National Library of Ireland £9.95 0907328199), is a very useful collection of 19th century documents, all relating to Parnell, and is the ideal starting point for historical research. The Historical Association of Ireland have produced the 'Life & Times' series which, aimed at the student as well as the general reader, places the lives of many important 19th Century figures against the background of new research in the period. Titles available in the series include **D.P. Moran** (1869-1936) by Patrick Maume (Dundalgan Press pb £6.00 0852211252); **William Martin Murphy** (1844-1919) by Thomas Murphy (Dundalgan Press pb £4.00 0852211325) and **John Redmond** (1856-1918) by Paul Bew (Dundalgan Press pb £6.00 0852211309). **Immortal Dan: Daniel O'Connell in the Irish Folk Tradition** by Rionach Ui Ogain (Geography Publications pb £9.95 0906602408) captures the 19th century reaction to O'Connell in poetry and song and demonstrates what a powerful figure he was in the Irish imagination. **William O'Brien & the Irish Land War** by S. Warwick-Hailer (Irish Academic Press hb £9.95 0716524589) is not only a biography of O'Brien but also discusses his involvement with the Land Wars of the late 19th Century. Probably most famous for his defence of the Marquis of Queensberry against Oscar Wilde in 1895, Dublin-born lawyer Edward Carson, became solicitor-general for Ireland in 1892, the same year he was elected MP for Trinity College, Dublin. In **Edward Carson** (1854-1935) (Blackstaff Press pb £8.99 0856406139), A.T.Q. Stewart examines Carson's life as a lawyer and as a successful politician who rose to fame during the debates on Home Rule.

Other books on the period worth reading include **The Origins of Modern Irish Socialism 1881-1896** by Fintan Lane (Cork University Press pb £16.95 185918152X) which demonstrates how the Socialist tradition was well established in Ireland long before James Connolly founded The Irish Socialist Republican Party in 1896, and **A Labour History of Ireland, 1824-1960** by Emmet O'Connor (Gill & MacMillan pb £12.99 0717120163) which illuminates the roles of trade unions in Ireland labour history. **The Miasma: Epidemic & Panic in 19th Century Ireland** by Joseph Robins

(Institute of Public Administration pb £7.99 187200282X) discusses the public reaction to the Typhus epidemic of 1816-1819 and the Cholera epidemic of the 1840s which was to compound the effects of the Great Famine. It also discusses the differing and divisive reactions in the medical profession to the cause of both epidemics. **How the Irish Became White** by Noel Ignatiev (Routledge pb £12.99 0415918251) is a fascinating study, arguing that the success of the Irish diaspora in 19th Century America society was a result of their almost total embrace of white supremacist views.

## Hannah Sheehy Skeffington and Irish Women's History
## By Anne Griffin Waterstone's, Dawson Street, Dublin

**Hanna Sheehy Skeffington: A Life** by Margaret Ward (Cork University Press pbk£14.95 1859181651) is the story of one remarkable woman's life, but it is also much more. Like many other of Ward's great works (**Unmanageable Revolutionaries,** for instance and **Countess Markievicz**) it highlights the strength and power of women in early twentieth century Ireland. These women, all born in the late nineteenth century, were highly educated and acutely aware of the discrimination they suffered despite their abilities. As a result they set out to force Ireland out of the dark ages. They demanded that their country give women degrees equal to those of men, jobs in male domains and votes and positions in Irish Politics. Over the course of a period up until the 1937 consitution they badgered Ireland into becoming one of the most advanced and modern countries of its time by being amongst the first of its European neighbours to allow such revolutionary change. These women pushed the powers to their limits and left them no choice but to shake off the cobwebs and grudgingly allow women's voices to be heard.

The histories of these times and the stories of women such as Skeffington, Mary Hayden, Gretta Cousins, Helen Curran, Louie Bennett and many more are fascinating. They were revolutionaries, freaks to many and annoying to most, and yet they are some of the greatest heroes Ireland has ever known. Skeffington's story is one of great bravery and boldness. From an early age she was aware of what Ireland meant for her as a woman. She had few rights and few chances to be what she wanted. It was a far cry from the Ireland under Brehon Law. Ireland was unashamedly discriminatory. Hannal fought all her life to change this. She fought not just Ireland's English rulers but also her nationalist colleagues. Skeffington had a deep commitment to a self-ruling Ireland and yet she refused to bow to the discrimination that was rife in the nationalist movement. Skeffington was not content to be a member of Cumann na mBan, the female wing of the Irish Volunteers. To have any kind of division based on sex in a political organisation was stupidity to her. For the Irish Volunteers to remain silent on the issue of Female Suffrage was moreover an insult to its female members. Skeffington protested that being a woman in this organisation meant one was to be treated as 'The ministering angel of the ambulance class, who provides the pyjamas and the lint, but who sinks below the human the moment she asks for the vote'.

The freedom of Ireland was of importance to her but the freedom of women even more so. Hannal's greatest tragedy was to befall her in the rising of 1916 when her husband Francis Sheehy Skeffington, renowned pacifist and feminist, was killed. Hanna continued to fight during the rest of her life against the injustice of this murder by British soldiers and their attempt to cover it up.

Hanna Sheehy Skeffington was a remarkable woman and Margaret Ward's biography is a remarkable read. The reader will be not just in awe of this woman's strength and determination but also aware that the story of Ireland in the early

*Anne Chambers*
**Granauaile: The Life and Times of Grace O'Malley**
Wolfhound £7.95 0863276318

*Anne Chambers*
**As Wicked a Woman: Eleanor, Countess of Desmond**
Wolfhound £8.95 0863271901

*Mary Cullen and Maria Luddy*
**Women, Power and Consiousness Cork**
University Press £17.95 1855940787

*Mary Daly*
**Women and Poverty**
Cork University Press £7.95

*Maria Luddy*
**Women in Ireland 1800-1918 Cork**
University Press £17.95 pb 1859180388

*Maria Luddy*
**Women and Philanthropy in 19th Century Ireland**
Cambridge University Press £12.95 pb 0521483611

*Maria Luddy*
**Hannah Sheehy Skeffington**
Dundalgen £6.00 0852211260

*Margaret MacCurtain & Mary O'Dowd*
**Women in Early Modern Ireland**
Edinburgh University Press £19.95 0748602410

*O'Ceirin*
**Women of Ireland (Dictionary of Biography)**
Tir Eolas £9.95 1873821069

*Mary O'Dowd & Mary Ann Valiulis*
**Women and Irish History**
Wolfhound £17.99

*Rosemary Cullen Owens*
**Smashing Times**
Attic Press £8.99 0946211086

*Ruth Taillon*
**Women of 1916**
Beyond the Pale £6.95 0951422987

*Margaret Ward*
**Unmanageable Revolutionaries**
Pluto £13.99 0745310842

*Margaret Ward*
**In their Own Voice**
Cork University Press £8.99

# Twentieth Century

## General

Dermot Keogh's **20th Century Ireland: Nation & State** (Gill & MacMillan pb £14.99 0717116247) is the last volume of the New Gill History of Ireland and is one of the few comprehensive histories of the whole period available. Keogh's emphasis is on the south of the country and the foundation of the Free State. He examines both social and political history, looking at the awful effect that emigration has had on several generations of Irish people. **Settlements & Divisions: Ireland 1870-1972** by Pauric Travers (Educational Company pb £6.85 0861670698), part of the Helicon History of Ireland, gives valuable background information to the Act of Union and the eventual Partition of Ireland. Joseph Lee's **Ireland 1912-1985: Politics & Society** (Cambridge University Press £17.99 0521377412) is a highly readable and comprehensive survey of the relationship between political activity and Irish public affairs. Lee argues that politics must be examined in the light of historical events and, using original sources, he examines the roles played in 20th century Irish history by key political figures. **Ireland in the Twentieth Century** by John Murphy (Gill & MacMillan pb £8.99 0717116948) blends historical fact and acute observation of events in Ireland from 1918 onwards with clarity and precision. The scope of this book is wide, spanning domestic areas such as coalition parties, legislative decisions, economic recovery, Northern Ireland and world events, yet it manages to be concise and highly readable. **Ireland This Century** by Tony Gray (Little Brown pb £7.99 0751513911) provides a year by year, decade by decade chronology of events in Irish history. Each year is preceded by an outline of events on the world stage. **Ireland: A Social and Cultural History 1922-1985 by** Terence Brown (Harper Collins pb £8.99 0006860826) is an innovative and thorough examination of a nation moving from colonial and civil war to Free State, through World War to European Union. Themes discussed include the inter-relationship of economic and industrial revival, demographics, language and literature. **Great Speeches of the Twentieth Century** by Michael McLoughlin (Poolbeg £12.99 1853716138) is one volume of many voices from defining moments in Irish history with orations from Taoisigh, insurgents, presidents, and poets, from James Connolly to Nelson Mandela and W.S. Churchill to Pope John Paul II.

**Sinn Fein: First Election 1908** by Ciaran O'Duibhir (Drumlin pb £3.00 1873437021) concentrates on the first election that Sinn Fein contested. This new party, led by Arthur Griffith, was running against John Redmond's Irish Parliamentary Party. O'Duibhir uses as its focus the North Leitrim by-election but also looks at the national situation as it pertained to the local in the North-West of the country. The Great War had enormous effect on Ireland. **Orange, Green & Khaki: The Story of the Irish Regiments in the Great War** by Tom Johnstone (Gill & MacMillan pb £17.99 0717119947) is a history of all of the Irish regiments that fought for England. In all over 300,000 Irishmen fought in Europe and roughly 50,000 lost their lives. Johnstone traces the history of the seventy two battalions involved and has greatly added to the history of the Great War. Cyril Falls's **History of the 36th (Ulster) Division** (Constable hb £17.95 0094766304) is a book about the battalion in which he served, from its inception in 1914 through its heroic efforts at the Somme, Ypres and Courtrai to its disbandment in 1919. First published in 1922, Falls's work had the benefit of many first hand experiences and is a comprehensive account of life in the trenches as well as a history of some of the bloodiest battles in the Great War. After the Great War ended in 1918, the question of Irish sovereignty raised its head once more. Many of the Irish soldiers serving in British regiments began to ask themselves why they were fighting for the side that were terrorising their friends and family at home. This feeling was especially heightened when the Black & Tans were deployed in Ireland. Anthony Babington, in his **Devil to Pay: Mutiny of the Connaught Rangers India 1920** (Airlift hb £17.50 0850523273), examines the most famous of the mutinies and explores the background events that led to this very dramatic action.

Roger Casement was born in 1864 and while on Colonial Service for the British Government in the late 19th Century, he strongly objected to the abuse of native people by the European colonisers in both Africa and South America. He became involved with the Gaelic League, but realised that a rebellion without sufficient munitions would be futile. He went to Berlin in 1915 to secure help from the German Government. He was very disappointed and dismayed at the little amount of help the Germans were prepared to offer and returned to Ireland to try and postpone the 1916 Rising. He was, however, arrested and tried as a traitor. The trial for treason of Roger Casement is one of the most infamous in 20th Century Irish and British history due to the fact that portions of his diaries, containing explicitly homosexual detail, were circulated during the trial, thus swaying the jury. Montgomery Hyde brilliantly reconstructs the events surrounding the trial in his **Famous Trials: Roger Casement** (Penguin pb £6.99 140021248). The famous 'Black' diary has recently been published as **Roger Casement's Diaries:**

**1910 The Black & the White** (Pimlico pb £10.00 071267375X) edited with an introduction by historian Roger Sayer. Angus Mitchell at the same time has edited and published **The Amazon Journal of Roger Casement** (Lilliput Press pb £18.00 1901866076) which he claims is the true diary, according to Mitchell, The Black diaries were an elaborate forgery perpetrated by the British government to discredit Casement. Both books make fascinating reading.

Other books look at other important figures in the period immediately before and after the 1916 Rising and the War of Independence. **Douglas Hyde: A Maker of Modern Ireland by** J.E. Dunleavy & G.W. Dunleavy (University of California Press hb £32.00 0520066847) is the only full-length biography of the first president of Ireland available. Detailing his cultural, literary and political success, the two authors have provided the general and academic reader with a very good biography as well as a history of late nineteenth and early twentieth century Ireland.

**John Chartres: Mystery Man of the Irish Treaty** by Brian Murphy (Irish Academic Press hb £14.95 0716525437) is an investigation of the role played by Chartres in the treaty-making process in London in 1921. Chartres had been a member of British intelligence and it was never made clear whether he forsook his role as a spy or whether he went over completely to the Irish side. **Hazel: A Life of Lady Lavery 1881-1935** by Sinead McCoole (Lilliput Press pb £15.00 1874675554) is the first full-length biography of Hazel Lavery whose face on the old Irish £1 note made her one of the most familar women in twentieth century Ireland. Born in Chicago, she married the painter Sir John Lavery and became friends with such various people as Michael Collins, Kevin O'Higgins, Winston Churchill and Evelyn Waugh. Her salon in London in the 1920s became the common ground where English and Irish politicians involved in Treaty negotiations could meet. This beautifully illustrated biography is essential reading for anyone interested in a hitherto untold background to 20th century Irish history. **Erskine Childers** by Jim Ring (John Murray pb £12.99 0719556872) is an entertaining biography of Childers (1870-1922). Though born in England and a veteran of the Boer War, Childers became involved in the Irish republican movement, using his boat the Asgard to smuggle guns into Howth in 1911. He was appointed the publicity director of the Irish Republican Army in 1918 and fought against the pro-Treaty forces in the Civil War. He was captured and executed in 1922.

When members of the Irish Republican Brotherhood and the Irish Citizen Army seized the GPO and other strategic public buildings in Dublin in a rise in arms against Britain on Easter Monday 1916, few envisaged the revolution in Nationalist spirit that would spring from their insurgence. The trading and social activities of the city were halted and the city centre left in ruin. It became a defining event in Irish history. The subsequent execution of the leaders of the Rising bequeathed to their cherished country a national pride and purpose, forging a renewed Nationalist movement in Ireland, as Yeats later wrote, 'all changed, changed utterly.'

**The 1916 Rebellion Handbook** (Mourne River Press pb £14.99 1902090055), with an introduction by Declan Kiberd is a complete narrative history of the 1916 Rising with details of all skirmishes throughout the country. It is also a sourcebook listing correspondence, casualties, official statements and a full record of sentences received. It is an invaluable introduction and reference work. **Insurrection in Dublin** by James Stephens (Smythe pb £4.95 0861403584) has the immediacy of Stephens' journal, written day by day as the events of the Easter Rising unfolded, and captures the mood of the public towards the undemocratic revolution and that of the insurgents. Events leading up to the Rising and its aftermath are discussed by Prof. John Murphy. **Dublin Burning** by Brennan-Whitmore (Gill & MacMillan pb £9.99 0717124134) is another first hand account of the Easter Rising by the Commanding Officer of the Volunteers at an outpost in North Earl Street which he held for 72 hours before he was captured and interned. This soldier's memoir of the historic week includes insightful pen-sketches of enigmatic leaders such as MacDermott, Plunket, Clarke, Pearse and Collins. **On the Easter Proclamation & Other Proclamations** by Liam de Paor (Four Courts Press pb £22.50 1851823200) is concerned with the text of the Proclamation read by Padraig Pearse at the beginning of the insurrection. It examines the underlying ideology and intent in a domestic context and in relation to Declarations of Independence further afield. An illustrated day by day account of the Rebellion, timelines, numerous maps, photographs and key biographical accounts of the leaders in **Easter Rising** by Richard Killeen (Gill and MacMillan pb £5.99 017123413) provide a concise introduction to the events of the Rising. **Easter Rebellion** by Max Caufield (Gill and MacMillan pb £12.99 071712293X) is an authoritative account of the Rising, drawing its strength from interviews conducted with participants and from its atmospheric writing. Insightful also are the two publications by Fr. Leo Coughlan, **Memories of Easter Week 1916** (O.L pb £14.99) and **Rebirth of a Nation** (Narsdl Tsee £4.99). The significant role played by Irish women during the Easter Rebellion is highlighted in **Women of 1916** by Ruth Taillon, (Beyond the Pale pb £6.99 ISBN 0951422987). This is a flagship publication which accounts for over 200 women, many of whom endured prison sentences for their work in the Nationalist movement.

Unrest had spurred the Easter Rebellion. It had been severe but revolution and war was yet to come. Sinn Féin claimed a decisive victory throughout the Republic and their policy of abstention from Westminister led to the foundation of Dail Eireann, which sat for the first time on 21 January 1919. **Revolutionary Government in Ireland: 1919-1922** by Arthur Mitchell (Gill & MacMillan pb £18.99 ISBN 0717120155) focuses on the construction and work of the Irish administration, the development of courts of law, a police force and government departments by men who carried a price of their heads. Personal interviews with eminent figures (General Mulcahy, Collins's Chief of Staff, E. de Valera, Col. N. Broy) and valuable archival material are skillfully combined in **Troubles** by Ulick O'Connor (Mandarin pb £8.25 0745311237) to form a gripping account of Michael Collins and the Irish Volunteers from 1917-1922. **Revolution in Ireland: 1917-1923** by Conor Kostick (Pluto Press pb £12.99 0745311237) is the first study of the militant mindset of the working people of Ireland who turned their back on freedom through negotiation and influenced decisions made by British authorities and Irish leaders such as Collins, Griffith and de Valera.

New chapters of bloodshed, random arrests, torturous reprisals and arson attacks were written when Lloyd George's cabinet unleashed armed but undisciplined troops in Ireland in 1920. **Black and Tans** by Richard Bennett (Roberts hb £6.99 1566198208) deals with this harrowing, merciless period preceding the Truce of July 1921. **From Public Defiance to Guerilla War: The Experience of Ordinary Volunteers in the Irish War of Independence** by Joost Augusteijn (Irish Academic Press pb £17.50 0716526077) traces the progression of the Volunteers from a traditional national organisation to the guerrilla fighting IRA, presenting much detail on participation on a local level based on public reports, IRA communications and interviews with veterans of the War of Independence.

The Truce of July 1921 brought temporary cease-fire. The Irish delegation now faced formidable British negotiators in London. The Treaty was ratified but engendered a split and the country was plunged into Civil War. Allegiance to the Crown was unpalatable and seen as a sell-out. By his own admission, Collins had signed his death warrant – prophetic also for many Irish citizens as former comrades and even blood relations waged a savage war on each other. Publications dealing with this bitter episode between June 1922 and April 1923 include: **Irish Civil War Illustrated** by Helen Litton (Wolfhound pb £6.99 0863274803), **Green Against Green** by M. Hopkinson (Gill & MacMillan pb £16.99 0717116301) and Ireland's Civil War by Calton Younger (Harper Collins pb £9.99 0006860982). **Who's Who in the Irish War of Independence 1906-1923** by Padraic O'Farrell (Lilliput Press pb £9.99 1874675856) provides biographical notes on 3,000 British and Irish soldiers, politicians and civilians of prominence and of marginalised stature. Irish women are salvaged from the margins of Irish Nationalist history in **Unmanageable Revolutionaries** by Margaret Ward, (Pluto Press pb £13.99 0745310842) which assesses women's involvement in the Land League, Inghinidhe na hEireann and Cumann na nBan. **Retreat from Revolution: The Dáil Courts 1920-1924** by Mary Kotsonouris (Irish Academic Press pb £8.95 0716526131) is the sole comprehensive account of the court system set up by the first Dáil in June 1920 which signaled a defining stage in the formation of the Irish Free State. **1922: The Birth of Irish Democracy** by Tom Garvin (Gill & MacMillan pb £14.99 0717124398) examines the features of the newly founded Irish state at the crucial juncture of modern Irish history. Garvin deals with the influence of European and American political ideas and contests assumptions on national identity.

Biographies of the major figures in the War of Independence and the Civil Wars abound. The number of accounts written by contemporaries, and in more recent years, is indicative of the extent of the legacy Michael Collins' short but controversial life has left on Irish history. By the age of thirty-one he had been deeply involved in the Easter Rising, War of Independence, Civil War and the Free State Government. His life is steeped in stories of risk-taking, infiltration, courage and ruthlessness as Director of Organisation of the Irish Volunteers, architect of urban guerilla warfare, mastermind behind the crippling of the British Intelligence system, Commander in Chief of the Free State Army, Irish plenipotentiary and Minister for Finance. Collins's articles and speeches on the Rising, Irish civilisation and culture, the Treaty, Civil War and economic development are published in **Path to Freedom** (Mercier Press pb £6.99 ISBN 1856351483). Francis Costello provides the historical context to Collins's letters, public statements, speeches, comments to colleagues and assessments of contemporary British and Irish politicians during the crucial years of the Irish Free State in **Michael Collins In His Own Words** (Gill and MacMillan pb £8.99). **Michael Collins** by Leon O'Broin (Gill & MacMillan, pb £6.99 0717119254) is a concise biography of the enigmatic leader written by an active member of the Nationalist movement., Frank O'Connor's account **Big Fellow** (Poolbeg pb £6.99 1905169840), written fifteen years after the death of the rebel leader is alive with human character and turbulence. **Michael Collins: The Lost Leader** by Margaret Forester (Gill & MacMillan pb £12.99) retains the authoritative text of its 1971 publication but its bibliography has been expanded to keep apace with subsequent research. It draws on much personal material and first hand accounts from surviving comrades. **In Great Haste: Letters of Michael Collins & Kitty Kiernan** (Gill & MacMillan hb £19.99 0717123987) edited by Leon O'Broin is a lavishly illustrated book of 300 letters, chronicling the love affair between Michael Collins and Kitty Kiernan, published to coincide with Neil Jordan's film based on Collins' life. The book also includes facsimile reproductions of some of the letters. As previously unreleased material has come to light so too have subsequent biographical works such as **Michael Collins** by Tim Pat Coogan (Arrow £9.99 0099685809), **Michael Collins** by James MacKay (Mainstream pb £9.99 185158949X), **Collins and the Brotherhood** by Vincent MacDowell (pb £9.99 ISBN 1901658058) and A.T.Q. Stewart's **Collins' Secret File** (Blackstaff pb £10.99 0856406147). From numerous primary resources, fascinating anecdotes and extensive archival material Tim Pat Coogan has fashioned an in-depth and captivating biography, written with a vigour reminiscent of the 'Big Fellow.' McKay provides a thorough work on the life of the charismatic leader and charming man of action with reference to new material. MacDowell discloses revelations about Collins personal life and involvement with the London Hostess Moya Ilelwyn Davis which led to a situation that left Collins unable to reject the Treaty and forwards an opinion on the ambush refutes other accounts. Recently released papers including handwritten notes and official reports on Collins's family history, his whereabouts and associates are reproduced in **Michael Collins' Secret File.** These documents were read by Collins himself read during his auda-cious entry into the HQ of the Dublin Metropolitan Police in 1919 and convey the intense surveillance mounted by the police from December 1916 to April 1920 in their attempt to track down the most wanted man in the British Isles. **Michael Collins: The Women in His Life** by Meda Ryan (Mercier Press £9.99) documents the fundamental role played by Collins' girlfriends, society hostesses, sister and secre-tary – all of whom were allies, some providing safe-houses, several enabling him to infiltrate the British intelligence system as conduits of information and others pleading his cause in British cabinet circles. **Michael Collins: the Final Days** by Justin Nelson (pb £9.95 ISBN 190091302X) contains the first account by Michael Collins's nephew and namesake to appear in print, historic photos (Dublin in ruin after 1916, photos of Collins's life and death) and articles published during and after the dramatic period. The manner of Collins's death in an ambush at Béal na Bláth has become as controversial as his life with speculation and conjecture fueled by a lack of hard evidence. Meda Ryan meticulously reconstructs the final four days of Collins's life, tracing his movements and his journey through Cork to the site of the ambush, in **The Day Michael Collins Was Shot** (Poolbeg pb £6.99 ISBN 185371738X). Her writing is based on the account of an eyewitness. **The Dark Secret of Béal naBláth** by Patrick Twohig (Tower Books pb £9.95 ISBN IR00002052) presents conflicting 'stories' and actual testimonies from veterans, their comrades or descendants from which the author forms a fresh account of the ambush and the individual who triggered the fatal bullet. **Two Leaders** by Martin Lester (Boyne Publications pb £5.99 0952942909) honors the lives of Collins and Arthur Griffith, closely linked by career rather than character. It contains written tributes by fellow Nationalists Richard Mulcahy, Kevin O'Higgins and Alice Stoppford Green, poetry inspired by their gallantry and a visual commemoration of their lives as orators, soldiers and politicians.

**Arthur Griffith** by Arthur Maye (Griffith College Publications hb £25 0953161102) is the only recent study of the prestigious Irish Nationalist and founding father of the democratic state. Maye sheds light on the long-term significance of Griffith's writing and radical newspapers, the pacifist embroiled in turbulent times and the distinctly public figure who remained essentially private. After the Easter Rebellion Ernie O'Malley abandoned his medical studies and became an IRA organizer, working closely with Collins and Mulcahy. **On Another Man's Wounds** (Anvil Books pb £7.95 0900068442) is his memoir of the War of Independence and it evokes the excitement, peril, hardship and strong vision of Irish Freedom fighters. Opposed to the Treaty, HQ of the IRA and Dáil Eireann, O'Malley recounts his harrowing struggle of an 'Irregular' during the Civil War and subsequent imprisonment in **The Singing Flame** (Anvil Books pb £7.95 ISBN 0900068418). **General Richard Mulcahy: Portrait of a Revolutionary** by Maryann Valiulis (Irish Academic Press pb £12.50) focuses on his most significant years (1916-1924) in Ireland's emergence as a nation state, his role as director of the War of Independence, Minister for Defence in the Post-Treaty Dáil and Chief of Staff during the Civil War.

## Marie-Louise Donnelly of Waterstone's, Dawson Street, Dublin examines the historical debate known as revisionism.

Every nation needs an inheritance of the past to validate itself and produce a sustaining image of the present. However, opinion is sharply divided on how the past should be examined, written, interpreted and presented. The discovery of previously undocumented material or the release of sources (reports, diaries, government papers etc.) makes re-examination of historical events and a fresh delineation of historical figures inevitable but is the rewriting of history, in our own times, beneficial or destructive? This question forms the pith of the revisionist debate.

In an Irish context, the revisionist debate dates from the 1930s when T.W. Moody and R.D. Edwards espoused a purer and more scholarly style of writing of Irish history than the prevalent version. Central to their theory was the distinction between history and myth and an obligation on the part of the historian to tackle anomalies and misconceptions. They promoted a 'constructive and instrumental' reformation, fostering research and refining its methods in relation to well-known and neglected areas. Later historians F.S.L. Lyons and Roy Foster embraced this mindset by questioning authoritative interpretations and writing with a clearer perspective. By writing decades if not centuries after an event, historical writing offers judicious assessment; removed are the strong allegiances to characters or political parties that may have marred the accuracy of accounts written at definitive moments. Areas of taboo can be more readily approached and individuals that may have been ill-treated or neglected by history can earn the credit that is their due.

The Revisionist theory has provoked dissension. As new light is shed, revered figures may be dispossessed of the limelight and closely held analogies may be exposed as little more than myth. Revisionism can be seen as Anti-Nationalist – an approach which de-sensitizes Irish events and undermines achievement – or as an assault on National heroes, purposefully dismantling inherited history and debunking the Irish Nationalist tradition, for which our ancestors, gave their lives by questioning its use in serving the good health of a nation. Bygone days are in danger of being rewritten with a different term of reference and moral interpretation to that which was cherished during the time of insurgents and mavericks and the validity of assessing morality with the aid of hindsight is questionable. History should be made intelligible in our own time but it is dangerous to allow it to fall victim to present day ideologies and the prevailing political climate, to suggest that it should provide instant answers or be rewritten to fit an ideological mould or validate political theories. Complexity should not be reduced to simplicity and events should not be assessed with a particular theory in mind.

**Interpreting Irish History: The Debate on Historical Revisionism** edited by Ciaran Brady (Irish Academic Press pb £14.95 ISBN 0716525461) traces the history of the Revisionist school from the 1930s, discusses the role of the historian and presents cases from both sides of the ongoing debate. Included are writings by Moody and Edwards from the 1930s and 1970s, and by F.S.L. Lyons, Oliver MacDonagh, Roy Foster, R. Fanning and S. Ellis. Opposing arguments are put forward by Moody's adversary B. Bradshaw and historians D. Fennell, K. O'Neill, B. Murphy, S. Deane, H. Kearney, A. Jackson, C. O'Grada, A. Coughlan and M.A.G. O'Tuathaigh.

**The Making of Modern Irish History** edited by Boyce and O'Day (Routledge pb £14.99 ISBN 041512171X) sets the revisionist debate in a broader context by highlighting debates and cases outside Ireland. Seven contributors from numerous countries and of varying backgrounds deal with Revisionism of events in Ireland from the eighteenth century onwards (the Irish Famine, Home Rule, the 1916 Rising), presenting the problems and areas of discussion and providing their own interpretation of each specific event.

## De Valera

Eamon De Valera was a dominant figure in the country's life from the 1916 Rising to his death and a number of books on him should be highlighted. **De Valera: Long Fellow, Long Shadow** by Tim Pat Coogan (Arrow Books pb £ 9.99 009995860) in its title alone presents the complex legacy of de Valera's political tactics which extend from 1916 far beyond his retirement in 1959. It confronts the dominant personality in post-independent Ireland, founder of Fianna Fail and its political weapon The Irish Press, chief architect of the Constitution and Ireland's leader during the Second World War. **De Valera and His Times** by John O'Carroll (Cork University Press pb £9.95 0902561448) provides an inter-disciplinary reappraisal of the life and times of de Valera. This publication incorporates a wide range of viewpoints on his political ideology, economic development, church and state, the IRA and the constitution with papers by experts in the fields political science, history, law, folklore and sociology. **De Valera's Constitution and Ours** by Brian Farrell (Gill & MacMillan hb £ 9.95 ISBN 0717116123) is a highly readable examination of the operation and function of the constitution in our times which examines the institutions devised and the religious ethos, the role of women and fundamental rights espoused by the charter for the Irish people.


## Roy Foster on the importance of F.S.L. Lyons' book, Culture and Anarchy in Ireland 1890-1939


This short and elegant book began life as the Ford Lectures which Lyons delivered at Oxford exactly twenty years ago; I went up from London each week to hear them. He had published his magisterial **Ireland since the Famine** a few years before and had recently been appointed authorised biographer of Yeats.
The lectures, and the subsequent book, came as something of a shock. Lyons' preoccupation was with the intellectual and political life in Ireland from the *fin de siécle* to the outbreak of World War II; or, put another way, from the fall of Parnell to the death of Yeats. He approached it by means of a coruscating analysis of the mentalities, achievements, visions and myopias of literary revivalists, poet-revolutionaries, cleric-politicians, and state-builders north and south. The tone of *Ireland since the Famine* had been conventionally nationalist in a measured, liberal, cautiously optimistic way; *Culture and Anarchy* was by contrast, bleak, sceptical and ultimately pessimistic. 'The new nation', he wrote in his last chapter, 'was turning in on itself, and in its anxiety to establish a cultural as well as political independence was intent upon the creation of an exclusively Gaelic-Catholic model. And, although illogical, it was also human that the more obviously out of line with contemporary reality this proved to be, the more bitterly and doggedly it was likely to be pursued; and the more it was pursued, the more blinkered and introverted the pursuers were likely to become'.

This was a sharp note to strike in 1978: 'pluralism' and 'inclusivity' were not the buzzwords they have since become, and the book's emphasis falls decisively on

Irish antipathies and antagonisms. But it was not depressing, partly because so much of the material was so pointedly funny: the use of D.P. Moran's polemical journalism, or episcopal pronouncements against dancehalls in the 1930s, or Yeats' most magniloquent *ex cathedra* statements, was a revelation. *Culture and Anarchy* was and remains an object-lesson in how to make erudition both accessible and entertaining. It was also liberating to read 'cultural history' pitched at this level. Lyons' work up to then, like that of much of his generation, had been resolutely 'high-political'. There had been a hint in Ireland since the Famine, notably in the marvellous section on the Literary Revival, that this approach was turning elsewhere. But *Culture and Anarchy* – which would, tragically and unexpectedly, be his last book – brought poetry, journalism and theatre straight into the mainstream of Irish history, using creative writing to illuminate the central thesis of a collision of cultures. Lyons wrote that Ireland by the twentieth century was the site of competing cultures: 'a diversity of ways of life which were deeply embedded in the past and of which the much advertised political differences are but the outward and visible sign. This was the true anarchy that beset the country. During the period from the fall of Parnell to the death of Yeats, it was not primarily an anarchy of violence in the streets, of contempt for law and order, such as to make the island or any part of it, permanently ungovernable. It was rather an anarchy in the mind and in the heart, an anarchy which forbade not just unity of territories but also unity of being, an anarchy that sprang from the collision within a small and intimate island of seemingly irreconcilable cultures, unable to live together or to live apart, caught inextricably in the web of their tragic history'.

It seems odd that this unpromising look at Irish life, and Irish possibilities, should be inspirational: but I find myself returning to these six short and compressed chapters over and over again, and always with a sense of excitement, even when I disagree. It is not necessary to follow Lyons' pessimistic line implicitly: looking at the same period of Irish history, I have come to believe, more than he did, in the possibility of fusion and interpenetration, and to question the predetermined 'collision of cultures' within the island. For all the horrors, events both north and south have given cause for hope over the two decades since Lyons published his book. But this is partly so because both sides are now more prepared to confront popular ideas and to face up to things not as they would like them to have been, but as they probably were. Work like Lyons's helped this process along. *Culture and Anarchy* also casts new light by concentrating on the ideas of the future which were mistakenly held by people who thought they knew what was going to happen. In Ireland from 1890 to 1939, the expected future changed bewilderingly: neither the parliamentary nationalists under Redmond, nor the cultural avant-garde grouped around Yeats, nor the Gaelic enthusiasts grouped around Hyde, nor the agrarian co-operativists led by Horace Plunkett and AE, nor even the political revolutionaries who followed Pearse into the Post Office in 1916 got the future they expected. What Lyons does in this book is to assemble their expectations, activities, prejudices and ideals and show how they wove together into the great outburst of cultural energy which made life in early twentieth century Ireland one of the upward curves in European civilisation. But as an envoi, he adds Yeats's lines: –

'Out of Ireland have we come,

Great hatred, little room,

Maimed us at the start'.

Still, for all its bitterness, prejudice and savagery of the years he surveys, what emerges is the concentration of talent, energy and imagination infusing Irish life in this period: handled with a sardonic flourish that is almost Gibbonian.

After *Culture and Anarchy* had collected prizes and become an immediately-recognised classic, Lyons affected some bewilderment: 'Although I'm quite fond of that little book, it was never designed to bear the weight that appears to being put on it'. It was certainly more controversial and hard-hitting than his earlier work, and dared to connect past with present more decisively; it reflected not only his enthusiasm for the history of culture rather than 'pure' politics, but also his engagement with Irish life, rediscovered since he had returned to Dublin as Provost of Trinity College. Some who questioned him about the difference in approach between *Culture and Anarchy* and the relatively sunny landscape of *Ireland since the Famine* received the saturnine answer: 'You must remember I was living in England then'. The book fascinated me because it showed how Lyons was coming to think about Irish history in the light of his work on Yeats's biography; I did not know then that his terribly premature death a few years later would prevent that book from being written, nor that I would be eventually be appointed to the task in his stead. But even aside from this personal identification, I still think *Culture and Anarchy* fits into its own 'little room' great wisdom as well as an anatomy of the roots of hatred; it also, perversely and perhaps unintentionally, allows some space for hope. In some ways, it has never read more relevantly than now.

## Thirties and Forties Ireland

Books on thirties and forties Ireland include **Blueshirts and Irish Politics** by Mike Cronin (Four Courts Press pb £19.95 ISBN 1851823336) which clears up the nebulous and scant study of the Blueshirts to date, exploring the movement's ideology and conflicting opinions among members, simultaneous developments on a European level and their role in domestic opposition politics. **In Time of War** by Robert Fisk (Gill & MacMillan pb £14.99 0717124118) is an essential read on Ireland's role during World War II. War time documents, memoirs and memoranda are skillfully studied for the first time and Fisk provides an elucidating account of Anglo-Irish relations of partition and suspicion. **The Lost Years: Emergency in Ireland** by Tony Gray (Little Brown pb £9.99 0316881899) is both a recollection and an assessement of the changes – in supplies, employment, power, transport, banking, literature – in Ireland during the period of enforced isolation. With personal insight, Gray underlines how development was born from restrictions marking the coming of age of a young nation. **Guests of the State** by T. Ryle Dwyer (Brandon Press pb £7.95 ISBN 0863221823) recounts the story of Allied and Axis servicemen interned in Ireland during World War II in extraordinary prison conditions which provided sporting facilities and permitted daily parole. Equally fascinating are incidents of attempted escape and mutiny. **Clear the Way!: A History of the 38th (Irish) Brigade, 1941-47** (Gill & MacMillan pb £12.95 0716525429) by Richard Doherty is the story of this brigade, formed by Churchill, which fought with great distinction in both Tunisia and Italy during the Second World War. Giving accounts of the whole campaign including the battles at Cassino and Spaduro, Doherty creates a fascinating and noble testament to the Irishmen who fought for England during the War. **Ireland & the League of Nations** by Michael Kennedy (Irish Academic Press hb £27.50 0716525496) is the first in-depth study of Ireland's role in this international organisation. Based on records from the department of Foreign Affairs, Kennedy's study looks at the parts played by Eamon de Valera and Patrick McGilligan amongst others and at the policies of both Cumann na nGaedheal and the Fianna Fáil parties. This book is a valuable addition to Irish history between the wars. **The Storm Passed By: Ireland & the Battle of the Atlantic 1941-42** by Trevor Allen (Irish Academic Press hb £17.50 0716526166) is a clear account of this important year of World War II, when Hitler changed his strategy and ordered the Luftwaffe to attack Britain's ports in order to help the U-Boat campaign. As a result, Belfast suffered huge bombings. Basing his book on German documentation that has not been seen before, Allen has reconstructed the story, supplying context and discussion.

## Contemporary Ireland – 1945 to the Present Day
## (see also Politics section)

**Modern Irish Lives** (Gill & MacMillan hb £19.99 0717121984) edited by historian and journalist Louis McRedmond is an extremely useful biographical tool, giving details of many 20th Century Irish literary, political and business figure.

Contemporary Ireland – 1945 to the present day, is an essential reference book for anyone interested in Modern Ireland. There are two good studies available on the life of Seán Lemass (1899-1971) who saw active service in the 1916 Rising, was instrumental in the founding of the Fíanna Fáil Party and in 1959 succeeded Eamon de Valera as party leader and Taoiseach. He held that position until 1966 and these years are looked upon as the years in which Ireland caught up with the twentieth century, with rapid modernisation and the development of Irish industry. The books are **Sean Lemass** by Michael O'Sullivan (Blackwater Press pb £7.99 0861217896) and **Sean Lemass: The Enigmatic Patriot** by John Horgan (Gill & MacMillan £19.99 0717120791). **Rocky Road: Irish Economy Since the 1920s** (Manchester University Press pb £13.99 0719045843) is a more recent companion volume to Cormac O'Grada's magisterial and comprehensive **Ireland: A New Economic History** (Oxford University Press pb £14.99 0198205988). Concentrating on the 20th Century, in this new work, O'Grada argues that the last seventy years have been a good study in economic experimentation, with different governments employing and implementing sometimes contradictory fiscal strategies. Joseph Morrison Skelly's **Irish Diplomacy at the United Nations 1945-65: National Interests & the International Order** (Irish Academic Press hb £32.00 0716525747) presents the fascinating account of the huge influence that Ireland's delegation to the united Nations had. Fronted by Frank Aiken, Frederick Boland and Conor Cruise O'Brien, the delegation over 20 years (amongst other things) promoted decolonisation in Africa, initiated what became the Nuclear Non-proliferation Treaty of 1968 and started the peacekeeping tradition, whereby thousands of Irish troops have helped keep the peace in some of the 20th century's worst trouble spots.

**Boss: A Biography of Charlie Haughey** by Joyce and Murtagh (Poolbeg pb £7.99 1853718912) concentrates on the 1982 General Election and is a very good study of the Irish political scene in the early eighties. **Fallen Idol** by T. Ryle Dwyer (Mercier Press pb £7.99 1856352021) looks at Haughey's career from the 1960s to date and is a lively account of the scandals in which the former Taois each was involved, including the payments to politicians and the tapping of the phones of two prominent journalists. Mary Robinson, who was elected first woman head of the Irish State in 1992 had previously led an impressive career as a lawyer. She also served as a Senator. When she became president, she had a high profile internationally and she became a great ambassador for the country. She visited many trouble spots during her time in office, including Rwanda and Somalia, and met world leaders such as Clinton and Nelson Mandela. After deciding not to serve a second term and stepping down as president she became the United Nations High Commissioner for Human Rights. There are two unofficial but very thorough biographies available – **Mary Robinson: The Woman Who Took Power in the Park** by Lorna Siggins (Mainstream hb £14.99 1851588051) and **Mary Robinson** by John Horgan (O'Brien Press hb £14.99 0862785405). Other biographies of contemporary figures include **The Mighty Healy-Rae** by Hickey (Marino pb £7.99 1860230687) which is the story of the indomitable spirit of Jackie Healy-Rae who was elected as an independent TD in the 1997 General Election. Ivan Fallon's **The Player** (Hodder & Stoughton pb £6.99 0340639792) is a lively biography of Tony O'Reilly, probably Ireland's most successful and profitable businessman ever. It chronicles O'Reilly's rise to the chairmanship of the Heinz Corporation and his more recent acquisition of the Independent newspaper group.

## Northern Ireland

General books on the North and the Troubles are plentiful. In **The Narrow Ground: Aspects of Ulster 1609 – 1969** (Blackstaff Press pb £8.99 0856406007), A.T.Q. Stewart goes back into history to examine the often unconscious motivation which has led to such conflict between Catholic and Protestant people in the North. Stewart has also examined the difficult period 1912-1914 when the British Liberal government was under attack from the Conservative Party because of its determination to grant Home Rule in the North in **The Ulster Crisis: Resistance to Home Rule 1912-1914** (Blackstaff pb £9.99 085640599X). This book also examines how Edward Carson was ready to defend Northern Ireland with an army of 100,000 men. **Explaining Northern Ireland** by McGarry & O'Leary (Blackwell pb £13.50 0631183493) is a cogent and full analysis of the problems and resultant stereotypes in the North. Thomas Hennessy's **History of Northern Ireland, 1920-1996** (Gill & MacMillan pb £12.99 0717124002) discusses, in a very balanced fashion, the sequence of events in Northern Ireland from the 1920s to the present and provides a very useful overview of the political debate which has taken place. **Northern Ireland since 1968** by Arthur Jeffrey (Blackwell pb £12.99 0631200843) is a concise overview of the Troubles since 1968. Although the last edition was published in 1980 **Northern Ireland: The Orange State** by Michael Farrell (Pluto Press pb £14.99 0861043006) remains one of the most cogent works on the historical and political background to the Troubles and its central argument that peace cannot be achieved unless there is a change in British Government policy has since been proved correct. **Northern Ireland Politics** by Aughey & Morrow (Longman pb £12.99 0582253462) demonstrates how many changes have taken place in the North despite the political intransigence in a discussion that spans the areas of history, ideas, representation, administration, politics and society. **Irish-America & the Ulster Conflict 1968 – 1995** by Andrew J Wilson (Gill & MacMillan pb £14.30 0856405639) is a very good study of the role that the Irish community in America have played in the North. It begins by giving a brief overview of the background from the 1800s to 1968 and then goes into detailed analysis of how the Irish American community has raised money to pay for a large proportion of the IRA's weapons, how they have provided shelter for people escaping from justice and probably most importantly how they have kept up a very strong political pressure on the American government to keep Northern Ireland high on its agenda.

J. Bowyer Bell has written four very valuable books on Northern Ireland. His massive and comprehensive **The Irish Troubles** (Gill & MacMillan pb £14.99 0717122018) is one of the leading accounts of the last thirty years in the North. **Back to the Future: The Protestants & A United Ireland** (Poolbeg pb £6.99 1853716928) gives the Protestant point of view on this, the fundamental crux of the Troubles. And his **In Dubious Battle** (Poolbeg pb £7.99 1853712795) asked many of the unanswered questions about the 1974 Dublin and Monaghan bombings which left thirty three people dead. **IRA: Tactics & Targets** (Poolbeg pb £4.99 1853716030) is an analysis of the IRA's terrorist policy over the last thirty years which covers individual acts such as the murders of Lord Louis Mountbatten and Christopher Ewart-Biggs. **Interpreting Northern Ireland** by the late John Whyte (Oxford UP£14.95 0198273800) is based mainly on his teaching on the subject in University College, Dublin and is undoubtedly the best survey of research, interpretations and possible solutions to the Northern Irish problems. Erudite, shrewd and succinct, this book both summarises and challenges traditional and radical views on the North. **The Troubles** by Tim Pat Coogan (Arrow pb £9.99 009946571X) will undoubtedly become the standard one-volume work on the last thirty years in Northern Ireland. Over its 500 pages, the book gives the background to all of the main events in Northern Ireland up to and including the breakdown of the first IRA ceasefire in 1996. Combining his journalistic and biographical skills, Coogan also provides detailed portraits of all the political players involved, from both sides of the border.

Other books, both academic and general, look at different aspects of the North, its history and its politics, past and present. **Two Lands on One Soil: Ulster Politics before Home Rule** by Frank Wright (Gill & MacMillan hb £40.00 0717121798) very usefully mixes history, political science and sociology to examine political life before the 1880s and argues that colonial structures that were put in place then, are still enduring and divisive. **Democracy Denied** by Desmond Wilson (Mercier Press pb £8.99 1856351777) is a controversial book which argues that the British Government has purposely manipulated both Protestant and Catholic communities in the North for their own political and economic gain. Wilson, a diocesan priest in Ballymurphy, one of the poorest areas of Belfast, also argues that the Irish Government and the Catholic Church have done very little to help. John Brewer's excellent **Crime in I reland, 1945-95** (Oxford University Press hb £40.00 0198265700) is one of the very few criminological studies of Northern Ireland. Looking at the ways paramilitary violence has affected 'ordinary' crime over the last twenty five years, Brewer also provides statistical and comparative evidence of crime on Belfast and Dublin. Much of his research is also based on interviews with people from East and West Belfast, asking their opinion on paramilitary and British Army activity. **Women Divided: Gender, Women & Politics in Northern Ireland** (Routledge pb £14.99 0415137667), by R. Sales, discusses the role of women in a society shaped by very obvious sectarian and gender inequality and examines how women have fought for their own agenda within both Protestant and Catholic communities over the last thirty years. **Dynamics of Conflict in Northern Ireland: Power, Conflict & Emancipation** by Joseph Ruane (Cambridge pb £16.00 052156879X) is a comprehensive examination of the particular system of sectarian relationships which, the book argues, add to the complexity of the Northern Ireland troubles. **Facets of the Conflict in Northern Ireland** by Seamus Dunn (MacMillan pb £12.99 033364252X) argues that the termination of the violent conflict and the resultant political cooperation is only the start of the long-term reconstruction of a society. **Clashing Symbols: A Report on the use of Flags, Anthems & Other National Symbols in Northern Ireland** by Lucy Bryson & Clem McCartney (Institute of Irish Studies pb £6.50 0853895384) is based on many interviews with various people in Northern Ireland and as a result is a fascinating and illuminating analysis of the roles played by National symbols. **Edge of the Union: The Ulster Loyalist Political Vision** by Steve Bruce (Oxford University Press pb £6.99 0198279760) is one of the few books that concentrates its examination on the viewpoint of Loyalist terrorists and the fanatical supporters of Ian Paisley. **Peacemaking Strategies in Northern Ireland: Building Complementarity in Conflict Management** by David Bloomfield (MacMillan hb £40.00 0333674324) skillfully analyses current peacemaking strategies and defines the two main approaches. The cultural approach seeks harmonization between the different cultures in the North and the structural approach looks to find and implement new structures of government and administration.

Since the late 1960s and the start of the Troubles, Derry has been one of the centres of conflict. It was in Derry that the first riots occurred and as a result the first place that British troops were sent. Niall O'Dochartaigh's book **From Civil Rights to Armalites: Derry & the Birth of the Irish Troubles** (Cork University Press pb £15.95 1859181090) takes Derry as its focus, examining the years 1968 to 1972, from the Civil Rights marches to the height of the conflict in the early 1970s. He also looks at the difficult confrontation that occurred between Catholic and Protestant people in the city. The international and British news media comes under close scrutiny in **Don't Mention the War: Northern Ireland, Propaganda & the Media** by David Miller (Pluto Press pb £14.95 0745308368). Miller analyses the handling and management of information by the media which has led to much disproportionate reporting of the Troubles. David Miller with Bill Rolston has edited **War & Words: Northern Ireland Media Reader** (Beyond the Pale pb £12.95 1900960001) which collects the best of the journalistic writing about the North with essays by, among others, Paul Foot, Robert Fisk and Peter Taylor, all examining the media's reaction to the troubles. **In Search of a State: Catholics in Northern Ireland** by Fionnuala O'Connor (Blackstaff Press pb £8.95 0856405094) is a fascinating book based on in-depth interviews with many Catholics in the North and presents the Catholic point of view on topics such as the IRA, Great Britain, the Irish Republic and the Catholic Church. **Between War & Peace: The Political Future of Northern Ireland** by Paul Bew (Lawrence & Wishart pb £11.99 0853157715) points out the repeated failure of understanding between Protestant and Catholic communities in Northern Ireland and how neither sides of the political and religious divide have a perspective which can achieve peace. Paul Bew has also written a very useful reference book. **Northern Ireland: A Chronology of the Troubles 1968-1993** (Gill & MacMillan pb £9.99 0717120813) gives a day to day account of the political and criminal events over twenty five-years. **The Sas in Ireland** by Raymond Murray (Mercier Press pb £4.99 085342991X) presents strong evidence that the SAS operated a Shoot-to-Kill policy in Northern Ireland, while also providing a detailed history of their operations. Murray also describes the links that this unit had with British Intelligence, MI5 & MI6. **The Shankill Butchers** by Martin Dillon (Arrow pb £6.99 0099738104) chronicles the brutal life and times of a Protestant paramilitary gang in 1970s Belfast. Led by fanatical unionist Lenny Murphy, the Shankill Butchers were responsible for the death of thirty Catholics. Journalistic in approach, this book provides all the motives and details of these brutal killings and present a horrifying picture of the violent depths that have been reached in Northern Ireland's recent history. Martin Dillon's latest book, **God & the Gun** (Orion hb £17.99 0752810375) is the first of its kind to explore the inherent relationship between religion and violence in Northern Ireland. Interviewing both churchmen and terrorists as the basis for his research, Dillon asks all of his interviewees how they can reconcile Christian beliefs with the condoning of acts of violence.

There are a number of books available specifically on the IRA. Martin Dillon in his **Twenty Five Years of Terror: The IRA's War against the British** (Bantam Books pb £5.99 0553407732) has the only comprehensive account of the IRA's bombing campaign against the British both before and after the World War II. He discusses the IRA's flirtation with Nazism and how this, along with Irish Neutrality, influenced British policy from the late 1940s onwards. Dillon also gives accounts of the bombing atrocities perpetrated by the IRA in Britain in the 1970s and 1980s, including Brighton, Warrington and London. **The Politics of Illusion: A Political History of the IRA** by Henry Patterson (Serif pb £14.99 1897959311) clearly sets down and explains the differences between the Provisional and Official IRA and the relationship of both to Sinn Fein. The book charts the progression of this republican movement from the 1920s to today and discusses the huge impact on Northern Ireland of militant nationalism mixed with left wing political views. Brendan O'Brien has written a **Pocket History of the IRA** (O'Brien Press pb £4.99 0862785111) which, although concise, gives a very comprehensive overview from 1916 to the collapse of the ceasefire in 1996. O'Brien has written a more expansive book on the same subject, **The Long War: The IRA & Sinn Fein from Armed Struggle to Peace Talks** (O'Brien Press pb £9.99 0862784255) which details the rise of Gerry Adams to leadership of Sinn Fein as well as examining terrorist strategy and looking forward to prospects of peace. **The Provisional IRA** by Patrick Bishop & Eamonn Mallie (Corgi £5.99 055213337X) is another very useful and informative book on the IRA. Mainly based on careful and illuminating interviews with IRA members by Eamon Mallie, Patrick Bishop has written a detailed account of the IRA leadership and tactics. **Killing Rage** by Eamon Collins (Granta hb £15.99 1862070083) is remarkable in its honesty and in its aim to debunk the popular notion that the IRA is a professionally run organisation and shows both the squalid and insular emotions that lead people to carry out atrocities against their neighbours. **Rebel Hearts** by Kevin Toolis (Picador pb £6.99 0330346482) is a moving attempt by Toolis to examine paramilitary nationalism by interviewing people directly involved with the IRA as well as looking at his own republican feelings to try and understand his own 'rebel heart'. Interviewing different people involved with the IRA, he writes of the horrific violence which has affected and divided so many families. Peter Taylor's **Provos: The Ira & Sinn Fein** (Bloomsbury hb £16.99 074753392X) examines the IRA and its relationship to Sinn Fein over the last thirty years. Based on many interviews with both gunmen and politicians, it provides a very valuable overview of the IRA.

**Nor Meekly Serve My Time: H-Block Struggle** edited by Brian Campbell with Lawrence McKeown and Felim O'Hagin (Beyond the Pale pb £9.95 0281049335) is the inside story of the Republican prisoners who refused to be treated as criminals and insisted on being treated as political prisoners. In 1976, a new regime was brought into play for political prisoners in Long Kesh and the following five years of deprivations and brutality led to the 1981 hunger strike which is brilliantly described by David Beresford-Ellis in his **Ten Men Dead: Story of the 1981 Hunger Strike** (HarperCollins pb £5.99 0586065334) which is the most comprehensive account of the action which led to the deaths of ten Republican prisoners. During the Widgery tribunal on the killings of Bloody Sunday, over 500 personal accounts were given, of which only fifteen were used. On the 25th anniversary of this atrocity, **Eyewitness Bloody Sunday: The Truth** edited by Don Mullan (Wolfhound Press pb £8.99 0863275869) was published. This book contains many of the eyewitness accounts which have never before been in print and contains some of the most moving personal testaments about the worst atrocity committed by the British Army in Northern Ireland. This, with Eamon McCann's detailed examination of the context of this atrocity, **Bloody Sunday in Derry** (Brandon Press pb £5.99 0863221394), is the best book available on the subject.

Some biographies of individuals on all sides of the troubles in the North are worth highlighting. **Persecuting Zeal: The Life of Ian Paisley** by Dennis Cooke (Brandon Press pb £9.99 0863222420) is the only full length biography of the religious and political leader. Cooke discusses Paisley's career from his ordination, through his involvement in the loyalist counter-demonstration to the Civil Rights movement in the early 1960s, his founding of the Democratic Unionist Party in 1971 and his outspoken engagement with Ulster politics ever since. **John Hume: A Biography** by Paul Routledge (Harper Collins hb £20.00 0002556707) is the authorised biography, written with Hume's approval and cooperation. The book profiles the founder of the nationalist Social Democratic Party who many feel is the real hero to emerge from the years of troubles in Northern Ireland. Through his staunch principles of non-violence, which were laid down the 1960s when he was involved with the civil rights movement in Derry, he has gained great respect and gravitas with both sides of the political and para-military divide. Hume's personal thoughts on Northern Ireland have been published as **John Hume: Personal Views** (Town House pb £9.99 1860590241). **Gordon Wilson: An Ordinary Hero** by Alf McGreary (Harper Collins pb £6.99 0551030267) tells the story of Gordon Wilson the ordinary man who shot to fame after he openly forgave the IRA bombers who killed his daughter Marie in the Enniskillen Remembrance day bombing in 1987. Wilson quickly became a symbol for hope between the two communities in Northern Ireland, because of his untiring belief that there could be peace in Northern Ireland. Wilson went on to hold a seat in the Irish Senate. **Phoenix: Policing the Shadows** by Jack Holland & Susan Phoenix (Coronet pb £6.99 0340666358) is a biography of the late Ian Phoenix (head of Northern Ireland police counter-surveillance unit) by his wife and the journalist Jack Holland. Phoenix was killed in 1994 with twenty four of his colleagues when their helicopter crashed into Mull of Kintyre. The book is also hugely informative about the nature of covert police operations in Northern Ireland. **Man of War: Man of Peace? Gerry Adams** by David Sharrock (MacMillan hb £16.99 0333698835) is the unauthorised biography of the president of Sinn Féin, examining and questioning his role in the political conflict. It portrays the 'real' Gerry Adams as well as providing a history of the Troubles. Adams's own views are put forward in two books, his **Selected Writings** (Brandon Press pb £8.99 0863222331) which include his political writings, stories and memoirs and **Free Ireland: Towards a Lasting Peace** (Brandon pb £7.95 0863222072) in which his political views are put down clearly and concisely. **Writings from Prison** by Bobby Sands (Mercier Press pb £6.99 185635220X) contains the prison memoirs, poetry and stories of this MP who died on hunger strike in Long Kesh prison in 1981 whileserving time for terrorist activity. Mainly written on toilet roll and smuggled out of the prison, these writings have left an astonishing inside view of the conditions in Long Kesh.

**Unionist Politics & the Politics of Unionism Since the Anglo-Irish Agreement** by Fergal Cochrane (Cork University Press pb £17.95 1859181392) is an essential book for anyone who wants an understanding of the Unionist frame of mind between November 1985 and July 1996. As well as analysing Unionist thought and political activity throughout the period, Cochrane also examines the demise of the political career of James Molyneaux and the rise to leadership of David Trimble. Martin Dillon has written a profile of loyalist paramilitary Michael Stone in his **Stone Cold** (Arrow pb £4.99 009922951X), which describes the events of March 1988 when Stone went on a killing rampage at the funerals of the three IRA volunteers shot dead in Gibraltar by the SAS. At the funeral, Stone killed three people and injured at least fifty others before he was caught. As a direct result two British soldiers were stripped, battered and eventually shot by the angry mob of mourners. Stone has used his extensive interviews with Stone to write this brilliantly realised exploration and portrait of a cold-blooded killer. **The UVF** by Jim Cusack & Henry McDonald (Poolbeg pb £9.99 1853716871) and **The Redhand: Protestant Paramilitaries** by Steve Bruce (Oxford University Press pb £8.99 0192852566) are both based on interviews with people directly involved and provide very good details of methods, motives, recruitment and finance of this terrorist organisation. **Fight for Peace** by Eamon Mallie & David McKittrick (Mandarin pb £7.99 0749322616) clearly and concise presents the details of the peace process. The book's great value is that it comprehensively presents all the prime movers on both sides of the border and the Irish Sea and rigorously reports on all the debate that has taken place.

**Pardon & Peace: A Reflection on the Making of Peace in Ireland** by Nicholas Frayling (Sheldon pb £10.99 0951422952) is an appeal by the Anglican rector of Liverpool for peace in the North of Ireland. Frayling argues that the only way forward is a whole hearted repentance by Great Britain. **Error of Judgement: The Truth about the Birmingham Bombings** by Chris Mullins (Poolbeg pb £9.99 1853713651) is the best account of this grave injustice paid to the six men who were tried, found guilty and convicted of the Birmingham bombings in the 1970s. After sixteen years in prison, they were released when the judgement was overturned. **Fifty Dead Men Walking: The Heroic True Story of a British Secret Agent Inside the IRA** by Martin McGartland (Blake pb £6.99 1857822013) is the incredible true story of a man who spent four years as an informer to British Intelligence. After being found out, he escaped torture and death by jumping through a third storey window. The fifty men of the title refers to the number of people whose lives were saved as a direct result of the information supplied by McGartland. **Enniskillen Remembrance Sunday Bombing** by Denzil McDaniel (Wolfhound Press pb £8.99 0863276113) examines the significance of this 1987 bombing which left eleven people dead. The book is based on interviews with survivors, the bereaved and politicians.

**Scorpions in a Bottle: Conflicting Cultures in Northern Ireland** by John Darby (Minrig pb £11.99 1873194161) is a very interesting examination of the Northern Troubles focusing on the cultural, ethnic and resulting political differences. The book also examines the inequalities inherent in this culturally divided society. **The Northern Ireland Peace Process: 1993-1996: A Chronology** by Paul Bew & Gordon Gill (Serif pb £9.99 1897959281) brilliantly clarifies the process by presenting all the political discussion and agreement in a diary form. This is the only reference book of its kind. **May the Lord in His Mercy be Kind to Belfast** by Tony Parker (Harper Collins pb £7.99 0006382541) is one of the most fascinating contributions to the literature of Northern Ireland. Taking as his premise that the best way to understand the troubles is to get the views of the people living in the North, Parker has compiled a catalogue of interviews with ordinary people, churchmen and terrorists from every side of the community which are illuminating in their content. **The Ruc 1922-1997: A Force Under Fire** by Chris Ryder (Mandarin pb £8.99 0749323795) is the only comprehensive book on the Royal Ulster Constabulary, which has fought terrorism in Northern Ireland with great dedication. For the 75th anniversary of the organisation, Ryder has updated his study which narrates the history of the force from the 1920s to the present day.

# Literary Criticism

*Hubert Butler* was born in Co. Kilkenny in 1900 and was eductaed in England. He travelled extensively throughout Europe during the 1920s and 30s and then came home to live at the family seat of Maidenhall in 1941. He was a founder member of the Kilkenny Historical Society. His essays were only discovered when he was in his 80s and three volumes appeared before his death in 1991. A fourth volume appeared posthumously. His essays are an extraordinary achievement in their scope, range and style. Whether writing about Sarajevo, the Holocaust, his maiden aunts or Kilkenny history, Butler has always produced essays that are compelling in their wisdom. An acute literary critic, he has written a brilliant essay on Graham Greene and Stephen Spender and has also translated Chekhov from the Russian. Volumes of his essays currrently available are **Escape from the Anthill** (Lilliput Press pb £5.95 0946640165), **Grandmother and Wolfe Tone** (Lilliput Press hb £16.95 0946640440) and **In the Land of Nod** (Lilliput Press hb £15.95 1874675538).

**Writing Ireland: Colonialism, Nationalism & Culture** by *David Cairns* (Manchester University Press pb £14.99 0719023726) is a lively post-colonial study of Irish culture, literature and identity. It starts off with a chapter on Spenser and Shakespeare; moves on to examine Arnoldian Celticism and concludes with a detailed look at the authors of the early 20th Century Revival, authors compared with contemporary propagandists Pearse and Griffith.

**The Hidden Ireland: A Study of Gaelic Muster in the 18th Century**
by *Daniel Corkery* (Gill& MacMillan pb £7.50 0717100790) is the by now classic
account of the lives of Aodgán Ó Rathaille, Eoghan Rua Ó'Súilleabháin
and Brian Merriman, the three most important 18th Century Irish poets.

*Neil Corcoran*, in his **After Yeats and Joyce** (Oxford University Press pb £8.99
0192892312) looks at authors of the later 20th Century and their reaction to
Ireland's most famous writers. Looking in detail at the work of Beckett,
Kinsella, Kate O'Brien, Seamus Heaney and Roddy Doyle, Corcoran
examines the relationship between rural and provincial writing and looks
at the Big House theme.

*Patricia Coughlan* and *Alex Davies* have edited a book of essays, **Modernism
and Ireland: Poetry of the 1930s** (Cork University Press pb £14.95 1859180612),
concerned with modern Irish writers who rejected the revival and whose
work is much more comfortable with the European tradition. The work of
writers like Thomas McGreevy, Brian Coffey and Denis Devlin, among others,
is studied by a range of contributors including Terence Brown, Anne Fogarty
and J.C.C. Mays.

*Gerald Dawe* is well-known as poet and critic. **Against Piety** (Lagan Press pb
£7.95 1873687753) is the most recent collection of essays and reviews to reveal
the range of his interests and sympathies. His recent **The Rest is History**
(Abbey Press pb £7.95 1901617033) examines Belfast culture through the early
lyrics of Van Morrison and Stewart Parker's dramatic masterpiece, Pentecost.
He also includes some shards of illuminating memoir about his early life and
the Belfast literary scene in the 1970s.

**Strange Country: Modernity & Nationhood in Irish Writing Since 1790**
(Oxford University Press hb £25.00 0198183372) by *Seamus Deane* is based on the
Clarendon lectures that he gave at the University of Oxford in 1995.
Starting with the works of Burke, Griffin, Stoker and finishing with Yeats,
Joyce and Synge, Deane convincingly argues that the reason we are a 'strange
country' is that we have manged to produce a literature that is both 'national'
and 'colonial'.

Edited by the poet *Theo Dorgan*, **Irish Poetry Since Kavanagh** (Four Courts Press pb £7.99 1851822402) is a collection of essays examining the relationship with and reaction to Kavanagh by the next generation of poets. Contributors include Augustine Martine, Terence Browne & Gerald Dawe.

*Terry Eagleton,* author of a standard introduction to Literary Theory, has always written sympathetically and insightfully about Irish literature. **Heathcliff & the Great Hunger** (Verso pb £13.99 1859840272) explores the relationship of Irish literature to Irish history and discusses a wide range of topics from the nature of language to the nature of the Celtic Revival.

*Robin Flower's* **The Irish Tradition** (Lilliput Press £7.99 1874675317), first published in 1947, and recently re-issued, is a set of lectures surveying Irish Literature and Culture from the 7th to 17th Centuries.

**Colonial Consequences: Essays in Irish Literature and Culture** (Lilliput Press pb £12.50 0946640475) by *John Wilson Foster* surveys Irish literature starting with the 18th Century. Foster's subjects include Irish Modernism, Yeats and 1916, close readings of Patrick Kavanagh and John Hewitt and essays on John Monatgue, Thomas Murphy and Seamus Heaney.

**Transformations in Irish Culture** by *Luke Gibbons* (Cork University Press pb £14.95 1859180590) is a series of essays examining the relationship between culture and politics, Nation and State, periphery and centre in contemporary Ireland. Gibbons argues that we have a very complex National Identity which we must redevelop and rethink. He examines literature, film and television and his two essays on the work of film-maker Pat Murphy are particularly strong.

Nobel Laureate *Seamus Heaney* is, of course, one of the great Irish poets of the century. He has also published a number of volumes of his prose writings. **Preoccupations** (Faber pb £7.99 0571133126) is a collection of early prose, from 1968 to 1978. **The Government of the Tongue** (Faber pb £7.99 057114151X) is a further collection of critical writings which includes the 1986 T.S.Eliot Memorial lectures. **The Redress of Poetry** (Faber pb £8.99 0571175376) is the series of lectures Heaney gave as Professor of Poetry at Oxford and includes his thoughts on Wilde, Yeats, Larkin and Dylan Thomas. **Crediting Poetry** (Gallery Press pb £5.00 1852351845) is the text of his Nobel lecture.
*Robert Hogan's* **Dictionary of Irish Literature** (Aldwych hb 2 Vols. £102.50 0861721020)

is a huge reference work to Irish writers from past and present and includes a chronology and bibliography as well as the dictionary entries.

Although best known as a poet, *Brendan Kennelly* has also written lucid, engaging prose about the literature that has impressed him most. **Journey into Joy: Selected Prose** (Bloodaxe pb £10.95 1852242108) is a collection of articles discussing Yeats, Joyce, MacNeice, Kavanagh to name but a few. It is wonderful to read a poet reading other poets and writers with such insight

**Inventing Ireland: The Literature of the Modern Nation** (Vintage pb £8.99 009958221X) by *Declan Kiberd* is a magnificent one volume survey of Irish literature from the 18th Century to the present. Arguing convincingly that the formation of the identity of the modern nation-state was left in the hands of its authors who literally 'invented' the idea of Ireland, Kiberd also provides historical 'interchapters' which provide informative context.

*Thomas Kinsella's* **The Dual Tradition** (Carcanet pb £9.95 1857541820) is a re-examination of Irish writing arguing that a dual approach has to be taken in any study because the literature exists in two languages, Irish and English. Reflecting on a huge range of writings from the earliest times to the present, Kinsella also examines the way in which writing from Ireland is published today.

*Joep Leerssen* has written two important studies on Irish literature and culture. **Mere Irish and Fior Ghael** (Cork University Press pb £17.95 1859181120) examines the development of the Irish ethnic image and self-image before 1800. His **Remembrance and Imagination** (Cork University Press pb £15.95 1859181112) is a study of cultural nationalism in the writings of Charles Maturin, Thomas Moore, Thomas Davis and W.B. Yeats.

*Edna Longley's* **Poetry in the Wars** (Bloodaxe pb £10.95 0906427991) is study of Northern Irish poetry, but placing it in the context of 20th Century English poetry. Longley asks whether poets from the North of Ireland should engage with the political and terrorist troubles. Using English poets who didn't write about the World Wars as example, she argues that Northern Irish poets shouldn't have to write about political violence. Poets studied include Louis MacNeice, Seamus Heaney and Derek Mahon.

Belfast-born poet *Derek Mahon* has had a varied career as academic, journalist, screenwriter and editor as well as publishing volumes of his oblique, ironic verse. The unambiguously titled **Journalism** (Gallery pb £10.95 1852351780) is a collection of his prose writings over a number of years.

**Bearing Witness: Essays on Anglo Irish Literature** (UCD Press pb £16.95 1900621029) by the late *Augustine Martin* is a selection of his work over three decades, selected and introduced by Anthony Roche. Lucid, text based analyses of Yeats, Joyce Kavanagh and Eavan Boland are followed by a number of his fine book reviews from various journals.

*S. Matthews'* **Irish Poetry: Politics, History, Negotiation** (MacMillan pb £14.99 0333643364) examines the influnce of Yeats on a number of contemporary poets including Ciaran Carson, Paul Muldoon, Seamus Heaney and John Montague and places detailed studies of some of the poems in their historical and political context.

*W.J McCormack's* **From Burke to Beckett: Ascendancy, Tradition & Betrayal in Literary History** (Cork University Press pb £18.00 0902561944) examines the huge contribution made to modernism by Irish writers. First published in 1985, the book has been expanded to include material on Elizabeth Bowen, W.B.Yeats and J.M. Synge. McCormack's **Battle of the Books: Two Decades of Literary Debate in Ireland** (Lilliput Press pb £3.95 0946640130) is a concise summary of contentious literary issues in the 1970s and 1980s.

**Twentieth Century Irish Drama: Mirror up to a Nation** (Manchester University Press pb £15.99 0719041570) by *Christopher Murray* is a very comprehensive overview of Irish Drama since the foundation of the state in 1922. Starting with Yeats, Lady Gregory, J.M. Synge and Seán O'Casey and covering contemporary dramatists like Sebastian Barry, Dermot Bolger and Marina Carr, Murray's is the best narrative history of Irish Drama this century.

*Tom Paulin* is well known as a fiery poet, controversialist and critic. **Writing to the Moment** (Faber pb £8.99 0571) is a collection of his critical writings from 1980 to 1995 which demonstrates his commitment both to artistic excellence and to both the Irish and the English traditions of political dissent.

In **Contemporary Irish Drama** (Gill & MacMillan pb £13.99 0717122409) *Anthony Roche* has written a lucid and clear study of contemporary Irish drama starting with the influence of Beckett and Yeats on dramatists this century and also tracing the Irish dimension in Beckett's drama. Roche also looks at the drama of Brendan Behan. He follows the careers and work of Brian Friel, Tom Murphy and Thomas Kilroy in detail and closes with an excellent chapter on the contemporary drama of Northern Ireland, in particular Stewart Parker, Frank McGuinness, Anne Devlin and the productions of the Field Day Theatre Company.

Edited by *Éibhear Walshe*, the collection of essays **Sex, Nation and Dissent in Irish Writing** (Cork University Press pb £16.95 1859180140) covers a previous uncharted area in critisism. Concentrating on writers like Somerville & Ross, Kat O'Brien and Mary Dorcey, amoung others, this book traces the development of dissident ideas in writers, both gay and straight, who are included in the mainstream tradition. The contributors include Declan Kiberd and Anne Fogarty.

**Oxford Companion to Irish Literature** (Oxford University Press hb £25.00 0198661584) by *Robert Welch* is an essential book for anyone interested in the rich fund of Irish writing. This alphabetical guide runs from entries on the Abbey Theatre to Zozimus, pseudonym of 18th Century balladeer Michael Moran and includes entries on all the major Irish writers. Ideal for the general reader to dip in and out of or for the scholar to use as a starting point for more expansive work.

# Local History

## General

**Irish Country Towns** (Mercier Press pb £9.99 1856350886) and **More Irish Country Towns** (Mercier Press pb £9.99 1856351211) by Ann Simms are a great introduction to the history of many towns. Giving details of origins and locality of many towns these books are a very good general reference. **The Dictionary of Irish Place-Names** (Appletree hb £6.99 086281460X) edited by Adrian Room contains details of over 3,000 names from both the Republic and Northern Ireland. Room shows the true names of many places that were re-named by the English when translating the old Irish. Deirdre Flanagan's **Irish Placenames** (Gill & Macmillan pb £6.99 071712066X) is also a very good introduction to the area. One of the most ambitious publishing projects in Ireland this century has been the History and Society series  published by Geography Publications. Each volume focuses on a different Irish County, and when complete will constitute, in thirty two volumes, the finest such history ever produced. History, archaeology, sociology and literary studies are all present in each volume and all of the books are a joy to read, produced to the highest of standards. Well illustrated with maps and line drawings, these books are definitive histories of each county. Titles currently available are:-

*Pat O'Flanagan*
**Cork History And Society**
(Geography Publications hb £40.00
090660222x)

*James Nolan*
**Donegal History And Society**
(Geography Publications hb £40.00
0906602459)

*Lindsay Proudfoot*
**Down History And Society**
(Geography Publications hb £40.00
0906602807)

*Gererd Moran*
**Galway History And Society**
(Geography Publications hb £40.00
0852090660)

*William Nolan*
**Kilkenny History & Society**
(Geography Publications hb £40.00
0906602130)
**Tipperary History And Society**
(Geography Publications hb £40.00
0906602033)

*Whelan Kevin*
**Wexford History And Society**
(Geography Publications hb £40.00
0906602068)

*Ken Hannigan*
**Wicklow History & Society**
(Geography Publications hb £40.00
0906602300)

*William Nolan*
**Waterford: History And Society**
(Geography Publications hb £40.00
0906602203)

# Dublin

The range of publishing on Dublin is, of course, enormous. **The Encyclopedia of Dublin** by Douglas Bennett (Gill & MacMillan pb £9.99 0717122921) is a very comprehensive historical A-Z of Dublin streets. Well illustrated, it gives the detailed history of most of the city centre streets and is thus indispensable for a thorough understanding of the development of the city. Daniel Hynes's **A Short History of Dublin** (Killeen pb £4.99 1873548397) is a very informative, concise study and an ideal narrative companion. **Dublin: City And County From Prehistory To Present** edited by Kevin Whelan (Geography Publications hb £30.00 090660219X) is a comprehensive history of the whole city of Dublin from 5000 B.C. to the 1990s. With chapters ranging from the development of Viking settlements to the evolution of Catholic parishes, this book covers every aspect of the city's history in detail. **Georgian Dublin** (Smythe pb £4.95 0851054250) is a collection of twenty-five aquatints of the flowering period of Dublin's architectural history. These 18th century images by James Malton with an accompanying text by urban historian Maurice Craig provide valuable views into the Dublin of 200 years ago. Deirdre Kelly's **Four Roads to Dublin** (O'Brien Press hb £19.95 0862784239) is a great history of Rathmines, Ranelagh and Leeson St. which comprise the main thoroughfares into the south city centre. The three areas are rich in architecture and were the most popular and, indeed, still are the most fashionable suburbs from the 18th century on. **Building Stones of Dublin: A Walking Guide** by Patrick Jackson (Town House pb £6.95 0946172323) is a very interesting look at the various types of stone that went into building Dublin city centre. The book contains instructions for four two-hour walks and illustrates the origins of the granite or limestone used.

Kevin Kearns has made an enormous and invaluable contribution to the understanding of Dublin local history. In his **Dublin Tenement Life** (Gill & MacMillan pb £9.99 0717124681), Kearns presents the oral history of the social lives, deterioration, and communities of the Dublin tenements both North and South of the Liffey. His **Stoneybatter: Dublin's Inner Urban Village** (Gill & MacMillan pb £12.99 0717124533) records the history of this modern community which was originally the Viking settlement of Oxmantown. This was to become a major trading centre for over a thousand years and earned its name as Cowtown. In both his **Dublin Pub Life and Lore** (Gill & MacMillan pb £9.99 0717126099) and his equally entertaining **Dublin Street Life and Lore** (Gill & MacMillan pb £12.99 0717126110) Kearns presents the oral reminiscences of old publicans, punters and street merchants.

Other books look at particular areas of the city, at the outlying areas of Dublin or at specific topics of local history. Edited by Jane Meredith, **Around and About the Custom House** (Four Courts Press pb £9.95 1851823085) is a beautifully illustrated series of images of this Gandon-designed building. The Custom House and Quay is presented as it has been seen by painters and photographers over the last two hundred years. **Around the Banks of Pimlico** by Mairin Johnston (Attic Press pb £5.95 0946211159) is both a tribute and history to the people and place situated in the heart of Dublin's Liberties. Johnston relates the life, lore and anecdotes of this area situated just outside the south inner city between 1850 and 1950. **Dublin Slums, 1800-1925** by Jacinta Prunty (Irish Academic Press hb £22.50 0716526905) focuses on the slums of Dublin's inner city between 1800 and 1925. Drawing on source materials like public inquiries and property valuation, Prunty recreates the geography and topography of the slum areas, while discussing issues like the awful disease and overcrowding which were rife. First published in 1912, **The Neighbourhood of Dublin** (Hughes hb £17.99 0708999999) by W. St. John Joyce is still the classic topographical guide to outskirts of the city. It is very interesting nowadays as the city is continuing its sprawl to look back at the Dublin 'villages' of the early 20th Century which have now become very close to the city centre. In his **Dalkey: A Town of the Archbishop** (Irish Academic Press pb £4.95 0716525968) Charles V. Smith looks at this now suburb's Viking origin and its use as a deep water bay during the middle ages. It became the home of local Dublin gentry and Smith examines the origins of one of the city's more prestigious villages. **An Early Toll Road: The Dublin-Dunleer Turnpike, 1731-1855** (Irish Academic Press pb £4.95 071652595X) by David Broderick is a history of the foundation and development of the main road out of Dublin to the North of the country. Discussing the building, traffic and the travellers on the road over its first hundred years, this is a great contribution to the understanding of early Irish traffic. **Dublin's Meath Hospital** by Peter Gatenby `tells the story of this hospital which was closed down in 1998. Founded in 1753, it found fame in the 19th century when John Cheyne, Robert Graves and William Stokes became renowned physicians. The author, a doctor himself, worked in the hospital for seventeen years and has examined minute books and records extensively. Put together by the Curriculum development unit, **Dublin, 1913: A Divided City** (O'Brien Press pb £4.50 0862780233) is a social history of the city during one of its most difficult periods, the 1913 lockout. Desmond J. Byrne's **The Talbots of Malahide 1630-1680** (Irish Academic Press pb £5.95 0716526298) is a family history of the Talbots who managed to keep all their lands during this time of confiscation. Combining Old English views with Catholicism they managed to keep most of their estates in north Co. Dublin. John Crawford's **St Catherine's Parish, Dublin, 1840-1900: A Portrait of a Church of Ireland Community** (Irish Academic Press pb £4.95 0716525933) is a very focussed study of one small parish in the Church of Ireland community. Taking a detailed look at socio-economic and church going trends, Crawford provides the modern reader with a valuable view of a Southern Protestant microcosm. **Thomas L Synott: The Career of a Dublin Catholic 1830-1870** by Robert Cullen (Irish Academic Press pb £5.95 0716526301) is a detailed examination of the career of Synott, who was very involved with Famine relief during the 1840s and was appointed governor of Grangegorman female prison in 1848. Synott's career is of historical interest because he achieved much more than most of his class contemporaries.

Finally there are two books which look at the Dublin of one of its most famous sons who memorialised the city in **Ulysses. James Joyce's Dublin Houses** by Vivien Igoe (Wolfhound Press pb £6.99 0863275885) gives a fascinating insight to the lives and background of both Joyce and his wife. Well illustrated throughout, it is both a good introduction and an aid to the interpretation of Joyce's work. **Ulysses Guide: Tours Through Joyce's Dublin** by Robert Nichols (New Island pb £5.99 0749309377) is a series of walks for the tourist and Dubliner alike, tracing the routes walked by the characters in Dublin's most celebrated novel. Walks around Sandycove, Sandymount Strand and through the city centre recreate the movements of both Leopold Bloom and Stephen Dedalus.

## Leinster

There are a number of interesting books available on the ancient towns and counties of Leinster. One of the Maynooth Monographs in Local History, **Carlow: The Manor and Town 1674-1721** (Irish Academic Press pb £5.95 0716526344) by Thomas King examines the foundation of the town, its population, type of employment and the various trades that were practised there during the late 17th and early 18th Centuries. **Cavan: Essays on the History of an Irish County** edited by Raymond Gillespie (Irish Academic pb £9.95 0716525542) is a selection of illuminating essays about this border county. Covering both social and economic history, this is the definitive history of the county. Desmond O'Dowd in his **Changing Times: The Story of Religion in 19th Century Celbridge** (Irish Academic Press pb £5.95 0716526352) discusses the not always easy relationship between the Catholic Church and the Church of Ireland in the town of Celbridge during the last century. Starting with examinations of the roots of both churches in the community, O'Dowd then looks at both the cooperation and conflict experienced as the century wore on. **A University For Kilkenny** (St. Canice's Press pb £4.95 0952807602) by John Leonard tells the story of the plans made to found a Royal college in Kilkenny during the late 17th Century. Plans were being made during the 1680s but were blocked by the victory of William of Orange and the Battle of the Boyne in July 1690. **Window on a Catholic Parish: Granard, County Longford 1933-1968** by Frank Kelly (Irish Academic Press pb £4.95 0716525941) is an illuminating look into the religious practices and life of this Longford parish. Kelly's findings are based on the parish records, which contained the surveys initiated by the Reverend Denis O'Kane in 1959. **County Wexford in the Rare Ould Times** edited by local historians Nicholas Furlong and John Hayes (Wexford pb £10.00 0951281224) is a wonderful pictorial celebration of the music, farming, sea and characters of Wexford county. It also features photos of the visits paid to Wexford by Eisenhower and John F. Kennedy. Art Kavanagh in his two volume study of the Wexford Gentry (Irish Family Names Vol 1 hb £15.95 0952478501) and (Irish Family Names Vol 2 hb £15.95 0952478536) examines the lives of many of the gentrified , land-owning families of Wexford. Families like the Redmonds, Boyds, Talbots and Alcocks are documented with all their idiosyncracies. In **Ballyknockan: A Wicklow Stone Cutter's Village** (Woodfield pb £9.99 0952845350) Sean O'Martíu & Tom O'Reilly examine the lives of the people who for over one hundred and seventy years provided stone for building in Dublin. Highlighting examples of the stone-cutting craft and recreating the daily life in as accurate a fashion as possible, the authors have produced a unique portrait of this essential craft.

## Munster

**Ennis in the 18th Century: Portrait of an Urban Community** (Irish Academic Press pb £4.95 0716525712) by Brian O'Dalaigh is part of the Maynooth studies in Local History and focuses on the topography, social structure and the local government of the town during the 18th Century. **West Cork: 'a sort of local history, like'** (Kestrel pb £9.95 1900505150) by Tony Brehony is a great run through the history, fable, myth and tales of West Cork. Brehony also relates the various anecdotes endemic to certain towns and villages.

The **Cork Anthology** (Cork University Press pb £11.95 090256188X) edited by Seán Dunne is a wonderful mixum-gatherum of poetry and prose connected with Cork life over twelve centuries. Selections from authors as varied as Edmund Spenser, Frank O'Connor, Paul Durcan, Alice Taylor and Daniel Corkery make this eclectic anthology a joy to both dip into and read closely. **Voices of Cork** (Blackwater Press hb £14.99 0861219368) are the transcripts of interviews about Cork conducted by Vincent Power. Personalities like actor Joe Lynch, sports commentator Bill Herlihy and chef Darina Allen all relate tales, opinions and anecdote to a very receptive interviewer. **The Murphy Story: History of Lady's Well Brewery** (Mercier Press hb £20.00 0953143104) by Donal & Diarmuid O'Driscoil is the only study available of this historic brewery. Lavishly illustrated and explaining brewing processes as they are used in the brewery; this makes for fascinating reading. **The Book of Kerry: Towns and Villages in the Kingdom** (Wolfhound pb £9.99 0863273726) by Arthur Flynn is a great introduction to the history, architecture, archaeology, people and landscape of the whole Kerry region.

Also focussing on many of the towns in 'the kingdom', Flynn brings the reader through the main streets of Listowel, Tarbert, Castlegregory and Kenmare. Muiris Macconghail in his **The Blaskets: People & Literature** (Town House pb £9.99 0946172447) takes the reader on two separate tours of these islands. The first part of the book sees him travelling by boat across the treacherous Blasket Sound and examining the landscape of the Islands and narrating the stories of the community that inhabited the island. The second half of the book is an astute exploration of the amazing literary heritage of the Great Blasket, with lucid comment on th writings of Peig Sayers and Thomas O'Crohan. Judith Hill's **The Building of Limerick** (Mercier Press pb £9.99 1856351912) is the only architectural study available of this city on the mouth of the Shannon which was founded by the Vikings, was walled during the Middle Ages and was a very important commercial centre during the 18th Century.

**The Limerick Anthology** (Gill & MacMillan pb £10.99 0717124584) edited by the late, great local politician Jim Kemmy is a great big book of reminiscences about Limerick by many people including Kate O'Brien, Gerald Griffin, Richard Harris, Eamon DeValera and more unlikely people like Harold Pinter, Heinrich Böll and Siegfrid Sassoon. Kemmy's follow up volume, The Limerick Compendium (Gill & MacMillan pb £10.99 0717126730) is just as interesting and was compiled in response to the great critical and commercial success of the former. **More of Nenagh's Yesterdays edited** by Murphy & O'Brien (Relay pb £10.00 0946327238) is a great book of photos commemorating the town of Nenagh between 1850 and 1950. Taken from parish and school records, these photos represent a great portrait of a town over a century.


## Connaught


J.F. Quinn's enormous and exhaustive three volume History of Mayo (Vol 1 Quinn hb £25.00 0951928007, Vol 2 Quinn hb £25.00 0951928015, Vol 3 Quinn hb £25.00 0951928023) is a complete and comprehensive history of this western county, full of statistics, topographical detail and anecdote. **In the Shadow of Benbulben: A Portrait of our Storied Past** by Joe McGowan (McGowan pb £9.95 0952133415) is a lively history of Co. Sligo, which focuses on the great dramatic events of the county's history. Recounting stories of the Spanish Armada, the Great Famine, the Land League, Mass Rocks and Hedge Schools, McGowan's anecdotal history makes for great reading.

Artist and mapmaker Tim Robinson has made a huge contribution to the study and understanding of the West of Ireland. His two volume **Stones of Aran** is the largest historical, topographical & archaeological study of Árainn (the largest of the Aran Islands) available and is a stunning achievement. The first volume, **Pilgrimage** (Penguin £7.99 014011565X) follows the coast clockwise around the island, taking note of flora and fauna and also expanding on the many tales told to him by the locals in each area. The second, larger volume, **Labyrinth** (Penguin £8.99 0140115668) charts the interior of the island and again is exhaustive in its recording and expansion of local history. Robinson's **Setting Foot on the Shores of Connemara** (Lilliput £10.00 1874675740) is a collection of fascinating essays about many topics, including map-making, fractal theory, archaeology, language and J.M. Synge. His most recent book **The View From the Horizon** (Coracle 090663007X pb £12.95) is a reflection on his work as an installation artist in the 1970s and the links between that and the map-making he does today. His award winning maps of Connemara and the Aran Islands are also available, **Connemara** (Folding Landscapes £12.00 0950400254) and **Oileán Áraínn Companion & Guide** (Folding Landscapes £10.00 0950400270).

## Ulster

Jonathan Bardon's enormous **History of Ulster** (Blackstaff Press pb £14.95 0856404764) is an incredible feat of scholarship. Spanning the history of all nine counties in the province, from 7000 B.C. to 1992, Bardon guides the reader through the turbulent history of this province, through the Elizabethan conquest, through the plantations, and both World Wars. He finishes with a chapter on the troubles from the late 1960s the early 1990s. This book is also available as a **Shorter Illustrated History of Ulster** (Blackstaff Press pb £14.99 0856405868). Bardon has also written **Belfast: A Pocket History** (Blackstaff Press pb £14.99 0856405884) Another shorter, but informative book on the North of Ireland is **A Pocket History Of Ulster** by Brian Barton (O'Brien Press pb £5.99 086278428X). **Shaping A City: Belfast In The Late 20th Century** edited by Frederick W. Boal (Institute Of Irish Studies pb £10.00 0853896054) is a fascinating history of and comment on the urban development of Belfast. Starting with an historical introduction, the book traces the housing, employment and population trends of the city since the 1960s. Beautifully illustrated with line drawings, colour photos, and maps, this is a book for both the student and general reader. In the Place-Names Northern Ireland series , there are two volumes on Co. Antrim. Volume 1 is **The Baronies of Toome** edited by Pat McKay (Institute Of Irish Studies hb £8.50 0853895694) and Volume 2 is **Ballycastle and North East Antrim** and is edited by Fiachra Macgabhan (Institute Of Irish Studies pb £8.50 0853896658). Both of these books are very comprehensive in their treatment of the placenames, parish by parish. These books look at the origins of the names and discuss early spelling in the hope of finding the true meaning.

**Tory Islanders: A People of the Celtic Fringe** (University Of Notre Dame Press pb £13.99 0268018901) by Robin Fox is a study of the people who inhabit this Irish speaking island which is nine miles off the Donegal coast. First published in 1978, the book discusses how the people of the island maintained a way of life which had all but vanished on the mainland because of their isolation.

# Music

When people think of Irish music they do not immediately think of rock music but there are a couple of books which chronicle the country's enthusiasm for the subject. **My Generation: Rock'n' Roll Remembered** edited by Anthony Farrell, Vivienne Guinness & Julian Lloyd (Lilliput pb £12.00 1874675511) is a wonderfully entertaining anthology of short prose pieces from various literary and visual and musical artists which explores their own relationship to and first experiences with Rock 'n' Roll. A diverse A-Z of contributions from Dermot Bolger to Marianne Faithful and Frank McGuinness to Ron Wood all tell their stories with enthusiasm, good humour and panache. **U2: At the End of the World** by Bill Flanagan (Bantam Books pb £7.99 0553408062) is the author's account of two years spent on the road with Ireland's biggest ever rock'n'roll band. U2 gave Flanagan full access to the tour and the result is a funny, affectionate but true portrait of the nuts and bolts of touring with a super group. The book also gives details of the many personalities met along the road people like Bill Clinton, Salman Rushdie and Bob Dylan. The book features places as far apart as Tokyo, Sarajevo, Sellafield and Mexico.

The boundaries between modern popular music and traditional music are not always clear-cut and there are acts which straddle the two. **Riverdance** (Deutsch hb

£14.99 0233990585) by award winning journalist Sam Smyth is the only full account of this incredibly successful show which has been performed on five continents. Smyth had full cooperation with all of the show's producers, performers and musicians. With stunning live photographs, this book is a very good record of the most recently successful Irish music phenomenon. **The Chieftains** by John Glatt (Century hb £16.99 0712676295) is the authorised account of the band's rise to become one the most successful Irish cultural exports. Written with the full cooperation of all of the band members, Glatt's book tells the Chieftains' story from when a group of enthusiastic and talented Irish musicians decided to play together, to the group's international success and their becoming the most successful and influential Irish traditional music group.

   **Traditional Music In Ireland** (Ossian pb £16.95 0946005737) by Tomás O'Canainn is a very clear study of traditional music in Ireland today. The book surveys collectors of music, the structure and style and focuses on Sean No's (traditional singing in Irish). It also examines the social context. O'Canainn concentrates on the style of three musicians, the piper Paddy Keenan, fiddler Matt Cranitch and singer Diarmuid ÓSuilleabháin using examples from their work. **Between the Jigs and the Reels** by Caomhín Mac Aoidh (Drumlin pb £9.99 1873437080) is the only comprehensive history and study of the great fiddle tradition of Co. Donegal. Charting the early influences, continuing changes and people and places involved, the book is invaluable for any one interested in Irish fiddle playing. **Toss The Feathers:Irish Set Dancing** by Pat Murphy (Mercier Press pb £8.99 1856351157) is a very comprehensive book of many dance styles, giving musical notation and clear explanations of the practicalities involved with dancing the 'Walls of Limerick' or the 'Siege of Ennis' while **Folk Music and Dances of Ireland** by Brendán Breathnach (Ossian pb £6.99 1900428652) is a study of the history, development and current state of Irish dancing with reference to the fiddle, uilleann pipes and tin whistle. HarperCollins also publish **Irish Dancing** by Tom Quinn in their pocket reference series which is a handily sized instruction book (Harpercollins pb £5.99 0004720695) as is **Irish Dances** by Terry Moylan (Ossian pb £5.00). **The Irish Whistle Book** (Ossian pb £3.95 0946005907) by Tom Maguire is the definitive guide to playing the whistle, probably the most portable of the traditional Irish musical instruments.

There are many Irish Songbooks currently available. The following is a selection of some of the most interesting. **Ireland: The Songs,** published by Waltons (0000335010 pb £12.95) is the first of four volumes of songs which gives both guitar chords and music score for such classics as the Rocky Road to Dublin and Danny Boy. These books also introduce each song, giving its background as does **The Songs and Ballads of Ireland,** published by Ossian (0946005532 pb £5.99) which gives the music score and lyrics to a similar selection including the Fields of Athenry and the Irish Rover. Bill Meek has selected many of the Irish favourites like the Orange Maid of Sligo, Whiskey in the Jar and the Arrest of Parnell in his **Irish Folk Songs** (Gill & Macmillan pb £3.99 0717125335).

Frank Harte has put together a great book **Songs of Dublin** (Ossian pb £12.95 0946005516). Born and bred in Dublin, Harte's family owned a pub where he first heard many of these songs. He set about collecting as many of the songs as he could and **Songs of Dublin** is taken from that collection. Songs like The Oul' Triangle, Raglan Road and Molly Malone are presented with music score. James Healy has edited **The Songs of Percy French** (Mercier pb £3.99 0853426953) which brings together a good selection of the work of probably Ireland's most famous traditional songwriter. The author of songs like Are Ye Right There Michael and Phil the Fluter's Ball, French was born in Co. Roscommon in 1854 and died in 1920. James Healy includes the score, guitar chords, lyrics and context of all of the songs included. **The World of Percy French** by Brendan O'Dowd (Blackstaff Press pb £10.99 085640604X) is a beautifully produced book of biography and song. A lifelong enthusiast of French's, O'Dowd has written both a warm biography of his musical hero and has collected a very valuable catalogue of songs, providing both words and music. John Healy has edited **Ballads from the Pubs of Ireland** (Mercier Press pb £3.99 1856350479) which includes guitar chords, lyrics and score of Finnegan's Wake and De Night Before Larry Was Stretched. Healy's other contributions to the collection of Irish Song are his **Irish Songs of The Sea** (Ossian pb £3.95 1900428458) and **Love Songs of The Irish** (Mercier pb £3.99 085342697X). **The Christy Moore Song Book** edited by Frank Connolly (Brandon pb £5.99 0863220630) presents a definitive collection, with guitar chords of Ireland's most popular folk singer.

The poet Ciaran Carson writes on the power of the anonymous authors of folk songs

The first bits of poetry I ever heard were folk songs. My mother would sing

> I'm going down the town and I know who's going with me
>
> I have a wee boy of my own and his name is Ciaran Carson
>
> He wears a wee top coat, he wears it in the fashion
>
> But he has to lie in bed while his Sunday shirt's a washin'

My father had a wider repertoire - songs of love and murder, songs of unrequited love and re-united lovers, Orange songs and Green songs, nonsense songs, songs of '98. Many of these he had learned from his mother, and one of my grandmother's favourites was 'The Grave of Wolfe Tone'

> In Bodenstown Churchyard there lies a green grave
>
> And wildly around it the winter winds rave
>
> Small shelter I ween are the ruined walls there
>
> When the storm clouds sweep down on the plains of Kildare

Listening to her singing it again in my memory, I am transported back to her tiny kitchen room, and see her sitting by the fire with her eyes closed. I remember how the scene described in those lines would flash into my inward eye with the clarity of a dark steel engraving, like those in my father's Book of Psalms, where the Godforsaken poet sprawls beneath a rack of nimbostratus, transfixed by one shaft of redeeming light. I loved to wallow in that gloomy ruin of defeated hope, of aspirations never to be realised.

Technically 'The Grave of Wolfe Tone' may not be a folk song - it is attributed to Thomas Davis - but folk songs were all made by people, though we may not know their names. Davis's lyrics (if they are his) are inspired by the genre, and have been absorbed by it. They are part of a collective memory of '98 as surely as Henry Joy McCracken, and I cannot look at the Napoleonic profile of Cave Hill, which dominates the north of the city where I live, without the first lines of that song coming to mind:

> It was on the Belfast mountains I heard a maid complain
>
> And she vexed the sweet June evening with her heartbroken strain
>
> Saying, Woe is me, life's anguish is more than I can dree
>
> Since Henry Joy McCracken died on the gallows tree

I would hear an echo of the song when my father brought me to the Ulster Museum. After we had viewed the stuffed Orang-Utan and the Egyptian Mummy, we would stand reverentially before McCracken's jacket draped on a headless torso: At Donegore he proudly rode and he wore a suit of green. It is there still, part of an exhibition commemorating the 1798 rebellion. I am struck now by how this heroic figure is diminished by the smallnesx of his sloped shoulders, and the poor quality of the faded cloth; it looks like an amateur dramatic prop.

Of course songs like Henry Joy speak to a political agenda but they also engage with a wider realm, of the narratives implicit in the human condition. Their protagonists jump vividly into the imagination, stark and emblematic as the woodcuts which accompany their printed broadsheet versions. We are faced by these characters who buttonhole us with their tales of lawlessness and wild endeavour, of faithful love and desperate circumstance. Soldier, sailor, tinker, tailor, they occupy their tragic or triumphant roles with beautiful conviction. It is up to the singer, and the listener, to invest them with their own experience, to deliver on the promise of their introductions:

> Come all you young fellows that follow the gun...
>
> I am a bold, undaunted youth, my name is John McCann..
>
> In comes the captain's daughter, the captain of the Yeos....

Oh who will plow the field now or who will sell the corn?

They may talk of Flying Childers, and the speed of Harkaway...

Young men that have your liberty, I pray you now draw near...

'Tis of a famous highwayman a story I will tell....

The figures in these dramas, and the cadences in which they are invested, lie continually at the back of my mind, resurrecting themselves fully on occasions. By their deeds of courage and terror they demand to be known. As they confront us, they demand that we confront ourselves. Their ghosts populate the landscape, flitting in and out of the present hedges of our conversation. As if every crossroads had its gallows. As if every road led to a port, and that port to a far-off country. As if the future was determined by the past.

In March of this year, 1998, I completed a sequence of sonnets which will be published in November as **The Twelfth of Never**. The first sonnet is called Tib's Eve which Brewer's Dictionary of Phrase and Fable defines as 'St. Tib's Eve; Never. A corruption of St. Ubes. There is no such saint in the calendar as St. Ubes, and therefore her eve falls on the Greek Calends (q.v.), neither before Christmas Day or after it.' The poem goes like this :

There is a green hill far away, without a city wall,

Where cows have longer horns than any that we know;

Where daylight hours behold a moon of indigo,

And fairy cobblers operate without an awl.

There, ghostly galleons plough the shady Woods of True,

And schools of fishes fly among the spars and shrouds;

Rivers run uphill to spill into the starry clouds,

And beds of strawberries grow in the ocean blue.

This is the land of the green rose and the lion lily,

Ruled by Zeno's eternal tortoises and hares,

Where everything is metaphor and simile:


Somnambulists, we stumble through this paradise

From time to time, like words repeated in our prayers,

Or storytellers who convince themselves that truths are lies.

The twelve - sometimes fourteen - syllables of the line were initially based on the French alexandrine but it seems to me that its cadences are not that far off Irish ballad metre. And the sonnet form itself offers anecdotal, ballad-like possibilities. Writing these poems was partly a homage to the tradition of ballads in Ireland. I'll count myself lucky if a few of them are half as memorable.

Note : Some of the songs referred to in this article can be found in **The Complete Irish Street Ballads** (Pan). Also of interest is Ciaran Carson - **Pocket Guide to Irish Traditional Music** (Appletree Press 0862811686).

# Poetry

by Pat Cotter, Waterstone's, Patrick Street, Cork

## Anthologies

Irish poetry anthologies have taken on a highly politicised, almost manifesto-type function in Ireland through the 90s. A flurry of anthologies from major British and American publishers caused major ructions with counter accusations of exclusivity flying all about the place. Since then various *de rigueur* criteria have emerged for an Irish poetry anthology: there must be adequate representation of both sexes, unless of course the anthology is exclusively a female one; there must be representation from both language groups, unless of course the anthology is exclusively an Irish language one. Where translations of Irish-language poems appear in an anthology aimed at an English-language readership, they must always be accompanied by the original texts. Some of these criteria make sense, others threaten to make the whole process painfully cumbersome.

In the **Penguin Book of Irish Verse** (Penguin pb £8.99 0140585265) Brendan Kennelly produces a good representative anthology of poems from earliest times right down to poets who began to publish in the 70s. Poems from both the Hiberno-English and Gaelic traditions are represented. **The Penguin Book of Contemporary Irish Poetry** (Penguin pb £8.99 0140586091) was edited by Peter Fallon and Derek Mahon. Despite the fact that this anthology appeared before the explosion of poetry publications by women throughout the nineties (and therefore does not include many of them) it remains the most representative of all the anthologies currently available. **The Faber Book of Irish Verse** (Faber pb £11.99 0571112188), edited by John Montague, is probably the best overall view of Irish poetry from both traditions from earliest times to the late 70s. Montague includes generous selections from the Irish, translated by various voices. An interesting feature of the anthology is the large tracts given over exclusively to love poetry. **The New Oxford Book of Irish Verse** (Oxford Up pb £9.99 0192826433) was edited by Thomas Kinsella. Kinsella's aim in this anthology was to tie the two literary traditions of Ireland together and present them as a unified whole. The book distinguishes itself from Montague's anthology by including more poems by less poets, by finishing up with poets who all began publishing in the late 60s, by not including any living women and by presenting all poems from the Irish exclusively in Thomas Kinsella's own translations. Kinsella's masterful versions from the Irish, including Merriman's Midnight Court in its entirety, are reason enough to buy the book. **Irish Poetry Now** (Wolfhound pb £8.99 0863273793), edited by Gabriel Fitzmaurice is an anthology of poems written in the 1990s by poets not found in either the Penguin or Faber anthologies. Sean Dunne, Greg Delanty, Caithlin Maude, Dennis O'Driscoll, Patrick Galvin and Cathal O Searcaigh are among the notables included. **The Faber Book Of Contemporary Irish Poetry** (Faber pb £8.99 057113761X) was edited by Paul Muldoon. Muldoon decided to present only ten poets in this anthology, rather than give a representative overview. It really should be called Contemporary Ulster Poetry as Kinsella and Durcan are the only poets of the ten not from the northern province. The selection of Tom Paulin to the exclusion of masterful fellow-Faber poet Richard Murphy is, at the very least, debatable. However it is, undoubtedly true that an amazing confluence of poetic talent emerged from Ulster in the 1960s. Poets like Seamus Heaney, John Montague, Derek Mahon and Michael Longley have carved-out well-deserved international reputations for themselves. **Poets from the North of Ireland** (Blackstaff pb £10.99 0856404446), edited by Frank Ormsby, takes the opportunity to present younger Ulster poets alongside the aforementioned. **Jumping Off Shadows** (Cork University Press pb £12.95 090256191X), edited by Nuala Ní Dhomhnaíl and Greg Delanty, is ostensibly an anthology of poets who were former students at UCC. However it includes so many of the key younger Southern players (Ni Dhomhnail and Delanty themselves, Durcan, Thomas McCarthy, Michael Davitt and Seán Dunne) that it stands as a good introduction to readers who may wish to balance their reading of many of the Ulster-centric anthologies of the last 20 years. Two collections of poems from the Irish are worth investigation. **An Duanaire 1600-1900: Poems of the Dispossessed** (Dolmen pb £11.50 0851053645), edited by Sean óTuama and Thomas Kinsella, is a marvellous selection of poems from the Irish following the collapse of the Gaelic Order and the great Bardic Courts. Dispossessed professional court poets are placed here along with a wonderful, vibrant, peasant folk tradition stretching from the beginning of the 17th century to the end of the 19th. **An Crann Faoi Bláth/The Flowering Tree** (Wolfhound Press pb £9.99 0863272320), edited by Gabriel Fitzmaurice and Declan Kiberd is the essential text for the English language reader wishing to discover the brilliant poets now writing in Irish. A generous representative selection is made and all translations are accompanied by original texts.

Other collections show how poetry can still appeal to the general reader. The **Lifelines** anthologies, edited by Niall MacMonagle (Lifelines 1 Townhouse pb £10.99 0948524464; Lifelines 2 Townhouse pb £9.95 0948524766; Lifelines 3 Townhouse pb £10.99 1860590497) are almost like a Golden Treasury for our own time. Originally begun as a school project to raise money for charity, this series of anthologies consists of poems drawn from all across the canon by hundreds of different Irish and British celebrities. Each choice comes with an explanation of what the poem means to the selector. The enormous sales of the series shows how popular poetry can still be with the general reader. Another best-selling series which exploits that repository of love the general reader has for poetry consists of **Favourite Poems We Learned In School** (Mercier pb £5.99 1856350517), **More Favourite Poems We Learned At School** (Mercier pb £5.99 1856350878) and **Favourite Poems We Learned In School As Gaeilge** (Mercier pb £5.95 1856351068). The books are edited by Thomas Walsh. As the title explains, the selection is limited to favourites from old school textbooks and includes many poems learnt by people by rote half a century ago but which otherwise are not generally available. Finally three miscellanies of Irish poems and verses are the perfect chocolate boxy selection to be given as a gift to those who only rarely read poetry. These are **Treasury of Irish Verse** (Gill hb £19.99 0717120007), **Popular Irish Poetry** (Gill pb £13.99 0717122700) and **Remembered Kisses** (Gill hb £12.99 0717124460).

## SARA BERKELEY
### (b. Dublin l967)

Berkeley first came to notice while still at school and precociously published her first collection at the age of nineteen. Stylistically her work is associated with that of Paul Durcan. She has also published a collection of short stories.

**Home Movie Nights**
Raven Arts Press pb £4.50
1851860509

## EAVAN BOLAND
### (b. Dublin 1944)

A precocious beginner, Boland had her first book **New Territory** published in 1967 to a favourable reception. She has since become one of Ireland's most famous poets. Her work is distinguished by an intellectual disposition and a strong awareness of technical restraints on themes. A poet who is a woman rather than a 'woman poet', she has nevertheless become an emblematic figure to many of Ireland's women; a great number of whom she has encouraged to write through the large number of workshops she gives. A re-examination of the feminine as portrayed in the patriarchal literary tradition is a core part of her work, particularly as used in the personification of landscape and national identity. She has variously explored motherhood, daughterhood, the alienating experience of being Irish abroad, as well as a host of other themes. To describe her work as feminist would be to suggest her poetry is doctrinaire and reductionist in a way that it is not.

**Collected Poems**
Carcanet pb £9.95 1857542207
**In a Time of Violence**
Carcanet pb £6.95 1857540670
**Outside History**
Carcanet pb £6.99 0856358991
**Selected Poems**
Carcanet pb £5.99 0856357413
**Object Lessons**
Vintage pb £6.99 0099580616
(memoir)

## PAT BORAN
### (b. Portlaoise 1963)

Boran won the Kavanagh Award in 1989. He has published three full collections with Dedalus. He published a collection of stories with Salmon and his interest in narrative and anecdotes are in evidence in his poems

**Familiar Things**
Dedalus pb £4.95 1873790325
**The Shape of Water**
Dedalus pb £5.95 1873790856

## MOYA CANNON
### (b. Donegal 1956)

In **The Parchment Boat**, Moya Cannon reflects on her life and the world around her in a collection of short, elegant poems. Using a varied range of images, from archaeological artefacts to wind-fallen hazelnuts, Cannon very effectively explores the world she knows.

**The Parchment Boat**
Gallery pb £5.95 1852352019

## CIARAN CARSON
**(b. Belfast 1948)**

Carson's first book published in 1976 introduced yet another competent but conventional poet from the North of Ireland. All presumptions of ordinariness however were smashed with the appearance of **The Irish For No** from Gallery in 1987. Carson had discovered a thrillingly long, Whitmanesque line with which he could expansively treat his obsession with his native city. Comparisons with the American poet C. K. Williams were not unwarranted but in reality Carson is superior to his supposed precursor, displaying a deeper love of verbal music and wordplay. Recent periodical poems show him returning to a shorter line, which may be a good thing as the long line is appearing a little exhausted now after four books. Carson has also published an idiosyncratic account of Irish traditional music, **Last Night's Fun,** and a memoir of the Belfast in which he grew up.

**Belfast Confetti**
Gallery pb £6.00 1852350423
**First Language**
Gallery pb £5.95 1852351284
**The Irish for No**
Gallery pb £5.95 1852350164
**The New Estate and
Other Poems**
Gallery pb £5.95 1852350326
**Opera Et Cetera**
Gallery pb £6.95 185235187X
**Last Night's Fun**
Pimlico pb £9.99 0712662529
**The Star Factory**
Granta hb £13.99 1862070725 (Memoir)

## EILÉAN NÍ CHUILLEANÁIN
**(b. Cork 1942)**

Another Kavanagh Award winner, an editor of the periodical **Cyphers** and lecturer of English at TCD. A fine craftsman who has controversially not taken part in a number of prominent anthologies. She has written convincingly about subjects as varied as Independence War ambushes and feelings about her native city of Cork.

**The Brazen Serpent**
Gallery pb £4.95 185235139X
**The Magdalene Sermon**
Gallery pb £4.95 1852350504
**The Second Voyage**
Gallery pb £5.95 1852350008

## AUSTIN CLARKE
### (1896–1974)

Clarke was one of the most accomplished of twentieth century Irish poets and an important influence on Thomas Kinsella. Despite (or maybe even because of) his rigorous fidelity to craft Clarke did not export well to Britain and with a dearth of Irish publishers, self-published much of the time. Clarke's earliest work is most influenced by Yeats. Later work reproduces in English the intricate consonantal and assonantal rhyme schemes of Gaelic Bardic poetry. A Southern, Protestant Nationalist, Clarke, like Yeats, found himself riled by the petty world created by the Catholic petit bourgeois in the wake of national independence and much of his work is satirical. There is an air of intellectual discipline in Clarke not found in the more emotionally expressive Kavanagh. Together they represent an important post-Yeatsian legacy for contemporary Irish poets. Hugh Maxton's selection from Austin Clarke's work, published by Lilliput, is currently out of print.

**Austin Clarke Remembered**
Dardis Clarke Bridge pb £7.50
0951941720

## HARRY CLIFTON
### (b.Dublin 1952)

Kavanagh Award winner Clifton has produced several books with Gallery Press. 'Monsoon Girl' about sex in an Asian setting is his most famous and anthologised poem. Other subjects have included Thomas Merton and James Joyce. It appears as if Clifton has not been interested in consistently exploring recurrent themes as his contemporaries Dunne and McCarthy do; nor does he appear to be as interested in language play as Muldoon or Carson but his interest in social issues is arguably greater.

**Night Train through the Brenner**
Gallery pb £5.95 1852351225
**Office of the Salt Merchant**
Gallery pb £4.95 0902996835
**The Walls of Carthage**
Gallery pb £4.95 0902996509

## MICHAEL COADY
### (b. 1939)

**All Souls** is a hauntingly moving mix of prose, poetry and photographic images, which is part memoir and part poetic engagement with memory, both personal and collective. It centres around the long title poem, whose narrator remembers the people dead and gone from his home town, and 'The Use of Memory', Coady's powerful memoir about the last four generations of his family.

**All Souls**
Gallery hb £13.95 1852352124

## PADRAIC COLUM
### (1881–1972)

Poet, playwight, novelist, friend of Joyce, Colum was a considerable figure in Irish literature from the first decade of the century to his death. His poetry, which appeared in many volumes through the years, was particularly successful when he spoke in the voice of others, often those marginalised by society.

**Poet's Circuits**
Dolmen Press pb £6.50
0851053904
**Selected Poems**
Syracuse UP pb £17.95
0815624581

## BRIAN COFFEY
### (1905–1995)

Dedalus deserve great credit for keeping in print Coffey's collected poems. Coffey, like Devlin and Beckett, went into exile and wrote in the 'high Modernist' mode. The main Irish tradition developed without as much as a nod in the direction of Modernism, viewed by many as an aesthetically dead-end early twentieth century experiment. As a consequence not many people take the trouble to read any of it now, which is a pity because Coffey's work includes gems such as 'The Death of Hektor' which reward the diligent, dedicated reader.

**Poems and Versions 1929-1990**
Dedalus pb £8.95 1873790023

## ANTHONY CRONIN
### (b. Co. Wexford 1925)

Cronin once described himself as the most neglected poet in Ireland. Certainly he deserves more credit for wonderful work such as his long poem 'RMS Titanic' and his sonnet sequence 'The End of the Modern World'. Sadly much of his best work is currently out of print.

**Relationships**
New Island Books pb £4.95
1874597065

## PADRAIG J. DALY
### (b. Co. Waterford 1943)

Published by Dedalus and a priest by profession, Daly has written work which displays a spiritual concern allied to a need to name hurts and pay praise where it is due.

**Out of Silence**
Dedalus pb £4.95 1873790260
**The Voice of the Hare**
Dedalus pb £5.95 1873790961

## GERALD DAWE
### (b. Belfast 1952)

Now living in Dublin, Gerald Dawe has written four collections of poetry, the most recent of which is **Heart of Hearts**. Divided in two, the first half concerns the poet's Belfast childhood and the second half is a collection of quietly lyrical poems which reflect on the everyday with gentle power.

**Heart of Hearts**
Gallery pb £5.95 1852351535
**The Lundys Letter**
Gallery pb £4.95 0904011844
**Sunday School**
Gallery pb £5.95 1852350636

## JOHN F. DEANE
### (b. Achill 1943)

Deane is the proprietor of Dedalus Press and, in this role, he has encouraged the lapidary Modernist line in Irish poetry. He is an accomplished translator of contemporary European poets. His own work displays an interest in the spiritual.

**Christ the Urban Fox**
Dedalus pb £5.95 1873790988
**Far Country**
Dedalus pb £5.95 1873790171
**Stylized City: New and Select Poems**
Dedalus pb £5.95 0948268891

## SEAMUS DEANE
### (b. Derry 1940)

Critic, novelist and poet, Deane has a critical intelligence which is everywhere evident in his poems perhaps to a degree detrimental to feeling and playfulness. Political issues dominate and his poetry is often more accessible and pleasurable than the even more intellectualised Paulin. His novel **Reading in the Dark** may point in a more creatively fruitful direction for this writer of ideas.

**Selected Poems**
Gallery pb £5.95 1852350288

## GREG DELANTY
### (b.Cork 1958)

Delanty has been the recipient of prizes from early in his career. Resident in America, his work shows him to be torn between the formalistic British tradition and the looser American tradition. In his collection **The Hell-Box,** the more formal poems win out by the brilliance of their craft and the powerful exploration of the traditional printing-trade as metaphor.

**American Wake**
Gill and McMillan pb £5.99 0856405493

## DENIS DEVLIN
### (1908–1959)

A friend and associate of Brian Coffey, Devlin was one of the leading members of the small but accomplished movement of Irish modernist poets. Devlin was an avid translator of French poets and their influence is greatly in evidence in his own work.

**Collected Poems**
Dedalus pb £9.95 0948268492

## KATIE DONOVAN
### (b. Dublin 1962)

Donovan has published two collections where, among other themes, she has written about sexual relationships with a refreshing frankness.

**Entering the Mare**
Bloodaxe pb £6.95 1852242159
**Watermelon Man**
Bloodaxe pb £5.99 1852244291

## MARY DORCEY

One of Ireland's most accomplished short story writers, Dorcey has produced work which is one of the few examples of gay love explored in Irish poetry.

**Moving into the Space Cleared by Our Mothers**
Salmon pb £5.99 1897648251
**The River that Carries Me**
Salmon pb £6.99 1897648626

## THEO DORGAN
### (b. Cork 1953)

Dorgan has published two collections of poems. His 'The Match Down the Park' from **Rosa Mundi** is a tour de force of a poem recounting the excitement and fervour of a hurling match. Other poems which stand out include 'Kilmainham, Easter' and 'Seven Versions of Loss Eternal'.

**Rosa Mundi**
Salmon pb £6.99 1897648642

## SEÁN DUNNE
### (1956–1995)

Dunne published three collections of distinguished poems before dying unexpectedly at thirty nine. A strong musicality and sense of form are inherent in his poems. The domestic life, its dangers, rewards and fragility forms his most prevalent subject matter. His later work displayed a dedication to metaphor and an almost Japanese-like sensitivity to the image.

**Road to Silence**
New Island pb £4.95
187459712X
**The Sheltered Nest**
Gallery pb £5.95 1852350849
**Time and the Island**
Gallery pb £5.95 1852351802

## PAUL DURCAN (b. Dublin 1944)

Durcan is one of Ireland's most popular and controversial poets. Ever since his first prize-winning collection Durcan has found detractors among the admirers of the 'well-made poem'. But though much of his work has a structural looseness suggestive of many Eastern European poets he has written many beautiful formal lyrics such as 'Memoirs of a Fallen Blackbird'. Durcan's work has been popular for its zany outlook, its commitment to social comment, its strong narrative impulse and its sensitivity to women. Durcan has been an animated performer of his own work – a fact which has made him stand out on the poetry-reading circuit. He has been an important critic of the social restrictions found in 70s and 80s Ireland whether it be the oppression of women or the social power of the Catholic Church. He has been a most vocal critic of the use of murder as a political instrument. Durcan is now one of the most imitated of poets prompting even Derek Mahon to attempt a Durcan pastiche as humorous tribute. **The Berlin Wall Cafe** recounting the collapse of his marriage was a major tour de force and sold like a best-selling novel. Meditative sequences on paintings followed and consolidated his position as a hugely popular and bestselling poet.

In 1993, the Harvill Press published **A Snail in My Prime** which contained new and selected poems and was a major publishing event, summing up his poetic career to date. The winter of 1996 saw the publication of **Christmas Day,** his most recent work, which is a moving meditation on the joys, fears and disappointments of life focussing on the festive season.

**The Berlin Wall Cafe**
Harvill pb £6.99 1860460887
**Christmas Day**
Harvill pb £6.99 186046288X
**Christmas Day Book and tape**
Harvill pb £10.00 1860464580
**Crazy About Women**
National Gallery pb £9.95
090316258X
**Daddy Daddy**
Blackstaff pb £5.95
0856404462
**Going Home to Russia**
Blackstaff pb £4.95
0856403865
**Jesus and Angela**
Blackstaff pb £5.95
0856404071
**O Westport in the Light of Asia Minor**
Harvill pb £6.99 1860460879
**A Snail in My Prime**
Harvill pb £7.99 0002713241

"Look – for me the equivalent of the Easter
Rising Is to be accosted by a woman whom I do not know
And asked by her to keep an eye on her things."
Paul Durcan – Bewley's Oriental Café, Westmoreland Street

## JOHN ENNIS
### (b. Co. Westmeath 1944)

Ennis has been described as Ireland's most neglected poet by Seamus Heaney. He is a poet of high ambitions who has frequently produced long narrative poems. His work displays a consistent dedication and sensitivity to language as a medium.

**Burren Days**
Gallery pb £4.95 0904011887
**In a Green Shade**
Dedalus Irish pb £5.95
1873790007
**Selected Poems**
Dedalus pb £7.95 1873790929
**Telling the Bees**
Dedalus pb £5.95 1873790775

## PETER FALLON
### (b.Germany 1951)

Fallon is the proprietor of the Gallery Press. A deep concern for rural matters, whether it be animal husbandry or the manner of countryside gossip informs his work. Poems written on the death of a son are particularly moving. He has just published a volume of new and selected poems.

**Eye to Eye**
Gallery Press pb £5.95
1852351004
**News and Weather**
Gallery Press pb £4.95
1852350105
**News of the World: Selected and New Poems**
Gallery Press pb £6.95
1852352140

## GERARD FANNING
### (b.Dublin 1952)

Fanning's work is quiet and serious. The 'Dolmen Mandarin short line' is common in much of his imagistic, unshowy poems concerned with subjects like cartography, God and politics.

**Easter Snow**
Dedalus pb £4.95 1873790155

## PADRAIC FIACC
### (b. Belfast 1924)

Born in Belfast but raised and educated in New York, Fiacc is one of Ireland's most committed political poets. His work faces issues of class and tribal politics head-on without any reticent fence-sitting. Structurally he appears to have learnt a great deal from French and German poets as well as William Carlos Williams.

**Ruined Pages**
Blackstaff pb £7.99
0856405299

## GABRIEL FITZMAURICE
### (b. Co. Kerry 1952)

Fitzmaurice has published over a dozen books of poems. It would be difficult for any poet to sustain consistent high achievement over such a large body of work in a twenty year period. Fitzmaurice is no exception. However, there are gems amongst his works including a very powerful translation of a long Michael Hartnett poem 'The Purge'.

**The Village Sings**
Taylor Publishing pb £8.80
1885266294

## ROBIN FLOWER
### (1881–1946)

Flower's translations of poems from the Irish language are masterful and an essential part of our literary culture. He is also well known for his memoir **The Western Island** about life on the Great Blasket.

**Poems and Translations**
Lilliput pb £5.99 1874675325

## PATRICK GALVIN (b.Cork 1927)

Galvin is an important precursor for the likes of Nuala Ni Dhomhnaill and Michael Hartnett. They have in common a love of folksy narrative with a humorous twist. Consciously or unconsciously Galvin's work has much in common with the structures and concerns of Gaelic folk poetry. The fact that he started publishing such work before it became popular to do so did not help his stature early on and he is mysteriously absent from most of the major anthologies to this day. Galvin first came to prominence with his powerful long poem 'Heart of Grace' an account of the brutalising of a young boy by borstal. Galvin is one of the few poets of working class origins from before the advent of free secondary school education and his poems recount the experience of the Irish urban poor like no other. He is also a songwriter and has recorded several albums of his songs. His most famous song covered by Christy Moore recounts the execution of James Connolly. Galvin also has a strong interest in Spanish culture and his later work shows the influences of Lorca and other Spanish Surrealists. More recently he has been the author of a best-selling series of surreal memoirs.

**New & Selected Poems
of Patrick Galvin**
Cork University Press pb £7.95 1859180914

## OLIVER GOLDSMITH
### (1728–1774)

The son of a clergyman, Goldsmith is better known as a playwright and novelist than poet but his **The Deserted Village** has endured as a sentimental favourite of the general reader. His influence in the Irish literary tradition, however, is quite small.

**The Deserted Village**
Goldsmith Press pb £6.00
090498429X
**Selected Poems**
Carcanet pb £5.95 0856356239

## ROBERT GREACEN
### (b. 1920)

This long under-rated poet, who won the Irish Times literary award in 1995 with the publication of his **Collected Poems** was born in Derry. He was educated in Belfast and in Trinity College, Dublin and lived in London for many years. His poetry examines, among other things the middle class protestant sensibility, especially in his recent collection **Protestant Without a Horse**. His memoir, **The Sash My Father Wore**, is a gently evocative book about the North of Ireland and his adventures in literary London and Dublin.

**Collected Poems**
Lagan Press pb £5.99
1873687559
**Protestant Without a Horse**
Lagan Press £5.95 1873687370
**The Sash My Father Wore**
Mainstream hb £15.99
185158923640

## EAMON GRENNAN
### (b. Dublin 1941)

Grennan teaches in the US but his frequent visits to Ireland would preclude one calling him a writer-in-exile. He is perhaps the most successful exponent of American-style *vers libre*. His work is highly meditative and ruminations on nature and family predominate. His work displays a large vocabulary buzzing with dynamic verbs giving his poetry a vibrancy lacking in the more noun-based language of much Hiberno-English writing.

**So It Goes**
Gallery pb £6.95 1852351705

## KERRY HARDIE
### (b. Singapore 1951)

Hardie is of an Ulster Protestant background and now lives in Leinster. She is published by Gallery but her frequently prize-winning poetry is reminiscent of the more accomplished Salmon poets in style if not sensibility. Family heritage and the refreshed focus on life forced on an individual who has undergone serious illness are her main themes.

**A Furious Place**
Gallery pb £5.95 1852351950

## ANNE LE MARQUAND HARTIGAN

Hartigan has published four collections of poetry as well as the ambitious long poem 'Now is a Moveable Feast'. Her poems have been frequently anthologised.

**Immortal Sins**
Salmon pb £5.99 1897648170

## MICHAEL HARTNETT
### (b. Co. Limerick 1941)

Hartnett is a versatile and exciting poet. He is the only major Irish poet to publish a collection of haiku and he has also done a very personalised version of the Tao Te Ching as well as translations from Gaelic poets such as O'Bruadair. Half way through his career he abandoned English altogether to write only in Irish. But his vocation as an English-language poet eventually reasserted itself. Hartnett is one of the few poets who know how to experiment and innovate within our dual tradition. His openness and receptivity to poetry in other languages have contributed to the invigoration of his own.

**Farewell to English**
Gallery pb £5.95 090299669X
**Haicead: Translations from the Irish**
Gallery pb £6.95 185235108X
**Killing of Dreams**
Gallery pb £5.95 1852350865
**The Necklace of Wrens**
Gallery pb £6.95 B1852350083
**Poems to Younger Women**
Gallery pb £6.99 1852350229
**Selected and New Poems**
Gallery pb £6.95 1852351187

## FRANCIS HARVEY

Francis Harvey is a quiet assured poet of mainly nature and rural themes. His work shows a very diligent and sensitive intelligence at work.

**The Boa Island Janus**
Dedalus pb £5.95 1873790287

## DERMOT HEALY
### (b.Co. Westmeath 1947)

Healy is one of our most accomplished novelists and short story writers. (See also entry in Fiction section).
**The Ballyconnell Colours** shows him to be a formally adventurous poet in love with music and storytelling.

**The Ballyconnell Colours**
Gallery pb £5.95 1852351020

## SEAMUS HEANEY (b. Co. Derry 1939)

A Nobel laureate, former Oxford Professor of Poetry, Heaney is the pre-eminent, living, English-language poet and the greatest Irish poet since Yeats. He was one of the so-called Northern poets who formed the nucleus of Philip Hobsbaum's workshop. But where Mahon and Longley would see MacNeice as their literary precursor, for Heaney, the work of Kavanagh was seminal in revealing the poetry in everyday rural concerns. Heaney burst onto the scene in 1966 with **Death of A Naturalist** - a book weighed with a physicality and heaviness of language which owed allegiance to the early Kavanagh and Hughes. The book's nature themes endeared Heaney to a wide general readership while his unfaltering technique earned him the admiration of his peers. Each of his subsequent volumes revealed an astonishing ability to develop and augment previous achievements. Heaney's latest work exhibits the same structural strengths he has had from the first, but in less busy language, devoid of a young poet's compulsion to prove himself or show off.

Seamus Heaney

**Death of a Naturalist**
Faber pb £6.99 0571090249
**Door into the Dark**
Faber pb £6.99 0571101267
**Fieldwork**
Faber pb £6.99 0571114334
**The Haw Lantern**
Faber pb £6.99 057114781X
**New Selected Poems 1966-1987**
Faber pb £11.00 0571143725
**North**
Faber pb £6.99 057110813X
**Seeing Things**
Faber pb £6.99 0571144691

**Spirit Level**
Faber pb £7.99 0571178227
**Station Island**
Faber pb £6.99 0571133029
**Sweeney Astray**
Faber pb £6.99 0571133037
**Sweeney's Flight**
Faber hb £20.00 0571160158
(Poetry and Photographs)
**Wintering Out**
Faber pb £6.99 0571101585
**The Cure at Troy: Version of Sophocles' Philoctetes**
Faber pb £6.99 0571162304

## JOHN HEWITT
### (1907–1987)

Hewitt was until his death the grand old man of Ulster Letters. Although he has a summer school dedicated to his memory he is not now considered especially influential and was surpassed even in his lifetime by the achievement of Ulster poets born in the Thirties and Forties. Still he was a very accomplished versifier and his work displays a strong interest in social issues concerning tribal identities and class struggle. Apart from his fourteen collections of poetry he published some literary criticism and writings on painters.

**Collected Poems**
Blackstaff pb £14.95
0856404942
**Selected Poems**
Blackstaff pb £5.95
0856402443

## RITA ANN HIGGINS
### (b. Galway 1955)

Higgins started to write for the first time in her thirties as a mother and housewife attending the Galway Writers' Workshop. Her work was subsequently published by Galway-based Salmon Publishing and Bloodaxe in Britain. Not concerned with the formal expectations of the literary establishment, Higgins' work reads like Eastern European poem-fables where all of the poetry is, as Heaney puts it, in the plotting. Her subject matter concerns itself mainly with the urban working-class, especially working-class women. Her work has been widely anthologised and forms the basis for many courses on Irish women writers.

**Goddess on the Mervue Bus**
Salmon pb £4.99 189764809X
**Higher Purchase**
Salmon pb £5.99 1897648987
**Philomena's Revenge**
Salmon pb £4.99 1897648103
**Sunny Side Plucked**
Bloodaxe pb £8.95 1852243759
**Witch in the Bushes**
Salmon pb £4.99 1897648081

## PEARCE HUTCHINSON
### (b. Scotland 1927)

Huthinson is one of that handful of poets equally at ease in both English and Irish. He is also at home in other European languages. His first book of poems was a translation from the Catalan of Josep Carner. Iberian influences have been prevalent in his work ever since. He once even considered composing in Spanish. Personal themes have informed most of his latest work.

**Barnsley Mainseam**
Gallery pb £6.95 1852351551
**Climbing the Light**
Gallery pb £4.95 0904011860
**The Soul that Kissed the Body**
Gallery pb £6.90 1852350601

## PAT INGOLDSBY
### (b. Dublin)

Ingoldsby was the only living Irish poet along with Heaney to reach the top ten in a national radio poll of favourite poems. Ingoldsby is a prolific versifier now in the habit of producing a volume of poetry every year. He is a frequent reader of his work to a cult following around the country. His work is primarily humorous with sometimes tragic touches. Much of it is sentimental but frequently he hits upon stunningly original insights and observations. In many ways his work holds a position analogous to that which the Liverpool poets and John Cooper Clarke have in Britain.

**How was it for You Doctor**
Willow pb £5.95 0952305208
**If You don't Tell Anybody I Won't**
Willow pb £5.99 0952305224
**Poems So Fresh and So New Yahoo**
Willow pb £5.95 0952305216
**Scandal Sisters**
Anna Livia pb £4.95 187131108X
**See Liz She's Pins In**
Willow pb £6.99 0952305232

## FRED JOHNSTON
### (b. Belfast 1951)

A Northerner who has chosen to live in the Republic, Johnston is a poet of wide subject matter dedicated to form. He co-founded Irish Writers Co-op with Neil Jordan among others and he was also founder of the Galway-based national poetry festival Cuirt. More recently he has been a no-nonsense reviewer of Irish poetry in various outlets.

**True North**
Salmon pb £5.99 1897648804

## PATRICK KAVANAGH
### (1904–1967)

Patrick Kavanagh is the most influential Irish poet after Yeats. His influence is most obvious in the works of Seamus Heaney and John Montague. Kavanagh was the son of a small, subsistence farmer. He left school at thirteen and was largely self-educated. His lack of formal education, his largely uncultured, penurious background and a strong non-conformist personality all contributed to produce a poetry which, by the originality and individuality of its idiom, its uncompromising refusal to romanticise the brutality of rural poverty and its celebration of parochial place, cut a swathe through much of the callow, derivative, Literary Revivalist verse produced by poetasters in Dublin at that time. His first poems were published in AE's *The Irish Statesman*. His first book **Ploughman and Other Poems** appeared in 1936, three years before his move to Dublin in 1939. In that book, in such poems as 'Inniskeen Road' and 'Spraying the Potatoes',

Kavanagh displays from the outset his love for the particular place and everyday routine which would distinguish his lifework and provide such succour to a later generation of poets. Seamus Heaney, by reading Kavanagh, came to realise that the everyday experiences of a small farmer's son were material as valid for poetry as any experience an Anglo-Irish aristocrat, Oxbridge graduate or war veteran might have had. Kavanagh's later poem 'Epic' in which he talks about having lived in important places and important times and where he equated local farmers' boundary disputes with the 'Munich bother' has been often cited as a mini-manifesto by contemporary poets. His crowning achievement is undoubtedly his long poem 'The Great Hunger' which ruthlessly relates the desperate existence of a middle-aged farmer married to his land and his religion while starved of sexual companionship. A volume of autobiography **The Green Fool** and an autobiographical novel **Tarry Flynn** failed to provide the steady living Kavanagh hoped to derive from his great literary talent. This failure to live comfortably from his writing combined with a personal insecurity derived from his lack of formal education and a sense of being an outsider in literary Dublin led to Kavanagh becoming deeply embittered in himself. His embittered state created many enemies and exacerbated his bad luck, culminating in an infamous libel case which he brought and lost and which wore him down to a degree where he developed lung cancer and almost died. Restored to health after an operation Kavanagh underwent a transformation in personality and consequently literary style. His later poems, such as his canal bank sonnets, show him to be concerned with quieter priorities and writing in a more assured style. He died in 1967, his health much dissipated by alcohol. He left an important legacy, without which one would be unable to conceive how Irish poets would have dominated English poetry at the century's end.

**Selected Poems**
Penguin pb £7.99 0140184856
**Tarry Flynn**
Penguin pb £6.99 0140181164
(Fiction)
**The Green Fool**
Penguin pb £7.99 0140181156
(Memoir)
**The Great Hunger: Poem into Play (Poem Adapted into Play By Tom MacIntyre)**
Lilliput Press pb £4.95
0946640327

(Kavanagh Criticism)
*Antoinette Quinn*
**Patrick Kavanagh: Born Again Romantic**
Gill & MacMillan pb £14.99
0717121143

"Who owns them hungry hills
That the waterhen and snipe must have forsaken?
A poet? Then by heavens he must be poor.'
I hear and is my heart not badly shaken?"
Patrick Kavanagh – Shancoduff

## BRENDAN KENNELLY (b. Co. Kerry 1936)

Kennelly is a university lecturer by profession. He is probably the most famous poet in Ireland by virtue of his frequent television and radio participation, including appearing in TV adverts for Toyota cars. Kennelly exudes openness and sincerity, and such candour is everywhere evident in his poetry, sometimes to a degree approaching sentimentality. But one gets the impression that Kennelly is only too aware of his occasional sentimentality and is not the least bothered by it. Kennelly is not concerned with entering the canon: he's having a good time, but he is producing some damn fine poetry along the way, especially in **Cromwell** and **Moloney Up and At It**. In his long sequences **Cromwell** and **The Book of Judas** Kennelly shows himself capable of detailed investigation of modern Ireland's many ills, its relation to Britain, its past and its present.

**Breathing Space**
Bloodaxe pb £8.95 1852242124
**Cromwell**
Bloodaxe pb £8.95 1852240261
**The Love of Ireland: Poems
From the Irish**
Mercier pb £6.99 0853428883
**Moloney Up and It**
Mercier pb £6.99 1856351297
**Poetry My Arse**
Bloodaxe pb £11.99
1852243236
**Time for Voices: Selected
Poems**
Bloodaxe pb £8.95 1852240970

**Euripides: Trojan Women
(Trans. Kennelly)**
Bloodaxe pb £6.95 1852242418
**Sophocles: Antigone
(Trans. Kennelly)**
Bloodaxe pb £6.95 1852243643
**Lorca's Blood Wedding
(Trans.Kennelly)**
Bloodaxe pb £6.95 1852243554

## THOMAS KINSELLA (b. Dublin 1928)

In the 1950s and 1960s, Kinsella, along with Montague, led a vanguard of Irish poets, who, faced with the choice, chose to be published in Dublin rather than abroad. Kinsella's early work exhibits a poetic line possessed of a musical, Yeatsian vigour. Over the years Kinsella has gradually shed this style in favour of a spare line whose music is less predictable and assuaging in tone. In so doing Kinsella has shirked a large reading public in favour of a commitment to an aesthetic ideal which recognises that poetic truth is sometimes better expressed in a language which threatens to be hermetic. Kinsella's body of work requires a greater trust and commitment than the average reader is usually prepared to give. His strong commitment to the dual Gaelic/Anglo-Irish tradition, the greater influence of Clarke rather than Kavanagh and a preference for 20th Century American poets over contemporary British poets distinguishes him from the so-called school of Northern poets whom (although he probaly admires individuals), he has dismissed collectively as a 'journalistic entity'.

**Butchers Dozen**
pb £4.50 1873790082
**Blood and Family**
Oxford £6.99 0192821822
**Collected Poems**
Oxford pb £11.99 0192825267
**The Pen Shop**
Peppercanister pb £5.95
1901233006

# FRANCIS LEDWIDGE
## (1891–1917)

Ledwidge is a rare favourite of both the literateur and the general reader. Born into modest circumstances he was active in the trade union movement as he began to write his first poems. Lord Dunsany, the novelist, arranged for the publication of his first book **Songs of the Field**. Delicate love lyrics and appreciations of the rural countryside predominate his work which probably accounts for its popularity. Strongly Georgian in his style Ledwidge is nevertheless an original poet whose life and career was tragically cut short in the Great War.

**Complete Poems**
Goldsmith Press pb £15.00
1870491475
**Selected Poems**
New Island pb £4.95
1874597103

# MICHAEL LONGLEY (b. Belfast 1939)

Although a student at Trinity College, Dublin, Longley was a member of Philip Hobsbaum's Belfast workshops. Like all distinguished members of that group his work shows a respect for the classical 'well-made poem'. Longley has never been tempted by the Whitman-Williams aesthetic path like Montague, Kinsella and Durcan. Ever since his first book **No Continuing City** in 1969 Longley has received his fair share of respect. Only with his inclusion in Muldoon's **Faber Anthology of Contemporary Irish Poetry** in 1986 and Penguin's publication of his collected poems to date in the same year did Longley's work reach a wider audience. This audience's expectations were not disappointed by the appearance of **Gorse Fires** in 1991 or **The Ghost Orchid** in 1995. These collections show Longley's latest work invested with a maturity and confidence which brings a poignancy and vigour of expression lacking to the same degree in his earlier work. **The Ghost Orchid** includes Longley's brilliant versions of Ovid's Metamorphoses which many commentators believe to be superior to the more famous versions by Ted Hughes.

**The Ghost Orchid**
Cape pb £7.50 0224041126
**Gorse Fires**
Secker & Warburg pb £6.99 0436256746
**Poems 1963-1983**
Secker & Warburg pb £8.00 0436256762

Francis Ledwidge

## TOM MCINTYRE
**(b. Co. Cavan 1931)**

A gifted playwright and short story writer, McIntyre's unconventional and experimental verse sometimes perplexes but always thrills. The Gaelic tradition of storytelling is very much in evidence in his poems.

**Fleurs-Du-Lit**
Dedalus pb £4.95 0948268832
**The Harper's Turn**
Gallery Press pb £9.95
0904011291 (fiction)

## JAMES CLARENCE MANGAN (1803–1849)

Chronically impoverished and stricken with alcohol Mangan was as much caught up with living the romantic stereotype of the poet's life as he was in producing fine poems. Considered by many to be the first distinctly Irish poet in English (as distinct from Irishmen such as Swift and Goldsmith writing within the English tradition) he was an avid translator and adapter not only from the Gaelic but also from Asian languages such as Arabic, Turkish and Farsi. He edited the first anthology of Munster poets concentrating primarily on Jacobite poets. He also published an autobiography which castigated his father and family life generally.

**Collected Poems Vol 1**
Irish Academic Press hb £35.00
0716525607
**Collected Poems Vol 2**
Irish Academic Press hb £35.00
0716525755
**Collected Poems Vol 3**
Irish Academic Press hb £35.00
0716525763
**Selected Poems**
Carcanet pb £7.95 185754059X

*Ellen Shannon-Mangan*
**James Clarence Mangan: A Biography**
Irish Academic Press hb £35.00
0716525585

## AIDAN CARL MATHEWS
**(b. Dublin 1956)**

Mathews first established himself as a poet before going on to make a name for himself as an internationally acclaimed novelist and short-story writer. For many years he appeared to have abandoned poetry until the appearance of a new collection from Joyce's old publisher Jonathan Cape in 1998. His early work is accomplished and pleasing in a whimsical manner. A new maturity and sense of depth are apparent in the latest work. He has also written plays.

**According to the Small Hours**
Cape pb £8.00 0224051253
**Minding Ruth**
Gallery pb £5.95 0904011402

## THOMAS MCCARTHY (b. Co. Waterford 1954)

Considered by Dennis O'Driscoll to be, along with Muldoon, the most important Irish poet of his generation, McCarthy is a poet primarily of politics and family. His work's importance lies in its unremitting and detailed examination of the Republic's failures and successes as an independent state. Described by Eavan Boland as the first poet born into the Republic to write about it critically, McCarthy has done so from the perspective of a family dedicated and loyal to the state's most successful and powerful political party: Fianna Fail. But his poems are not eulogies to the party or apologies for its policies; they are more like an exploration of the party as object of loyalty and devotion (like a lover objectified) with all the potential such an object has for empowerment and betrayal. McCarthy has attracted much lazy and inattentive criticism including one reviewer who presumed he was writing about the Soviet Communist Party. Love poems and more recently poems about children predominate as McCarthy unfolds the developmental struggles of one lived life in his work.

**The Lost Province**
Anvil pb £7.95 0856462764

## CATHERINE PHIL MACCARTHY
### (b. Co. Limerick 1954)

MacCarthy is a graduate of UCC and a drama teacher by profession. She has published two collections with Salmon. She is a recipient of the Patrick Kavanagh Award and winner of the National Woman's Poetry Competition. A very short line and a love of sensuous adjectives distinguishes her work.

**This Hour of the Tide**
Salmon pb £6.99 1897648197
**The Blue Globe**
Blackstaff pb £6.99
0856406198

## ROY MCFADDEN
### (b. Belfast 1921)

A solicitor by profession McFadden is prominent as one of a number of Ulster poets who first published in the 40s and were associated with the periodical *Rann*. Political questions and issues surrounding ethnic identity make frequent appearances in his work and he has also written interesting biographical treatments of figures such as Behan and Synge.

**Collected Poems**
Lagan Irish pb £7.95
1873687168

## THOMAS MACGREEVEY
### (1893–1967)

Renowned as a member of the Irish modernist group and as a close friend of Samuel Beckett, MacGreevey was not very prolific. He spent most of his life working in the visual arts either as a critic or as a gallery director and his poems reflect his deep interest in that area.

**Collected Poems**
Anna Livia pb 1871311128

## MEDBH MCGUCKIAN
### (b. Belfast 1950)

McGuckian's work is primarily a poetry of celebration of life's mysteries and little rewards while they are constantly under threat from forces fixed on their destruction. Her poems are very much products of the intuitive side of the brain rather than the rational and any attempt to reduce her poems to rational statements misses their point and their pleasure principle and is doomed to failure. Her language is dense, hermetic in effect if not in design and undeniably Irish. McGuckian's voice is a strong, exotic isolated instrument within the Irish literary tradition.

**Captain Lavender**
Gallery pb £6.95 1852351411
**Marconi's Cottage**
Gallery pb £6.95 1852350814
**On Ballycastle Beach**
Gallery pb £5.95 1852351578
**Selected Poems**
Gallery pb £7.95 1852352035
**Venus and The Rain**
Gallery pb £5.95 1852351438

## LOUIS MACNEICE (1907–1963)

There is no denying the magnificent achievement of MacNeice, unfairly evaluated by many as a minor member of the 30s Auden gang. His work exhibits a subtlety of intelligence and a sense of intellectual independence superior to Auden's in many respects. Born in 1907 in Belfast to Southern parents, his father was the only Protestant cleric not to take the Ulster Covenant, prefiguring MacNeice's own spirited non-partisanship. MacNeice was educated at Marlborough and Oxford and lived most of his life away from his Ulster birthplace. He has been hailed as a progenitor of a separate Northern poetic tradition to the bafflement of most Southern readers. It is true that Derek Mahon's acerbic wit would owe much to MacNeice but no more than it would to Marston's and Marlowe's Ovid. It is possible that MacNeice's mere fact of being, his being the first world-class writer to emerge from north-east Ulster is of more emblematic import than any aesthetic strategy or tradition he might present. Auden once said: 'Even the most formal and elevated styles of poetry are more conditioned by the spoken tongue, the language used by the men of that country, than by anything else.' To most ears MacNeice does not write in Hiberno-English. It is true that his poems include much Irish local colour, but then so do poems of Spenser, Betjeman and Larkin. MacNeice's place in Irish Literature will cause many a disputation to come.

**Autumn Journal**
Faber hb £8.95 057117776X
**Collected Poems**
Faber pb £14.99 0571113532
**Selected Poems**
Faber pb £7.99 0571152708

## "My childhood is preserved as a nation's history, my favourite fairytales the shells leaded by the hermit crab."
### Medbh McGuckian – Slips

## DEREK MAHON (b. Belfast 1941)

Educated at Trinity College Dublin, Derek Mahon is an exciting, accessible poet whose work deserves a more popular readership. He is undoubtedly the most musical poet now writing in English. Increasingly described as a poet's poet, his uncompromising dedication to form, his astute, analytical intelligence and a stirring tendency to take risks, make him essential reading. Readers can detect his influence in the work of younger Irish poets such as Sean Dunne and Justin Quinn. Early influences include Beckett and MacNeice but it is the Romans who seem to be Mahon's guiding lights in his most recent work. In **The Hudson Letter** and **The Yellow Book** versions of Ovid and Juvenal are appositely prominent. Mahon writes now like a latter-day Ovid in exile; not only exiled from his green homeland but also from a less philistine, decadent time. No one else of equal stature is dealing with the questions raised by globalisation and the proliferation of new technology. With a style which is classical, Mahon is exploring the most contemporary and pressing and relevant of themes.

**The Hudson Letter**
Gallery pb £6.95 1852351764
**Selected Poems**
Penguin pb £8.99 0140586636
**The Yellow Book**
Gallery pb £6.95 1852352051

**The Chimeras: Translations from Nerval**
Gallery pb £4.95 0904011321
**High Time: After Moliere**
Gallery Press pb £5.95 0904011801
**Racine's Phaedra: A Version**
Gallery Press pb £5.95 1852351659

## PAULA MEEHAN
### (b. Dublin 1955)

Meehan has shot to prominence during the late 90s. Her earliest work appeared in the mid-Eighties and has gained in strength and accomplishment since then. Her poems are very much concerned with intimacy, between mother and daughter and between lovers. There is a fairytale-fable feel to much of her work.

**The Man Who was Marked by Winter**
Gallery pb £5.95 1852350717
**Pillow Talk**
Gallery pb £6.95 1852351330

## JOHN MONTAGUE (b. New York 1929)

Although born in America Montague was raised in County Tyrone by his mother's people. Montague's poetic ouevre (he is also the author of three volumes of short fiction) divides into two main concerns. Firstly, the position of the poet amid his personal heritage and the place of that personal heritage amid a larger, more complex national heritage and secondly a significant body of love poetry. The long sequences **The Rough Field** and **The Dead Kingdom** both treat the poet's concerns with national history, with a Kavanaghesque sensitivity to the formative influences of place and family; and a consciousness of a lost Gaelic culture replaced by the 'grafted tongue' of English. Both sequences display in structure and style the strong influences of American poets (such as William Carlos Williams and Ezra Pound) that mark out Montague along with Kinsella from the company of the more British-influenced Heaney, Mahon and Longley. Most critics single out **The Rough Field** as Montague's crowning achievement, although he himself prefers **The Dead Kingdom**. His large body of love poetry may yet be the work which endures longest and with the most affection in the minds of the general reader. Montague's love poetry constitutes one of the most moving collections of courtly love lyrics after Robert Graves.

**Collected Poems**
Gallery pb £13.95 1852351594
**New Selected Poems**
Gallery pb £5.95 1852350407
**The Rough Field**
Gallery pb £5.95 185235044X

## SINÉAD MORRISSEY (b. Portadown 1972)

Sinéad Morrissey's first book, **There was Fire in Vancouver**, is a very effective collection revolving around large themes of childhood, love and death without being heavy handed.

**There was Fire in Vancouver**
Carcanet pb £6.95 1857542304

## PAUL MULDOON (b. Co. Armagh 1951)

Muldoon qualifies as one of the most original poets writing in English this century. A wide, exotic, vocabulary, daring pararhyme schemes and a witty, sometimes sardonic, tone are the unmistakable hallmarks of his work. The engaging sardonic tone and the quirkiness of his narratives have spawned a whole generation of less talented British imitators. Most admiring young Irish poets have avoided sounding like Muldoon in the same way that an earlier generation scrambled to get away from the influence of Yeats.

In Shakespeare's day Spenser was considered to be the greatest living poet. If any contemporary Irish poet could be elevated above the reputation of Heaney by subsequent generations of readers it would probably be Muldoon. His strong lyric impulse has given away in recent years to longer and longer poems of mock-heroic proportions. **Madoc** with its 'dum-de-dum' lines showed Muldoon playfully cocking a snook at all those who expect, in Graves's terms, perfect 'smithwork' in a poem. Even many dedicated Muldoon admirers failed to appreciate this particular gesture and in drawing negative attention to it, hinted that Muldoon has perhaps become over self-indulgent. In a way Muldoon's uncompromising development mirrors the aesthetic direction of Thomas Kinsella. The radical originality of each poet's individual voice helps to disguise that fact.

**Annals of Chile**
Faber pb £7.99 0571172067
**Kerry Slides**
Gallery hb £14.95 185235190X
**Madoc: A Mystery**
Faber pb £7.99 0571144896
**Meeting the British**
Faber pb £4.99 057114859X
**New Selected Poems**
Faber pb £8.99 0571177840
**New Weather**
Faber pb £6.99 0571102336
**Quoof**
Faber pb £4.99 0571131174
**Six Honest Serving Men**
Gallery Press pb £5.95
1852351683
**(Muldoon Criticism)**

*Tim Kendall*
**Paul Muldoon**
Seren pb £9.95 1854111612

## AIDAN MURPHY
### (Cork 1952)

Murphy has published four collections with Bolger's Raven Arts Press and its successor New Island Books. A strongly confessional poet, his most recent work sees him dealing frankly and effectively with marital breakdown.

**Stark Naked Blues**
New Island pb £4.99
1874597677

## GERRY MURPHY
### (b. Cork 1952)

Gerry Murphy is a popular performance poet whose anarchic vision and humour translate well to the page. Sex and socialism have been his main concerns and he has frequently juxtaposed the symbolism of the Soviet Union with courtly love situations. More recently he has written about the Spanish and American Civil Wars.

**The Empty Quater**
Dedalus pb £5.95 1873790716

## RICHARD MURPHY
### (b. Co. Galway 1927)

As a member of the Anglo-Irish Ascendancy, the aesthetic strategies of either the Catholic peasant Kavanagh or the lower bourgeois Protestant MacNeice were unavailable to Richard Murphy. Murphy is instead a classicist; an extremely successful and unembarrassed exponent of a tenuous Yeatsian tradition. His work deals extensively with the guilt of a colonist whether it be in Ireland or Rhodesia. He first established his reputation with moving lyrics about the sea around Galway. His most ambitious work would be 'The Battle of Aughrim' which deals with the ultimate defeat of the Irish during the great Jacobean wars and the relevance of those historic events to the ethnically divided Ireland of the 1960s. Its episodic structure prefigured the long sequences later produced by Montague and Heaney. More recently a stunning sonnet sequence entitled The Price of Stone, has confirmed him as one of the front-ranking Irish poets this century. Shamefully most of his work is currently out of print.

**New Selected Poems**
Faber hb £10.99 0571154824

## NUALA NÍ DHOMHNAILL
### (b. England 1952)

One of the crucial Innti group which emerged in University College Cork in the 1970s. The Innti group's importance stems from their continuation of O'Riordain's development of a radical modern idiom in poetry in the Irish language. Ni Dhohmnaill is the most translated of contemporary Irish poets and her work now holds an important position straddling the dual tradition. She has used the imagery and conventions of contemporary folktale in Irish to good effect. Her idiom in Irish is highly individualistic and ingenious. Her achievement is reflected in the calibre of translators drawn to her work. A large body of her work was first translated by Michael Hartnett. More recently Muldoon, McGuckian and Ni Chuilleanain have reproduced a substantial body of versions. Her work is especially favoured by a wide audience for the delight and frankness it displays on sexual themes.

**The Astrakhan Cloak**
Gallery pb £6.95 1852351047
**Pharaoh's Daughter**
Gallery pb £6.95 1852350563
**Selected Poems**
Raven Arts pb £6.95
1851860274

## AINE NÍ GHLINN
### (b. Co. Tipperary 1955)

A radio journalist by profession Ni Ghlinn is prominent as a writer in Irish. **Unshed Tears** contains translations of poems which pull no punches in dealing with the harrowing effects of child sexual abuse.

**Unshed Tears/Deoran Ar Caoin**
Dedalus pb £5.95 1873790678

## CONOR O'CALLAGHAN
### (b. Co. Down 1968)

One of the more interesting of the younger poets. His work displays a fine sensuous sensibility. He has also produced accomplished translations from the Italian.
**The History of Rain**
Gallery pb £5.95 1852351160

## ULICK O'CONNOR
### (b. Dublin 1928)

Journalist, historian, playwright, poet. His best-selling book is probably a retelling of Irish sagas illustrated by Pauline Bewick. He has written plays in the Japanese No form. His published poems are primarily translations, mainly from French and Irish.

## MARY O'DONNELL

Monaghan-born O'Donnell has returned to the border of her youth in her most recent collection **Unlegendary Heroes**. This volume also contains a group of poems examining the rituals of love with a rare sensuousness of language.

**Spiderwoman's Third Avenue Rhapsody**
Salmon pb £5.99 1897648006
**Unlegendary Heroes**
Salmon pb £5.99 1897648960

## BERNARD O'DONOGHUE
### (b. Co. Cork 1945)

O'Donoghue lives in Oxford where he has taught English at Magdalan College. A Kavanaghesque celebration of his West Cork homeland and its traditions is his main distinction. Family life and the experience of the Irishman in Britain (one poem recounts watching an All Ireland Hurling match on a big screen in a London cinema) also feature. O'Donoghue won the Whitbread Award for poetry with his second collection

**Gunpowder**
Chatto pb £6.99 0701163313
**The Weakness**
Chatto pb £6.99 0701138599

## JOHN O'DONOHUE

Best-selling author of the Celtic spiritual text *Anam Cara*, O'Donohue previously published a collection of poems notable for their European, especially German influences. Paul Celan is an abiding presence in these poems, especially the very effective poems concerning love and sex.

**Echoes of Memory**
Salmon pb £5.99 1897648189

## MARTIN Ó DIREÁIN
### (1910-1988)

Not as accomplished as his contemporary Sean O'Riordain in either his use of language or breadth of reference, O'Direain is nevertheless recognised as one of the most important poets writing in Irish this century. His early work was sentimental in outlook but as it developed a bleakness of vision and expression took hold.

**Tacar Danta 1939-79**
Goldsmith Press pb £5.95
1904084893

## DENNIS O'DRISCOLL
### (b. Co. Tipperary 1954)

O'Driscoll is an uncompromising and demanding critic and poetry journalist. His own work is characterised by an Eastern European-style preoccupation with image and narrative plotting. Death and taxes, the only certain things in life, predominate as his themes.

**Long Story Short**
Dedalus pb £5.95 1873790473

## DESMOND O'GRADY
### (b. Limerick 1935)

An acquaintance of Ezra Pound, in his youth, O'Grady is an accomplished technician and tireless translator. 'The Dark Edge of Europe' is probably his best work, bristling as it is with wonderful sound effects and complex prosody. More recently translations from Arabic and all the major European languages predominate. His work has a strong Classical feel to it which is not surprising considering his long sojourn during the 70s on a Greek island.

**Sing Me Creation**
Gallery pb £4.95 0902996568

## FRANK ORMSBY
### (b.1947)

Frank Ormsby was born in Enniskillen and currently teaches at the Royal Belfast Academical Institution. He has edited a number of anthologies and has written three collections of poetry, the most recent of which is The Ghost Train, published in 1995. Both humorous and elegiac, the poems in this collection displays Ormsby's talent for mixing personaliy, politics and anecdote to great effect.

**The Ghost Train**
Gallery Press pb £6.95
1852351721

## MICHÉAL O SÍADHAIL
**(b. Dublin 1947)**

O Sí`adhail first wrote and published in Irish. A linguist by profession his work in Irish is noted for its elegance and technical virtuosity. His work in English reveals a mind Rilkean in its ambitions but which can border on the sentimental. OSíadhail's best poems are those where he appears least self-conscious and obsessed.

**A Fragile City**
Bloodaxe pb £6.95 1852243341

## SEAN Ó TÚAMA
**(b. Cork 1926)**

A student of Daniel Corkery, O Túama's poetry reflects the high ideals of his former mentor but is far superior to any poetry Corkery wrote himself. As well as being a fine poet O Túama is a critic of rare intelligence. He has been an important mentor and facilitator to Innti poets such as Ní Dhomhnail and Davitt whom he lectured in UCC.

**Rogha Danta/Death in the Land of Youth**
Cork University Press pb £7.99 1859181589

## TOM PAULIN
**(b. England 1949)**

Although he was born and has lived most of his life in England, Paulin spent his formative years growing up in Belfast. He is of Protestant background but identifies with the Nationalist cause in Northern Ireland. Better known as a social commentator and critic, his intelligence is, arguably, too analytical and didactic in nature to suit the production of great poetry. **The Liberty Tree** is his best and most readable book in that it shows a musicality and fluency not always seen in his other work.

**Fivemiletown**
Faber pb £5.95 0571149154
**The Liberty Tree**
Faber pb £4.99 0571130259
**Selected Poems**
Faber pb £5.99 0571149413
**Walking a Line**
Faber pb £6.99 0571170811

## PÁDRAIG PEARSE
**(1879–1916)**

Patriot, revolutionary and educationalist, Pearse was executed by the British for his part as leader in the 1916 rising. Pearse's poetry is competent stuff and his life and work will continue to hold a central place in Irish Nationalist mythology.

**Selected Poems**
New Island pb £5.99 1874597502

## JUSTIN QUINN
**(b. Dublin 1968)**

Quinn is one of a number of new formalists who are recent graduates of TCD. His first book presents a technical accomplishment which is admirable.
**The ó ó á á bird**
Carcanet pb £7.95 1857541251

## W.R. RODGERS
**(1909–1969)**

A clergyman by profession, Rodgers' slim output includes two of the greatest poems written by an Irish poet this century: 'The Net' and 'Lent'.

**Poems**
Gallery pb £7.95 1852351063

## JAMES SIMMONS
**(b. Derry 1933)**

Simmons has written effectively about the tenuousness of human relations and most effectively on the subject of marital breakdown.

**Mainstream** Salmon pb £7.99 1897648278

## PETER SIRR
### (b. Co. Waterford 1960)

Sirr won the Kavanagh Award and published his first collection **Marginal Zones** when still in his early twenties. That first book displayed a technical prowess, an almost classical, authoritative tone and a dazzling vocabulary which Sirr appears to have played down in his three subsequent books. His latest poems now have a strong narrative, anecdotal impulse in ragged free verse.

**The Ledger of Fruitful Exchange**
Gallery pb £6.95 1852351756
**Marginal Zones**
Gallery pb £5.95 0904011704
**Ways of Falling**
Gallery pb £5.95 1852350733

## JO SLADE
### (b. England 1952)

Limerick painter and poet Slade has produced two quietly accomplished books displaying a gentle music and refined sensibility.

**Certain Octobers**
Salmon pb £7.99 2950877915
**The Vigilant One**
Poolbeg pb 1897648324

## EITHNE STRONG
### (b. Co. Limerick 1923)

Strong has written in both Irish and English. A mother of nine children her work has been seminal in dealing with domestic struggles and subsequent liberation.

**Spatial Nosing: New and Selected Poems**
Salmon pb £6.99 1897648049

## MATHEW SWEENEY
### (b. Co. Donegal 1952)

Sweeney lives permanently in England but his work displays mainly American influences. He has displayed virtuosity in many forms but a plain conversational free verse style seems to suit him best. His poems very often seem like short-short stories and show an affinity through their plainness of language with the work of Raymond Carver.

**The Bridal Suite**
Cape pb £7.00 0224043285

## WILLIAM WALL

Wall is a teacher by profession and his one book so far deals with the original theme of maths. His poems have a strong Modernist feel to them.

**Mathematics and other Poems**
Salmon pb £6.99 1898256268

## DAVID WHEATLEY
### (b. Dublin 1970)

A prize-winner and a young poet of serious intent. His first collection has many fine accomplished poems as well as number of less successful ones. He is one of the young New Formalists.

**Thirst**
Gallery pb £6.95 1852352078

## VINCENT WOODS
### (b. 1960)

Although better known for his plays, Vincent Woods has written one collection of poems which combines witty satire and haunting reflection.

**The Colour of Language**
Dedalus pb £5.95 1873790562

Eavan Boland on her discovery of Yeats's poetry and the lifelong pleasure it has given her.

I remember buying my first copy of Yeats' *Collected Poems*. I was fifteen. I took the bus one empty September weekend in from Killiney, where I was in boarding school, and went into the bookshop which is now Waterstone's: the old Hodges Figgis, with its airy interiors and round tables piled with magazines. I wasn't a particularly bookish teenager. And so I remember the long bus journey, the sight of the coast when I was leaving and returning, the bracelet of lights in the distance towards Bray, much better than why I wanted to buy the book. But I did buy it. And went back to school clutching the handsome burgundy hardback with its cream milled covers. And read it. And read it. And when the darkness began to spread in from the sea into our dormitory, I got a flashlight out of my bedside locker and read more of it. And then I was sixteen. And then seventeen. And then wrote, with self-conscious and straight-faced earnestness inside the front cover: Eavan Boland, Her Best Book.

But why? I certainly wasn't his inevitable reader. I was hardly more than a stranded teenager, home from London and New York. Unable to name the country I came from. Unable to come from it until I could name it. I felt awkward, an impostor, waiting for my differences and mistakes to be noticed. And so what was it that made me connect so easily, obstinately, powerfully with this finished and magisterial poet who belonged so totally to his country that he felt free to invent it? What is it that makes me connect to this day across decades more knowledge and suspicion and understanding than I had then? Yeats has been the poet I have loved most, have understood most, have returned to most often. And the return is not enacted by going to my shelves and taking down that book with its childish inscription. It is a return made up of the continuous, shiny breakages of memory, of lines and of melodies that come in and out of my mind like Chekhov's instance of moonlight on broken glass.

The *Collected Poems* I read is still very much the standard version of Yeats' work. It is arranged chronologically. It goes from the first clipped-off lyrics of his London and Dublin years. And I like to think of him as he describes himself in those years: haunter of libraries and of cranky East End spiritualist meetings. Equally at the edge of The Cheshire Cheese and Grub Street. A young man who, if you had met him at Kensington or The Strand, might have seemed part fop and part country bumpkin. A young man however who went back to a succession of boarding houses and cold rooms and crafted and re-crafted his early poems on a strange frontier between the Pre-Raphaelites and the first stirrings of the Irish revival.

There are poems there I still like: To Ireland in the Coming Times and even The Lake Isle of Innisfree. They are a young poet's poems. He was critical of them himself. 'When I re-read those early poems which gave me so much trouble', he once wrote, 'I find little but romantic convention, unconscious drama. It is so many years before one can believe enough in what one feels even to know what the feeling is'. Then came the middle books. Then the late ones. And then there was the finished effect of this poet who had so touched my mind and went on doing so when the thick, pinkish covers were shut.

Always an epicentre, a place, as the French teacher-painters used to say, where the soul sits. For me it comes right smack in the middle of the Collected Poems. The poem is The Wild Swans at Coole. It comes from the volume of the same name, published in 1919. The date is important. After the Rising, after the war, out of the crucible of broken friendships and threatened art forms. The poet who wrote it and lived it is not at all the awkward and charming poseur of *fin de siècle* London. This is an older man: engaged, embittered. He returns in his middle years to the Galway woods, to the late summer twilight, to the freakish, distant white of the swans gathering and making noise and reminding him of a lost happiness. What he makes is the new Irish pastoral: a heartbroken dispossession to put all the easier poetry of place to shame.


I have looked upon these brilliant creatures
And now my heart is sore.
All's changed since I, hearing at twilight,
The first time on this shore,
The bell-beat of their wings above my head
Trod with a lighter tread.


Unwearied still, lover by lover,
They paddle in the cold
Companionable streams or climb the air;
Their hearts have not grown old.
Passion or conquest, wander where they will,
Attend upon them still.

Here is the Yeats I first knew. Fiercely musical. Lost in control. It seems impossible that a man and a poet could become more real the more he becomes a master of artifice. But that is precisely what his poems achieved. And, in my case, they achieved something to be treasured even more. Here in this gritty twilight, in this disillusioned and complicated series of rhymes and half-rhymes and repeating cadences, I began to hear something different: the sound, at last, of a place where I might no longer be an impostor. A place which could be made exact in language and therefore hospitable to the very degrees of estrangement I felt.

These discoveries, made in reading, can last a lifetime. But, of course, they aren't private and can't be exclusive. Things have changed. The bus in from the coast has shimmered and changed into the Dart. The Saturday traffic is as dense as a Friday afternoon. The buildings are bulkier, the cars sleeker and the streets more crowded. But someone else is taking down that book, even as I write this. Is bringing it back. Will read it after dark. Someone else will carry that exact magic with them forever. As I have. And always will.

**"Was it for this the wild geese spread
The grey wing on every tide;
For this that all that blood was shed
All that delirium of the brave?
Romantic Ireland's dead and gone,
It's with O'Leary in the grave."**
W.B.Yeats

# WILLIAM BUTLER YEATS (1865-1939)

Yeats is frequently declared (as an alternative to Eliot) the century's greatest poet writing in English. He first started writing at the age of fifteen and his first book *The Wanderings of Oisin and Other Poems* was published in 1889. Over the course of his life, as Yeats the man changed so too did his poetry to a degree where an early poem like 'The Lake Isle of Innisfree', so beloved of anthologists and the general reader to this day, was in later years viewed with distaste by the mature poet who wrote 'Sailing to Byzantium'.

Yeats was a multifaceted man with many enthusiasms; such as an idyllic view of peasant culture, an obsession with the occult and Oriental philosophy, the determination to forge an Irish national literature in the English language, an admiration for aristocracy and an active involvement in politics. Many commentators today find it easy to ridicule Yeats for his many disparate interests and try for instance to discredit his interest in Nationalist politics by associating it with his interest in automatic writing, seances etc. Whatever one might think of Yeats the man from all of this activity, Yeats the poet never failed to make good use of it as a basis for his poems. He defended his interests in these matters with all the vigour with which a great poet defends his aesthetics.

Yeats's wish to forge a National literature led him to invest his work with many references to Irish Mythology; other poems owed their genesis to his unrequited infatuation for Maud Gonne, to involvement in the struggle for National Independence, to Yeats's public life in later years and to the physically debilitating effects of old age.

Yeats was awarded the Nobel Prize in 1923 and his influence extends way beyond Ireland but his career and his opus retain an especially central position in the Hiberno-English Literary Tradition. In a way he established the tradition, through his own poetry, his thirty stage plays, his many prose works and his encouragement of writers such as Synge, Gregory and Sean O'Casey. Yeats was a consummate technician and exhorted young Irish poets to forgo writing poems that were shapeless. So pervasive and dominating was Yeats's influence that for years many Irish poets sounded like ersatz Yeats. Coffey, Devlin, McGreevy and Beckett reacted against him by forming a minor Irish Modernist movement abroad. It wasn't really until the arrival of Kavanagh with his radically different idiom and outlook that a pathway for post-Yeatsian development in Irish poetry became clear.

Yeats's involvement in politics established a precedent and an expectation of literary involvement in political affairs not dissimilar from the situation pertaining in many other European countries but curiously lacking in Britain. Various contemporary Irish poets have received criticism for not being more overtly political, if not downright partisan in their writings. Yeats's example remains an irritation for those who maintain that 'poetry makes nothing happen' and that contemporary poets should eschew all political expression.

**Collected Poems**
Macmillan pb £9.99
0330316389
**Collected Poems**
Vintage pb £8.99 0099723506
**Early Poems**
Dover pb £1.00 0486278085
**Heaven's Embroidered Cloths**
Pavilion hb £10.99 185793654X
**Love Poems**
Gill pb £6.99 0717118215
**Poems**
Macmillan pb £12.99
0333556917
**Poems**
Everyman pb £4.95
0460874284
**Poems**
Everyman hb £12.99
1857151038
**Poems (Ed.Jeffares)**
Gill pb £8.99 0717117421
**Selected Poems**
Bloomsbury hb £9.99
0747514046
**Selected Poems**
Everyman hb £9.99
1857157117
**Selected Poems**
Everyman pb £3.99
0460879022
**Selected Poems**
Penguin pb £6.99 0140586458

**Selected Poems**
Pan pb £4.99 033031520X
**Autobiographies**
Macmillan pb £13.99
0333306368
**Gonne-Yeats Letters 1893-1938
(Ed. Macbride & Jeffares)**
Pimlico pb £12.50 0712654348
**Representative Irish Tales (Ed. Yeats)**
Smythe pb £7.10 0901072842
**Selected Plays W.B. Yeats**
Penguin pb 9.99 0140183744
**Short Fiction**
Penguin pb £6.99 0140180028

# (Yeats Criticism / Biography)

*Keith Alldritt*
**W.B. Yeats The Man And The Milieu**
John Murray hb £25.00
0719553547
**Brodies Notes On Yeats Selected Poems**
Macmillan pb £2.99
0333582233

*Stephen Coote*
**W.B. Yeats: A Life**
Hodder & Stoughton pb £8.99
0340647116

*Elizabeth Butler Cullingford*
**Gender And History In Yeats' Love Poetry**
California University Press pb
£14.99 0815603312

*Elizabeth Butler Cullingford*
**Yeats: Poems 1919-1935**
Macmillan pb £10.99
0333274237

*Richard Ellman*
**Yeats: The Man and the Masks**
Penguin pb £9.99 0140113649

*R.F. Foster*
**W.B. Yeats A Life, Vol 1: The Apprentice Mage**
Oxford University Press hb
£25.00 0192117351

*Joan Hardwick*
**Yeats Sisters**
Pandora pb £8.99 0044409249

*Norman A. Jeffares*
**W.B. Yeats Man And Poet**
Gill & Macmillan pb £12.99
0717123855

*Anthony Jordan Willie*
**Yeats and the Gonne Macbrides**
Westport pb £17.95
0952444712

*Edward Larrissy*
**W.B. Yeats: Critical Study**
Oxford University Press pb
£13.99 019283083x

*John Stallworthy*
**Yeats' Last Poems**
Macmillan pb £9.99
0333020367

# Politics

## Politics

There are several general books on Irish government, politics and society worth highlighting. **Government & Politics of Ireland** by Basil Chubb (Longman pb £17.99 0582086248) is the, by now, classic study of Irish political processes. Functioning as an informative guide to the intricate details of elections and government policy as well as an astute analysis of governmental dealings, this is an essential text for both student and general reader. **Irish Society: Sociological Perspectives** (Institute of Public Administration pb £17.99 1872002870) edited by Patrick Clancy, provides a brilliant overview of the current social criticism of Ireland. Grouped into three sections – Population, Work & Social Change; Class, Politics & the State; Education, Culture, Social Movements – these essays are informative, engaging, and interesting. **Irish Government Today** by Sean Dooney (Gill & MacMillan pb £14.99 0717126692) is a study of changes in recent Irish Government. Dooney looks at the change in strategic management and parliamentary procedures in light of EU membership. He also examines the increased freedom of government information. **Irish Voters Decide** by Richard Sinnott (Manchester University Press pb £17.99 071904037X) is the definitive book on Irish voting patterns. In exploring the voting behaviour of the Irish people this century Sinnott has taken into account how changes in demography have altered the outcome of General Elections. Not just confining his study to Elections, Sinnott has also looked at the changing nature of recent referenda on abortion and divorce and has examined the role the membership of the EU has played in changing the way that the Irish vote. In what now has become the classic acount of every election, **Nealon's Guide to the 28th Dail: Election 97** (Gill & MacMillan pb £12.99 0717126757) has once again collated and presented all of the information concerning the 1997 General election. Ted Nealon has written profiles of all the politicians elected and has not just given the election results but demonstrated very clearly how second and third preference votes were distributed in the complicated process of Proportional Representation. In **Values & Social Change in Ireland** (Gill & MacMillan pb £14.50 0717119475), a collection of essays edited by Christopher Whelan, the large changes that have taken place in Irish religious, moral and political and family values are closely examined. Using the 1981 and 1990 European Values Survey as a starting point, the contributors ask why these changes have taken place in such a short space of time. Combining interview, history and political analysis, John Ardagh's **Ireland & the Irish** (Penguin pb £8.99 0140171606) is one of the most interesting examinations of Irish culture in recent decades. Starting his research by interviewing public figures like Gay Byrne, Bishop Eamnon Casey and Mary Robinson, Ardagh continued by interviewing ordinary people that he met all over the country and has sifted this data to produce a very readable if sometimes contentious view of the achievements and paradoxes of Ireland this century.

Other books look at more specific aspects of contemporary Irish society. **Under the Belly of the Tiger: Class, Race, Identity & Culture in the Global Ireland** (Irish Reporter Publications pb £17.95 1900900025) edited by Ethel Crowley & Jim MacLaughlin is a collection of essays examining the side effects of the recent economic success that Ireland has enjoyed. The essays argue correctly that many sections of the community have neither benefited from nor seen the rewards of the economic boom. This timely book also looks at the status of the Black and Jewish communities in this now 'global' country. Patrick Smyth & Ronan Brady, two of the founder members of Let in the Light, Ireland's anti-censorship organisation have argued very strongly for a freedom of information act to be passed in Ireland. In **Democracy Blindfolded: The Case for a Freedom of Information Act in Ireland**

(Cork University Press pb £4.95 185918040X) they set out their argument in a very clear manner and cut through much of the waffle that has become associated with anti-censorship writing. Published in conjunction with Trócaire, one of Ireland's largest Third World relief organisations, **Poverty Amid Plenty: World & Irish Development Reconsidered** by Kirby Peadar (Gill & MacMillan/Trócaire pb £7.50 0717126072) analyses the current major theories of World development and then goes on to apply this theory to Ireland and offer a revaluation of Nationalism in light of these theories. **Location & Dislocation in Contemporary Irish Society: Emigration & Irish Identities** (Cork University Press pb £15.95 1859180558), a series of essays edited by Jim MacLaughlin argues the emigration is not something that is endemic to the Irish people, but unfortunately is the response to the social and economic structures of late Twentieth Century Ireland. Through well argued essays, the authors dispel the myth of the Irish feeling a deep need to leave their homeland, and also examines the affect on the community that emigration has. Jim MacLaughlin has also written a pamphlet in Cork University Press's excellent Undercurrent series. **Travellers & Ireland: Whose Country, Whose History?** (Cork University Press pb £4.95 1859180949) looks at the relationship between the travellers and the settled community and argues that they are effectively a people without a history, while also examining the changes that have taken place in the travelling community this century. May McCann has edited a collection of essays **Irish Travellers: Culture & Ethnicity** (Institute of Irish Studies pb £8.50 0853894930) which examine the history, language and culture of the travelling people while also looking at the question of ethnicity and nomadism. In this, the second edition of his book, **Prejudice in Ireland Revisited** (Irish pb £12.00 0901519898), Micheal MacGreil gives a detailed analysis of the awful prejudice that exists in Irish society. This is without doubt the most comprehensive survey of Irish attitudes and values in print and also looks at the change in values over the last half century. Examining the changing attitudes toward Travellers, homosexuals, Jews and asking vital questions about the role of women in contemporary Irish society, MacGreil has provided the student and general reader with a valuable text. **Women & Work in Ireland** by Mary E. Daly (Dundalgan Press pb £4.00 0947897186) is a short study which charts the changing patterns of women's work over the last three centuries and tries to explain work trends in the pre and post Famine period and in this century. Daly also acutely examines the relationship between related issues such as the drop in fertility in working mothers in the last thirty years. **The Irish Raj** by Naindur Kapur (Irish pb £12.95 1870157249) tells the stories of the many Indian immigrants now living in Ireland, and as a result points out the many cultural and social similarities between Ireland and India, two countries that seem like they couldn't be more different. Following the great success of the L'Imaginaire Irelandaise festival 1997, Doireann Ni Bhrain, coordinator of the project has edited and introduced a lively collection of essays by many of the writers who took part. Eavan Boland, John Banville, John Hume & Julia O'Faolain and others all contribute to **Arguing at the Crossroads: Essays on a Changing Ireland** (New Island pb £7.99 1874597545) which examines the differences between the Ireland that they knew before and the country it has become.

Books on crime and corruption in the country include **The Joy** (O'Brien Press pb £6.99 0862784913), the story of life inside Mountjoy Gaol in Dublin as told to the journalist Paul Howard. Documenting the stories of drug use, bullying and suicide with harrowing detail, the book presents a good argument for the anti-reformative nature of prisons. Howard does try to keep some balance and tells the more upbeat details of the inmates' reactions to Ireland's World Cup success in 1990, without trying to sentimentalise the harsh reality of prison life. **The General: Godfather of Crime** by Paul Williams (O'Brien Press £6.99 0862784336) is the biography of Martin Cahill, the most notorious recent Dublin criminal who was assassinated by the IRA in 1994. Charting Cahill's rise to notoriety, from bank robbery to jewellery and art theft, while nearly always keeping one step ahead of the police, Williams narrates a fascinating story of a complex, brutal criminal. In **Wad of Notes: All Eyes on the Money** (Emerald pb £5.95 0952581302) Denis M. Lenihan looks at some of the recent financial scandals that have beset various governments. Giving details of the Beef tribunal, Greencore & Telecom Scandals, Lenihan provides a very useful overview of what has become a regularity in Irish politics. **Thanks a Million Big Fella** (Blackwater Press pb £9.99 086121952X) by former journalist of the year Sam Smyth is the definitive account of the dealings between former Taoiseach, Charles Haughey, Government Minister Michael Lowry and the supermarket millionaire Ben Dunne. Detailing the payments received by both politicians in exchange for potential political favours, Smyth also examines corruption at the highest level of Irish politics. **Banished Babies: The Secret History of Ireland's Baby Export Business** by Mike Milotte (New Island pb £7.99 1874597537) is the history of the illegal exporting of babies in the 1940s and 1950s and how illegitimate children were sold to couples abroad. The book also fingers the Catholic Church and the Government of the day as the main instigators and provides a frightening example of how misguided 'morality' can cause terrible hardship.

In a lively collection of essays collected by the editor of The Sunday Business Post Damien Kiberd, **Media in Ireland: The Search for Diversity** (Four Courts Press pb £6.95 1851823158) questions about media ownership are examined. Kiberd is concerned that media monopolies have had a huge affect on the way news items are reported, particularly the recent peace process in Northern Ireland and asks if we can have a representative and balanced coverage of news items if one or two people are controlling the press. The first television address was made in 1961 by the then President Eamon de Valera and the Catholic Primate Cardinal d'Alton. Both were apprehensive of the influence that this new form of media would have on the social and moral fibre of the country. In **Irish Television: The Political & Social Origins** (Cork University Press pb £16.95 1859181023) Robert J. Savage examines the founding of RTE in its political and social context while also examining the influence of politics, culture, economics and religion on the national television service.

A number of journalists have collections of their work in print. Fintan O'Toole's **Black Hole Green Card** (New Island pb £6.95 1874597014) is a collection based on his brilliant journalism for the Irish Times, which argues convincingly that the Irish nation has been replaced by a diaspora spread all over the globe and that Irish history has been quickly replaced by the tourist driven heritage/interpretive centre. The 'black hole' of the title refers to the place controlled by the Government and the international banks seems to have replaced the economy. O'Toole's argument leads to his conclusion that the Ireland invented by nationalist belief in the 1950s seems to have disappeared. This argument is continued and expanded in **The Ex-Isle of Erin** (New Island pb £7.99 1874597499). A selection from both book and his other journalism collection in **A Mass for Jesse James** (Raven Arts Press £6.99 1234567890) was published recently under the title **Lie of the Land: Irish Identities** (New Island hb £9.99 1874597723). During the Beef Tribunal of 1991 to 1993, which was the most expensive tribunal in the history of the state, O'Toole reported daily for the Irish Times from Dublin castle. Using his immense knowledge of the workings of the case, he has written the definitive history of the affair. **Meanwhile Back at the Ranch: The Politics of Irish Beef** (Vintage pb £6.99 0099514516) tells the story of how the Irish Government in the early 1980s fully backed Larry Goodman's beef export business with tax payers money. All of the key political and business players are mentioned and the case analysed and written up in a very clear style.

**The Trial of the Generals** (Raven Arts Press pb £5.95 1851860819) is a collection of Colm Toibin's witty and incisive journalism written between 1980 and 1990. Whether writing about such varied topics as lack of American relief for Sudan or the difficulty of buying condoms in Dublin after the 1979 Family Planning Act,

Toibin writes with a great mix of humour and appropriate seriousness. For many years Mary Cummins wrote a weekly column for the Irish Times. In **The Best of About Women** (Mercier pb £7.99 1860230474) she has collected her favourite pieces from her provocative and cogently argued journalism. Topics ranging from divorce, the Pope, Mary Robinson and Princess Diana all come under review in witty, engaging prose. Sean Duignan, news presenter, journalist and former spin doctor with the Fianna Fail Party has written a highly entertaining memoir **One Spin on the Merry-Go-Round** (Blackwater Press pb £9.99 0861217322) which details a lot of the background to contemporary Irish politics. In an age in which media manipulation plays such a huge role in any election campaign, Duignan's memoir is all the more valuable for presenting the fascinating 'spins' and tricks with such candour. **O'Machiavelli: Or How to Survive in Irish Politics** (Leopold pb £4.99 0952686511) by John O'Byrne is a biographical and political study of W.B. O'Carolan, one of Eamon deValera's key political and cultural advisers. O'Byrne discusses O'Carolan's political career in the context of his times and concludes that the secret of his success was a direct application of Machiavellian principles to Irish politics and policies. Paddy O'Gorman in his RTE radio programme Queueing for a Living has interviewed people queueing for various services and lengths of time. From dole queues to people waiting outside drug rehabilitation clinics, O'Gorman has presented life on the margins of Irish society in a fresh way. He has published two books, **Queueing for a Living** (Poolbeg pb £5.99 1853713554) and **Paddy's People** (Poolbeg pb £7.99 1853713511), both of which offer candid and revealing interviews.

Finally one writer has looked to the future. Paddy Walley has examined the current advances in technology, work practices and social issues and in this context has looked forward optimistically in his **Ireland in the 21st Century** (Mercier pb £6.99 1856351203). Arguing logically that all of these advances will have a profound effect on the country in the new millennium, Walley presents his evidence of the great advances to come with clear, cogent prose.

# Travel

## Travel Guides

There are many general travel guides to Ireland. The following guides all include information about history, culture, art and literature as well as a lot of practical information about places to stay and travel notes. All contain local maps. Although Let's Go, Lonely Plant and Rough Guides are geared more towards budget travel they are still very informative about the country. All have good information concerning the varied leisure activities available to visitors: –

**Let's Go Ireland 1998**
MacMillan £13.99 0333711742
**Ireland Lonely Planet Guide**
Lonely Planet pb £11.95
0864423527
**Rough Guide to Ireland 4th ed**
Rough Guide pb £9.99 1858281792
**Fodor's Ireland 1998**
Fodor's £14.99 0679034900
**Ireland 3rd Edition**
Cadogan pb £12.99 0947754644

**Ireland Baedeker**
Baedeker pb £12.99 0749514051
**Northern Ireland Guide**
Cadogan £10.99 1860110851
**AA All In One Guide**
AA pb £9.99 0749317646
**Ireland Insight Guide**
Insight pb £13.99 9624210381
**Ireland Insight Compact Guide**
Insight pb £3.99 9624213178

Of the more glossy guides with colour illustrations, Everyman and Dorling Kindersley are the best. Both of these books are lavishly illustrated and are closer to art books than to travel guides. They also include a lot of practical information.

**Ireland Everyman Guide**
Everyman £16.99 1857158865
**Ireland Eyewitness Travel Guide**
Dorling Kindersley pb £14.99 0751300047

Both of the standard Michelin guides (Red & Green) are available and are updated on a regular basis.

**Ireland Green Guide**
Michelin hb £8.99 206153502X
**Ireland 1998 Michelin**
Michelin hb £8.99 2060071898

For Dublin, the best of the basic guides is the **Dublin Street Atlas and Guide** (Causeway Press £3.95 1872600387) which has a full colour O.S. map with street index as well as having information about places to go, stay and eat. Other guides include **Globetrotter Dublin** (Globetrotter £6.99 1853688045), **Lonely Planet's Dublin City Guide** (Lonely Planet £5.95 0864423519), **Dublin Mini-Rough Guide** (Rough Guides £5.99 1858282942), which is a very handily sized pocket book, and the recent **Time Out Dublin Guide** (Penguin £8.99 0140266879) which is the ideal introduction to the city, strong on practical and historical/cultural information.

The Insider's series, published by Gill & MacMillan are excellent regional guides. All include clear information on where to stay, eat and drink as well as walking and cycling around the particular area. They also include details about museums: –

**Insider's Guide to Kerry and West Cork**
Gill & Macmilllan £7.99 0717120775
**Insider's Guide to Connemara**
Gill & Macmilllan £7.99 0717119041
**Insider's Guide to Dublin & Wicklow**
Gill & Macmilllan £7.99 0717121232

**Patricia Levy's Ireland: A Guide to Customs & Etiquette** (Kuper £8.95 1857331494) from the popular Culture Shock series is a solid introduction to the history, politics and culture of Ireland and is also valuable in that it explodes many stereotypes and popular myths about the country. For more trips around the country, Patricia Preston's **Daytrips Ireland** (Gazelle pb £12.99 080389385X) is full of different ideas and the necessary travel details. The Appletree Press has produced a small but informative **Irish Museums Guide** (Appletree Press £3.99 0862815487) which details collections and opening hours of museums and galleries throughout th country. And for the more active, Brendan Walsh's **Cycle Touring Ireland** (Gill & MacMillan pb £6.99

0717124452) is the best starting point for exploring the country on two wheels. There are three great books packed with information about activities for children in Ireland. Mary Finn's **Adventure Guide to Dublin** (Wolfhound £4.99 0863273556) is a great introduction to everything that's on in the capital city for a range of age groups from toddlers to teenagers. Fiona Mackenzie-Hook's **Ireland for Kids** (Mainstream hb £9.99 1851589201) covers the country and gives information about local festivals and entertainment. **Kids' Day Out** (Marino £8.99 1860230164) by Brídóg Ní Bhuachalla is a book full of ideas for keeping children occupied during the summer months. All of these books are suitable for both tourists and locals.

Peter Harbison's wonderful **Shell Guide to Ireland** (Gill & MacMillan £9.99 0717123103) is the ultimate A-Z gazetteer to places of cultural, historic and archaeological interest in Ireland. Well illustrated with maps and photographs, this is the ideal book for the glove compartment when driving around the countryside. **Ireland** (Gill & MacMillan £9.99 071712536X) by Max Caulfield is a well-illustrated guide to places of historic interest. Suggesting various possible routes to take, it is well served with photos of cities, towns and countryside.

There are plenty of books to guide people towards the best in Irish food and drink. Food experts John and Sally McKenna, under their Estragon Press imprint, have produced the most comprehensive guides to Irish food available. **The Bridgestone Irish Food Guide** (Estragon Press 1874076170) covers all aspects of food and its availability in Ireland, from chefs to growers, restaurants, cheesemakers and some recipes. Their **Bridgestone Dublin Food Guide 1997/1998** (Estragon Press £6.99 1874076219) covers the Dublin area and recommends delis, restaurants, pubs, butchers and wine. The other two titles in the Bridgestone series are **Bridgestone 100 Best Restaurants 1997/1998** (Estragon Press pb £7.99 1874076227) and **Bridgestone 100 Best Places to Stay 1997/1998** (Estragon Press pb £7.99 1874076200).

**The Bailey's Dublin Pub Guide** (Footprint £2.00 1860800122) is a very handy book which gives information about all the best pubs in Dublin. A useful companion volume is the **Dublin Literary Pub Crawl** by Peter Costello (A & A Farmar £5.99 1899047204) which gives all the information about the pubs in Dublin, like McDaid's, Davy Byrne's and the Palace Bar, that have literary connections. If you are going further afield to check out the pub scene **The Bushmill's Irish Pub Guide** (Appletree £9.95 0862813859) by Sybil Taylor is a very useful companion to the pubs around the country.

## "It is a city where you can see a sparrow fall to the ground, and God watching it."
Conor Cruise O'Brien on Dublin

There are guides available both for the country as a whole and for particular areas. Joss Lynam's **Best Irish Walks** (Gill & MacMillan £8.99 0717125890) is a guide to seventy six different walks in various parts of the country, giving detailed descriptions of the walks as well as best practice for safety in the hills. Lynam has also produced a guide specific to the Mountains of Connemara in Galway, which includes a detailed map and gazetteer – **Mountains of Connemara: Guide** (Folding Landscape £6.00 0950400246). **Irish Waterside Walks** (Gill & MacMillan £7.99 0717125327) by Michael Fewer is a series of suggested walks of varied lengths along the rivers and canals of the countryside. The walks range from half an hour to five hours in length and Fewer also writes very informatively about the history and architecture of the areas mentioned. He includes suitable spots for swimming and picnics. His companion volume to this is The **Way-Marked Trails of Ireland** (Gill & MacMillan £9.99 0717123863) which suggests walks along some of the 1500 km of trails marked by Cospóir (the Irish Sports Council). Most of the trails are along disused roads and paths and Fewer includes information on accommodation and good places to stop. One of the more unusual walking guides available is Kevin Cronin's **Off the Beaten Track: Irish Railway Walks** (Appletree Press £7.99 0862815630) which describes forty different walks around the 3,000 miles of abandoned railway track that exist in Ireland. Cronin gives the history of each line and also gives details of O.S. map location. He also provides information on various types of accommodation available.

David Herman has written a brilliant series of walking guides for various parts of the country. These small books include maps and detailed descriptions of different walks of various lengths:–

**Hill Stroller's Wicklow**
Shanksmare pb £3.50 0951454714
**Hill Walker's Donegal**
Shanksmare £3.50 0951454730
**Hill Walker's Kerry**
Shanksmare £3.75 0951454765
**Hill Walker's Wicklow**
Shanksmare £3.75 0951454757
**Hill Walker's Connemara & Mayo**
Shanksmare £3.50 0951454749

He has also written **Great Walks of Ireland** (Cassell £5.99 0706371526) and the **Walk Guide to the East of Ireland** (Gill & MacMillan £6.99 0717124282). Kevin Corcoran has written two very good walk guides, **West Cork Walks** (O'Brien Press 0862782546 £5.95) and **West of Ireland Walks** (O'Brien Press £5.95 0862783453). Both books give full instructions for starting and completing ten walks in both areas and include local maps with well researched information on local flora and fauna. Barry Keane has written three walking guides to different peninsulas on the South West Coast of Ireland. All published by the Collins Press, the books give great detail about a number of walks of various length. The books are **Ivereagh Peninsula** (Collins Press £5.99 1898256276), **Dingle Peninsula** (Collins Press £5.99 1898256284) and **Beara Mizen & Sheep's Head Peninsulas** (Collins Press £5.99 1898256292).

Vincent Godsil's **Walks Around Cork** (Collins Press £7.99 1898256195) is a charming mix of guide, anecdote and history. All of the walks contained are within twenty five miles of the city centre and Godsil matches appropriate anecdote to place. Folklorist Séan Ó'Suilleabháin has written a **Walk Guide to the South West of Ireland** (Gill & MacMillan £6.99 0717126358) which includes both practical information and local folklore about the Kerry Way, the Dingle Way and the Béara Way. J.B. Malone's **Complete Wicklow Way: A Step-By Step Guide** (O'Brien Press £5.95 0862781582) is the most comprehensive guide to this famous walk through the 'garden of Ireland'. Starting in the Dublin mountains and finishing in South Wicklow, the walk goes through some of the most scenic areas on the East Side of the country. Malone's book is complete with maps, history and botanical guide to the different areas and is indispensable to anyone attempting any part of the walk. **The Higher Lakes of Wicklow** (Phylax £5.99 0952409003) by John Mccormick is a guide to the five highest lakes in Wicklow, often overlooked because of the popularity of Glendalough and the lakes at Blessington. McCormick's book explains exactly how to get to Loch Ouler, Cleevaun, Firrish, Kelly and Arris and once you have found the lakes, suitable walks around them. The book also includes photographs and maps. Christopher Moriarty has written three books that are a lively and informative mix of natural and local history. His **Exploring Dublin** (Wolfhound £8.99 0863275907) examines the environs of the capital city while **On Foot in Dublin & Wicklow** (Wolfhound £4.50 0863272266) sees the author going further afield, walking around both Dublin and Wicklow counties. His **Down Along the Dodder** (Wolfhound pb £6.99 086327286X) is a wonderful exploration of this river from it source in the North Wicklow, through the west Dublin suburbs and to its mouth in Ringsend.

Ruth Delany has written two books on the inland waterways of Ireland which are histories of the canals but are also very useful as guides. Her **Ireland's Inland Waterways** (Appletree Press £7.99 0862813808) covers most of the canals in Ireland while her **Grand Canal of Ireland 1789-1992** (Lilliput Press £10.00 1874675651) is a fascinating history of the building and function of this canal over the last 200 years. The Office of Public Works have also produced their own guide to the Grand Canal, **Grand Canal Guide** (OPW £5.00 0707616255). **Nature in Ireland: A Scientific &**

**Cultural History** (Lilliput Press £20.00 1874675899) by John Wilson Foster is a fascinating collection of essays about this much neglected topic. These essays ask how nature has been expressed in popular culture throughout this century and also discuss the influence of political, economic and social change on the landscape. Specialised pieces include essays on field sports, nomenclature and histories of botany, geology and ornithology in Ireland.

From Beautiful History of Ireland

# Illustrated Books

There are many, very fine illustrated books on Ireland and its landscape, culture and history available. **Ireland Our Island Home** (Collins Press hb £19.99 1898256209) by expert photographer Kevin Dwyer is a beautiful book of aerial photographs. Starting at Carlingford Lough, 100 miles north of Dublin and working clockwise around the country, Dwyer has captured the splendid and varied beauty of the Irish coast. Including photographs of towns from the air as well, this is a unique book of photos all taken between 1992 and 1996. It has a lively introduction by Keith Floyd. **Ireland County by County** (Gill & MacMillan hb £19.99 071712584X) by Thomas Lee is an illustrated celebration, province by province, county by county of the rich historical and cultural traditions of the Irish counties.

**McGilloway's Ireland** (Blackstaff £14.99 085640540X) by Olly McGilloway is a beautifully illustrated book with clear text, examining the seasonal cycles of nature in Ireland and demonstrates McGilloway's passion for the natural world. With words by Peter Somerville-Large and stunning aerial photographs by Jason Hawkes, **Ireland from the Air** (Weidenfeld & Nicholson hb £25.95 0297834746) is a book of arresting images. Covering each province, Hawke's photos and Somerville-Large's commentary beautifully display the rich diversity of the Irish landscape. From the wilds of Inisheer, off the West coast to the centre of Dublin, this book paints a beautiful portrait of Ireland.

Elizabeth Healy's **Book of the Liffey: From Source To the Sea** (Wolfhound hb £16.95 0863271677) is a well illustrated guide to Ireland's most famous river. It combines comprehensive history with description of flora and fauna as well as illustrations, maps and pictures. **Liam O'Flaherty's Ireland** (Wolfhound hb £19.99 0863275508) by Peter Costello is not just a beautifully illustrated biography of O'Flaherty. As well as clear, informative text, Costello provides many colour photographs of both the Aran Islands and areas in the West. Terence J. Sheehy's **Irish Moment** (John Hinde hb £16.95 0862837685) is a beautifully illustrated book with clear text telling the story of Christianity in early Ireland from the 9th century to the Middle Ages. Stunning colour photographs from the John Hinde archive accompany the text.

In 1954, the American photographer Dorothea Lange came to Ireland. Staying in Co. Clare for two months she took over 2,400 photos of the region. These pictures, in her usual style, captured the daily lives of the people of Clare in the 1950s. In **Dorothea Lange's Ireland** (Aurum Press hb £19.95 185410411X) the best of these photographs are presented in beautiful duotone reproduction. The text of the book by Gerry Mullins expands on Lange's reasons for coming to Ireland and on the subjects of the photos. Over the last twenty five years, Dublin-based photographer Tom Lawlor has enjoyed a professional relationship with the Gate theatre. Taking pictures of cast and set, during rehearsal and production, Lawlor has perfectly captured the actors in various Irish and international productions. **Tom Lawlor at the Gate** (Lawlor hb £25.00 0953145204) is a stunning collection of photos and is both a tribute and testimony to the quality of productions at the Gate and to a photographer's art. John Minihan's **Shadows from the Pale: Portrait of an Irish Town** (Secker & Warburg hb £20.00 0436203472) is a stunning photographic record of Athy, Co. Kildare, taken over 35 years. The book cover all aspects of daily life in the town and at the heart of the book is Minihan's photo essay of the wake of Katy Tyrell, which is one of the most moving records of this Irish tradition available.

Born in Cork in 1880, Fr. Browne photographed over 42,000 images in his lifetime. As a Jesuit and Army Chaplain, he traveled the world taking pictures of his experiences. For a number of years the Wolfhound Press in Dublin have brilliantly restored some of this historically important archive to the public domain. Through these photographs, the modern observer can get an important glimpse into the lives and lifestyles of Ireland in the early 20th Century: –

**Father Browne's Titanic Album**
Wolfhound hb £20.00 0863275982
**Father Browne's Cork**
Wolfhound hb £19.99 0863274897
**Father Browne's Dublin**
Wolfhound hb £20.00 0863273661
**Father Browne's Ireland**
Wolfhound hb £19.95 0863272002

**Irish Traditions** (Abrams hb £14.99 0810980967) edited by Kathleen Jo Ryan and Bernard Share is a book of essays well illustrated with photographs, about the art, literature and history of Ireland. Contributors include Cyril Cusack, Séamus Deane, Benedict Kiely and Hugh Leonard. **Ireland in Old Photographs 1840-1930** (Thames & Hudson hb £19.95 1856690172) edited by Sean Sexton is a fascinating look back in time to the last century and the early years of the 20th century in Ireland.

These photographs show a mix of both rural and urban life and are a valuable reminder of ways of life that have all but disappeared.

Finally, **In an Irish House** edited by Sybil Connolly (Weidenfeld & Nicolson pb £9.99 0297796046), is a lavishly illustrated book about various houses around Ireland. All of the houses included are introduced by their inhabitants and they tell the story of how they found (and sometimes rebuilt!) their houses. Contributors include Desmond Guinness, Patrick Scott, Jacqueline O'Brien and Myrtle Allen. Each piece is accompanied by a number of recipes regularly made in the particular house. The book also comes with a foreword by Molly Keane. Sybil Connolly, with Helen Dillon, has also edited **In an Irish Garden** (Weidenfeld & Nicolson pb £9.99 0297795848), which, with accompanying photographs, gives a number of people the opportunity to introduce their splendid private gardens.

# Where to find your nearest Waterstone's

**ABERDEEN**
236 Union St
Tel: 01224 571655

**ABERYSTWYTH**
Arts Centre
University of
Wales
Tel: 01970 623251

**AMSTERDAM**
Kalverstraat 152
Amsterdam
The Netherlands
Tel: 00 312 0 638
3821

**ASTON
UNIVERSITY**
12 Gosta Green
Aston Triangle
Tel: 0121 359
3242

**ALTRINCHAM**
24 George Street
*(from Winter 1998)*

**AYLESBURY**
31-32 Friars
Square
Tel: 01296 423153

**BASINGSTOKE**
2 Castle Square
*(from Winter 1998)*

**BATH**
4–5 Milsom St
Tel: 01225 448515

University of Bath
Claverton Down
Tel: 01225 465565

**BEDFORD**
11-13 Silver Street
Tel: 01234 272432

Cranfield
University
Bookshop
College Road
Wharley End
Tel: 01234 754280

**BELFAST**
Queen's Building
8 Royal Avenue
Tel: 01232 247355

**BIRKENHEAD**
188/192 Grange
Rd
Tel: 0151 650
2400

**BIRMINGHAM**
24–26 High Street
Tel: 0121 633
4353
Fax: 0121 633
4300

Birmingham
University
Ring Road North
Edgbaston
Tel: 0121 472
3034

**BLACKPOOL**
4, The Tower
Shopping Centre
Bank Hey Street
Tel: 01253 296136

**BOLTON**
32–36 Deansgate
Tel: 01204 522588

**BOURNEMOUTH**
14/16 The Arcade
Tel: 01202 299449

Bournemouth
University
Talbot Campus
Fern Barrow
Poole
Tel: 01202 595528

**BRADFORD**
University of
Bradford,
Great Horton Rd
Tel: 01274 727885

Management
Centre Bookshop,
Emm Lane
Tel: 01274 481404

The Wool
Exchange
Tel: 01274 723127

**BRUNEL
UNIVERSITY**
Cleveland Road
Uxbridge
Tel: 01895 257991

**BRIGHTON**
55–56 North St
Tel: 01273 327867

71–74 North
Street
Tel: 02373 206017

**BRISTOL**
Computer Centre
University of
Bristol
Tyndall Avenue
Tel: 0117 925
4297

27–29 College
Green
Tel: 0117 925
0511

University of
Bristol
Tyndall Avenue
Tel: 0117 925
4297

Cribbs Causeway
33 Lower Level,
The Mall
Tel: 0117 950
9813

The Galleries
Broadmead
Tel: 0117 925
2274

**BROMLEY**
20–22 Market Sq
Tel: 0181 464
6562

**BRUSSELS**
Boulevard
Adolphe
Max 71-75
B1000 Brussels
Belgium
Tel: 00 322 219
2708

**BURY**
4 Union Arcade
Tel: 0161 764
2642

**CAMBRIDGE**
6 Bridge St
Tel: 01223 300123
Fax: 01223 301539

**CANTERBURY**
20 St Margaret's
St
Tel: 01227 456343

**CARDIFF**
2a The Hayes
Tel: 01222 665606

**CARMARTHEN**
Trinity College
Tel: 01267 238100

**CHELMSFORD**
The Meadows
Centre
High Street
*(from Winter 1998)*

**CHELTENHAM**
88–90 The
Promenade
Tel: 01242 512722

**CHESTER**
43–45 Bridge St
Row
Tel: 01244 328040

**CHICHESTER**
The Dolphin and
Anchor
West Street
*(from Winter 1998)*

**COLCHESTER**
16 Culver Precinct
Tel: 01206 767623

University of
Essex
Wivenhoe Park
Tel: 01206 864773

**CORK**
69 Patrick St
Tel: 00 353 21
276522

Boole Library
University College
Tel: 00 353 21
276575

**COVENTRY**
22 Cathedral
Lanes
Broadgate
Tel:01203 227151

Coventry
University
26 Earl Street
Tel: 01203 229092

Coventry
University
Bookshop
Earl Street
Tel: 01203 230880

**CRAWLEY**
83-84 County Mall
Tel: 01293 533471

**CROYDON**
1063 Whitgift
Centre
Tel: 0181 686
7032

**DERBY**
78–80 St Peter's St
Tel: 01332 296997

University of
Derby
Keddleston Road
Tel: 01332 331719

Chevin Avenue
Mickelover
Tel: 01332 511462

**DORKING**
54–60 South St
Tel: 01306 886884

**DUBLIN**
7 Dawson St
Tel: 00 353 1 679
1260

The Jervis Centre
Tel: 00 353 1 878
1311

**DUNDEE**
35 Commercial St
Tel: 01382 200322

**DURHAM**
69 Saddler St
Tel: 0191 383
1488

University
Bookshop
55-57 Saddler
Street
Tel: 0191 384
2095

**EASTBOURNE**
120 Terminus Rd
Tel: 01323 735676

**EDINBURGH**
128 Princes St
Tel: 0131 226
2666

13–14 Princes St
Tel: 0131 556
3034/5

83 George St
Tel: 0131 225
3436

**EGHAM**
Royal Holloway
College
Egham Hill
Tel: 01784 471272

**EPSOM**
113 High St
Tel: 01372 741713

**EXETER**
48–49 High St
Tel: 01392 218392

5 Isambard
Parade
St. Davids Station
Tel: 01392 273433
Tel: 01392 491250

**FOLKESTONE**
1–2 Guildhall St
Tel: 01303 221
979

**GATESHEAD**
17 The Parade
Metro Centre
Tel: 0191 493
2715

**GLASGOW**
153–157
Sauchiehall St
Tel: 0141 332
9105

**GUILDFORD**
35–39 North St
Tel: 01483 302919

**HANLEY**
Stoke-On-Trent
The Tontines
Centre
Parliament Row
Tel: 01782 204582

**HATFIELD**
University of
Hertfordshire
College Lane
Tel: 01707 284940

**HEREFORD**
18–20
Commercial St
Tel: 01432 275100

University of
Hertfordshire
Mangrove Road
Tel: 01707 285505

**HUDDERSFIELD
UNIVERSITY**
Queensgate
Tel: 01484 472200

**HULL**
University of Hull
Tel: 01482 444190

The Grand
Buildings,
Jameson St
Tel: 01482 580234

**ILFORD**
158-160 High
Road
Tel: 0181 478 8428

**INVERNESS**
50–52 High St
Tel: 01463 717474

**IPSWICH**
15–19
Buttermarket
Tel: 01473 289044

**KEELE**
University of
Keele
Tel: 01782 627001

**KETTERING**
72–76 High St
Tel: 01536 481575

**KING'S LYNN**
76–77 High St
Tel: 01553 769934

**KINGSTON-UPON-
THAMES**
23–25 Thames St
Tel: 0181 5471221

**LANCASTER**
2–8 King St
Tel: 01524 61477

Lancaster
University
Bookshop
Bailrigg
Tel: 01524 32581

**LEAMINGTON SPA**
1 Priorsgate
Warwick St
Tel: 01926 883804

**LEEDS**
36–38 Albion St
Tel: 0113 242
0839

93–97 Albion St
Tel: 0113 244
4588

6 Gledhow Wing
St. James Hospital
Beckett Street
Tel: 0113 243
3144

**LEICESTER**
21/23 High St
Tel: 0116 251
6838

**LIVERPOOL**
52 Bold St
Tel: 0151 709
0866

## LONDON

**BUSINESS BOOKSHOP**
72 Park Road
NW1
Tel: 0171 723
3902

**CAMDEN, NW1**
128 Camden High
St
Tel: 0171 284
4948

**CHARING CROSS RD, WC2**
121 Charing Cross
Rd
Tel: 0171 434
4291

**CHARING CROSS AND WESTMINSTER MEDICAL SCHOOL**
The Library
Reynold's
Building
St Dunstan's Road
W6
Tel: 0171 589
3563

**CHEAPSIDE, EC2**
145–147
Cheapside
Tel: 0171 726
6077

**CHISWICK, W4**
220-226 Chiswick
High Road
Tel: 0181 995
3559

**THE CITY, EC3**
1 Whittington Ave
Leadenhall
Market
Tel: 0171 220
7882

**CITY UNIVERSITY, EC1**
Northampton
Square
Tel: 0171 608
0706

**COVENT GARDEN, WC2**
9 Garrick St
Tel: 0171 836
6757

**EALING**
64 Ealing
Broadway Centre
Tel: 0181 840
5905

**EARL'S COURT, SW5**
266 Earl's Court
Rd Tel: 0171 370
1616

**ECONOMIST BOOKSTORE, WC2**
Clare Market
Portugal Street
Tel: 0171 405
5531

**GOLDSMITHS', SE14**
Goldsmiths'
College,
New Cross
Tel: 0181 469
0262

**HAMPSTEAD, NW3**
68 Hampstead
High St
Tel: 0171 794
1098

**HARRODS, SW1**
87 Brompton Rd
Tel: 0171 730
1234

**IMPERIAL COLLEGE, SW7**
Imperial College
Rd
Tel: 0171 589
3563

**IMPERIAL COLLEGE SCHOOL OF MEDICINE**
Charing Cross
Campus
Reynolds Building
St Dunstan's Rd
Tel: 0181 748
9768

Hammersmith
Campus
Commonwealth
Building
Du Cane Road
Tel: 0181 742
9600

**ISLINGTON, N1**
11 Islington
Green
Tel: 0171 704
2280

**KENSINGTON, W8**
193 Kensington
High St
Tel: 0171 937
8432

**KING'S COLLEGE**
Macadam House
Surrey Street
Tel: 0171 836
0205

**KING'S ROAD, SW3**
150-152 King's
Road
Tel: 0171 351
2023

**KINGSTON UNIVERSITY**
2 Brook Street
Tel: 0181 547
1221

**LONDON GUILDHALL UNIVERSITY, E1**
Calcutta House
Old Castle Street
Tel: 0171 247
0727

**NOTTING HILL, W11**
39 Notting Hill
Gate
Tel: 0171 229
9444

**OLD BROMPTON RD, SW7**
99 Old Brompton
Rd
Tel: 0171 581
8522

**QUEEN MARY & WESTFIELD, E1**
329 Mile End
Road
Tel: 0181 980
2554

**THAMES VALLEY UNIVERSITY**
St. Mary's Road &
Westel House,
Ealing
Tel: 0181 840
6205

**TRAFALGAR SQUARE, WC2**
The Grand
Building
Tel: 0171 839
4411

**WIMBLEDON, SW19**
12 Wimbledon
Bridge
Tel: 0181 543
9899

**LUTON**
University of
Luton
Park Square
Tel: 01582 402704

**MAIDSTONE**
19 Earl St
Tel: 01622 681112

**MACCLESFIELD**
47 Mill St
Tel: 01625 424212

**MAILING SERVICE**
Tel: 01225 448595
Fax: 01225 444732

**MANCHESTER**
91 Deansgate
Tel: 0161 832
1992

**MANCHESTER AIRPORT**
Terminal 1 Airside
Tel: 0161 489
3405

**MERRY HILL**
95/96 Merry Hill
Shopping Centre
Brierley Hill
Tel: 01384 751551

**MIDDLESBROUGH**
9 Newton Mall
Cleveland Centre
Tel: 01642 242682

University of
Teesside
Middlesbrough
Tel: 01642 242017

**MILTON KEYNES**
51-63 Silbury
Arcade
Tel: 01908 696260

570 Silbury
Boulevard
Tel: 01908 607454

**NEWBURY**
64 Northbrook St
Tel: 01635 569998

**MILTON KEYNES**
51-63 Silbury
Arcade
Tel: 01908 696260

**NEWCASTLE**
104 Grey St
Tel: 0191 261
6140

**NORTHAMPTON**
19 Abington St
Tel: 01604 634854

**NORWICH**
21–24 Royal
Arcade
Tel: 01603 632426

University of East
Anglia
Tel: 01603 453625

**NOTTINGHAM**
1–5 Bridlesmith
Gate
Tel: 0115 9484499

**OXFORD**
William Baker
House
Broad Street
Tel: 01865 790212

**PERTH**
St John's Centre
Tel: 01738 630013

**PETERBOROUGH**
6 Queensgate
Tel: 01733 313476

**PLYMOUTH**
65/69 New
George St
Tel: 01752 256699

**PRESTON**
3–5 Fishergate
Tel: 01772 555766

**READING**
89a Broad St
Tel: 01189 581270

Reading
University
Whiteknights
Tel: 01189 874858

**RICHMOND-UPON-THAMES**
2–6 Hill St
Tel: 0181 332
1600

**SALISBURY**
7/9 High St
Tel: 01722 415596

**SCARBOROUGH**
97-98
Westborough
*(from Winter 1998)*

**SHEFFIELD**
24 Orchard Sq
Tel: 0114 272
8971

Meadowhall
Centre
26 The Arcade
Tel: 0114 256
8495

**SHREWSBURY**
18–19 High St
Tel: 01743 248112

**SOLIHULL**
67-71 High Street
Tel: 0121 711
2454

**SOUTHAMPTON**
69 Above Bar
Tel: 01703 633130

Southampton
Medical School,
Southampton
General Hospital
Tel: 01703 780602

University of
Southampton
Highfield
Tel: 01703 558267

**SOUTHEND-ON-SEA**
49–55 High St
Tel: 01702 437480

**SOUTHPORT**
367 Lord St
Tel: 01704 501088

**ST. ALBANS**
8/10 Catherine
Street
Tel: 01727 868866

**STIRLING**
Thistle Marches
Tel: 01786 478756

**STOCKPORT**
103 Princes St
Tel: 0161 477
3755

**STOKE**
Staffordshire
University
Bookshop
Station Road
Tel: 01782 746318

**STRATFORD-UPON-AVON**
18 The High St
Tel: 01789 414418

**SUTTON**
71-81 High St
Tel: 0181 770
0404

**SWANSEA**
17 Oxford St
Tel: 01792 463567

Taliesin Arts
Centre
University of
Wales
Singleton Park
Tel: 01792 281460

**SWINDON**
27 Regent St
Tel: 01793 488838

**TAUNTON**
County Hotel
East St
Tel: 01823 333113

**TUNBRIDGE WELLS**
32/40 Calverley
Rd
Tel: 01892 535446

**ULSTER**
Central Buildings
University of
Ulster
Cromore Rd
Coleraine
Tel: 01265 324
735

**WATFORD**
174–176 The
Harlequin Centre,
High St
Tel: 01923 218197

Wall Hall Campus
Aldenham
Tel: 01707 285745

**WINCHESTER**
1/2 Kings Walk
Tel: 01962 866206

The Brooks
Middle Brook
Street
Tel: 01962 866206
*(from Winter 1998)*

**WOLVERHAMPTON**
13-15 Victoria
Street
Tel: 01902 427219

University of
Wolverhampton
Wulfruna Street
Tel: 01902 322435

Dudley Campus
Castle View
Tel: 01902 323374

Shropshire
Campus
Priors Lee
Telford
Tel: 01902 323815

**WORCESTER**
95 High St
Tel: 01905 723397

**WREXHAM**
9/11 Regent
Street
*(from Winter 1998)*

**YORK**
28–29 High
Ousegate
Tel: 01904 628740